Understanding Social Psychology
Across Cultures

SAGE SOCIAL PSYCHOLOGY PROGRAM

Senior Consultant Editor

Michael A. Hogg (University of Queensland, Australia)

Consultant Editors

Richard E. Petty (Ohio State University, USA)
Marilynn B. Brewer (Ohio State University, USA)
John M. Levine (University of Pittsburgh, USA)
Stephen Reicher (St. Andrews University, UK)
Vincent Yzerbyt (Université Catholique de Louvain-la-Neuve, Belgium)

SAGE Publications is pleased to announce the launch of a new program of titles in social psychology – both text and reference books – brought together by a team of consultant editors led by Michael Hogg: the *Sage Social Psychology Program*. Written or edited by leading scholars and infused with the latest research in the field, the program is intended to be a self-contained and comprehensive resource that meets all the educational needs of a social psychology program beyond introductory level.

The *Sage Social Psychology Program*'s remit has breadth and depth. Student textbooks are written by leading and experienced scholars in a style that is carefully crafted to be stimulating, engaging and accessible. They are scholarly, comprehensive and up-to-date, and are furnished with the appropriate pedagogical devices and supplements - thus making them appropriate to build courses around at a variety of levels. Reference works, including Handbooks and Encyclopaedias, survey the landscape with an even broader sweep and should become benchmark volumes for many years to come.

Forthcoming titles:

Work & Organisations – Robin Martin (University of Queensland, Australia)

The Social Psychology of Groups: Processes and Performance – Scott Tindale (Loyola University Chicago) & Christine Smith (Grand Valley State University, Michigan)

Applying Social Psychology – Bram Buunk (University of Groningen, the Netherlands) & Mark Van Vugt (University of Kent, UK)

Communication, Language and Society – Scott A. Reid and Howard Giles (both University of California, Santa Barbara)

Understanding Social Psychology Across Cultures

Living and Working in a Changing World

Peter B. Smith, Michael Harris Bond and Çiğdem Kağıtçıbaşı

SAGE Publications
London ● Thousand Oaks ● New Delhi

SAGE Publications Ltd
1 Oliver's Yard
55 City Road
London EC1Y 1SP

SAGE Publications Inc.
2455 Teller Road
Thousand Oaks, California 91320

SAGE Publications India Pvt Ltd
B-42, Panchsheel Enclave
Post Box 4109
New Delhi 110 017

British Library Cataloguing in Publication data

A catalogue record for this book is available
from the British Library

ISBN 1-4129-0365-3
ISBN 1-4129-0366-1 (pbk)

Library of Congress Control Number available

Typeset by C&M Digitals (P) Ltd., Chennai, India
Printed on paper from sustainable resources
Printed in Great Britain by TJ International, Padstow, Cornwall

Contents

Acknowledgements

This book supersedes our two earlier volumes, entitled, *Social Psychology Across Cultures*. Thirteen years have passed since the publication of its first edition, and during that time the study of cross-cultural aspects of psychology has been transformed. Consequently, the text of this book is almost entirely new. The overall structure remains, but our breadth of coverage is increased and we have endeavoured to include a clear account of those growth points in the field that are most relevant to the challenges posed by our ever-changing contemporary world. Just as the span of cross-cultural investigation has broadened, so has the cross-national collaboration involved in the production of this book. As a team of three, we have benefited from the diversity of our perspectives, and been stimulated to bring together aspects of the field that are too often considered in isolation. In discussing with others the content of this book, we are confident that you will have no difficulty in pronouncing the names of Smith and Bond. You may appreciate a little help in pronouncing Çiğdem Kağıtçıbaşı's name in a way that gives respect to the distinctive Turkish characters within it. Try saying it as chee-dam kut-cha-ba-sha.

We appreciate the permission granted to us by Dianne van Hemert to reproduce unpublished material in Boxes 3.7 and 4.3, and by Michele Gelfand for Box 4.7.

We are grateful to Pawel Boski, Joris de Bres, Mary Jiang Bresnahan, Rolando Diaz Loving, Ronald Fischer, Marta Fulop, Michele Gelfand, Gert Jan Hofstede, Heidi Keller, Mansur Lalljee, Elias Mpofu, Ype Poortinga, Floyd Rudmin, Shalom Schwartz, Andy Tamas, Nathalie van Meurs, Patricia Rodriguez Mosquera, Jim Nelson, Peter K. Smith, Evert Van de Vliert, Vivian Vignoles and Susumu Yamaguchi for their insightful comments and generous contributions, and to Anne Cathcart for her patience and support. The enthusiasm of many colleagues who read and adopted the first two editions of this text has confirmed and sustained us in our effort to improve our own understanding of social psychology across cultures. Thank you one and all.

Peter B. Smith
Michael Harris Bond
Çiğdem Kağıtçıbaşı
June, 2005

Part One

Establishing the Framework

1

Some Pressing Questions for Cross-cultural Psychology

The only true exploration, the only true fountain of delight, would not be to visit foreign lands, but to possess others' eyes, to look at the world through the eyes of others (Marcel Proust, *Remembrance of Things Past*)

In this book we seek to show how psychology can help us to understand and cope with the unparalleled processes of social change that are occurring in the world at the present time. This will not be an easy task, as it requires us to focus equally on two issues that are most often kept quite separate. Firstly, we shall need to show how psychologists can best address the diversity of the reality confronting the world's population. Psychology has most frequently been conducted by focusing on standardized and simplified settings. This type of focus can yield a sharply delineated understanding of what occurs within the few types of setting that are sampled, but raises problems if one wishes to apply those understandings to settings that are located in different cultural contexts. Secondly, we shall need to focus on change as much as on stability. Research methods that sample events at a single point in time, as most do, can give us an illusion of stability, even though our individual experiences tell us that things are in flux.

In this chapter, we commence our work by defining the problems with which we are concerned. The rest of the book will then develop a perspective on how cross-cultural psychology can best contribute to addressing these problems. Our focus can be defined in the following few sentences. Over the past 10,000 years, human evolution has differentiated a series of relatively small and relatively separate groups that we can describe as societies or cultures. These cultures were adapted to sustaining life in a wide variety of differing and hostile environments. Depending on how we might choose to define 'culture', several thousand cultures may be considered to have evolved. In the early part of the twentieth century, social anthropologists made detailed ethnographic studies of many of these groups. Their observations have been documented and summarized in the 'Human Relations Area Files' at Yale University, which contain information on 863 cultural groups (Murdock, 1967).

The fact that anthropologists were able to visit and document all these cultural groups was itself a symptom of an evolutionary process that commenced long before the industrial revolution and has been accelerating ever since. The development of modern technology has steadily increased the speed and ease with which we can travel the world and has virtually eliminated the time within which messages can in principle pass between two points located anywhere in the world. New technologies and the economic developments that they have engendered have unleashed a new stage in human evolution. Many of the several thousand languages that have evolved out of distinct cultural niches and traditions are in the process of being lost. In parallel with this reduction in linguistic diversity, a few languages are becoming more and more widely spoken. Many of the cultural groups studied earlier by anthropologists are no longer insulated from modern influences. Mass media ensure that the cultural products of a few industrialized nations are beamed into all corners of the world. Very large numbers of persons visit other parts of the world, as tourists, as workers for either non-governmental organizations or foreign governments, as students or for business purposes. Large numbers of persons migrate to other parts of the world, some as foreign workers, some as economic migrants, and some as refugees or as victims of persecution. Even larger numbers of people are moving from the countryside to cities, some of which are becoming very large indeed.

Boxes 1.1, 1.2 and 1.3 give some indication of the current magnitude of these movements. Box 1.1 lists those nations in the world that have received the greatest number of migrants in proportion to their population, averaged across the years between 1995 and 2000. Some nations that received large numbers of refugees during this period have been omitted from the table on account of war in a neighbouring nation. The greatest absolute number of migrants has gone to the USA, and other large nations such as Germany and Russia have also received more than 200,000 migrants per year in this period. Of course, there are many factors that determine what happens when migrants arrive at their destination, and we discuss these in Chapters 10 and 11. However, if we wish to understand the issues raised by high rates of immigration, the smaller nations listed in the table are likely to illustrate them more clearly. Migrants have a point of departure as well as a point of arrival, and nations that are losing large numbers of people are also susceptible to various forms of social disorganization, particularly because those leaving often include the most highly qualified, thus depriving their countries of rich social capital. Nations losing more than 1 per cent of their population annually during this period included Samoa, Albania, Kazakhstan, Guyana, Surinam and Tajikistan.

Box 1.2 shows the 18 nations that received the greatest absolute number of persons entering their country in 1997. Many countries do not record the reasons why entrants are visiting a country, so the figures here will comprise primarily tourists in some instances, and primarily business persons or students in others. Again, the more interesting statistic is the proportion between the number of entrants and the numbers of the existing population. Where entrants greatly exceed residents, we may expect to see the most evident signs of social transformation, either on the basis of tension and conflict or on the basis of willing incorporation of new values and behaviours into the

Box 1.1

The World on the Move: Permanent Migrants

Nation	Number of permanent migrants, per year	Proportion of existing population, per thousand persons
Singapore	74,000	19.6
Hong Kong	99,000	15.1
Kuwait	20,000	11.1
Luxembourg	4,000	9.4
Israel	52,000	9.1
United Arab Emirates	20,000	8.1
Bahrein	4,000	6.6
Costa Rica	20,000	5.3
Australia	95,000	5.1
Ireland	18,000	4.9
Lebanon	16,000	4.8
Canada	144,000	4.8
USA	1,250,000	4.5

Source: United Nations (2002). Migrant numbers are defined as number of inward migrants minus the number of outward migrants.

residents' nation. The nations most exposed to this type of impact are small nations located near to other large and rich nations.

Box 1.3 gives an overview of the massive and increasing rate at which people in developing nations have been leaving the countryside and moving to cities over the past decades, as well as predictions for the continuation of this trend. World population growth of more than two thousand million over the next 20 years is expected to occur almost entirely within cities. Of course, some of this growth will be partly attributable to the families of those already living in cities, but migration from rural areas will be so strong as to completely cancel out population growth in rural areas. Thus we may expect that very large and rapidly increasing numbers of persons will be living in contexts that divorce them from the contexts in which their families of origin have lived for generations. At the present time, we cannot be certain as to where these processes will lead, but we can anticipate that they will be momentous.

Box 1.2

The World on the Move: Entrants

Nation	Entrants staying at least one night, in millions	Percentage of the existing population
Austria	16.447	204
Hungary	17.248	173
Hong Kong	10.406	152
Switzerland	10.600	148
France	67.310	114
Spain	43.252	108
Portugal	10.172	102
Greece	10.070	95
Italy	34.087	59
Canada	17.636	57
Poland	19.520	51
UK	22.995	39
Mexico	19.351	20
Germany	15.837	19
USA	47.754	17
Turkey	9.040	14
Russia	17.463	12
China	23.770	2

Source: World Tourism Organization (1999).

How can we best understand these processes of social and cultural change and stability? The world is now organized as a system not of thousands of cultural groups, but of 200 or so nation states. The geographical locations and human histories of these nation states vary greatly, leading each toward their current circumstances. Nations are politically defined entities, containing a broad range of persons most of whom will share a single nationality, but who may well choose to describe themselves in terms

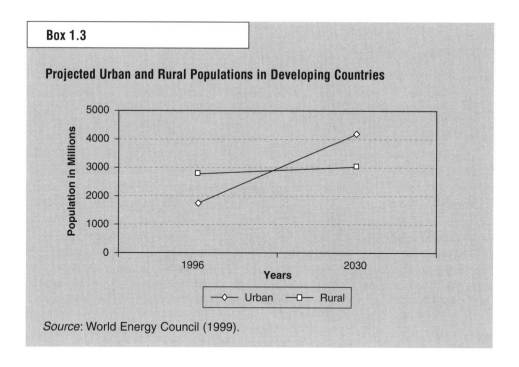

Box 1.3

Projected Urban and Rural Populations in Developing Countries

Source: World Energy Council (1999).

of differing genders, occupations, ethnic origins and skin colours. In some cases, one's nationality defines one's ethnicity, but skin colour, prior migration history and regional loyalties are frequently also involved. Whether a nation can be best understood as a society, as a culture or as an amalgam of ethnicities is a question that we shall discuss in Chapter 3. Until we reach that point we shall be referring to nations, not cultures.

In order to understand contemporary changes, we shall first need to consider how best to study and describe the existing similarities and differences between groups and between nations. Social scientists have devised many useful ways to do this, each of which can illuminate specific aspects of current stability and change. Our perspective stems from cross-cultural psychology. Cross-cultural psychologists resemble researchers in most other fields of psychology in that they favour research methods that entail quantitative forms of measurement, but they are distinctive in their emphasis on the need to test theories in a broad range of geographical locations. As we shall see in Chapters 2 and 3, they have developed measures that enable existing differences between nation states to be dimensionalized and hence compared. But will these differences persist, or will contemporary developments gradually create a global mono-culture? We can put the question in a more basic way: what is fundamental and basic about human nature, and what is malleable and likely to emerge in a different form, depending on the ways in which particular individuals are socialized?

Socialization is most typically studied as a process occurring during childhood, and in Chapter 5 we shall consider ways in which childhood socialization processes vary across nations. However, as individuals move through the life span and occasionally also from one nation to another, further socialization processes become more salient. Multinational businesses seek to socialize their employees to operate within a global organizational culture. Governments adopt a variety of practices concerning the provision of schooling within multiethnic contexts, and these schools in turn function as agents of socialization. Political alliances and conflicts create pressures for particular kinds of social change. Tourists make particular kinds of demands on local residents. People form relationships with, and sometimes marry, partners from nations other than their own. In doing so, they must confront the differences in the assumptions and values to which their prior lives have socialized them. Box 1.4 identifies one such pattern.

Box 1.4

Jan meets Maria

Jan grew up in a Dutch Protestant family. By the time that he completed his *doctorandus* degree at a university in the Netherlands, he, like his classmates, was a fluent speaker of Dutch, English, German, and French. He was keen to find a way to express his internationalist values and obtained a scholarship to study at a university in the UK for a doctorate concerning development issues in Brazil. Maria grew up in a Catholic family in Sao Paulo, Brazil. She learned English in school, and after completing a top-graded psychology degree in Sao Paulo, she was delighted to be awarded a Brazilian government scholarship to study for a doctorate in the UK.

The students in the doctoral programme at the UK university were drawn from all over the world. They soon found themselves in a friendship group that included British, American, German, Swedish, and Japanese students. In conversations among friends, they told one another that their different backgrounds were unimportant: they felt a sense of personal freedom. Jan was attracted to Maria's warmth and spontaneity. He said that he could respond to it much more freely when speaking English than he could have in Dutch. Maria was first attracted to Jan because of his evident concern and knowledge about Brazil. They became romantic partners, or as their friends put it, 'an item'.

As their studies progressed, they decided to marry, and to live in Brazil. Jan had done fieldwork for his dissertation in Brazil, and when their doctorates were completed, they married and set up home in Sao Paulo. Maria's mother immediately started to press her to start a family. Jan had initially found Maria's family delightfully welcoming. However, he soon began to feel that their demands on Maria and their all-encompassing sociability were smothering his individuality and interfering with their time together. He expressed his discontents to Maria in the open manner to which he had been socialized, but it did not seem to have any effect. He began to realize that he had not only married Maria, but had also chosen to live in a context that challenged his whole sense of who he was. If his relationship was to survive, he would need to talk and interact with Maria in ways that had not seemed necessary in their student days.

Psychologists mostly treat individuals as the focus of their studies. Their research methods are better adapted to doing so than are those mostly employed by sociologists, anthropologists or economists. However, if we study individuals without regard to their surroundings, physical, social and cultural, we will fail to understand many of the reasons why they behave as they do. It is for this reason that cross-cultural psychologists have recently developed measures of individuals' cultural context, for example the national system within which they live, in addition to measures focused on their social environment and on the individuals themselves.

This interplay between individual and context will be important throughout this book. Some of those theorists and researchers who define this reciprocal interplay as the central focus for psychology identify themselves as *cultural* psychologists. *Cross-cultural* psychologists differ from cultural psychologists in their somewhat stronger preference for obtaining separate measures of the individual and of the broader contexts such as the nation that they inhabit. Different levels of analysis tell us different things about patterns of human behaviour. In Chapter 4, we focus directly on the new and growing field of nation-level analyses in psychology.

Distinguishing levels of analysis is especially important in the types of settings upon which we focus, most especially in the later chapters of this book: intercultural settings. What happens when I from my nation meet you from yours? Do some aspects of the cultural milieu within which you are located make it difficult for you and me to relate effectively with one another? Do we make adjustments in our interpretations of the other, our language use and our actions towards one another? Whether we do or do not will contribute to the success or failure of that particular interaction. Whether failures or successes are typical of the interactions of you and me as individuals will determine the quality of our individual life experiences and the success of our joint enterprise. Box 1.5 illustrates some of the cultural issues that can arise. In one respect Box 1.5 is unusual in that the English speaker in the episode was able to speak the language of the other party. Native English speakers frequently underestimate the extent to which mastery of language is a prime contributor to failed cross-cultural interactions. Whether successes or failures are more typical of the millions of interactions that occur between members of two nations will contribute to the further evolution of those nations' cultures. Will they merge, polarize or remain as they are? What level of contact between nations can be expected to leave them as separate, self-sustaining entities and what will facilitate their integration?

Box 1.5

'C'est trop anglais, Monsieur'

Paul was a British senior manager, negotiating to sell machinery to a large French organization. A series of meetings took place in Paris, with Paul, often being the sole representative of the British firm, meeting a group from the French side. Paul felt that negotiations were going well, and commented that he was 'getting a feel for the French' and was taking the chance to improve his French language skills. He worked hard at anticipating possible problems that might arise in reaching agreement and was confident that there were none. Preparing for the next stage in negotiation, Paul

(Continued)

Box 1.5   Continued

arranged for a standard legal contract to be prepared, founded on the points agreed in previous meetings. There was no difficulty in translating the document into French by the French partner. At the next and decisive meeting, Paul was shocked when the French team rejected his draft contract. 'C'est trop anglais, Monsieur' ('It's too English'), they said. Paul was astonished.

After some time, Paul made contact with a French business consultant, trying to find a way forward. Taking account of the points that emerged from their discussion, he was able to reopen negotiations with the French company and to agree a contract without further difficulty. The consultant highlighted six issues that had contributed to the initial failure to secure a contract:

1   Paul had neglected the importance of hierarchy in France and had not ascertained whether those with whom he was dealing had been given appropriate authority to reach agreement.
2   Paul had assumed that the contract terms are not affected by cultural differences and simply required a literal translation from English to French.
3   The draft contract was written in a way that reflected the English preference for indirectness and flexibility. It contained non-specific phrases indicating, for instance, that possible future events would be handled by such procedures 'as may be agreed from time to time'. To the French, this undermined the basis for the creation of trust.
4   Paul had not arranged for the British and French lawyers who were involved to meet and discuss the much greater need for precision that exists in the French legal code.
5   The contract was lengthy, specifying many unlikely eventualities, but was so vague that the French would not be able to find specific codified elements within it that they could contest.
6   Paul had taken responsibility for the project overall, whereas it was important for the French to have representatives of various specializations involved. Consequently, Paul appeared to the French as more of an amateur, compared to their specialist strengths. While Paul had seen his solo trips to France as an effective way to cut costs, to the French it would appear that, by not sending a full team, the British were not giving them respect and investing sufficient resources in the collaboration to ensure its success and guarantee their sincerity.

Source: Harper & Cormeraie (1992).

The main concern of the later sections of this book is with the social psychological consequences of contemporary modes of transport and communication. These consequences are most evident (and have been most studied) among those who travel both between nations and from the countryside to the cities, as well as among those who communicate globally. In reviewing what is happening among this section of humanity, we need also to remember that these processes may barely touch those within all nations who continue to live in great poverty. Indeed, aspects of modernity such as the spread of AIDS, the long distance transportation of foodstuffs and timber, and the global arms trade may well be accelerating the growth of poverty and the gap between the rich and the poor, along with environmental degradation. A full understanding of what is universal about human nature requires that we focus not just on how humans cope with the context of modernity, but also on how they cope with a context of poverty and with disparities in the distribution of a cultural group's wealth.

In this book, we cannot answer all the questions that we have touched upon in the preceding paragraphs. If a full answer is possible at this time, input is also required from historians, anthropologists, demographers, economists, sociologists, political scientists and geographers. What we do claim to achieve is some insight into the processes that we have listed above, using the perspectives that have been developed over the past 30 years by cross-cultural psychologists. In the first nine chapters, we give most attention to the social psychology of the world as it is, because this provides a necessary basis for understanding our discussion of change processes in the remaining chapters. We conclude each chapter with a summary, suggestions for further reading and some study questions. We have also provided a glossary at the end of the book, in which you will find definitions of the technical terms that have proven useful for cross-cultural psychologists. Terms that are included in the glossary appear in **bold** throughout the text.

In Chapter 2, we describe the process whereby some psychologists have confronted the monocultural perspective of their discipline and developed new research methods that take better account of variations in culture around the globe. One lesson that has been learned, and which needs to be constantly relearned, is that researchers themselves are not immune to the processes that they seek to study. Psychologists' own cultural and educational histories have persistent, pervasive effects on what they find worth studying and how they choose to study it. Many well-known cross-cultural psychologists were themselves migrants or have married someone from a different cultural background and have benefited from their intercultural encounters (Bond, 1997a). One way to confront and minimize one's preconceptions is to work with others whose socialization yields a different but complementary perspective.

Thus it has been in the writing of this book. We draw on experiences arising from our work in the contexts of North America, in Europe, in Pacific Asia and in the developing nation of Turkey. As a further check on the ethnocentrism of our perceptions, we have asked leading cross-cultural psychologists from a number of nations to tell us very briefly what they see as one or two of the intercultural problems that they identify where they live and to which cross-cultural psychology can make a positive contribution. Their answers are summarized in Box 1.6. No doubt many of those who responded would also endorse issues that were identified by other contributors to the table. Overall, these are the key issues. In the chapters that follow, we shall develop a perspective on how cross-culturalists can best address them.

In the next two chapters, we explore the methods and theories of cross-cultural psychology. In Part 2, we review five core areas in which cross-cultural psychology can make a major contribution: social development, personality, social cognition, interpersonal relations, and organizational psychology. Finally, in Part 3, we draw on the perspectives outlined in Part 2 to explore the current global turbulence.

Box 1.6

Contributions of Cross-cultural Psychology to Key Local Issues

Nation	Potential Contribution
Canada	In parts of the nation where multiculturalism is a fact of life, finding ways to help institutions become less ethnocentric. In parts of the nation where there is less diversity, contributing to programmes that foster pluralism and equity of access to opportunity.
Germany	Providing information that is relevant to the creation of a multi-cultural society. Helping to manage intra-cultural conflicts and providing means to cope with contentious parts of German history.
Hong Kong	Helping multicultural work teams, comprising British, US and Hong Kong employees, become more effective. Improving the teaching of English as a second language. Finding ways to confront avoidance tactics of the Chinese government.
Hungary	Making Hungary more visible to others. Clarifying what is culturally distinctive about Hungary. Separating the effects of political and cultural transformation.
Israel	Helping groups to understand one another's worldviews and to seek ways to manage their differences.
Japan	Serving as a mirror through which Japanese can better understand themselves.
Mexico	Providing a way to understand regional and local realities. Contributing in a sensitive manner solutions to such issues as individual and social development, poverty, violence and a better way of living.
Southern Africa	Helping to address development issues, especially wealth, conflict resolution and the promotion of peace. Giving support to traditional institutions, such as spirituality and respect for elders, which can have a positive contribution to social and economic development.
Turkey	Providing a psychology that is appropriate and relevant to Turkish reality, thus enabling Turkish psychologists to do the psychology that accords with the priorities of the Turkish social development agenda.
United Kingdom	Confronting media stereotyping of minorities, particularly 'asylum seekers'. Promoting reasoned debate about European integration.

Summary

The purpose of this book is to provide an up-to-date analysis of the achievements of cross-cultural psychologists and to show how these achievements can be used to address the issues raised by the current impact of enhanced interdependence, mobility and communications.

Further Reading

There is an online website that contains short articles written by many of the leading contemporary cross-cultural psychologists. The website is located at Western Washington University, USA, and was established by Dr Walter Lonner and his colleagues. Lonner was also the founding editor of the *Journal of Cross-Cultural Psychology*, which is the premier journal in this field. This website can be freely accessed at www.wwu.edu/psychology/~culture. Take a look at the introduction to the website. Specific suggestions for relevant readings taken from this website are indicated after each of the chapters in this book.

Study Questions

1 How would you describe yourself in terms of nationality and ethnicity? Can you identify ways in which your national or ethnic identity affects the way that you behave?
2 What issues arise for you when you interact with persons of different nationality or ethnicity?
3 What contemporary problems can you identify where an understanding of culture may improve our capacity to improve the situation?

2 Improving the Validity of Cross-cultural Psychology

Our focus in this volume is primarily but not exclusively on what is typically considered to constitute social psychology. Indeed, since a main element in our perspective is that one cannot understand any particular behaviour without taking account of the context within which it occurs, one could argue that all of psychology is (or at any rate, should be) social psychology. However, some aspects of behaviour are much more context-dependent than others, and it is these that demand our closest scrutiny. In this chapter, we explore the ways in which the present understanding of how to do cross-cultural psychology has been achieved. This undertaking will entail a certain amount of historical review and a focus on methods of investigation. We must defer detailed consideration of theories and results until we have some confidence in the skills and techniques available to cross-cultural investigators. Throughout the chapter, we shall underline a series of methodological cautions that can be drawn from earlier experience.

Published accounts of the origins of psychological research are often written in a way that suggests a linear development towards a particular contemporary research method. Those who favour experimental research highlight the establishment of laboratories, for instance by Wundt in Leipzig, Germany in 1879. Those who currently favour qualitative or discursive methods point to the earlier foundation of a social psychology journal in Germany by Steinthal and Lazarus (Lück, 1987) and to descriptive accounts of crowd behaviour in France (Le Bon, 1895). English language authors typically identify the social psychology texts by McDougall (1908) in the UK and Ross (1908) in the USA as the first to be published, failing to note earlier texts by Tarde (1898) in French, and Orano (1902) in Italian. In a similar way, Triplett (1898), working in the USA, is often credited with having conducted the first empirical study of social influence processes, whereas Ringelmann had made studies on the same topic in France ten years earlier (Kravitz & Martin, 1986), as had Binet and Henri (1894). Even earlier discussions of how best to study social behaviour empirically were reported from Italy (Cattaneo, 1864). It may seem pedantic to point out these studies, which now have only archival significance. However, they serve to emphasize our first caution: **Guideline 1   Cross-cultural psychologists should not expect that all relevant studies will be published in English**.

Clearly there can be no definitive history of psychology, but rather a set of histories within which different authors highlight events that mark the way toward their own preferred present (Lunt, 2003). Our own account has a similarly selective perspective. While the work of most of those noted above implicitly assumes that human behaviour can be validly studied by sampling at a single location, we look instead for work that tests for universality by using some kind of comparative research design. Three rather separate paths towards this perspective can be discerned. One path leads us to social anthropology, one comprises a psychometric perspective, and the last has emerged from a primarily North American social psychology. We consider these in turn.

A Social-anthropological Perspective Based on Fieldwork

Accounts of the focus of Wundt's psychological laboratory and of the persons who visited him make it clear that the current specialist focus of the different social sciences did not then exist. He was a skilled generalist. In his later publications, Wundt espoused what he termed *Völkerpsychologie*, and his visitors included those who subsequently became well known as sociologists and social anthropologists, for instance Durkheim and Malinowski. Wundt's account of *Völkerpsychologie* was not based on observations, but was focused on analysis of such issues as language, myth, customs, religion and art. Although Wundt never drew on this material, through the first half of the twentieth century the developing discipline of social anthropology yielded a rich harvest of ethnographic studies of non-Western societies. Initially, it was seen as worthwhile simply to document the practices and social relationships characterizing a given society. As more and more studies were published, it was inevitable that attempts would be made to construct theories as to why societies differed in the ways that they did.

Thus was born the **culture and personality** school. The US anthropologist, Ruth Benedict, for instance characterized whole cultures in terms such as 'paranoid', which might be applied to individuals and which were derived from integrating observations about the typical individuals of that culture. As she put it:

> It is recognized that the organization of the total personality is crucial in the understanding or even in the mere description of the individual personality. If this is true in individual psychology where individual differentiation must be limited always by the short span of human lifetime, it is even more imperative in social psychology, where the limitations of time and of conformity are transcended. The degree of integration that may be attained is of course incomparably greater than can ever be found in individual psychology. Cultures from this point of view are individual psychology thrown large upon the screen, given gigantic proportions and a long time span. (Benedict, 1932, p. 24)

Drawing on this perspective, Benedict (1946) asserted that the national character of the Japanese was based on shame, in contrast to that of Western nations that was said to be more focused on guilt. She acknowledged that some individuals might not fit the overall pattern, but was primarily concerned with understanding the overall profile of a given society.

Psychological anthropologists, as they became known, were strongly influenced by psychoanalytic theories (Piker, 1998). Once the massive databank of the Human Relations Area Files had been assembled, it became possible to test hypotheses linking particular styles of child-rearing with the predominant practices of different societies. For instance, support was found for the hypothesis derived from psychoanalysis that societies in which weaning occurs relatively late would favour remedies for illness that are taken orally (Whiting & Child, 1953). The **culture and personality** school found particular applicability to societies that were small and homogeneous.

When we try to comprehend the social behaviour of those who live in contemporary societies, it becomes imperative to make a distinction between the experiences of the individual and the cultural context within which they live. There is simply too much variability across the characteristics of individuals within the same cultural group to justify the simplifications arising from the culture and personality tradition. We discuss the reasons for making this distinction more fully in Chapter 7, but for the moment we can simply note a second methodological guideline arising from the historical development of the field: **Guideline 2   Cross-cultural psychologists need a clear understanding of the distinction between individual-level analysis and culture-level analysis**.

An additional perspective drawn from fieldwork has been that which derives from the work of Vygotsky (1934/1962) in Russia. Vygotsky studied peasant communities in Central Asia, focusing upon the development of thought and language. He emphasized the manner in which learning derives from the socio-cultural context within which the child develops. For instance, the child acquires language skills from the more competent practitioners with whom he or she interacts. These models provide illustrations of ways of speaking and thinking that are slightly more complex than those the child has yet mastered, but still within its 'zone of proximal development'. The child first learns to speak in the new ways observed from his or her socialization models, and then internalizes these skills. This focus on cultural transmission of cognitive development of children has been an important precursor to contemporary **cultural psychology** (Cole, 1996; Valsiner, 1989; Rogoff, 1990; Segall, Dasen, Berry, & Poortinga, 1999; see also the recommended Further Reading by Valsiner). The focus of cultural psychology is no longer distinctively upon children, but highlights the reciprocal process by which everyday interactions between individuals transmit and reformulate our sense of what goes on around us.

The Psychometric Perspective

The basis upon which psychology became distinguished from neighbouring social sciences was through its emphasis upon studying samples of individuals within controlled settings, rather than focusing upon larger groups, organizations or nations. Experimentalists test the specific effects of changes within a controlled environment on the individuals in that environment, but there is an equally strongly developed set of procedures based simply upon psychometric testing of individuals. If the beginnings of psychological study are marked by the use of these types of methods, then the beginnings of cross-cultural psychology are to be found within the studies conducted by members of the Torres Straits expedition. Over 100 years ago, a group of social scientists visited the islands in the Torres Straits, which separate Australia and New Guinea. One member of the team, Rivers, focused his studies upon the islanders' perceptual processes. Rivers referred to his respondents as 'savages', and was influenced by a belief prevalent at that time that because 'savages' were less intelligent than Caucasians they might have superior visual skills:

> The natives were told that some people had said that the black man could see and hear better than the white man, and that we had come to find out how clever they were … (Rivers, 1901)

Despite whatever preconceptions Rivers may have held, he obtained some rather striking results. For instance he reported that susceptibility to visual illusions varied, depending on the perceiver's **ethnicity**. The islanders were indeed less susceptible to the Müller-Lyer illusion, namely that the vertical lines with outward and inward facing arrow heads in Box 2.1 differ in length. However, they were more susceptible than Caucasians to the illusion that the vertical line in Box 2.1 is longer than the horizontal line. Susceptibility to various types of visual illusions has been studied extensively by cross-cultural psychologists in more recent times (Segall, Dasen, Berry, & Poortinga, 1999). The results are not wholly consistent, but it appears that differential sensitivity to illusions is a product of the particular type of environment in which one lives. The presence or absence of particular types of routine visual stimuli in the environment is thought to give differential encouragement to the development of relevant types of perceptual discrimination. This line of research points to two further guidelines of key relevance to cross-cultural psychology. Firstly, **Guideline 3   If we wish to detect cross-cultural differences, tests are required that will validly detect those differences**.

Box 2.1

Visual Illusions

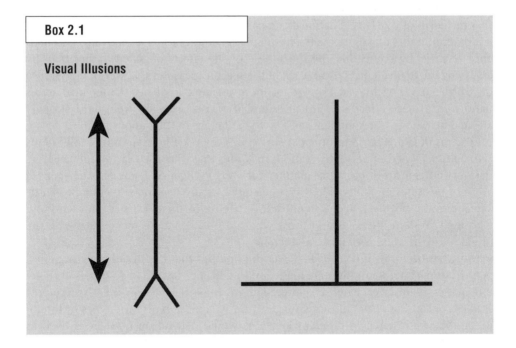

Rivers used a great variety of tests, not just those that have been mentioned here. He was perhaps lucky, in that he chose to include two different tests of visual illusion. Had he used only one, he might have been led towards a false and possibly racist conclusion about the greater susceptibility of one group to illusions. Secondly, in explaining his experimental procedures to his respondents, Rivers chose to deceive them. The tests must indeed have seemed strange to the islanders, and some form of explanation was clearly required. In more recent times, psychologists also sometimes tell lies to their research participants, in the hope that this deception will conceal from them the hypotheses that they wish to test and enable the psychologist to assess their responses more validly.

The particular issue that informing participants about one's research raises for cross-cultural psychologists is this: if research participants are told that they are part of a cross-national comparison, is this likely to cause them to respond differently? In the case of the Torres Straits studies of perceptual processes, the answer is probably no, but in relation to social behaviours the answer is less clear. What would happen, for example, if a cross-cultural social psychologist told his or her participants that the purpose of the research was to compare national levels of helping behaviour? This challenge leads to **Guideline 4   In conducting cross-cultural studies, care must be taken to explain one's study in ways that do not prejudice the validity of the data that are obtained.** Achieving validity does not require deception, but it may require an explanation that is only partial, if one is given at all.

Psychological research that involves testing of individual respondents' cognitive capacities has been very extensive in more recent times. Various types of intelligence tests have been frequently employed. Van de Vijver (1997) reported a **meta-analysis** that included fully 251 cross-national comparisons of cognitive abilities. **Meta-analysis** is a procedure that makes it possible to summarize studies using a wide range of different measures, by comparing the magnitude of the effects obtained, rather than by analysing the results separately for each of the specific measures that were used (see also the Further Reading by van Hemert for more on **meta-analysis**). Differences across nations in average effect sizes on measures of cognitive ability were most strongly affected by the age of respondents and by the affluence of the nations sampled.

In terms of Guideline 3 formulated above, the key issue in examining these results is to consider whether or not the various measures that were used can validly measure national differences in cognitive abilities such as intelligence. Some researchers used Western measures of ability, whereas others used locally developed measures. Van de Vijver did not, however, find a significant difference in the effect size between those who used Western measures and those who did not. For more social outcomes, the origin of the measure may make a difference.

There has been much controversy over the findings that certain ethnic groups and persons from certain nations score higher on intelligence tests than do others. It therefore matters a great deal whether 'culture-fair' measures have been used. The results of studies concerning visual illusions suggest that we might expect the types of intelligence that are fostered in different locations would depend on how life is lived in those locations. In other words, intelligence would need to be defined in terms of the abilities necessary to process information effectively that is relevant to the local context, rather than as an absolute quality of which one has either more or less. Western-style schooling may develop a focus on particular modes of logical, abstract thought. Other contexts may require other ways of thinking. Mundy-Castle (1974) interviewed West Africans as to the qualities that they perceived to make up intelligence and found that they considered social skills an equally important aspect of intelligence to what he called technological skills. Segall et al. (1999) note further studies that reach similar conclusions. Rather than treating cognitive ability as a unitary trait, it is preferable to study the way in which different environments encourage the development of the kinds of cognitive ability that are needed for survival in each context (Sternberg & Grigorenko, 2003). Although the tests of cognitive ability that are employed in most cross-national surveys continue to emphasize the Western focus on abstract reasoning, it is interesting to note the recent surge of interest in Western nations in 'emotional intelligence' (Goleman, 1996). This development suggests that what was first identified as social intelligence in Africa actually has a relevance that is not restricted to effective functioning in less technically advanced societies.

Box 2.2

When is a Difference a Cultural Difference?

National differences in scores on intelligence tests focus on abilities considered without reference to context. What happens if we make comparisons that include context? After one year of schooling, children in Finland, Germany, Italy, Spain and Greece all achieve accuracy levels of greater than 90% on reading of words and of non-words constructed by the researcher. Children in Portugal and Denmark achieve around 70% accuracy. Children in the UK achieve an accuracy of just 40%. It takes them three or four years to achieve 90% accuracy.

Why is this very large difference found? Is it because children in the UK often start school between the ages of four and five, while those in most other European countries start later? Is it because teachers in the UK are less well trained in the specific skills required to teach reading? Are UK teachers less motivated?

The principal explanation for the difference is that English is a much more difficult language to read. It is relatively easy for a Spanish or Greek child to learn to read because their languages are phonically consistent. In other words, a given combination of characters always has the same sound. In English, vowels are frequently pronounced in different ways depending upon the consonants with which they are paired. Consider for instance the sound of 'a' in 'cap', 'call' and 'car', or of 'o' in 'go' and 'do'.

Comparisons of rates of learning to read differ from comparisons of intelligence scores because languages differ from one another, whereas intelligence testers attempt to make their tests 'culture-fair'. Should differences in learning to read be considered as a cultural difference, or should differences only be attributed to culture when measures are used that are equivalent across cultures? Is language a part of culture? These questions are discussed in Chapter 3.

Sources: Seymour, Aro, & Erskine (2003); Goswami, Porpodas, & Wheelwright (1997).

The dilemmas faced by those seeking to measure cognitive abilities can be considered in light of a useful distinction proposed by Pike (1967) and popularized by Berry (1969). In attempting to learn a Mexican Indian language, Pike found that the use of differing pitches and tones influenced the meaning of specific sounds in that language. In terms of the concepts used in linguistics, phonetic production affects the meaning of specific phonemes. Drawing on this distinction, Berry contrasted two approaches to cross-cultural study. Firstly, one could start from the assumption that there are universals and proceed in that manner until evidence is found for differences. He termed this the **'etic'** approach, paralleling the universalist assumptions made in phonetics, the study of sounds. Alternatively, one can start by studying intensively the distinctive attributes of one specific cultural group. He termed this the **'emic'** approach, because it focuses on local meanings, and draws most readily on information provided by persons within that cultural group. This orientation parallels linguists' focus on the phonemic attributes of a specific language.

Berry suggests that most cross-cultural research is initially **'imposed-etic'**, that is to say, it is based on Western concepts and measures applied in non-Western contexts. The assumption is made that the concepts and measures will have the same meaning in new contexts. The global use of intelligence tests such as the Wechsler Intelligence Scale for Children (WISC) and Wechsler Adult Intelligence scale (WAIS) is a typical example. **Emic** studies such as that by Mundy-Castle (1974) can highlight the limitations of using **imposed-etic** measures. As a research field becomes more fully developed, an accumulation of emic studies can contribute to the development of improved 'derived-etic' measures, that have equal validity in a broad range of contexts.

A simple example of progress toward this goal can be found in cross-cultural studies of emotion recognition, which we shall discuss in Chapter 6. In early research, persons from many nations were asked to identify emotions portrayed in posed photographs of American faces. This procedure assumes that all possible types of emotional expression are to be found in US faces. In later studies, faces from all participating nations were included. Berry's concepts lead us towards **Guideline 5   Cross-cultural researchers need to ensure that their stimulus materials and measures are understood comparably in each location**.

The creation of measures that are understood equally well and in similar ways across different parts of the world is not simply a matter of using items that refer to issues or tasks that are familiar to respondents. There is also a need to ensure that translations from one language to another are done in a manner that yields items with equivalent meaning. The most widely accepted procedure for achieving this is back-translation (Brislin, Lonner, & Thorndike, 1973); that is to say, a translation is first made from the language in which the test was originally developed into the language of the society in which it is to be used. A second bilingual person is then asked to translate the items back into the original language, without having seen the original version. Comparison of the retranslated version and the original can then be used to detect problematic translations and to create an improved version through discussion between the two translators.

This discussion often focuses on the relative merits of a literal translation versus **'decentring'**. A decentred translation is one that does not use terms that have precise linguistic equivalence, but which draws on the cultural knowledge of the translators to use phrases that have equivalent meaning in the two languages. For instance, while English speakers discussing some misfortune might seek hope by claiming that 'every cloud has a silver lining', speakers of Mandarin Chinese would claim that 'every cloud has a pink edge'. A decentred translation would drop the specific descriptors in favour of a similar, more general saying, like 'something good comes from any misfortune'. Some of the problems of creating a measure that is understood in a similar way in a whole series of locations are illustrated in Box 2.3.

Box 2.3

Expressing Anger

Spielberger and his colleagues developed a measure of the different ways in which persons might handle their feelings of anger. Within the USA, he distinguished those who hold anger in, those who let anger out and those who are aware of their anger but actively control it. He used **factor analysis** to develop his State-Trait Anger Expression Inventory (STAXI). This measure has been translated subsequently into various languages and employed as an imposed-etic measure in studies in Canada, Norway, Austria, Italy and Singapore. However, it was found that there are fewer words in Norwegian describing the experience and expression of anger than in English. Some English metaphors concerning anger that are used in STAXI (e.g., burning up) have no direct equivalent in Norwegian; conversely some Norwegian metaphors 'Jeg r forbannet' ('I am cursed') have no direct equivalent in English. In Singapore, it was found that the 'anger-in' item 'I am secretly quite critical of others' loaded on the 'anger-out' factor. This occurred because Singapore Chinese respondents interpreted the item as referring to talking negatively behind someone's back, while Western respondents interpreted the item in terms of holding grudges and not talking about them. In designing measures with cross-cultural validity for comparative purposes, items with variable meanings need to be identified and discarded.

Sources: Håseth (1996); Tanzer, Sim, & Spielberger (1996).

Once a satisfactory translation of items to be included in a questionnaire has been accomplished, it is next necessary to determine whether responses to the separate items defining a scale correlate together in the same way as they did in the original language. Procedures that have been used to establish the adequacy of a measure in its country of origin must be repeated in the new locations where it is to be employed. Does the translated scale have adequate **reliability**, in other words a pattern of consistent responses to items that measure the same quality? **Reliability** may have been lost through the translation process. Furthermore, do responses to different scales differ in the same way that **factor analysis** in the country of origin had shown? Finally, is there evidence, such as correlations with other measures that supports the **validity** of the measures in the new context? **Guideline 6   Researchers require evidence that their measures are reliable and valid in each new cultural setting.**

The Experimental Perspective

While the fieldwork and the psychometric perspectives have both contributed substantially to the development of cross-cultural psychology, the most distinctive approach characterizing much psychological research has long been an emphasis upon some form of experimental method. Psychologists have favoured the experimental method because it offers the best chance for determining causal relationships between variables. Simplified settings are required if one is to set up an adequately controlled experiment, but this simplification has mostly been seen as a price worth paying for the development of a truly scientific psychology, one that can establish causal relationships.

Whilst the earliest applications of experimental method were not particularly influential, many of the key figures in the foundation of modern social psychology were those who did favour experimentation, particularly those who practiced in the USA. The political turbulence of the 1930s led to prominent researchers such as Kurt Lewin and Muzafer Sherif seeking refuge in the USA. Other key figures including Fritz Heider and Solomon Asch had migrated to the USA a little earlier. Furthermore, although the origins of social psychology were European, as a consequence of the widespread destruction and dislocation surrounding the Second World War, the practice of social psychology was for a time largely confined to the USA (Farr, 1996). Lewin, Sherif and Asch all espoused theories that emphasized the effect of the immediate social context on behaviour. The generation of US researchers that succeeded them sought ways to illustrate these effects of context experimentally. In order to do this, they created simplified settings in which experimental subjects were exposed to various kinds of social pressures. Over the years, these procedures and the theories that they were designed to test have become more sophisticated, but they all seek to explore the variable impact of the surrounding social field on those persons interacting in that setting.

A series of stages can be identified through which North American experimental social psychologists and those from other parts of the world have sought understanding of the similarities and differences between the outcomes of their studies. Initially, US researchers initiated collaborative work with researchers from other parts of the world, attempting to replicate the results that they had obtained back home. As we shall see, these studies often yielded problematic results. As social psychology became practised more widely around the world, a second stage became apparent. Various critiques of experimental methodology were formulated. In some nations, researchers argued in favour of the development of '**indigenous**' psychologies, abandoning experimental method and using more culturally appropriate methods. In other nations, especially in Europe, the critique was focused on improving the experimental method, rather than on abandoning it. The third and current stage in this process is one where social psychologists from different nations are increasingly collaborating on an equal basis, and draw on theories and methods that are explicitly formulated to explain cultural differences. We consider these three stages in turn.

Stage 1: Replications

Replication of research studies is a crucial element in the establishment of their validity. Even within a single nation, it is not always the case that the results of a study would prove replicable, since there are many ways in which one sample of participants in a study might differ from one another. Probably the most widely replicated experimental study in social psychology has been the Asch (1956) conformity study. Asch showed that when a group of experimental accomplices repeatedly all give incorrect judgements as to which of several lines matched another line, naïve experimental participants rather often also gave incorrect responses. Asch interpreted these effects in terms of conformity, but we should note that only 38% of the responses made by naïve respondents actually showed conformity. The study could also be interpreted in terms of the independence of the remaining 62% of responses.

R. Bond and Smith (1996) reported a **meta-analysis** of 134 published Asch conformity effects. Of these effects, 97 had been obtained with US respondents, while the remainder was drawn from 16 other nations. Bond and Smith used the US data to estimate the effect of variations in the types of experimental procedures that were used, the type of respondents, and the date of the study. They were then able to discount these sources of variance when examining the amount of influence that occurred within the studies done outside North America. As Box 2.4 shows, the degree of group influence on conformity responses was less within Europe than it had been in the USA, but it was greater in the rest of the world than it had been in the USA.

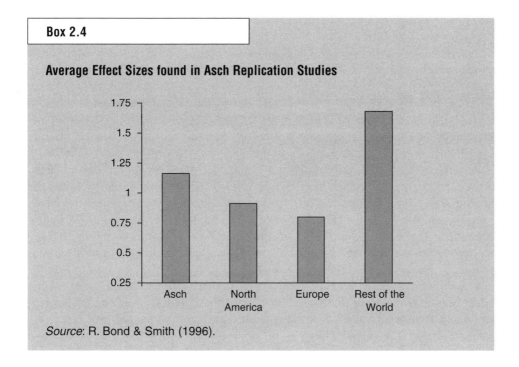

Box 2.4

Average Effect Sizes found in Asch Replication Studies

Source: R. Bond & Smith (1996).

The results of this extensive analysis pose two questions. Firstly, it appears that a standard experimental procedure produces different results in different parts of the world, even after all variations that could be detected within a great number of US replications have been discounted. We need a theory to explain why this change in effect size might occur. Bond and Smith tested various relevant culture-based explanations and we shall return to this study after cultural theories have been introduced in Chapter 3.

Secondly, it is necessary to consider what to call the specific experimental effect that Asch obtained. Asch called it conformity, and subsequent writers follow this usage. However, in differing cultural contexts, it is possible that the same behaviour may have different meanings. One possible way to investigate the meanings of a behaviour is by asking those who engage in that behaviour why they are doing it. Asch did so and obtained a variety of answers from his US respondents. Some said that they thought their eyesight must be defective; others wanted to avoid embarrassment by giving 'wrong' answers publicly. We lack similar interview data from other nations. One possibility is that respondents may have given incorrect answers not to save themselves from embarrassment, but to save the others from embarrassment! Confronted with a group of people who were obviously giving wrong answers, someone who valued tact or sensitivity might choose to reduce the others' humiliation by tactfully also giving wrong answers.

Other very well-known US studies have also been quite often repeated outside the USA, yielding results consistent with the Asch findings. For instance, Milgram's (1961) study of obedience to a destructive authority figure was repeated in eight other countries (reviewed in Smith & Bond, 1998, Chapter 2). The levels of obedience that were found varied, but the effect was obtained in all studies. However, when many other studies have been repeated in new locations, the results are sometimes non-significant and sometimes even in the opposite direction from those obtained in the USA. Amir and Sharon (1987) attempted to estimate the magnitude of the problem of non-replicability. Rather than focus on famous studies, they selected six studies that had been published in major US social psychology journals and attempted to replicate their results, using both high school and university students within Israel. They deliberately selected studies whose design and methods would be appropriate to Israeli respondents. The six original studies had yielded 37 significant effects. Amir and Sharon succeeded in replicating only 16 of these outcomes within both their Israeli samples, and nine more within just one of their samples. They also found 27 significant effects that had not been found in the original studies. Thus it appears that the replicability problem is very substantial, even when assessed in two cultural systems that many would regard as relatively similar.

A particularly striking instance comes from studies of the so-called social loafing effect. Studies have shown that, in the USA, individuals put less effort into a task when working with others than when working alone. Karau and Williams (1993) reported a **meta-analysis** of 147 social loafing effects obtained within the USA and 15 obtained in Pacific Asian nations. On simple tasks, such as clapping one's hands or shouting, social loafing effects were obtained equally in Pacific Asia and the USA. On more complex tasks, the Pacific Asian studies showed a complete reversal: people worked harder when they were in groups than when they were alone. Subsequent studies by Earley (1993) provided further insight into these results. Earley studied managers working on tasks in the USA, China and Israel. Both the Israeli and the Chinese managers worked harder when they believed that their tasks were part of a group effort, whereas the Americans worked harder when they believed that they were working alone. In addition, some of those participants who thought that they were working in a group were led to believe that the group comprised others known to them, whereas other participants were told that they were working with strangers. The enhanced social effort expended by Israelis and Chinese was found only when working with one's own group, not with strangers. This study begins to provide clues as to the nature of the cultural differences that may explain the reversal across nations of the social loafing effect, and will be explored further after we have considered the concepts of **individualism** and **collectivism** in Chapter 3.

One of the requirements of experimental method is that one needs a supply of participants who can present themselves at a psychology laboratory without too much difficulty. This consideration provides one reason why experimental social psychologists have often based their sampling on students. Students differ from the general population in many respects, even within a single nation. However, there are additional hazards in making cross-cultural comparisons based on student populations: the populations of students differ greatly across different countries. In Western nations, university education is undertaken by a relatively large percentage of the age cohort. However, in many nations participation in university education is achieved only by a small percentage of the age cohort, and is drawn disproportionately from elite families. Comparing student samples may give misleading results. Using other populations, as was done in Earley's studies, is preferable. **Guideline 7   Sampled populations should be comparable.**

Stage 2: Decentring Research Methods

We noted above that translators of research materials often need to use **decentring** to make a translation meaningful in another language. Likewise, the results of early attempts to replicate US studies in other locations indicated a need to decentre the research methods that were to be used in studies conducted in other parts of the world. Participation in a social psychology experiment requires one to treat as 'real' a staged event in which one typically interacts for a short period of time with one or more strangers. Valid responses to such a setting are much more likely within contexts where people habitually meet many strangers than in settings where they do not.

In developing their own studies, researchers from different parts of the world have put emphasis on the importance of what they saw as distinctive or **'indigenous'** perspectives. Markus and Kitayama (2003), for example, have concluded that, 'Psychology as we knew it was not yet a comprehensive psychology; it appeared to be the indigenous psychology of America or perhaps, more specifically, the psychology of secular, middle-class Anglo America' (p. 280). By examining other indigenous perspectives and the results they produce, we can form an opinion as to whether different methods suit different national contexts, or whether the debate about methods transcends national boundaries.

We first consider the case of Europe. The initial recovery of social psychology in Europe after the Second World War owed much to visitors from the USA (van Strien, 1997). Reflecting on numerous early US visitors to his research group at Oxford in the UK, Argyle (2001) wrote:

> all were a great source of stimulation, information and help. Our group became an important channel for the transfer of American social psychology to Britain. And yet we kept our distance from American social psychology. They had colonized us, perhaps intentionally, but we altered the message. We were impressed by their ingenious and well designed experiments,

but we found them too artificial, insufficiently related to real behaviour. We could not see how this kind of research could be applied to real problems. We were looking for a different way of doing it. The way we favoured could also be found in several places in the US, but not in the mainstream. (pp. 340–1)

Argyle's concern to address real problems and avoid artificial contexts was echoed by some of the early work in the USA. For instance, the series of field experiments of intergroup conflict conducted by Sherif and his colleagues each lasted several weeks (Sherif, 1966). However, these were exceptional. As European social psychology developed during the 1960s, critical perspectives were formulated of the way in which the experimental methods that were being used neglected the social context within which studies were being conducted (Israel & Tajfel, 1972). Tajfel, a leading proponent of this critique, argued that experiments were conducted 'in a vacuum', focusing only on the individuals and their response to a temporarily contrived, unrealistic social context. He argued for a greater role of small and large group affiliations in determining social behaviours. This challenge led to his formulation of social identity theory and its subsequent development into self-categorization theory (Tajfel & Turner, 1979; Turner, Hogg, Oakes, Reicher, & Wetherell, 1987). These theories have proved distinctly popular among European social psychologists. Researchers in this field continue to use experimental methods, but they test predictions that emphasize the impact of group affiliations in real-world settings.

A second and more radical critique of experimental method in social psychology was articulated by the French social psychologist, Moscovici (1972). Moscovici developed a viewpoint that has become known as the social representations perspective. In a way that recalls the work of Vygotsky, he argues that social knowledge does not reside within individuals, but in communally shared representations of the persons, ideas and objects within one's environment. Researchers who study social representations have mostly abandoned experimental methods, and rely more on interviews and observation to elucidate the way in which one or other concept is socially represented. For instance, specific studies examine social representations of health, illness, the European Union, or the individual. Work on social representations is widespread in Europe and in some regions of Latin America. Both social identity theory and the social representations approach can be thought of as having an indigenous European origin, but both now find adherents in other parts of the world (Smith, 2005).

Most other attempts to develop indigenous psychologies have involved a radical rejection of the experimental method and an attempt to develop methods appropriate to psychological study within a single nation (Kim & Berry, 1993; Sinha, 1997). The most extensive work of this kind is currently to be found in Taiwan and in the Philippines (Church & Katigbak, 2002). *Sykolohiyang pilipino* (Filipino psychology) entails distinctive methods of data collection built upon group participation and has yielded a set of indigenous concepts, among which *kapwa* is said to best describe Filipino social relationships. Enriquez (1993) cautions against inadequate translations of these concepts into English. He notes that while *kapwa* translates literally as 'others', the connotation of that word in English is one of exclusion, but in Tagalog *kapwa* implies inclusion with known, supportive others.

Part of the thrust of indigenous psychologists' work is exemplified by the fact that little of it is available in English. Many Taiwanese studies are published in the Chinese language journal *Indigenous Psychological Research in Chinese Societies*. Yang provides a series of ten 'Dos' and seven 'Don'ts', arising from some of the Taiwanese work. Some of these are listed in Box 2.5. Note how Yang chooses to describe Western psychology as an indigenous psychology, not as mainstream psychology or as universal psychology.

Box 2.5

How to do Indigenous Psychology

- **Do** tolerate ambiguous or vague states of understanding and suspend decisions as long as possible in dealing with theoretical, methodological and empirical problems, until something indigenous emerges in your mind during the research process.
- **Do** be a typical native in the cultural sense when functioning as a researcher.
- **Do** take the studied psychological or behavioural phenomenon and its socio-cultural context into consideration.
- **Do** give priority to the study of culturally unique phenomena.
- **Do** base your research on the intellectual tradition of your own culture rather than on that of a Western culture.
- **Don't** neglect Western psychologists' important experiences in developing *their own* indigenous psychologies, which may be usefully transferred to the development of non-Western indigenous psychologies (emphasis added).

Source: Excerpts from Yang (2000).

Translations of concepts said to be indigenous do not always confirm their uniqueness, however. For instance Diaz-Guerrero (1993) identified a series of more than 100 'historic socio-cultural premises' that are widely endorsed by Mexican respondents and which form the basis of the indigenous Mexican ethnopsychology that he and his colleagues have formulated. These premises comprise attitude statements in favour of what Diaz Guerrero terms affiliative obedience, *machismo*, respect over love and virginity. However, Ayçiçegi (1993) translated a selection of these statements into Turkish and found that Turkish respondents also endorsed them all. At various points in this book, we shall discuss several other indigenous concepts that are said to have meanings that do not apply to other cultures. There are likely to be many more that are not yet represented in the psychological literature and are fertile grounds for readers of this text to explore within their own cultural systems for possible overlap.

For the moment, it is more important that we focus upon the methodological dilemma that is raised increasingly by the fruits of indigenous research. How can we know whether concepts drawn from different languages do or do not have the same meanings? In the case of *kapwa*, there is a self-evident difference. Are such differences a major threat to the ultimate development of a unified psychology, or are the majority of differences a matter of nuance, which while important need not overshadow the presence of more general human universals? We can offer a provisional answer to these questions in the form of **Guideline 8   Evidence for universality is more likely** to be found from a series of parallel studies done within different nations to explore the meanings of a concept, rather than from direct cross-national comparisons of mean scores on that concept.

This is a more controversial guideline than those offered so far. Many cross-cultural studies involve direct comparisons of mean scores from one nation to another, as, for example, in the Asch 'conformity' studies discussed earlier. While studies of this type are important in identifying what appear to be cultural differences, they cannot tell us whether similar sounding concepts have the same meaning in different cultural contexts. To discover the meaning of a concept, we need to determine its correlates *within* each cultural context. The correlates of that concept define its '**nomological net**', the set of meanings that make sense of its usage and help social scientists build up a theory about the concept. If we find that a phenomenon has the same correlates in different cultural contexts, then we can be more confident that we are studying equivalent phenomena. As an example, let us revert to Earley's studies of social loafing. If we find that even though we get more loafing by groups in one nation and more loafing by individuals in another nation, the same predictors correlate with the presence or absence of loafing in both contexts, then we can be confident that we are comparing like with like. For instance, we might find that the level of endorsement of particular values in different nations could explain the change in loafing behaviours when alone or in a group.

Stage 3: Benchmarks for Contemporary Cross-cultural Studies

In the preceding section, we gave some illustrations of the ways in which researchers in different parts of the world have expressed reservations about a psychology that is built upon global application of the experimental methods that are favoured within mainstream US social psychology. Van de Vijver and Leung (1997) provide a much more comprehensive discussion of methodological issues in cross-cultural research (see also the Further Reading by van de Vijver). Our position here is neither for nor against particular methods. Each can illuminate aspects that other methods may well miss. We have hinted already at some of the ways in which studies can be done that bridge at least some of the gaps between the divergent methods that are currently employed. Here we highlight some further achievements that have arisen from cross-cultural research over the past few decades, and which can be useful in evaluating the quality of the studies that we report in later chapters.

The first achievement to be noted is that recent studies are much more frequently based upon equal collaboration between those from inside and those from outside those nations that are included in a cross-national study. Both internal and external perspectives are valuable in understanding patterns of social behaviour. It is easy for **emic** researchers to think falsely that some aspect of their culture is unique; it is equally easy for **imposed-etic** researchers to assume falsely that their measures capture all the important aspects of a particular culture. Together, they can provide a corrective to one another's blind spots. Equality is not always easily achieved because some researchers may defer to others on the basis of seniority or presumed greater expertise. However, in the matter of internal versus external perspective, no one is more expert than anyone else. **Guideline 9   A better study will show evidence of input from both emic and etic perspectives**.

The second achievement concerns measurement. The two types of study that have been discussed in most detail in this chapter relied on objective measurements. In the Asch studies, social influence was measured by actual recorded judgements. In the social loafing studies, measures of actual work performance were used. However, very many of the studies reported by cross-cultural researchers utilize survey measurements of attitudes, beliefs, values or abstract judgements. All of these responses are recorded on rating scales, most typically those known as Likert scales, anchored by phrases such as 'Strongly agree' to 'Strongly disagree' or 'Very much' to 'Not at all'.

The study by Hofstede (1980) has been a key influence on cross-cultural psychology and will be discussed extensively in the next chapter. One particularly important aspect of Hofstede's study was that he identified the varying propensity of respondents in different parts of the world to record agreement or disagreement with Likert-scale items. Hofstede overcame this problem by the use of **within-subject standardization** of scores, sometimes known as ipsatization. In other words, he reasoned that given a full range of mutually contradictory statements, a respondent could not logically agree with all of them. Consequently, in order to make a valid comparison of mean scores across different nations, a respondent's scores on each item must be made *relative* to his or her scores on all the other items. Hofstede made this type of correction for whole nations, but it can be done equally well for individuals. Studies will be discussed in later chapters that failed to make this type of correction and consequently drew conclusions about national differences that most likely reflected differences in **acquiescent response bias**, rather than the differences the researchers claimed to have studied. Box 2.6 illustrates the size of cultural differences that required correction in one recent study. **Guideline 10   A better study will be one in which the possibility of acquiescent bias has been taken into account, either by balancing items requiring positive and negative responses, or by estimating and discounting bias**.

Box 2.6

Yea-saying and Nay-saying

Business managers from 43 nations were surveyed. Respondents were asked to rate on 5-point scales to what extent they relied on each of eight sources of guidance in handling each of eight separate work events. Thus, each respondent provided 64 ratings, and it is not plausible that any manager would rely on all eight sources of guidance in handling all eight events. Below are shown the highest and lowest scores for what the researchers termed the 'culture mean'. This is the mean across all 64 ratings – the net tendency to agree or disagree with statements in general. Note that the difference of 0.82 between the highest and lowest scoring nations spans 20% of the whole 5-point scale, indicating that **acquiescent response bias** could be a major source of misunderstanding in interpreting cross-national comparisons.

(Continued)

Box 2.6   Continued

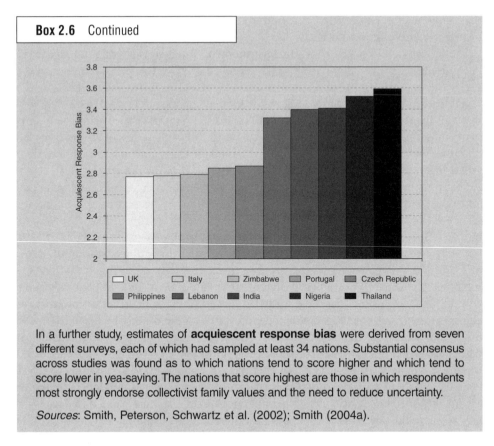

In a further study, estimates of **acquiescent response bias** were derived from seven different surveys, each of which had sampled at least 34 nations. Substantial consensus across studies was found as to which nations tend to score higher and which tend to score lower in yea-saying. The nations that score highest are those in which respondents most strongly endorse collectivist family values and the need to reduce uncertainty.

Sources: Smith, Peterson, Schwartz et al. (2002); Smith (2004a).

The third achievement is that cross-cultural psychologists do now have theories to guide their studies. In the early years, many studies were conducted which made simple comparisons between a certain effect in country A and country B, without any initial rationale as to why these particular nations should have been selected for comparison. In the next chapter, we outline the emergence of the theories that are currently available to guide cross-cultural investigations. Progress towards this point has necessarily required debate as to how best to conceptualize culture and how to measure its salient attributes. Studies selected for discussion in later chapters will be evaluated in terms of all the guidelines outlined in this chapter, but with especial focus on this last one – **Guideline 11   The studies of greatest interest are those that test relevant theories about how culture affects the outcome studied.**

Summary

Studying psychological phenomena in differing cultural contexts requires skills additional to those required for research within a single population. This chapter has formulated a series of eleven guidelines for effective research that have arisen from the successes and failures of earlier studies. We reproduce them here for easy reference.

1   Cross-cultural psychologists should not expect that all relevant studies will be published in English.
2   Cross-cultural psychologists need a clear understanding of the distinction between individual-level analysis and culture-level analysis.

3   If we wish to detect cross-cultural differences, tests are required that will validly detect those differences.

4   In conducting cross-cultural studies, care must be taken to explain one's study in ways that does not prejudice the validity of the data that are obtained.

5   Cross-cultural researchers need to ensure that their measures are understood comparably in each location.

6   Researchers require evidence that their measures are reliable and valid in each new cultural setting.

7   Sampled populations should be comparable.

8   Evidence for universality is more likely to be found from a series of parallel studies done within different nations to explore the meanings of a concept, rather than from direct cross-national comparisons of mean scores on that concept.

9   A better study will show evidence of input from both emic and etic perspectives.

10   A better study will be one in which the possibility of acquiescent bias has been taken into account, either by balancing items requiring positive and negative responses, or by estimating and discounting bias.

11   The studies of greatest interest are those that test relevant theories about how culture affects the outcome studied.

These guidelines can help us to evaluate the studies that are discussed in the rest of this book. Over the past century, some progress has been achieved towards designing and conducting studies that meet these criteria, but we have much more to learn before we can claim that we have a full understanding of culture's impact on social processes and behaviour.

Further Reading

1   Replications in other nations of early US studies are discussed in much fuller detail in Smith & Bond (1998, Chapter 2).

2   Bond, R., & Smith, P.B. (1996). Culture and conformity: A meta-analysis of studies using Asch's (1952b, 1956) line judgement task. *Psychological Bulletin, 119,* 111–137.

3   Valsiner, J. (2004). Culture and its transfer: Ways of creating general knowledge through the study of cultural particulars. www.wwu.edu/psychology/~culture

4   Van Hemert, D.A. (2004). Cross-cultural meta-analyses. www.wwu.edu/psychology/~culture

5   Van de Vijver, F.J.R. (1997). Meta-analysis of cross-cultural comparisons of test performance. *Journal of Cross-Cultural Psychology, 28,* 678–709.

6   Van de Vijver, F.J.R. (2002). Types of cross-cultural studies in cross-cultural psychology. www.wwu.edu/psychology/~culture

Study Questions

1   Should different research methods be used in studying different cultures or are there methods that can usefully be applied in all cultural contexts?

2   Which research method holds greatest promise for advancing our understanding of cross-cultural issues: fieldwork, psychometric tests and surveys, or experimentation?

3   Select any one of the 11 guidelines for cross-cultural research and explain why it is important in the study of social psychology across cultures.

3

Defining the Way Forward:
Theories and Frameworks

There is nothing so practical as a good theory (saying attributed to Kurt Lewin)

Thus far we have explored some of the ways in which cross-cultural studies might best be conducted, so now we need to address the questions that are most central to the field that we are exploring. In this chapter we discuss how best to define the concepts that are needed to guide the work of cross-cultural researchers and then evaluate initial progress in understanding how these concepts can be used to explain both cultural similarities and cultural differences.

Culture, Nations and Societies

There has been extensive debate over the past century about the most useful way in which to define the concept of culture. Psychologists have been relatively late entrants into this debate, drawing upon the earlier work of anthropologists. Anthropologists found particular value in the concept of culture as a way of encapsulating their under-standings of the relatively small and relatively isolated groups of people upon whom many of their early studies had focused, but were not all agreed as to how best to define what a culture is conceptually. An influential early definition was provided by Tylor in 1871. He saw culture as 'that complex whole which includes knowledge, belief, art, morals, laws, customs and any other capabilities and habits acquired by man as a member of society' (Tylor, 1871, Volume 1, p. 1). Subsequent critics favoured a variety of less all-encompassing definitions, leading to an outpouring of narrower definitions, so that by 1963 Kroeber and Kluckhohn (1963) could identify as many as 161. Herskovits (1948) provided an apt and concise summary of the anthropological perspective, describing a culture as 'the man-made part of the human environment', where 'man-made' included both physical artefacts and social systems. So, for example, in studying the Trobriand Islanders in the Pacific Ocean, Malinowski (1927) was able to survey both the behaviours and the physical structures that the islanders created, which together defined and sustained a particular way of life. Trobriand Islanders comprised a distinctive culture, which could be contrasted and compared with those found elsewhere.

More recently, psychologists (and many anthropologists) have focused their atten-tion on human behaviour within the more modernized world. For this rather differ-ent purpose, different approaches to culture may be appropriate. The modern world is organized at least in a political sense into nations, many of which are large and all of which enjoy substantial contact with one another. Is a nation the same as a society, and can it be said to have a culture? Rohner (1984) explored how best to answer these questions within a modern and changing world. He proposed that the essence of 'culture' lies in the shared way in which individuals interpret what goes on around them. These shared interpretations could cover both individual behaviours and the environment within which those behaviours occur. If you and I agree that a certain gesture indicates friendliness rather than aggression, or if we agree that that gesture is beautiful rather than ugly, we are interpreting the world around us in a similar manner. If those similarities are numerous, you and I can be said to share a culture.

Note that in principle this judgement could be applied at all levels of generality. We could identify the culture of a marriage, of a nuclear family, of a work team, of a whole organization, or of a whole nation. In each case we should need to find a criterion against which to judge how much similarity was required before we could say that it was useful to say that a culture was present rather than absent. Given the differing numbers of individuals involved, in deciding whether a family had enough consensus to indicate that it has a culture, we would probably set the criterion higher than we would when deciding whether a nation has a culture. The move over time from definitions that emphasize behaviour patterns to those that emphasize the sharing of the meanings that are attributed to behaviour parallels the evolution of behaviourist psychology into cognitive psychology. A similar evolution has occurred in anthropology. Thus the influential anthropologist Geertz writes: 'The study of culture, the accumulated totality of such patterns [of behaviour] is thus the study of the machinery individuals and groups of individuals employ to orient themselves in a world otherwise opaque' (1973, p. 363).

Culture defined in this way is a quality that entities inhabiting that setting have in relation to one another, not of the individuals that comprise that entity. Individuals are sometimes said to be cultured, but in the sense in which it is being used here culture can only be defined collectively. As Rohner put it, culture is 'the totality of equivalent and complementary learned meanings maintained by a human population, or by identifiable segments of a population, and transmitted from one generation to the next' (1984, pp. 119–20). In later chapters we shall rather frequently refer to individuals as having a particular '**cultural orientation**'. By this phrase we shall mean a propensity to interpret their surroundings in a way that is consistent with one or other of the dimensions of culture that we shall be exploring in this chapter. Speaking of individuals' '**cultural orientation**' acknowledges the continual interplay between a culture and the individuals who are socialized by it and in turn sustain it. This interplay is of particular interest to those who define themselves as **cultural psychologists**. Shweder (1991) for instance defines the goal of **cultural psychology** as the study of 'mentalities' and locates mentalities equally within individuals and within the larger population. His position is formulated in terms of two principles:

> The principle of existential uncertainty asserts that human beings starting at birth ... are highly motivated to seize meanings and resources out of a socio-cultural environment that has been arranged to provide them with meanings and resources to seize and use. The principle of intentional (or constitutional) worlds asserts that subjects and objects, practitioners and practices cannot be analyzed into independent and interdependent variables. Their identities are interdependent; neither side of the supposed contrast can be defined without borrowing from the specifications of the other. (Shweder, 1991, p. 74)

Shweder's sharply formulated perspective helps to clarify the distinction between the approaches used by **cultural psychologists** and cross-cultural psychologists. While cultural psychologists emphasize the way that the individual and culture are inextricably interwoven, cross-cultural psychologists see benefits in using different terms to characterize the perspective of individuals (cultural orientation) and to characterize the extent to which their understanding of events around them is shared by others (culture).

Rohner also emphasizes that it is important to distinguish between a culture and a social system. A social system comprises 'the behaviour of multiple individuals within a culturally-organized population, including their patterns of interaction and networks of social relationships' (Rohner, 1984, p. 126). Social systems can also be as small as a family or as large as a nation, but they are defined in terms of patterns of behaviour, not in terms of the meanings that are placed on those behaviours.

The meanings of most behavioural actions are not by themselves self-evident. If I stand close to you, you may interpret my behaviour in one culture as friendly, in a second as aggressive, and perhaps even in a third as a form of sexual harassment. Even if I hit you, you may depend upon a variety of contextual clues to interpret that physical contact as playful, as accidental or as hostile. Social systems define the patterns of behaviour whose meaning is provided by their cultural context. Social systems *have* cultures. Cultures do not have social systems; they make social systems comprehensible.

Contemporary cross-cultural psychologists frequently define their samples on the basis of respondents' nationality. It is evident that nations are social systems because they comprise extensive interconnected networks of people, but can they be thought of as cultures? A few nations, like Japan, are very homogeneous in the **ethnicity** of their population; many others, like the USA, Germany, Brazil, and Singapore have considerable and increasing ethnic diversity. China, for example, officially recognizes over 50 minority groups within its national borders. According to the definition advanced here, nations, as well as the ethnic groups that may be present within them, are only cultures if there is evidence that their members interpret the events around them in relatively similar ways. We need next to look at the ways in which cross-cultural psychologists can test for such homogeneity of outlook within any particular social system.

Values, Beliefs, and Behaviours

As we have seen, psychologists who are interested in culture tend to fall into one or other of two categories. Those who focus upon the moment to moment ways in which cultures create and reproduce themselves usually prefer to label themselves as **cultural psychologists** (Cole, 1996; Shweder, 1991). Those who focus upon the longer-term consistencies in cultures mostly prefer the label of cross-cultural psychologist. It will be apparent by now that this book stands primarily within this latter perspective. We share the view of those who find the two approaches complementary (Kashima, 2000; Kağıtçıbaşı & Poortinga, 2000). The perspective of cultural psychology is particularly useful when mapping the ways in which specific cultural groups make sense of what goes on around them and how change and development in their understandings may occur. The perspective of cross-cultural psychology has proved more attractive to social psychologists, primarily because it opens up ways of testing whether cultural variations can be explained in terms of processes that are more universal.

We shall need to discuss in later chapters both how the world's national cultures have arisen and how they are sustained. For the moment, let us assume that a certain culture exists as a steady state. How do its members interpret the actions that occur around them? We argued above that a cross-cultural psychologist cannot assume that a particular behaviour has a particular meaning. However, a member of a specific culture can often assign meanings to behaviours. The processes of socialization acting on both children and adults teaches one to interpret the most likely meanings of specific acts. One way for researchers to determine whether a nation could or could not be considered as a culture would be to survey culture members and determine the extent to which there is consensus about the meanings of particular actions. This would be an example of the type of **emic** research design that we noted in the previous chapter. However, one difficulty with this approach is to determine which of thousands of possible behaviours are the ones on which it would be best to focus.

A more parsimonious way to address this problem is not to focus on the meanings of specific behaviours, but on the more organized conceptual frameworks 'held' by culture members, which are likely to guide their interpretations of specific events. As cross-cultural psychology has developed, the most popular choice has been to focus on the values that are held by members of a culture. A person's values provide guidelines as to favoured goals to pursue in living. They are abstract and general and therefore easier to measure. A second basis for prediction is provided by the types of belief endorsed by members of a culture. While values concern what is desirable, beliefs concern what is thought to be true. If a social system is characterized by shared values and shared beliefs, it is very likely that behaviours will be interpreted in similar ways by its members, satisfying our criterion for defining the existence of a culture.

The culture of psychology as a discipline is one in which the formulation and testing of hypotheses is highly valued. Many cross-cultural psychologists share this perspective, and consequently we shall be discussing numerous studies in later chapters where hypotheses are tested asserting that an independent cultural variable (often defined as values or beliefs) will have predictable effects on a dependent variable (often behaviour). We need to remind ourselves that social systems are not composed in the manner of a laboratory experiment. It is rarely the case that we can be sure that one variable causes another to change. The multiple elements of a culture will over time all be acting upon one another. Patterns of behaviour may arise that cause values or beliefs to change, just as changing values or beliefs may cause behaviours to change. However, in order to get inside social systems and begin to understand this complex, dynamic interplay, we need defensible measures of the relevant elements in the system. As a start in this direction, we explore a sequence of key empirical studies that have emerged over the past three decades. These are studies in which researchers have sought to classify nations on the basis of their prevailing values, prevailing beliefs and prevailing behaviours.

The Hofstede Project

There can be little doubt that the single work that has most influenced the development of research into cross-cultural psychology has been the seminal study that was carried out by the Dutch social psychologist, Geert Hofstede. During the late 1960s and early 1970s, Hofstede was one of a team of researchers employed by the US company, IBM. The team was engaged in worldwide morale surveys of their employees in more than 70 nations and eventually accumulated a huge databank of some 116,000 responses. Hofstede conducted extensive analyses of these data, leading in 1980 to the publication of his classic study entitled, *Culture's Consequences*.

Hofstede's conceptualization of culture is similar to the position taken in our book. He defined culture as 'the collective programming of the mind that distinguishes the members of one group or category of people from another' (Hofstede, 2001, p. 9). His goal was to identify some dimensions that could be used to characterize the ways in which nations differed from one another. He was seeking to establish culturally for nations what latitude and longitude established for nations geographically, i.e., the tools for locating them in terms of useful coordinates.

In conducting his study, Hofstede was constrained by the fact that the IBM surveys had been designed to provide the type of information that the company required, rather than for the purposes of cross-cultural research. Most items tapped values, others tapped descriptions of behaviours or intentions to behave in certain ways. Nonetheless, the size of the existing databank gave him some advantages. For instance, he was able to construct samples from each nation that were similar to one another demographically, so that he could be sure that whatever differences he found were attributable to national differences rather than to differences in, for instance, type of job or gender. Once comparable samples had been created, his data set was reduced to 72,215 respondents and the number of nations had declined to 40. However, he was unable to control the number of respondents from different nations, which varied between 11,384 from Germany and 58 from Singapore.

The next step that Hofstede took was crucial. He reasoned that if he was to characterize whole nations rather than individuals, he must analyse his data not at the **individual-level** but at the **nation-level**, or as he termed it, the **'ecological'** level. In other words, taking the answers to each specific question, he *averaged* the scores of all the respondents from each particular nation. Some of the items in the IBM survey required answers on Likert scales anchored by phrases such as 'agree' and 'disagree'. Hofstede was also aware of the problem of cultural differences in **acquiescent response bias**, which we discussed in Chapter 2. He therefore standardized the averaged responses to each item. To do this, each nation's mean across all items was subtracted from each separate item mean and the resultant score was divided by the standard deviation of the item means. With this standardization accomplished, he was ready to determine whether the average answers to each survey item varied in ways that could be classified along any particular dimension.

By comparing correlations between specific item scores and conducting a factor analysis of some of the standardized nation averages to the questionnaire items, he succeeded in identifying four dimensions of national variation. He named these Power Distance, Uncertainty Avoidance, **Individualism-Collectivism**, and Masculinity-Femininity. Those who are familiar with **individual-level** factor analysis would argue that 40 cases are insufficient to conduct a valid factor analysis. However, within his **nation-level** analysis, most data points are the mean of hundreds and in some instances thousands of responses. Such numbers give these data points much enhanced stability, reducing the error of measurement and making the resulting analyses reliable. Each dimension was defined by the answers to between three and six questions from within the original survey. The items that define each dimension are shown in Box 3.1.

Box 3.1

Defining the Hofstede Dimensions

Dimension	Items
Power Distance	1 Employees are afraid to disagree with their managers. 2 My manager is autocratic, OR persuasive/paternalistic. 3 I prefer managers who are autocratic OR participative, but not those who consult and then make their own decision.
Uncertainty Avoidance	1 Company rules should not be broken, even when the employee thinks it is in the company's best interest. 2 I intend to stay with the company for at least five years. 3 I feel nervous and tense at work.

Individualism (versus Collectivism)	It is important for me to have:
	    Personal time, Freedom to use my approach, Challenge.
	Less important for me:
	    Good physical conditions, Training opportunities, Use of all my skills.

Masculinity (versus Femininity)	It is important for me to have:
	    High earnings, Recognition for good work, Advancement, Challenge.
	Less important for me:
	    Good relations with manager, Cooperating with others, Desirable living area, Job security.

Note: Wordings are not exact and have been modified for greater clarity.
Source: Hofstede (1980).

As with other factor analyses, there is some degree of subjectivity in deciding how to name the factors that emerge. Hofstede's choices have had substantial impact upon how others have later responded to each of the factors so named. The dimension that he first identified was labelled Power Distance, which he defined as 'the difference between the degree to which B can determine the behaviour of S and the extent to which S can determine the behaviour of B' (Hofstede, 2001, p. 83; B and S refer to Boss and Subordinate). Subsequent to his original analysis, Hofstede has provided additional scores for some additional countries. Drawing also on these data, the nations rated highest on Power Distance were Malaysia, Slovakia, Guatemala, Panama, Philippines, and Russia; those rated lowest were Austria, Israel, Denmark, New Zealand, and Ireland.

The second dimension was called Uncertainty Avoidance. This is defined as the shunning of ambiguity. Hofstede (2001, p. 148) notes that many writers have understood his concept as risk avoidance. However, he argues that this is a misinterpretation and that in high uncertainty avoidance cultures, risks may sometimes be taken, simply as a way to escape from uncertainty. High Uncertainty Avoidance nations were found to be Greece, Portugal, Guatemala, Uruguay, and Malta; those rated lowest were Singapore, Jamaica, Denmark, Sweden, and Hong Kong.

The third dimension was named **Individualism-Collectivism**. Individualist cultures are defined as those in which individuals see themselves as having relatively separate identity, whereas collectivist cultures are those in which identity is more strongly defined by long-lasting group memberships. The manner in which this dimension is defined lends itself to application within **individual-level** studies, and these are discussed extensively in Chapter 6. However, for Hofstede, **individualism-collectivism** is an attribute of nations, not of individuals. The most individualistic nations were shown to be the USA, Australia, the UK, the Netherlands, and Canada; the most collectivistic nations were reported as Guatemala, Ecuador, Panama, Venezuela, and Colombia.

Nation scores for collectivism correlate strongly and positively with those for power distance, but Hofstede argued that it is conceptually useful to keep them separate. This dimension of cultural variation has generated greatest interest among cross-cultural researchers and provides the basis for many of the studies to be discussed in later chapters. As Box 3.1 indicated, the actual survey items used by Hofstede to define individualism and collectivism concerned relative preference for differing work motivations. In nations defined as individualist, 'personal' time, freedom and challenge were favoured more strongly, whereas in nations defined as more collectivist nations use of skills, good physical conditions and training opportunities were more strongly endorsed. These items do not match closely the definitions of individualism and collectivism employed by Hofstede and by later researchers. However, as we shall see the distinction between nations with individualist and collectivist cultures has proved robust.

Hofstede's final dimension was named Masculinity-Femininity. This differentiates nations that value assertiveness from those that value nurturance. As with the other dimensions, Hofstede's concern is with nations, not with individuals, and he notes that his labels 'should not be taken to imply that men always actually behave in a more masculine manner than do women or that women behave in more feminine ways than do men' (Hofstede, 2001, p. 284). Nonetheless, many subsequent critics have had difficulty in accepting his labels for this dimension, as they appear to reify a gender distinction that has been much debated in recent times. 'Masculine' nations were found to be Slovakia, Hungary, Japan, Austria, and Venezuela; the most 'feminine' nations were Sweden, Norway, the Netherlands, Denmark, and Costa Rica.

Progress Check

Hofstede's study yielded four dimensions along which a substantial number of the world's nations could be located. Hofstede himself tested the predictive validity of these dimensions by exploring what he termed their 'consequences' through correlating them with other available measures that can be used to characterize nations. We provide a full discussion of the growing use of this type of validity check in Chapter 4.

For the moment, we need to explore some of the other issues raised by his study. The original study was completed before the current focus of interest on cross-cultural psychology had developed. Indeed, it contributed to the triggering of that development by providing a rich conceptual structure for these studies (Bond, 2002). How does it fare in terms of the criteria for good studies that were itemized in Chapter 2?

On the positive side, we can note that the samples from different nations were well matched, the survey was translated into local languages, **acquiescent response bias** was controlled, the appropriate level of analysis was correctly defined, and respondents were unaware that they were contributing to cross-national comparisons. On the negative side, the survey items were selected for other purposes and could well have missed important aspects of cultural difference. The items were also **imposed-etic**, being likely to reflect the preoccupations of the American-owned company. Indeed, it is interesting that the company was seeking at the time to create a *uniform* global company culture, and for this reason Hofstede's finding of cultural differences led him to publish the results using a company pseudonym, 'Hermes'. The dimensions were also defined by very few items each, thereby enhancing the risk that their meanings cannot be precisely determined.

While Hofstede's study matches up well to the majority of criteria, improvement of the measures can only be achieved within newer and more recent surveys, which we shall discuss shortly. There are some further issues to consider first. Some critics argue that the Hofstede country scores were obtained so long ago that they cannot any longer provide valid guidance as to differences between nations in the twenty-first century. Hofstede, however, sees cultural differences as rather robust and unlikely to change fast. In the revised 2001 edition of his book, he notes numerous instances in which his country scores are found to be significant predictors of effects measured by other researchers as much as 30 years later.

In the intervening years, many researchers have undertaken studies in which samples from two or three nations were compared on some attribute, and the results were then interpreted on the basis of Hofstede's scores for those nations. Interpretation is much more secure if it is based on data showing that the actual samples surveyed within a study did differ in terms of individualism, collectivism or whatever cultural dimension was used to formulate a hypothesis. It is risky to infer that because samples drawn from IBM employees 35 years ago differed in a certain way, contemporary samples of, for instance, students from the same nations will differ in the same ways sometime later.

Another issue that we need to consider has to do with diversity within nations. In undertaking his **nation-level** analysis, Hofstede controlled for the demographic variability of his samples. That does not mean that there is no variability to be found within his data. He reports additional analyses that showed variability in terms of gender and occupational role. Within nations we can expect subcultures based on regions, on social class, on professional subcultures, on **ethnicity**, and on gender. Such variations are all of interest, but they are not likely to be defined in terms of the same dimensions that were found to characterize national differences. The dimensions that emerge will be a product of the issues that define the differences between the categories being compared. For instance, when Hofstede, Neuyen, Ohayv and Sanders (1990) studied cultural differences between organizations in the Netherlands and in Denmark, they found that the dimensions defining variation in organizational cultures were quite different from those defining variation in national cultures. The 'cultural' unit being studied will determine the nature and type of the dimensions used to characterize their culture.

The final aspect of the Hofstede project that needs more discussion is fundamental and brings us back to the discussion of definitions with which this chapter began. If cultures are defined by shared meanings, does the IBM survey data actually provide us with information on the ways in which meanings of particular values were or were not shared in different nations? A social system with a certain national culture cannot by itself be shown to share meanings. It is individuals who do or do not share meanings. If we could show that individuals within a particular nation do share particular sets of meanings, then we should be in a stronger position to make more valid *cultural* comparisons between larger systems, such as nations. How would sharedness of meanings be established? The obvious approach would be to compare the levels of agreement across a cultural unit's members to establish the consensus around the value or belief in question. We thus need to do **individual-level** analyses to prepare the way for more valid **higher-level** analyses, whether these be analyses of marriages, families, organizations, or nations.

Alternatively, we could attempt to identify and compare cultures by measuring the constructs that produce 'sharedness' in the first place, namely, rules, norms, social conventions and the like. From the perspective of this approach, individual values, beliefs and so forth are the socialized products of these man-made 'culturing' processes. There will be some degree of consensus in the psychological consequences of the social system, but there will not be uniformity. The average level of endorsement of a value or belief in one cultural group, however, would probably differ from that in another because of the homogenizing influence of the social system characterizing each cultural group. Because of psychology's 'individualistic bias' (Sampson, 1981), however, we have only rarely compared cultures in terms of those variables, like rules, norms, and social conventions that make cultural groups into *cultures* instead of merely collections of individuals. We explore this 'top-down' perspective in Chapter 4.

Studying Individuals and Studying Cultures

While Hofstede considered the best way into the study of cultural differences was to focus on value differences at the **nation-level**, an alternative approach has been developed over the past 15 years by Shalom Schwartz in Israel. Schwartz (1992) emphasized that one cannot validly compare **nation-level** variations in endorsed values until one has first undertaken more basic research into the structure of values that are held by individuals. By checking how values correlate with one another among individuals in different parts of the world, we can check whether a values survey relies on the same psychological meanings in different parts of the world. Since cross-national surveys necessarily involve translations into numerous different languages, the scope for variation in meaning is large. How can we be sure that when persons in different parts of the world endorse values such as honesty, freedom or loyalty, they mean the same thing?

The Schwartz Value Surveys

Schwartz proposed that one could test for uniformity of meaning by doing a parallel series of **individual-level** studies of a set of specific values within different nations. His respondents were asked to rate the extent to which each of 56 values was a guiding prin-

Box 3.2

Schwartz's Analysis of the Individual-level Structure of Values

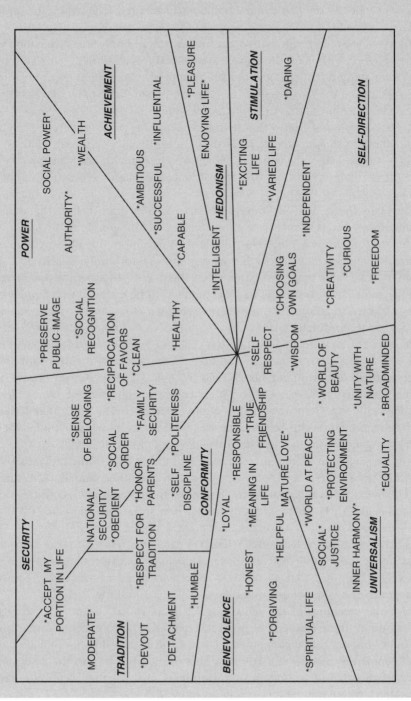

ciple in his or her life. Each value was stated as a single word or phrase, with a brief illustration or two provided in brackets, for instance: 'successful (achieving goals)' and 'social justice (correcting injustice, caring for the weak)'. The majority of these items were drawn from earlier surveys conducted by Rokeach (1973) in the USA, but further values were added from other cultural traditions in an attempt to reduce the **imposed-etic** nature of the measure. Separate samples of students and of schoolteachers from 20 nations were surveyed initially, with many further later additions. For each nation's data, Schwartz then undertook **smallest space analysis**. This is a technique similar in principle to **factor analysis**, which does not make parametric assumptions about the intervals between points on the rating scales. The output from **smallest space analysis** is a two-dimensional plot that portrays the proximity within the data of every value to every other value. Schwartz reasoned that if endorsement of a given value falls close to the same set of other values in other nations' data, then the values must have relatively close meanings within each of the nations represented. The figure in Box 3.2 shows the average of the results from each of 20 national groups averaged across those 20 nations (Schwartz, 1992).

As the figure shows, Schwartz interpreted his results by drawing lines that divide his 56 values into clusters of relatively similar values, defining each of these as a 'value type' or domain. This is a subjective procedure, equivalent to the subjectivity involved in assigning names to the factors that emerge from **factor analysis**. Schwartz identified ten separate value types and assigned a name to each. In assigning names, he was originally guided by a theoretical framework in which he reasoned that human values may be expected to reflect the three universal human requirements: biological needs, needs for social coordination, and needs for group welfare and maintenance. However, the value types that were identified do not clearly separate these three types of need.

The ten value types can also be summarized as two bipolar dimensions, which are represented vertically and horizontally in Box 3.2. The vertical dimension of Openness to Change versus Conservation contrasts endorsement of novelty and autonomy with endorsement of tradition and conformity. The horizontal dimension of Self-Enhancement versus Self-Transcendence contrasts individual striving for individual ends against cooperation with others for supra-individual ends.

Across his sample of 20 nations, Schwartz found that 75% of the individual values fell within the same value type as that found in the other samples. Schwartz and Sagiv (1995) extended this analysis to 88 samples from 40 nations. Schwartz, Melech, Lehmann et al. (2001) reported that by using a new and simpler measure, the Portrait Value Questionnaire, they were able to obtain a similar structure of values. These results make clear that at least after Schwartz's detailed attention to back-translations of his survey, most individual value items do have equivalent meanings in most nations. He concluded that 44 of his original 56 items had adequately equivalent meanings across a wide sample of nations. As Box 3.3 indicates, analysis of the ways in which the meanings of the remaining 12 items varied can provide some **emic** insights into distinctive aspects of particular nations. The consistency of meaning of most values implies that measurements based upon these values do provide a useful way of comparing nations and cultures. This opened the way to the next stage in his project, which was to undertake **nation-level** analyses that were more directly comparable to those that had been conducted by Hofstede.

Box 3.3

Japanese Friendship and Australian Loyalty

'True friendship' and 'loyalty' were among the values that Schwartz and Sagiv (1995) found to have meanings that varied across nations. Among the value types shown in Box 3.2, 'true friendship' is typically found within the benevolence value type. However, analysis of data from 542 Japanese students placed 'true friendship' within the security value type. This indicates that its meaning among this sample falls closer to the other values located within the security value type, including 'sense of belonging' and 'healthy'. In other samples, the values falling closer to 'true friendship' are 'mature love' and 'meaning in life'. Thus, it appears that friendship in Japan has more overtones of inclusion than of intimacy.

Within the Australian student data, endorsements of loyalty and responsibility were associated with favouring obedience and politeness, whereas elsewhere they link with honesty and helpfulness. This difference in meaning could possibly be interpreted in terms of the distinctive Australian concept of 'mateship'. Being honest or helpful is evidently not thought of as being a requirement or obligation. These examples provide illustrations of the way in which Schwartz's data can yield ideas for more focused **emic** studies.

After adjusting the scores for possible differences in **acquiescent response bias** and averaging the responses for each separate value within each country, a **nation-level smallest space analysis** was conducted (Schwartz, 1994). As the figure in Box 3.4 indicates, the structure which emerged was not identical to that obtained in the **individual-level** analyses, partly because it is based on 44 data points rather than 56. Seven **nation-level** value types were identified, which could be summarized as three bipolar dimensions. These are named as Autonomy-Embeddedness, Hierarchy-Egalitarian Commitment and Mastery-Harmony. Schwartz chose to assign different labels to his **nation-level** dimensions of values than those assigned to his **individual-level** dimensions because he wanted to emphasize the importance of distinguishing the separate levels.

The availability of Schwartz's two separate analyses enables us to address one of the most central and vexing questions in contemporary cross-cultural psychology, and one that many people find difficult to comprehend. How can it be that when the same data are analysed at two different levels, the results are not the same? Look carefully at the results for endorsement of the values 'humble' and 'authority' in Boxes 3.2 and 3.4. In Box 3.2, 'humble' appears in the value type for tradition, whereas 'authority' appears in the value type for power. The two values are located on opposite sides of the plot, which indicates that endorsement of them is negatively correlated. In other words, those who endorse authority as a guiding principle in their life are not at all likely to be the same as those who see being humble as a guiding principle in their life. Contrast this with the results in Box 3.4. At the **nation-level**, both 'humble' and 'authority' appear in the value type for hierarchy. Nations in which there is strong average endorsement for authority tend to be the same as those in which there is strong average endorsement of being humble.

Box 3.4

Schwartz's Nation-level Structure of Values

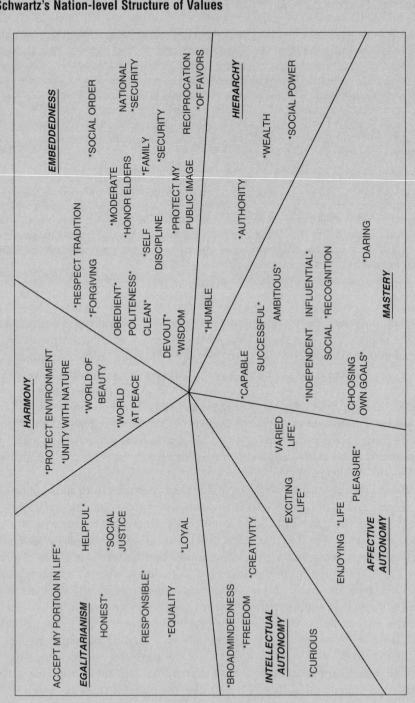

Putting results for both levels together, the picture is clear enough: in certain nations there is a relative preponderance of some individuals who endorse authority and of other individuals who endorse humility. These individuals are likely to relate to one another through a system of hierarchically ordered roles. These nations can be predicted to be those whom Hofstede identified as high on power distance. Conversely, in some other nations there are lesser numbers of individuals who endorse authority and humility and these should be the nations in which power distance is relatively low. Within any given nation, however, individuals who endorse the value of authority do not endorse the value of humility, and vice versa. Nations are not individuals.

The positionings of values in Schwartz's two analyses do not all differ between levels. The ones that do are those that have to do with the reciprocal role relationships found in hierarchical nations, for instance 'devout' and 'obedient'. The important point to draw from these observations is that there is no *logical* reason why the structure of values should be the same at different levels. Sometimes they are; sometimes, not. Whether or not different values (or other attributes of cultures) go together at each level will depend upon the factors operative at each level. At the **individual-level**, we may expect genetic dispositions and individual socialization histories to be strong predictors of the way that different values go together. At the **nation-level**, we may expect variation in different aspects of social systems to predict the values that are particularly salient within each nation. To construct a valid cross-cultural psychology we need to draw on both perspectives. Above all, we need to ensure that our analysis is done at the level that matches our hypotheses. To infer that a relationship holds at the **individual-level** because it has been found true at the **nation-level** is illogical and has been termed the '**ecological fallacy**' by Hofstede and others; to infer that a relationship holds at the **nation-level** because it has been found true at the individual-level is likewise illogical and has been termed the 'reverse **ecological fallacy**'.

In discussing Schwartz's studies, we have so far only considered his analyses of the *structure* of values. While this is essential groundwork if values are to provide the conceptual framework for cross-cultural studies, the reward for establishing a reliable structure is that one may then proceed to make comparisons between different samples and different surveys, at a given level of analysis. The techniques used to plot the structure of values can also be used to plot the distribution of each nation's scores. Several kinds of comparison are possible. We already noted the nations that scored high or low on each of Hofstede's dimensions. Box 3.5 shows the location of 67 nations in relation to Schwartz's seven **nation-level** value-types (Schwartz, 2004). Later in this chapter, we consider how much convergence there is between means from all of the published surveys that have included large numbers of nations.

Schwartz and Bardi (2001) provide a different type of comparison, focusing upon which **individual-level** value types are most endorsed within each of the 123 samples of teachers and students for which data were available. A remarkable consensus was found across these samples. The two most favoured value types were benevolence and self-direction and the two least favoured value types were tradition and power. Since cross-cultural psychologists most frequently study and try to explain *differences* between the samples that they study, these results help to provide a necessary overall perspective. While most members of most nations do favour benevolence, the priority that they give to benevolence *relative* to the other values that they may endorse varies, and it is this variation upon which cross-cultural psychologists mostly focus.

Box 3.5

Schwartz's Map of 67 Nations on Seven Cultural Orientations

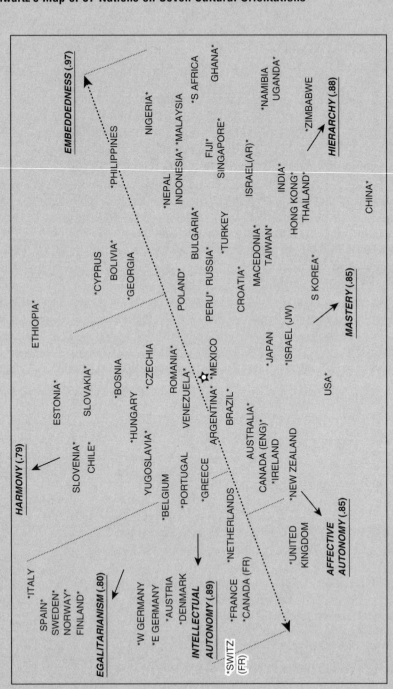

Further Values Surveys

Several further large scale surveys of values have been reported. The study published as Chinese Culture Connection (1987) was conducted as a test of the extent to which the Western origins of Hofstede's survey items had influenced the dimensions of **nation-level** variation that were found. Michael Bond in Hong Kong asked a group of Chinese scholars to identify values important in Chinese society. He then used these values as the basis for a survey that was administered to samples of university students from 23 nations. Following Hofstede's procedures, he then aggregated item scores for each nation and performed a **nation-level factor analysis**. Of the four dimensions that emerged, three replicated Hofstede's dimensions in the sense that the scores on these three dimensions closely predicted the scores on three of Hofstede's dimensions. However, there was no replication of the Uncertainty Avoidance dimension. In its place, a dimension that Bond named 'Confucian Work Dynamism' was found. Items loading strongly on this dimension included traditional Chinese values such as perseverance and thrift. Hofstede (2001) concludes that this dimension should be added to his four to yield a more comprehensive characterization of **nation-level** differences, but he renamed the dimension as Long Term Orientation.

Bond (1988) also analysed the Chinese Culture Connection data at the **individual-level**. Anticipating the later results of Schwartz, he found a different factor structure for values at the **individual-level**. It should be noted that Bosland (1985) had earlier attempted to analyse the Hofstede values at the **individual-level**, but had not been able to detect an equivalent structure for these values across the national groups included in the analysis. Success in finding such **individual-level** similarity in the structure of the values is necessary for drawing comparisons, but is not a guaranteed outcome. The more specific and concrete the items, the less likely that cross-cultural equivalence in item groupings will be found.

Another large database that yields **nation-level** means for values is that derived from the World Values Survey (Inglehart, 1997). The World Values Survey comprises a coordinated set of opinion surveys that are repeated every few years and which draw on representative national populations. Commencing within Europe in the 1980s, the survey now spans most of the world. Inglehart has analysed the changes over time that are most relevant to political preferences. **Factor analysing** individual responses to 47 variables, he identified two dimensions of variation across nations: focus on Self-expression versus Survival and preference for Rational-legal versus Traditional Authority. The items constituting each of these two factors are grouped in the same way by respondents within each of his now 67 nations, thereby meeting the requirement emphasized by Schwartz that national averages only be compared for those value items whose meaning is the same across individual persons in all cultural groups.

Finally, Smith, Dugan, and Trompenaars (1996) analysed a databank comprising a survey of the values of organizational employees in 43 nations. However, these authors did not make such a clear distinction between levels of analysis. Multidimensional analysis of all the **individual-level** data regardless of the respondent's nation revealed two principal dimensions of variation. The first contrasted individuals whose involvement in their organization was based on loyalty and those whose involvement was more utilitarian. The second dimension contrasted conservatism values against more egalitarian values. Smith et al. computed average scores for each nation along these dimensions. This analysis was done at the **individual-level** without using the **nation-level** types of analysis that Hofstede, Schwartz and Inglehart employed. For this reason, Smith et al's scores for each country cannot be considered as validly computed **nation-level** scores. Many researchers have computed scores of this type and in this book we shall be referring to them as '**population means**'.

In drawing the distinction between **individual-level** means and **nation-level** means, we make it possible to advance a little further our discussion of how best we can understand the nature of culture. If *shared* values are an indicator of the existence of a culture, then knowing the values of the average person will give only a weak indication of the context within which that person is operating. We will do better if we know more about the way that an overall average set of values is distributed among the population.

Box 3.6

Are Hofstede's Dimensions Replicable? Correlations across Different Surveys

Newer Dimensions	Power Distance	Uncertainty Avoidance	Individualism (versus Collectivism)	Masculinity (versus Femininity)
Chinese Culture Connection				
Moral Discipline	.55**		−.54**	
Integration	−.58**		.65***	
Human Heartedness				.67
Confucian Work Dynamism				
Schwartz				
Autonomy (versus Embeddedness)	−.52***		.64***	
Hierarchy (versus Egalitarianism)	.41**	−.29*	−.50***	
Mastery (versus Harmony)	.29*			
Smith et al.				
Loyal Involvement	.67***		−.77***	.37*
Conservatism	.63***		−.74***	
Inglehart				
Self-expression (versus Survival)	−.72***	−.55**	.74***	−.39*
Rational Authority	−.56**		.49**	

Note: The direction of these correlations refers to the dimension names that are not placed in brackets.

The five large-scale values surveys described above each sampled a rather different range of nations. Inglehart's data were derived from nationally representative surveys, while all the others sampled distinctive sub-samples from within nations. They also used different measures, were conducted at different times, and analysed their data in different ways. This range of variation makes it difficult to identify the extent to which their results confirm or contradict one another. It would certainly be remarkable if their results were to converge with one another.

However, as Box 3.6 indicates, there is in fact considerable convergence. As Hofstede's original analysis indicated, his dimensions of **individualism-collectivism** and power distance are significantly and negatively correlated with one another. Each of the more recent surveys has identified dimensions that are strongly associated with this same polarity. Correlations of around +0.6 between two measures indicate that less than half of their variance is shared, but correlations of this magnitude are nonetheless encouraging. As Hofstede also noted, nation scores for **individualism-collectivism** are strongly correlated with a nation's wealth. Thus it appears that the **nation-level** values surveys that we have explored have succeeded primarily in identifying the values that predominate in rich nations in contrast to those that prevail in less rich nations. There is also some evidence for the replicability of Hofstede's other dimensions, but as we shall see, these dimensions have thus far exercised a lesser influence upon subsequent research.

Cultures as Systems of Shared Beliefs

Rather than focus on values, some researchers have looked at the extent to which nations can be characterized by sets of shared beliefs. Research in this field has paralleled developments in the study of values, progressing from measures that are purely **imposed-etic** to those that have greater **emic** content and which take account of the need to differentiate **individual-level** and **nation-level** data analysis. Within the USA, Rotter (1966) developed a measure of 'locus of control', that is to say a generalized belief in internal versus external control over events. Put more simply, to what extent did respondents expect that the events occurring around them were amenable to influence by themselves, rather than being due to external agencies, such as powerful others or fate? Rotter's scale has proved popular among researchers from many nations (Dyal, 1984). Smith, Trompenaars, and Dugan (1995) analysed locus of control data from 43 nations. After standardization, **individual-level** multidimensional scaling revealed three dimensions of beliefs. The first dimension contrasted belief in personal efficacy with belief in the efficacy of politicians. Scores on this dimension correlated strongly with Schwartz's nation scores for mastery values. The second locus of control dimension contrasted belief in personal autonomy with belief in the need to depend on others. Scores on this dimension correlated strongly with Schwartz's nation scores for autonomy and Hofstede's scores for individualism. This provides a preliminary indication of links between the values and beliefs that prevail in nations, but because they refer to different levels of analysis, **population means** and **nation-level** means cannot validly be compared in this way. We must turn our attention to studies that have addressed the levels of analysis problem correctly.

More recently, a survey of widely endorsed social axioms or beliefs has been devised. Initially, Leung, Bond, de Carrasquel et al. (2002) identified an extensive list of several hundred social axioms that are prevalent in Venezuela and Hong Kong, adding some from established scales of beliefs, such as that of Rotter. After translation and pilot testing, responses to 60 of these axioms by students were then surveyed in Hong Kong, Venezuela, Japan, Germany, and the USA. Five comparable, **individual-level** factors were identified within each of these nations. The survey was then repeated with further student respondents from 41 nations (Leung & Bond, 2004). The five factors of widely held **individual-level** beliefs were confirmed as Social Cynicism (a negative view of human nature), Social Complexity (belief in multiple solutions to problems), Reward for Application (belief that effort and knowledge will be rewarded), Religiosity (belief in positive functions of religious practice and institutions) and Fate Control (belief that events are predetermined but can be influenced).

The same data were next aggregated to the **nation-level**, in order to determine the structure of beliefs at that level (Bond, Leung, et al., 2004). As had been the case with Schwartz's analyses of values, the **nation-level** structure of beliefs differs in some respects from the **individual-level** structure. At the **nation-level**, four of the five **individual-level** factors merge into one strong factor, which Bond et al. label as Dynamic Externality. This cluster of beliefs is focused around religiosity and a belief that effort will ultimately lead to justice. The second **nation-level** factor was named Societal Cynicism, and was constituted almost exclusively by items that defined the factor of social cynicism at the **individual-level**. In relation to values, nations' scores on dynamic externality are highest where Schwartz's measure of embeddedness values is high. Endorsement of societal cynicism was significantly associated with Hofstede's collectivism measure. Once again, some consistency is found between endorsements of values and beliefs at the **nation-level**.

Since scores on Hofstede's collectivism and Schwartz's embeddedness are strongly correlated with one another, these results create an initial impression that the values and beliefs surveys all point toward a single dimension of cultural variation, distinguishing nations that are wealthy, individualistic, secular and taking a positive view of human nature, in contrast to nations that are less wealthy, more collectivistic, more traditional, more religious, and more cynical. However, this is too simple a reading of these results. Just because two measures correlate with one another at +0.5 or +0.6 does not mean that they are identical. Variance in common between two measures correlating at 0.6 is the square of 0.6, namely 0.36, or only 36%. In Chapter 4, we explore the extent to which national differences in beliefs and values can explain separate variance in other measures.

How do we interpret the divergent structure of beliefs at the two levels of analysis? The consistency across levels in the structure of societal cynicism indicates that in nations where social cynicism is high, there will be some individuals who endorse all of the cynical beliefs that comprise the overall factor and others who endorse none of these beliefs. In contrast, in nations where dynamic externality is high, we may expect to identify differentiated subcultures or sets of individuals where for instance those who endorse religiosity are not necessarily the same ones as those who believe more strongly in reward for application.

Culture as Patterns of Behaviour

Two further large-scale surveys have been reported, each of which yields population means on measures that are more directly related to behaviour than those considered so far. Smith, Peterson, and Schwartz (2002) surveyed managers in 47 nations. Respondents were asked to what extent they had relied on various sources of guidance in handling different events that arose at work. Smith et al. computed an index of verticality, which reflected reliance on one's superior and on formal rules, rather than reliance on oneself or one's subordinates. Verticality was significantly higher for nations scoring higher on Hofstede's power distance and on Schwartz's measures of hierarchy, mastery, and embeddedness. Again, there seems to be meaningful convergence of results at the **nation-level**.

House, Hanges, Javidan, Dorfman, and Gupta (2004) surveyed behaviour related to leadership by managers in 62 nations. Respondents were asked to describe their nation 'as it is' and 'as it should be' on rating scales comprising nine dimensions of national culture, many of which were based upon the earlier work of Hofstede and others. The 'should be' ratings could be considered as measures of values, but the 'as is' ratings comprise the most extensive survey to date that has focused upon description of behaviours. House et al. found marked differences between the 'should be' and the 'as is' responses.

Another innovation in this project was that in addition to recording their own ratings on some scales, respondents also rated how most other people in their nation would respond on other scales. The measures derived from these latter ratings may have greater potential to detect shared meanings given to behaviours in a nation, since respondents are reporting on typical behaviours. Typicality may reflect normative pressures in a cultural system, thereby bringing our measures closer to the definition of culture itself. This survey differed from all the others discussed in this chapter in that none of the ratings referred to beliefs or values as a guide to one's own life, focusing instead on perceptions of how *others* are perceived to act, or how they should act. Despite this, significant correlations at or above +0.6 were found, particularly between House et al.'s 'as is' scores for collectivism and power distance and Hofstede's scores with the same names.

Putting the Picture Together

Bringing Our Terminology into Better Focus

So far in this chapter, we have argued for a particular way of defining culture and social system, and have then reviewed a series of studies that can lead us towards an application of these definitions. However, in the process, we have raised as many questions as we have resolved. In particular, we have opened up the crucial question of how to relate our understandings of individuals and of large cultural entities such as nations. Reflecting on the studies that we have reviewed, we can differentiate not two but three ways of describing the data that arise from cross-cultural comparisons. Firstly, we can study a sample of individuals. The respondents may be drawn from a single nation, but within cross-cultural psychology, they are more typically drawn from at least two nations. As Box 3.7 emphasizes, even if the data are drawn from two or more nations, this does not mean that comparison between mean scores from nation A and nation B is a **nation-level** comparison. If the analysis treats *each individual as a separate case*, this is an **individual-level** comparison of **population means**. Many cross-national comparisons of this kind have been published and we shall be discussing relevant examples in later chapters. Comparison of **population means** between different nations is only likely to be valid if checks have been made that the measures that have been used have the same structure at the **individual-level** in both nations, and account has been taken of possible differences in **acquiescent response bias**.

Box 3.7

Measures Created by Researchers Comparing Nations and their Uses

Type of Measure	What is a Case?	How Computed?	Uses/Weaknesses
Population Sample	An Individual	Average the items comprising a scale and then compare means, without any check on the equivalence of their structure across samples	Cross-national comparisons likely to be invalid
Citizen Mean (Individual or 'psychological' level)	A Nation	Factor analyse the items comprising each scale for individuals in each nation separately. If factors are stable, compare means across nations	Provide a single score per nation depicting the average respondent within each nation
Nation-level Mean (Cultural or 'ecological' level)	A Nation	Compute a national average for each item separately, then factor analyse the item means across nations	Summarize the national context within which individuals are located

---

One popular procedure for checking the similarity of the structure of scales is **factor analysis**. We noted earlier that Schwartz (1994) prefers to use **smallest space analysis**. Whichever technique is used, analysis is first done within each nation's data separately. If convergence is found, the basis for **nation-level** comparisons is established. The next step is to *aggregate* data from each sample before testing a hypothesis. Aggregation will yield what we here call a **citizen mean** for each sample. The scale mean from a sample *is* its **citizen mean**, but if we use the **citizen mean** as a data point, we shall have *only one score for each nation that is sampled*. Consequently **citizen means** can only be compared statistically when large numbers of nations have been sampled.

The alternative procedure, pioneered by Hofstede (1980) is first to aggregate individuals' responses and then test the **nation-level** structure of the items. We call means computed in this way **nation-level** means. Many studies in the published literature do not make clear which type of analysis was undertaken, or else identify their method in a way that uses terms confusingly. Box 3.7 also contains the alternative terms (**ecological mean**, psychological mean) that have been employed by some authors to distinguish levels of analysis.

Relating Individuals and Cultures

What is the usefulness of each of these types of data and how do they relate to one another? If culture is defined in terms of shared meanings, then their usefulness to us depends on how much they reflect the sharing of meaning rather than simply providing us with an individual's values, beliefs or other attributes. The variation around a **population mean** can provide us with a reminder that characterizing a whole nation as individualist or collectivist is at best a convenient shorthand. Measurement of **population means** also provides an invaluable way of testing whether a researcher's specific samples are similar to the ways in which previous **nation-level** researchers have categorized the nations from which their present samples are drawn. For instance, do the students whom researchers rather frequently sample actually have the collectivist or individualist values that one might expect from Hofstede's **nation-level** scores for these nations? As we will discover in Chapter 6, Oyserman, Coon, and Kemmelmeier (2002) have documented some surprising reversals of such expectations.

Citizen means become useful only if they are drawn from a wide variety of nations. A **citizen mean** gives us an estimate of whether or not there are a substantial number of persons within a given population having a particular psychological attribute. A higher mean necessarily means that that attribute is shared with a good many others. Being based upon measures of psychological attributes such as values, beliefs or behaviours, **citizen means** lend themselves to the types of comparisons that are most relevant to psychological theories, which mostly refer to individuals, not to larger entities. However, what they fail to do is to give us any indication of how the elements of a culture are integrated with one another.

The meaning of **nation-level** scores is less immediately clear. Even though researchers in this tradition start with measures of psychological constructs like values, by averaging these responses before **factor analysing** them, they create non-psychological higher-order groupings, in this case national groupings. These groupings bear no necessary logical or empirical relation to groupings developed at the **individual-level** of analysis (Leung & Bond, 1989). **Nation-level** analysis has been adopted by many social scientists (e.g., Chinese Culture Connection, 1987; House et al., 2004; Smith et al., 1996), in part because it sidesteps the requirement to establish metric equivalence of the constructs at the individual level. These researchers often compound the potential for confusion by giving their **nation-level** constructs psychological sounding names, like 'Human-heartedness', 'Assertiveness', and 'Loyal Involvement'. However, it is individuals, not nations who possess these types of qualities, and mis-labelling nation-level factors in these ways perpetuates the confusion.

Addressing this dilemma in general terms, Schwartz (1994) has argued that:

Individual-level value dimensions presumably reflect the psychological dynamics of conflict and compatibility that individuals experience in the course of pursuing their different values in everyday life ... In contrast, culture-level dimensions presumably reflect the different solutions that societies evolve to the problems of regulating human activities, the different ways that institutional emphases and investments are patterned and justified in one culture compared with another ... The culture-level values that characterize a society ... must be inferred from various cultural products [e.g., folktales] ... these cultural products reflect assumptions about the desirable that are built into the institutions of the society and are passed on through intentional and unintentional socialization. ... The average of the value priorities of societal members reflects these commonalities of enculturation. Individual variation around this average reflects unique personality and experience. Thus, averaged values of societal members [and their factor groupings], no less than their folktales or textbooks can point to cultural values. (p. 92)

The current use of **nation-level** scores by cross-cultural researchers may thus represent a temporary compromise between the use of truly psychological measures such as **citizen means** and measures that derive directly from a nation's social structure, such as wealth, social class and institutional structures. The only aspect of the individual's broader social context that has been given sustained attention by psychologists is the family. Detailed study of other aspects of social systems has for the most part been relinquished to sociologists, political scientists and so forth. However, if cross-cultural psychology is to deliver on its intention to show how cultures affect individuals, deeper exploration will be required of the way in which the **nation-level** means for values and beliefs computed by cross-cultural researchers relate to the broader qualities of nations identified by other groups of social scientists. As Whiting (1976) put it long ago, we need to **unpackage** the concept of culture, showing how the various elements come to make up the whole. This exploration is taken up in Chapters 4 and 5. In preparation for this exploration, we outline in Box 3.8 a model of the ways in which the different types of measures that we have discussed relate to one another.

At the bottom of the figure, we note that the institutions that arise within nations are a reflection of the fundamental ecological context with which they have had to contend. Ecological and institutional processes can only be represented as **nation-level** variables. In Chapter 4, we explore the way in which these **nation-level** attributes are related to the factors represented in the upper parts of the figure. In that chapter, you will find a more detailed figure, which 'unpacks' the abstract model given in the present figure. The processes whereby **nation-level** attributes influence the practices and consequent psychological outcomes of the individuals within a nation comprise various forms of socialization. These provide the focus for Chapter 5.

Evaluating Progress

The studies reviewed in this chapter have revealed a surprising consensus in the findings of the various surveys. Despite differences in methods, survey contents and

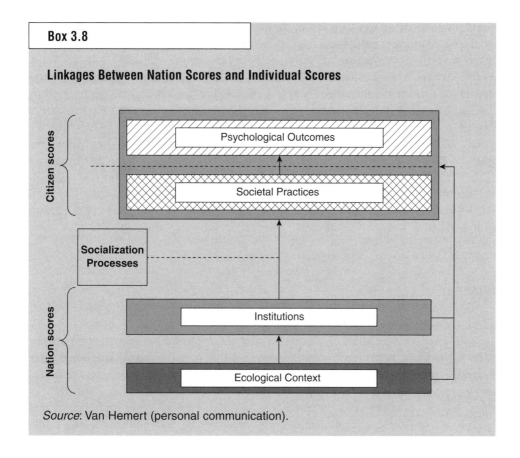

Box 3.8

Linkages Between Nation Scores and Individual Scores

Source: Van Hemert (personal communication).

samples, results often concur to a significant extent. Although this is encouraging, we need to consider several limitations to what has been achieved. Firstly, we do not know whether the dimensions of cultural variation that have been identified are the most important ones. They may be the easiest to identify, especially where they prove to be correlated with such major attributes as the wealth of a nation. Secondly, we need to consider how accurate observers are in judging the qualities that go to make up our existing measures of culture. As Heine, Lehman, Peng, and Greenholz (2002) point out, we can only make judgements that are relative to our own experience. Someone who has grown up in a hierarchical culture may perceive hierarchical behaviour as less autocratic than would someone who has grown up in a culture favouring equality. It is better to seek out measures that are more firmly anchored to phenomena that can be judged objectively. Thirdly, we need to take greater account of the varying contexts in which life is lived. We can show that one nation is more collectivist or hierarchical than another, but there may be equally strong sources of variation within nations. For instance, it may be that work organizations everywhere are more hierarchical than families are everywhere. The ways in which we act upon our values and our beliefs may be tempered by the differing contexts within which we operate and from which we receive feedback in the course of daily living. Fourthly, few of the studies reviewed in this chapter took account of diverse **ethnicities** within the nations sampled. Members of groups perceive greater diversity within their own group than they see in other groups (Linville, Fischer & Yoon, 1996), and this effect is as typical of nations as it is of small groups. Despite this perceptual enhancement of differences, where comparisons have been made across ethnic groups within a single nation, they show surprisingly small differences. For instance, a mapping of Israel's profile of values using the Schwartz (1994) survey looks much the same using the Druze, Muslim, Christian Arab, or Jewish populations to locate Israel relative to other national groups (Bond, 1996b). In a similar way, Cashmore and Goodnow (1986) showed that when socioeconomic status was held constant, ethnic divergences in Australian parental values disappeared. Whether wealth is something separate from culture that should be discounted in this way, or whether it is an integral part of the system of shared beliefs and values that we have been discussing will be discussed further in the next chapter.

Summary

Culture can be defined as the shared meanings found within a given social system. Psychologists have provided a conceptual framework for studies involving culture by surveying endorsements of values, beliefs and the differential occurrence of behaviours. Progress has been dependent upon obtaining a clear conceptualization of the different levels of analysis involved in doing cross-cultural psychology. Valid characterizations of nation-level differences can only be achieved if prior individual-level studies show that measures are equivalent across samples. Measures derived from individual-level rather than nation-level studies are required for predictions about individuals. Nation-level measures define the contexts within which individuals are socialized. Their relation to objective indices derived from other social sciences is of major interest.

Further Reading

1 Kağıtçıbaşı, Ç. (1997). Individualism and collectivism. In J.W. Berry, M.H. Segall, & Ç. Kağıtçıbaşı, (Eds.) *Handbook of cross-cultural psychology* (2nd ed., Vol. 3, pp. 1–49). Needham Heights, MA: Allyn & Bacon.
2 Smith, P.B. (2002). Levels of analysis in cross-cultural psychology. www.wwu.edu/psychology/~culture .
3 Smith, P.B. & Schwartz, S.H. (1997). Values. In J.W. Berry, M.H. Segall, & Ç. Kağıtçıbaşı (eds.) *Handbook of cross-cultural psychology* (2nd ed., Vol. 3, pp. 77–108). Needham Heights, MA: Allyn & Bacon.

Study Questions

1 What would you say are some of the salient values and beliefs of the nation within which you reside? How do these relate to the dimensions of cultural difference that researchers have identified?

2 Is it preferable to define culture in terms of shared values, beliefs and meanings, or should a greater emphasis be given to behaviours?

3 What value do nation-level dimensions have for psychologists, given that psychology tries to understand individuals?

4 What is a citizen score, as the concept is used in this chapter? Give an example and speculate how a nation's citizen score on this variable may be related to some aspect of its national institutions.

4   Nations as Cultures and their Consequences for Social Psychology

Internalization is rather the reabsorbtion into consciousness of the objectivated world in such a way that the structures of this world come to determine the subjective structures of consciousness itself (Peter L. Berger, *The sacred canopy*, 1967, p. 14–15)

Increasingly, cross-cultural studies in psychology are becoming the study of nations and of their inhabitants. This emerging practice makes sense: many cross-cultural psychologists are trained in the West, and return to practise psychology in their non-Western country of origin, conducting research with the citizens of their nation. The West, especially the USA, and the psychology of Westerners, especially North Americans, becomes the implicit standard against which they compare the results of their research and practice. This dynamic led to bi-national studies becoming the standard format for cross-cultural research in the last three decades of the twentieth century. Increasingly, data from broader samples of nations are now being collected, enabling us to sharpen the conclusions we can draw about national influences on social-psychological processes.

Most nations are characterized by language policies mandating a *lingua franca* (one or more common languages) for use in education or government, in addition to whatever mother tongues its inhabitants learn from birth. Many nations are also small enough to be subject to relatively uniform geographical conditions, ecological supports and vulnerabilities. National policies of education are frequently applied across the spectrum of primary and secondary education, permitting only slight regional variations in curricula or procedures. Legal systems and enforcement policies likewise have a common core around which there may be some local variation. In all these respects, nations may be considered as systems of constraints and affordances, in other words, as societies whose institutions press their inhabitants towards greater cultural unity, despite their increasing ethnic diversity.

In Chapter 3, we noted that nations are certainly social systems, but indicated that they could only be thought of as having a culture if we find evidence for shared ways of interpreting the diverse events that members of a nation experience. Using such a definition, would it not be better to say that most nations do not have a single culture, but are more like a mosaic of separate cultures, constrained by a set of socializing forces from various societal institutions, each applied with varying degrees of effectiveness? Is it not then a distortion to consider any given nation as having a single culture? We present here some arguments claiming that for some purposes, it is not only convenient but also sensible to treat nations as a unit of analysis. In particular, by focusing on nations we can help to redress psychology's neglect of the context within which our lives are lived.

Currently, 191 nations are members of the United Nations. Within their borders and subject to their jurisdiction is the vast majority of the world's population. Nations are political units whose boundaries and political prerogatives have gradually been defined historically. Within a given nation, its institutions channel and empower interpersonal exchanges to shape the socialization processes that affect its inhabitants. Some **ethnic groups** are more engaged with their national institutions than are others, by virtue of their geographical spread and concentration, their traditional practices, their integration into work, military, or religious organizations, their ideologies for or against integration, and national policies and practices that encourage or discourage ethnic integration. Through these varying degrees of engagement, the **ethnic groups** within a nation will be more or less responsive to the shaping of their members' socialization by institutional structures. Each community will show differences among themselves of course, just as social classes may show different profiles within and across nations (e.g., Kohn, Naoi, Schoenbach, Schooler, & Slomczynski, 1990). Indeed, some **ethnic groups** differ from one another not only in their **ethnicity**, but also in their social class, occupational profiles and education. In some nations, this patterning results in distinctive ethnic group specializations.

Despite these potentials for difference, however, a nation's various **ethnic groups** do often produce similar profiles on psychologically relevant measures vis-à-vis those from other nations. For instance, Schwartz (1994) reports that 'the three teacher samples from across China had quite similar profiles' (p. 118), despite the geographical-linguistic separation of these groups. This closer grouping of within-nation samples also occurs for self-reports of emotional experience, even when different languages are used (Kuppens, Kim-Prieto, & Diener, in press). Such results have encouraged social scientists to explore the impact of nationhood on the psychological profiles of its inhabitants. In doing so, it is important to ensure that respondents' **ethnicity** is noted, so that they may be categorized into their group of cultural origin and its importance for the psychological outcome in question assessed. Singelis, Her, Aaker et al. (2003) grouped their US respondents by **ethnicity** when measuring the five dimensions of social axioms identified by Leung and Bond (2004). They found differences in these beliefs among Mexican-American, Black-American, Asian-American and Caucasian-American populations. When the profiles of their Japanese-American and Chinese-American respondents were included in a cluster analysis of the profiles from 40 other national groups, the Japanese-American group showed close similarity with the Caucasian-American group, but the Chinese-American group did not. Instead, the Chinese-American group had greater similarity to the Hong Kong Chinese group and formed part of a larger cluster some distance from the Caucasian-American cluster.

So, whether different **ethnic groups** from the same nation show the same psychological profile is an open question. The outcome will probably depend on the types of psychological construct being considered, and upon the particular **ethnic groups** being sampled. The conclusion drawn from such results, however, is clear: social scientists must sample the **ethnic groups** constituting a nation as widely as possible, recording their **ethnicity** for subsequent analytic purposes.

In characterizing the psychological profile of a nation, representative samples should ideally be used. Relying on the profile of the numerically dominant group can only be accepted as a temporary convenience to locate that nation in psychological space vis-à-vis other nations. In a similar vein, we know from the pioneering work of Kohn and his associates that there are dramatic differences in values along the conservatism versus openness axis across the class divide within the USA, and that this difference is found also within nations such as Canada and Poland, which were also sampled (Kohn et al., 1990). Most cross-national comparisons of psychological data involve university student samples, a middle- to upper-class sample. We must be cautious in using such highly selected groups to represent their fellow citizens, and only use their scores for the sake of temporary convenience, and if they position a nation in sensible and theoretically meaningful ways.

Psychological Characterizations of National Culture

The Accuracy Problem

As a first approximation of a nation's true score, social scientists typically use an equivalent, but unrepresentative sample of the nation's inhabitants to characterize its **citizen mean** on the psychological characteristics being studied. It is often impractical to gather fully representative samples in cross-national research, and only the rare project, like the World Values Survey (Inglehart, 1997), approaches such an achievement. The results of surveys using equivalent but unrepresentative samples must then be judged in terms of their **validity** – what features of nations predict the resulting psychological profile, and do these linkages between institutional features and psychological outcomes make theoretical sense?

As an example of such a test for validity, consider the correlation of +0.81 that Hofstede (1980) reported between a nation's wealth as measured by its Gross National Product per capita (GNP) and its individualism score, derived from the responses of IBM employees. He argued that this result made sense because greater national wealth filters down to a nation's populace, giving each inhabitant of that nation greater purchasing power. This personal wealth thereby enhances individuals' authority in directing their consumer, occupational and leisure choices. Such freedom is consistent with, and encourages, individualism in a nation's citizens. Schwartz (1994) found a somewhat weaker correlation between autonomy values and GNP. Other scholars (e.g., McClelland, 1961) interpret whatever correlation is found in the opposite way, claiming that it is individualistic values that drive economic activity. The basic issue, however, is clear – can the cross-national data, from whatever group of respondents, be made to test a social scientific hypothesis persuasively?

Of course, a correlation does not establish causation, nor does a correlation confirm the direction of influence between the variables associated with one another. However, repeating the survey across considerable time periods can help support one's reasoning. So, Hofstede (1980) took two measures of GNP per capita and individualism, one set from 1967 and the other from 1971. By using a technique known as **cross-lagged**

panel analysis (see e.g., Yafee, 2003), it is possible to determine whether it is the GNP at time 1 that is more likely to drive the individualism at time 2, or vice versa. Using this logic, Hofstede concluded that wealth spurred individualism. Again, causation cannot be established with certainty, but one of the two directions of influence becomes the more probable as a result of such data processing. Since these conclusions are plausible, we can argue that it is more likely that Hofstede's sampling represented nations accurately. We explore the cultural impact of changing global wealth in Chapter 12.

The Stability Problem

It is resource-intensive to repeat surveys, and this is rarely done without strong institutional support and researcher persistence. When it has been done, there is remarkably high stability in the positions of nations relative to one another. For example, the Inglehart (1997) team has collected measures of two dimensions of values taken from the analysis of individual responses, traditional versus rational-legal values and survival versus self-expressive values. Inglehart and Baker (2000) report high stability across nations in rank ordering of **citizen means** on these dimensions over two decades. Similarly, Schwartz, Bardi, and Bianchi (2000) report high degrees of similarity in the ordering for **nation-level** value profiles on the Schwartz value domains using cross-sectional comparisons in East and West European nations across six- to eight-year periods. National values thus appear to be relatively stable across considerable time spans.

Box 4.1

Cultural Values and Communism

Schwartz, Bardi, and Bianchi (2000) addressed the question of whether the political system in a country influences the importance that its citizens ascribe to basic human values. To do so, they compared Schwartz's (1994) measures of nation-level values in the formerly communist nations of Central and Eastern Europe with those of democratic Western European nations. They argue that the imposition of communism affected values by altering the opportunities and constraints within which citizens had to function. Specifically:

> When the attainment of values concerned with material well-being and security is largely beyond personal control, a compensation mechanism operates ... Deprivation increases the strength of such needs and, correspondingly, of the valued goals to which they point ... For example, people who have endured economic hardship and social upheaval attribute more importance to the attainment of wealth and the preservation of social order. (p. 219)

(Continued)

Box 4.1   Continued

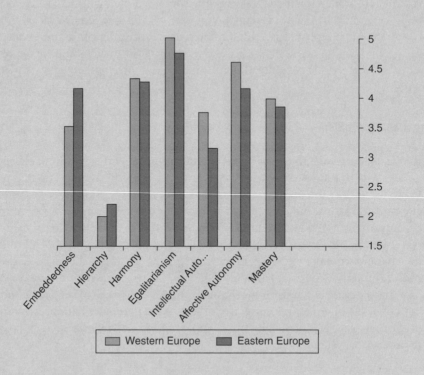

Consistent with this analysis, the chart shows that teachers in Eastern European nations attributed greater importance to embeddedness and hierarchy values and lower importance to egalitarianism, intellectual and affective autonomy values, when compared with West European samples. These same contrasts appeared when comparing East European countries in which communism had penetrated more versus less deeply … Autonomy and mastery values are not widely endorsed, suggesting reluctance to assume responsibility, to take risks, and to work hard to apply one's talents assertively. (p. 232–3; 'conservatism' changed to 'embeddedness' to reflect Schwartz's current usage)

The researchers explain these differences in national value profiles as arising from 'people's adaptations to the day-to-day reward contingencies and opportunities present under communist regimes …' (p. 232). Having controlled for alternative influences, such as economics, history and religion, Schwartz et al. conclude that '40 years of pervasive communist rule sufficed to influence people's basic values' (p. 233), and had left formerly communist Europe 'ill-suited for the development of democracy [since a] commitment to egalitarianism and autonomy values is required to provide the moral basis of social responsibility needed to maintain a democratic system' (p. 233).

Conceptual Groupings of National Characteristics

Encouraged by this evidence for stability, social scientists have begun to compare across different surveys taken at different time periods from different samples. As we reported in Box 3.6, high and significant correlations have been found between the **nation-level** means obtained from each of the existing multiple nation surveys. High correlations are not uncommon in **nation-level** research and this has stimulated social scientists to speculate about the meaning of the underlying national construct being assessed. Bond (1996b) went further with this approach, factor analysing the results from three value studies, those of Hofstede (1980), the Chinese Culture Connection (1987), and Schwartz (1994). He extracted four factors from this higher-order **factor analysis**. The first factor contrasted universalistic, open values with traditional, authoritarian emphases, which, it was argued, distinguish nations from one another. This conclusion was speculative, given the limited number of nations common to all three samples. Nonetheless, such a deeper way of characterizing social systems is an emerging possibility, given the increasing number of cross-national value studies that are sampling an ever wider set of countries.

How Should Psychologists Characterize Nations?

True psychological constructs are those assessing individual psychological variables, like values, motivations, traits, beliefs, cognitive styles, etc., and forming measures of these constructs by grouping **individual-level** data. If these groupings of items are similar across national or other cultural groupings, then comparisons of citizen profiles can be made across nations. We argued in Chapter 3 that averages across the individuals of a nation should be called **citizen means**. It is these profiles, differing across nations, that constitute the typical individual outcome of cultural processes of socialization. This inculcation is what Berger (1967) and others before him (Durkheim, 1898; Freud, 1923/1971) termed 'internalization' and we explore this process more fully in Chapter 5.

In practice, how do **citizen means** relate to **nation-level** constructs? Answering this question requires developing a body of pan-culturally usable psychological constructs that have been defined and measured at the **individual-level**. The daunting challenge in achieving this scientific resource base is to escape the risks of using **imposed-etic** measurement by establishing the equivalence or at least similarity of each psychological construct across the various national groups that one samples. To our knowledge, this equivalence has been established in five or more national groups only for measures of values (Bond, 1988; Schwartz, 1992; Inglehart & Baker, 2000), beliefs (Leung & Bond, 2004), general self-efficacy (Scholz, Dona, Sud, & Schwartzer, 2002), personality (Allik and McCrae, 2004), allocentrism/idiocentrism (Triandis et al., 1993), independent/ interdependent self-construal (Gudykunst et al., 1996), depression (van Hemert, van de Vijver & Poortinga, 2002), subjective well-being (Diener & Oishi, in press) and the value of children (Kağıtçıbaşı, 1982a). Even this small collection could be challenged by scholars demanding more stringent levels of similarity than was achieved by these investigators.

Box 4.2 shows the range of **nation-level** indicators found to correlate significantly at a probability-level of less than .01 with **nation-level** scores for the beliefs that were

Box 4.2

Nation-level Indicators and Nation-level Dimensions of Belief

Dynamic Externality	Societal Cynicism
Low Gross Domestic Product per capita High daytime temperature More women than men More persons per room Higher population growth Lower life expectancy Lower human development index Less human rights	Lower job satisfaction Lower life satisfaction Faster pace of life Lower church attendance
Lower status for women Less 'Freedom' Less unemployment More work hours per week Lesser % of Gross Domestic Product spent on health Lesser alcohol consumption Lower 'Quality of Life' index	

Source: Bond et al. (2004).

surveyed by Bond et al. (2004). The table excludes linkages with measures of values. We noted already in Chapter 3 that **nation-level** measures of values and beliefs do show substantial linkages with one another. We can now see evidence that these ways of characterizing nations also converge with less 'psychological' **nation-level** indicators.

Citizen means based on single-item measures, like Inglehart's (1997) measure of trust, are problematic in terms of this approach, since it is uncertain what construct is being tapped across cultural or national groups by any single item measure. 'Trust' may have different meanings in various populations, a question that can only be resolved by establishing the degree of similarity in its grouping with other related items within the populations of the various groups being examined. Until that question is addressed empirically, we must interpret single-item measures of any social psychological phenomenon with caution when doing cross-national comparisons.

The linking of **nation-level** constructs like individualism to **individual-level** constructs such as **independent self-construal** is an agenda for future research. So, too, is the linking of a society's institutional features to both **nation-level** and **individual-level** psychologically based constructs. As an aid to making one's way through the maze of constructs relevant to these various levels of analysis, Box 4.3 provides a fuller version of the table that was presented at the end of Chapter 3. The model treats ecological context as the basic causal agent in channelling the ways in which institutions are constructed with these institutional structures in turn eliciting particular patterns of psychological processes.

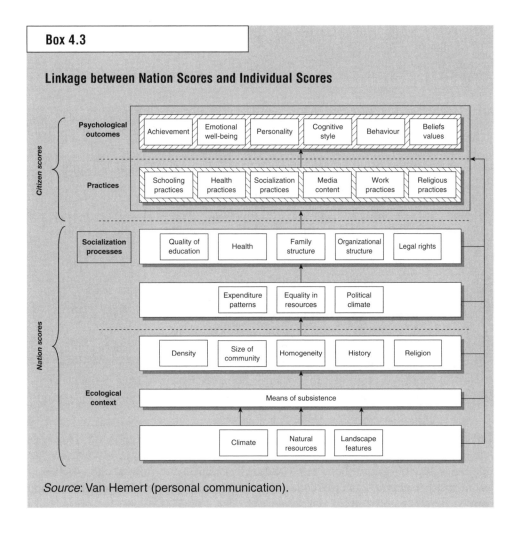

Box 4.3

Linkage between Nation Scores and Individual Scores

Source: Van Hemert (personal communication).

We will now consider various ways that social scientists have attempted to understand and measure the institutions of society, the national contexts within which a nation's inhabitants are subjected to socialization pressures by its institutions.

The Eco-politico-socio-economic Context of Nations

If nations are construed as contexts for the socialization of their inhabitants, how may we characterize these national contexts? As Smith (2004a) has argued, the discipline of cross-cultural psychology needs 'a framework that clusters nations with common ecological and social elements. Focus on these elements, rather than on countries simply identified by nationhood, should help us order nations in terms of key contextual parameters' (p. 11). For psychologists, our interest in these dimensions of nations is instrumental, enabling us to describe and then predict social-psychological outcomes: 'The similarity or dissimilarity of nations on these parameters can then be employed in cross-cultural studies to generate *a priori* hypotheses about how and why the observed similarities in psychological variables are found' (p. 11).

In this search, cross-cultural psychologists were initially inspired by the insights of other social scientists – anthropologists, political scientists, sociologists, and economists. Many of these scholars worked to develop dimensional systems that would allow them to map nations in terms of variables deemed important in their discipline. Sawyer (1967), for example, extracted 236 social, economic, political and geographic indicators from various sources to measure the position of 82 independent nations in 1955. He factor analysed these indicators, extracting three independent dimensions of national variation – size, wealth, and politics. The dimension identified as national size was represented most strongly by measures of population, amount of arable land and extent of energy resources. The dimension of national wealth was tapped by measures of GNP per capita, the percentage of the population in manufacturing and life expectancy. The dimension of national politics was defined by whether the nation was Communist, neutral or Western in its political practices. Sawyer's decision to extract three factors resulted in a three-dimensional space that located countries with respect to one another. This typology could be used as a basis for generating predictions about how the citizens of these nations might differ from one another with respect to values, beliefs, political attitudes like ethnocentrism, ways of construing themselves, self-efficacy and the other psychological constructs of interest to social psychologists. However, later researchers have favoured the use of more explicit theory in defining dimensions of national variation.

The Eco-cultural Framework

In a series of publications, Berry (1976, 2001) has argued that cultural and psychological diversity is a consequence of collective and personal adaptations to environmental context. This **eco-cultural** framework posits:

> two fundamental sources of influences (ecological and sociopolitical) and a set of variables that link these influences to psychological characteristics (cultural and biological adaptation at the population level and various 'transmission variables' to individuals – this includes enculturation, socialization, genetics and acculturation). (Georgas, van de Vijver, & Berry, 2004, p. 75)

Georgas et al. attempted to simplify the host of ecological and sociopolitical factors into a manageable typology. To do so, they culled a wide variety of national indicators, and grouped these **eco-cultural** indicators into categories of ecology, (e.g., highest monthly level of precipitation), economy (e.g., percentage of population employed in services), education (e.g., enrolment ratios in tertiary education), mass media (e.g., telephones per 1,000 inhabitants), and population (e.g., rate of population increase). The measures in each of these categories were factor analysed, yielding a single factor solution for each category. A secondary **factor analysis** of these five factor scores also yielded a single factor, accounting for almost 80% of the variation in the various ecological indices. A single factor thus appears to unify this multitude of **eco-cultural** indices.

However, all outputs from factor analyses of this sort are constrained by the available inputs used to generate the solution. In this case, the inputs are skewed towards measuring the subsistence and production bases of a nation. There seems to be a single factor running through these kinds of indicators, formally labelled as Affluence by Georgas and Berry (1995). Does this discovery indicate that there is only one important way to distinguish nations, one from another? If so, such a finding would give support to economic determinists who argue that the means of production drive all key aspects of culture (see e.g., Harris, 1979).

An indication that there may be more to national variation than affluence is provided by Georgas et al. (2004), who also assigned a religious classification to each nation. Inspired by Huntington's (1996) identification of eight major civilizations (Western, Confucian, Japanese, Islamic, Hindu, Slavic-Orthodox, Latin American, and African), but using the cultural zones identified by Inglehart and Baker (2000), they isolated six religious groupings: Muslim, Christian Catholic, Christian Protestant, Christian Orthodox, other Christian, Buddhist, and traditional. Georgas et al. considered it important to separate nations by religious type because of Inglehart and Baker's assertion that, 'A history of Protestant, Orthodox or Islamic or Confucian traditions gives rise to cultural zones with distinctive value systems that persist after controlling for the effects of economic development' (2000, p. 49). They predicted that a nation's religious categorization would relate to its values, and relate differently than would its level of affluence. Thus, from a social scientific perspective, it would be important to know more about a nation than just its level of economic development. Their intuition was substantiated, as we will see below, and provides a lead to researchers seeking additional ways to distinguish nations from one another.

Linking Nations' Eco-politico-socio-economic Factors to Citizen Outcomes

Such analytic frameworks, however complex and all-encompassing, are merely descriptive. For cross-cultural psychologists, the over-riding issue with such derived taxonomies has been how they may be linked to psychological phenomena that differ across the inhabitants of these nations. The crucial consideration is whether the dimensions of nations may be plausibly linked by theory to the outcomes of interest for psychologists. In an early test of such a linkage, Berry (1976) argued and showed that subsistence practices promoting qualities of either independence or conformity from a group's members result in socialization for either independence or conformity, with consequently higher or lower levels of field independence in perceptual functioning (see Chapter 6 for an elaboration and extension of this argument). Likewise, Ember and Ember (1994) showed that a history of recent warfare in cultural groups resulted in greater current levels of aggressiveness in the population, through the previous stronger socialization of young males in those cultures for aggressiveness (see also Archer & Gartner, 1984). Furthermore, Rohner (1975) showed that greater social system complexity led to greater demands on parents, resulting in somewhat higher levels of parental rejection of their children in child-rearing.

The Georgas et al. (2004) study mentioned above focused on the values of a nation's population as a function of their levels of affluence and religious type. They sampled widely from existing value studies, including both those providing **nation-level** means (Hofstede, 1980; Smith et al., 1996; Schwartz, 1994) and **citizen scores** (Inglehart, 1997; Diener & Diener, 1995). The statistical analyses required to disentangle the overlap between affluence and religion type were complex, but enabled Georgas et al. (2004) to conclude that:

> Affluence is positively associated with self-enhancing values (such as individualism...) Religion was found to be less salient for these values, and if religious clusters or cultural zones were significant, these were often the zones or clusters associated with the highest levels of affluence. Power distance was associated negatively with affluence and positively with various religions. The psychological variables associated with religious cluster membership (and not with affluence) were hierarchy, involvement, and uncertainty avoidance ... the data suggest a view in which religion is associated with vertical relationships, not just between the believer and the Supreme Being but also between humans with unequal power or resources. (p. 90)

Affluence is important for individualistic values, as Georgas et al. (2004) have shown, by their cross-sectional analysis of national data. Using time series measures over the last 20 years, Inglehart and Oyserman (2004) conclude that, 'One important way that culture changes is under the impact of economic development' (p. 74). As we discuss more fully in Chapter 12, 'experiencing prosperity minimizes survival concerns, making societal values associated with survival less important and allowing for increased focus on social values associated with self-expression and personal choice' (p. 74). This observation confirms the Georgas et al. result with a longitudinal research design, the basic conclusion supporting Hofstede's (1980) original finding.

There is more to be derived from the Georgas et al. (2004) findings: this important study points our discipline beyond the economic determinism of Marx to the domains of the spiritual-philosophical legacy characterizing nations through historical diffusion. Over time, societal systems are introduced that are based on the teachings of these legacies, for example, the use of open examinations for selecting magistrates and advisors to the court in China was introduced during the Former Han Dynasty in 124 BCE (Dawson, 1978). Such institutions establish a social starting point upon which subsequent adaptations are added as society advances. In the Chinese case, political order was extended, societal wealth increased, and the provision of basic education was broadened. A national system of academic assessment is now operated by the Chinese Ministry of Education, but remains rigorous and elitist, selecting only the best students and sending them to the best schools for further study and eventual release into the nation's civil service and professions. With these kinds of institutional structures in place, is it any surprise that Singapore's Prime Minister, who is ethnic Chinese in a predominantly Chinese nation, is the most highly paid head of state in our contemporary world? These contemporary institutions imprint the marks of earlier socialization influences on those socialized into the contemporary realization of these legacies. In the Chinese case, this mark is the distinctively high endorsement of power or self-enhancement values among contemporary Chinese persons, both within and beyond China itself (Bond, 1996b).

The projects discussed above took a single, albeit broad dimension of the eco-social context and related it to a broad range of outcomes of interest. Box 4.4 explores the more specific issue of how we may best draw on the results of **individual-level** and **nation-level** studies to explain national levels of coronary heart disease.

Box 4.4

Nationality, Values and Health

Friedman and Rosenman (1975) showed a powerful relationship between the Type A personality profile of American men and their susceptibility to developing coronary heart disease and of suffering from angina pectoris or myocardial infarction, together known as CHD. The connection between personality and this threat to physical health remained strong even after controlling for other factors with known relations to heart disease like smoking, diet and exercise. Levine and Bartlett (1984) extended this work into the cross-national arena by arguing that, if a sense of time pressure is a component of the Type A personality, then nations whose citizens have a faster pace of life should have correspondingly higher rates of death by heart attack. To their surprise, Japan, which showed the highest pace of life in their study of six nations, showed the lowest rate of death by heart disease.

It is now believed that the operative component of the Type A personality syndrome for CHD is anger, specifically anger expression (Siegman, 1994). This insight at the level of individual pathogenesis will help focus our explorations at the national level of those factors that might best predict the incidence of CHD in a country. Specifically, any cultural factor that operates to inhibit the expression of anger in mundane living should show a negative correlation with CHD. In 1988, Triandis, Bontempo, Villareal, Asai, and Lucca integrated the literature on collectivism and concluded that, 'other things being equal (e.g., GNP per capita), the levels of disease in collectivist countries should be lower than those in individualistic countries' (p. 328). Chan (1995) correlated national levels of acute myocardial infarction, diseases of pulmonary circulation, and cerebrovascular disease with Schwartz's (1994) nation-level value domains, partialling out GNP per capita, using data from 23 nations. She found that higher levels of mastery were associated with higher levels of pulmonary disease.

It is alternatively possible to focus on individual-level measures of collectivism (or low independence, as we shall label the concept at the individual-level). Then, controlling for GNP per capita, would citizen scores on some measure of **interdependence** predict national rates of CHD? Bond (1991b) argued that the individual-level value dimension of social integration (Bond, 1988) resembled interdependence, so that countries with citizens showing higher levels of social integration should show higher levels of CHD, after controlling for national wealth. As predicted, citizen scores on social integration predicted one category of CHD, cerebrovascular disease positively, but for 'other circulatory system diseases' the relationship was negative. This conflicting result, combined with Chan's (1995) findings, suggests that the specific sub-type of a given disease may be related to citizen interdependence, and that we require different theorizing to explain these opposing outcomes.

Bond (1991b) also showed that a different dimension of citizen values, morality *versus* reputation, related to the national rate for the most typical type of heart disease, acute myocardial infarction. Is a concern with reputation the psychological factor driving this type of heart disease? If so, how? Is a concern for reputation an aspect of

(Continued)

Box 4.4   Continued

psychological interdependence (an individual-level reflection of national-level collectivism), and does it drive this type of CHD through generating the expression of anger when one's reputation is challenged (Felson, 1978)? If this is the case, then nation-level collectivism, after controlling for national wealth, would predispose towards higher levels of this type of CHD, not lower levels, as Triandis et al. (1988) hypothesized.

Answers to this and similar questions about national health require both a more extensive sampling of countries than was possible with this early study, and also careful control of other possible causal agents for CHD at the nation-level, such as levels of cholesterol in the bloodstream. Additional health problems may be considered: Cohen, Doyle, Turner, Alper, and Skoner (2003) have shown experimentally that susceptibility to the common cold is lower for more sociable persons, 'independent of baseline immunity (virus-specific antibody), demographics, emotional styles, stress hormones, and health practices' (p. 389). Given that citizen scores for sociability differ across nations (Allik & McCrae, 2004), would we therefore expect to find national differences in catching cold and its associated consequences, such as work absenteeism, associated with these differing levels of sociability across nations? Such research requires that measures of these less dramatic health problems be taken, but the suggestiveness of careful work, such as that by Cohen et al., may inspire their collection.

Do we need a separate theory for each type of health outcome? Lynn and Hampson's (1975) classification of national rates of disease types and social pathology suggests that some simplification may be possible: they factor analysed 12 of these rates across 18 developed nations and extracted two broad factors, labeled 'neuroticism' and 'extraversion'. Their neuroticism factor combined high psychosis, low suicide, high caffeine consumption, low alcoholism, low crime, high calory intake, high CHD, and low accidental death. 'Cultural' explanations for a national difference in one of these constituent rates, e.g., CHD, may then also be applicable to any one of the other 'health' problems included in this factor. Again, a much wider sampling of nations is needed, but there is promise that disease types do group together and hence may be responsive to the same societal variations.

More complex **eco-cultural** models are now being developed and tested against psychological outcomes of interest. Van de Vliert, Huang, and Levine (2004), for example, use both national temperature and national wealth to predict citizen levels of motivation to do volunteer work. These researchers argue that national wealth is a proxy measure for the abundance of resources generally available to a nation's citizenry:

> For voluntary workers in higher income countries with abundant tangible resources, self-serving and altruistic motivations might well be positively linked because self sacrificing is a way of 'establishing one's self-identity, confirming one's notion of the sort of person one sees oneself to be and expressing the values appropriate to this self-identity' (Katz & Kahn, 1978, p. 361) ... By contrast, voluntary workers in countries with scarce tangible resources might face a salient and serious trade-off between serving one's own interests and acting out altruistic or humanitarian concerns, given that they receive no, or hardly any, remuneration to offset their work-related expenses. (2004, p. 64).

Thermal climate is then hypothesized to enter the predictive mix as an amplifier of this wealth effect on the two motivations driving voluntary activity:

> countries with less comfortable climates require greater national wealth, which may be used to provide for one's own needs and for helping others in need. In comfortable climates on the other hand, there is little need to make resources available to cope with climate-contingent concerns.
>
> As a result, in uncomfortably colder or hotter climates, the hypothesized positive link between self-concern and other-concern in higher income [i.e., resource abundant] countries and the hypothesized negative link between self-concern and other-concern in lower income countries will gain strength ... (2004, p. 64–5)

In this sophisticated argument, a psychological outcome, the balance between self-concern and other-concern, is affected by the interaction of two basic national variables, wealth and climate comfort. Van de Vliert et al. (2004) argue that the ecological features of a country, its resource base and its temperature, conspire to shape the pattern of pro-social motivations in its citizens, presumably through the socialization of values in various institutional settings. These ecological conditions operate by directing human effort in different directions, towards self-survival or towards other-assistance.

The empirical support that van de Vliert et al. (2004) obtained for this hypothesis lends credence to the potential importance of linking dimensions of nations to the social-psychological outcomes of its citizens. National context matters, although drawing out the pathways of linkage is a challenging exercise, requiring scientific imagination. Critics have challenged the model advanced by van de Vliert et al., pointing out that there is considerable within-nation climatic variation, and that a few countries are very large with a considerable range of latitude, for example, China, Russia, Australia. Van de Vliert (personal communication) responds that, 'The geographical within-country variance in temperature is negligible compared with the between-country variance. In other words, results are basically the same no matter whether you use the northernmost or the southernmost city's temperature.' Furthermore, 'The number of big countries is small relative to the number of smaller countries, with the consequence that their erroneous impact is modest at best.' In further studies, van de Vliert and his colleagues have shown that this same interaction between average national temperature and affluence can also predict national wage levels (van de Vliert, 2003), happiness (van de Vliert, Huang & Parker, 2004) and the prevalence of different styles of leadership (van de Vliert & Smith, 2004; van de Vliert, in press). The type of results obtained in each these studies is illustrated in Box 4.5, which shows variations by nation in leader styles. Van de Vliert's empirical results present a case to be answered, a case that will require the same conceptual sophistication that was used to frame his original hypotheses, now supported with fuller data. National variation in climate makes a difference!

A Case Study of Nationality and Homicide

One of the challenges faced by **nation-level** research such as that described above is giving it psychological substance by identifying behavioural outcomes. In van de Vliert et al.'s (2004) research, for example, how do the researchers go beyond their

Box 4.5

Leadership as a Joint Function of Demanding Climate and National Wealth

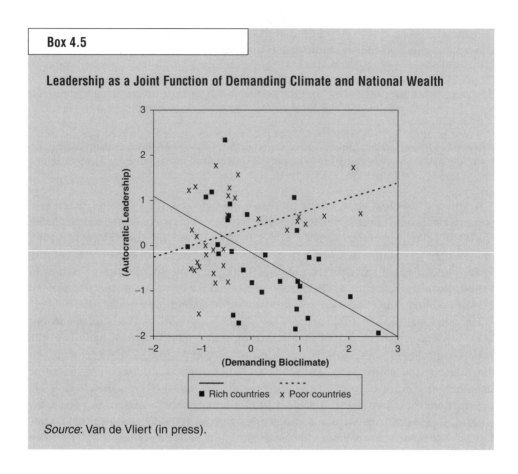

Source: Van de Vliert (in press).

finding that the self-concern and other-concern driving volunteer work varies across nations of varying temperatures and resource bases?

Lim, Bond, and Bond (2005) have attempted to address this challenge empirically while examining the outcome of national homicide. The World Health Organization (2002) reports that 1.6 million people die premature, violent deaths each year. Of these, 32% are victims of homicide. Lim et al. gathered homicide rates from 56 nations across a minimum of three years between 1992 and 1995. Rates varied from a low of about 1 per 100,000 inhabitants in Japan to a high of over 80 for Colombia. Consistent with results of previous sociological studies, the researchers found that this homicide rate could be positively predicted by a combination of three national indices: a nation's level of poverty, its inequality in resource distribution, and its gender ratio (the number of females per 100 males).

In attempting to explain such outcomes, social scientists have frequently proposed social psychological explanations, such as the stress arising from economic hardship (Linsky, Bachman, & Strauss, 1995) or the weakening of inhibitory restraints through a lack of social trust among a nation's members (Wilkinson, Kawachi, & Kennedy, 1998). How might one confirm such reasoning? Cross-cultural psychology has now developed to the point where equivalent measures of social psychological constructs have been gathered in a number of nations. Lim et al. (2005) argued that multiple regression techniques could be used to discover if these social psychological constructs are found to mediate the effect of the three societal variables they had identified as predicting national homicide rates. The application of the concepts of **mediation** and **moderation** to cross-cultural psychology is explored in Chapter 6.

Lim et al. (2005) found that the effect of a nation's gender ratio on the homicide rate was completely mediated by the preference for status rather than love in one's criteria for a preferred mate. This dimension of mate preference was one of the factors identified by Shackelford, Schmitt, and Buss (2005) in a re-analysis of ratings on qualities that might be desired in a mate that were made by respondents in 37 nations (Buss, 1989; see Chapter 8). The effect of poverty was also completely mediated by the preference for a mate's status rather than love. The effect of relative inequality was partially mediated by the mate preference of status over love. An emphasis on acquiring mates who could improve one's social position was thus the common denominator to all three linkages between a nation's characteristics and its level of homicide. Lim et al. argued that social systems dominated by the pressure to accumulate valued resources socialize their members to be competitive with one another, resulting over numerous daily interactions across a number of years in more killing. The generally higher preference for a mate who confers status rather than one who gives love is one socialized manifestation of this general societal emphasis on power.

Variability of Life Satisfaction within Nations across Nations

Reported subjective well-being varies between nations. Box 4.6 explores why this may be so. **Citizen means** for any measure of happiness are averages. Within a given nation, there will be variations around this average score, such that in some nations citizens will show similar levels of happiness, while in other nations there will be a wider latitude of difference. This **nation-level** variable is called intra-cultural variation (ICV), and has been explored as a predictor of a variety of social psychological constructs (Au, 1999).

Box 4.6

Are Scandinavians Happier than Asians?

Diener and Oishi (2004) attempt to explain why citizens from various countries differ in their level of happiness. They begin by pointing out that the broad term 'happiness' is construed by many social scientists as 'subjective well-being' (SWB), i.e., 'people's assessments of the quality of their lives' (p. 1). It is important to note that well-being may be construed more broadly to include living in a good environment, being able to cope with life, being of worth for the world, along with enjoying life (Veenhoven, 2004). Social psychologists like Diener and Oishi (2004) tend to focus more specifically on the subjective component of well-being. These assessments are made by asking respondents to evaluate their lives across the various roles they

(Continued)

Box 4.6 Continued

have played to date, i.e., their general satisfaction with life, and also by their levels of positive and negative affect and by their self-assessed level of happiness. Nation-level scores for these four indicators overlap highly. However, positive and negative affect relate somewhat differently to life satisfaction in the members of different nations, an issue to be examined in Chapter 7. Discussion here focuses on assessments of life satisfaction or happiness across nations.

Conveniently, the World Values Survey included measures of life satisfaction in general and across various role domains, such as the family, and job. Citizen scores for life satisfaction are derived from probability samples of adults in each nation (Inglehart & Klingemann, 2000), and so give a broad representation of a nation's citizenry on this basic social psychological variable. The score used is the national average to the question, 'All things considered, how satisfied are you with your life-as-a-whole now?' along a nine-point scale bounded by the adjectives 'dissatisfied' and 'satisfied'.

Diener and Oishi (2004) conclude that three factors affect citizen ratings of life satisfaction: higher affluence (most strongly), declines in political-social stability, and cultural tendencies to focus on the more negative domains of one's life satisfaction. The affluence of a nation is, however, highly correlated with many national characteristics like citizen longevity, literacy levels, level of human rights observance, degree of political freedom, and the relative status of women. These societal characteristics are aspects of what Veenhoven (1999) describes as, 'Living in a good environment', and it is difficult to know which among these many factors leads to higher life satisfaction among a nation's citizenry. The same uncertainty bedevils the association of political-social stability with life satisfaction, as there are many correlates of political-social instability, such as income loss, higher rates of crime, widening gaps between the rich and the poor, earlier death by disease, and so forth, that may be responsible. The cultural tendency to focus on the less positive appears to be an aspect of Confucian social philosophy rather than collectivism, since, although Latin American nations are collectivist, Latin Americans focus on the more positive domains of life in determining their level of life satisfaction.

So, Scandinavians (Norwegians, Swedes, and Finns) are more satisfied with their lives than Asians, at least Confucian East Asians (Japanese, Hong Kong Chinese, Taiwanese, Singaporeans, Mainland Chinese, and South Koreans). This appears to derive from the greater affluence and social-political stability of Scandinavian nations combined with a general tendency of their citizens to focus on the most positive domains of their lives rather than upon the most negative in assessing their life satisfaction. This last cultural issue may be responsible for the persistence of national differences in happiness levels across ethnic groups in the United States. The stability of these effects across generations and even nationality is suggested by the discovery that differences in happiness among these groups may be predicted from the happiness scores of people from the nations of their immigrant forefathers, even though the respondents are now living in a wealthier and more politically stable environment (Rice & Steele, 2004).

ICVs are different properties of their nations than their **citizen means**, and may therefore be considered as a separate feature of nations. Like nation scores for any set of variables, they may themselves be factor analysed. In the case of life satisfaction, ICVs for a nation on satisfaction with life as a whole, with my job, with my home life and with the financial situation of my home life all loaded on the same factor, labelled by Au (2000) as 'satisfaction variation'. Calculating factor scores on this dimension, Au showed that the Netherlands had the lowest level of satisfaction variation and Austria the highest.

It is possible then to correlate these scores on satisfaction variation with some of the **eco-cultural** indices discussed earlier. One could predict, for example, that nations with higher variation in citizen satisfaction would have higher variation in wealth, which is assessed by what is known as a 'GINI' score; that is, the greater the range of incomes within a nation, the greater the range of satisfaction scores will be within that nation. Au (personal communication) confirms that this correlation is strong and positive ($r = +0.53$) across 35 nations.

Au (2000) does not provide **eco-cultural** results for measures such as GINI, but instead focuses upon **nation-level** value scores taken from the work of Hofstede (1980) and Schwartz (1994). He reports that satisfaction variation is most positively associated with Schwartz's embeddedness and most negatively with his egalitarianism. Thus, there is more variation in satisfaction judgements in nations with greater embeddedness, less in more egalitarian nations. This contrast can be explained if one argues that nations high in egalitarianism manifest their commitment by ensuring a more egalitarian distribution of the very resources associated with higher levels of life satisfaction, namely, affluence, human rights observance, freedom, and so forth. Embedded nations are nations divided into a collection of segregated, more tightly knit in-groups, more indifferent to the well-being of other groups. In consequence, the greater differences across these various groups in their levels of life satisfaction arising in part from a high GINI are tolerated or ignored. Consistent with this reasoning, Au and Cheung (2002) showed that across 42 nations, high ICV in reported job autonomy predicted low reported health and lower job satisfaction.

An Integrative Model

Although suggestive about possible psychological processes, the approach taken by Lim et al. (2005) did not include **individual-level** data, but used **nation-level** average scores taken from other studies. Such research cannot therefore directly assess the processes leading to the individual outcome of interest. As Hofstede (1980) reminded us, 'Eco-logic differs from individual logic' (p. 31). To tap into individual logic requires that an **individual-level** outcome is selected for examination. The national and psychological processes leading to this outcome are predicted by theory and then measured in respondents from a number of nations. Such an approach is discussed next, first theoretically and then empirically.

Theoretical Example

Gelfand, Nishii, Raver, and Lim (2004) have developed a multi-level model of 'situational constraint'. This theory 'illustrates the complex interplay between eco-cultural and historical factors, the structure of social situations, and psychological processes' (p. 2). They propose this model as a complement to the strong focus on cultural values that permeates the cross-cultural literature. Gabrenya (1999) was one of the first to argue that an exclusive focus on values in cross-cultural psychology to the neglect of the larger social structure amounted to an 'idealist bias' in the field. Gelfand and colleagues responded to this critique by advancing their model, which makes the structure of situations a central focus of cross-cultural psychological theorizing.

Gelfand and colleagues aptly point out that there is little theorizing on the nature of social situations in psychology in general. They draw on Mischel's (1977) notion of *strong versus weak* situations, arguing for the first time that nations can be differentiated on the degree to which situations are generally strong versus weak. They argue that strong situations will be generally found in *tight* rather than *loose* cultures – a crucial distinction among social systems that had first been highlighted by Pelto (1968), whose anthropological explorations alerted him to groups varying widely in terms of their level of compliance with norms. Gelfand et al. begin by noting that, 'Culture is fundamentally a *system* of interrelated and dynamic forces that span different levels of analysis' (p. 5, emphasis in original). Given this premise, Gelfand et al. then proceed to identify the macro-level precursors and micro-level correlates of the structure of situations across cultures. At the most macro level of analysis,

> certain ecocultural and historical factors create an increased need for predictability and coordinated social action within cultures. For example, factors such as high population density, lack of natural resources, extreme temperatures, and/or a history of external threat are associated with the need to create social structures to facilitate order and coordinated action within the social environment. (Gelfand et al., 2004, p. 6)

These 'distal' background contextual factors conspire to influence the structure of situations that comprise the cultural context, producing a preponderance of strong or weak situations:

> Strong situations create order and coordinated social action by having many clearly defined norms wherein there are a limited number of behavioural patterns that are acceptable, and by increasing the propensity for censuring inappropriate (deviant) behaviour. By contrast, weak situations have few clearly defined norms, permit a wide range of acceptable behaviour, and afford much latitude for individuals' behavioural choices. (Gelfand et al., 2004, p. 6)

Individual members of such cultural systems are socialized to develop social psychological characteristics that then enable them to function effectively within the typical situations that characterize their cultural group:

> individuals in societies with high situational constraint will generally have a greater need for structure, greater impulse control and conscientiousness, and a greater concern for sanctioning of inappropriate behaviour as compared to individuals in societies with low situational constraint ... Individuals in societies with high situational constraint will generally have more chronically accessible *ought* self-guides and a *prevention* regulatory focus, as compared to individuals in loose cultural systems who will generally have more chronically accessible *ideal* self-guides and a *promotion* regulatory focus (Higgins, 1987). Cognitive styles or 'preferred ways of gathering, processing, and evaluating information' (Hayes & Allinson, 1998, p. 850; Kirton, 1976) are also expected to vary across societies with strong versus weak situational structure, with individuals in systems with high constraint being more likely to

have *adaptor* cognitive styles and individuals in systems with low constraint being more likely to have *innovator* cognitive styles (Kirton, 1976). Finally, we argue that individuals' schemas will reflect the predominant strength of situations, with cognitive schemas evidencing less variability across individuals (i.e., higher socially shared cognition) in systems with high versus low situational constraint. (Gelfand et al., 2004, p. 7)

Gelfand et al.'s (2004) model is graphically represented in Box 4.7:

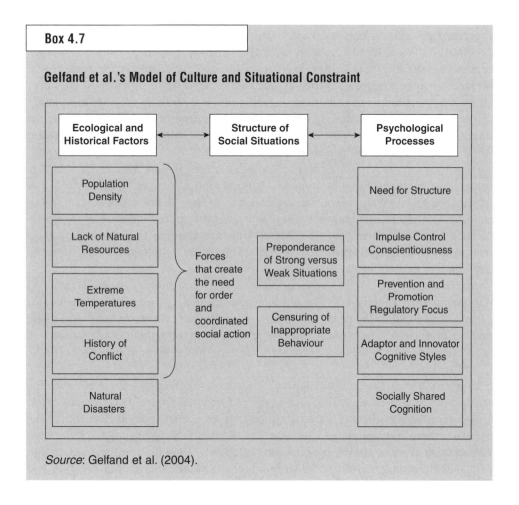

Box 4.7

Gelfand et al.'s Model of Culture and Situational Constraint

Source: Gelfand et al. (2004).

In this model, the structure of social situations **mediates** between the distal level of ecological-historical influences and the proximal level of adaptive individual-level processes. Such comprehensive theorizing is needed in cross-cultural psychology, where our research is necessarily multi-levelled, requiring that we develop models reflecting the specific constructs involved and the mutually causal relations across the various levels (Gabrenya, 1999). Note that this model, in contrast to the one in Box 4.3, specifies two-way causal influences between ecological factors and psychological processes. While causation may historically have operated from ecological factors to psychological processes, current research into global warming serves to remind us that human activity can and does affect even the most basic aspects of the environment to which we shall subsequently need to adapt once more.

Empirical Example: Nationality and Self-esteem as a Determinant of Life Satisfaction

Gelfand et al.'s (2004) complex and sophisticated reasoning linking culture to psychological processes points the way towards the constructs and operationalizations necessary for the scientific validation of their theory. Essentially, authors of such theories are arguing that culture exercises a moderating effect on the relationship between social psychological variables, such as the link between perceived employee effort and that employee's performance evaluation. It does so by varying the strength of some aspects of the cultural system, like the structure of social situations or the importance of self-guides, that enhance or weaken the salience of some key process variable, in the above case perceived employee effort.

Empirical demonstrations of this process are rare. They require the collection of data from respondents socialized in numerous cultural groups, nations in the present case. At least two social psychological variables must be measured, the strength of their relationship assessed in each cultural group, and then the strength of that linkage compared across the national groups. This varying strength can then be explained by relating it to that **nation-level** variable deemed by theory to influence the relationship between the two social psychological variables. The classic study in this mould is Diener and Diener's (1995) examination of self-esteem and life satisfaction in 31 national groups. They argued that a major part of the social agenda in individualist cultures is to enhance the perceived importance of the self as an actor in a world where one has been freed from binding association with collectivities. One's self-esteem will reflect one's success at achieving this goal, and one would be more satisfied with life in consequence.

To test this idea, Diener and Diener (1995) simply correlated self-esteem with life satisfaction for individuals within each of their 31 national groups. This correlation was always positive regardless of national group, but its strength varied. The size of the correlation was itself correlated with a nation's level of individualism – the more individualistic the nation, the stronger the correlation between self-esteem and satisfaction with life. The strong correlation between a nation's wealth and its individualism had already been established by Hofstede (1980) and subsequently confirmed, so one could thus argue that increasing wealth leads to increasing individualism in a nation's socializing institutions and hence to the stronger valuing of individualism. This individualism makes self-esteem a more salient concern throughout socialization and ties it more strongly to a sense of satisfaction with one's life. National culture can then be construed as a sensitizing agent, enhancing certain social processes, diminishing others.

This is a new role for national culture – it not only positions its members on a given social-psychological construct, but it also tightens or weakens the connection between such social-psychological constructs. As another example, Fu, Kennedy, Tata et al. (2004) found that belief in fate control, i.e., the belief that important outcomes are determined by external forces like luck, chance or karma, was posi- tively associated with higher rated effectiveness of using assertive strategies of con- trol among persons from 12 nations. However, the strength of this association varied across nations, from a high of +0.38 in the USA to a low of –0.07 in China. This asso- ciation was found to be stronger for persons from countries higher in GNP per capita (Fu, personal communication). So, the **nation-level** construct of affluence appears to moderate the **individual-level** impact of perceived fate control on the rated use- fulness of assertive tactics in organizations. As more and more multi-nation data sets become available, we will increasingly need to theorize about how national culture acts as a highlighting force, moderating how social factors affect one another in different locations.

Summary

Nations are political units with distinctive ecological, historical, political, educa- tional, legal, regulatory, social, and economic characteristics. As such, they con- stitute systems and have cultures. The consequences of national cultures for the socialization practices and the subsequent psychological characteristics of their citizens and the social-psychological processes occurring within their boundaries thus become the appropriate focus of the typical cross-cultural study conducted today. These studies may be conducted at the national or the individual level of analysis, but nation-level studies carry no necessary implications for the under- standing of individual-level phenomena. This chapter has analysed the different ways that social scientists have examined nations as cultures, presented a general framework for integrating these various types of studies, and given examples of how these approaches have been empirically tried to date. The ideal type of study conceptualizes and then measures both national characteristics and individual processes. Such research is one of the current active growth points in cross-cultural social psychology.

Further Reading

1 Bond, M.H., & 68 co-authors. (2004). Culture-level dimensions of social axioms and their correlates across 41 cultures. *Journal of Cross-Cultural Psychology, 35*, 548–70.
2 Inglehart, R., & Baker, W.E. (2000). Modernization, cultural change and the persis- tence of traditional values. *American Sociological Review, 65*, 19–51.
3 Leung, K., & Bond, M.H. (2004). Social axioms: A model of social beliefs in multi- cultural perspective. In M.P. Zanna (ed.), *Advances in Experimental Social Psychology*. San Diego, CA: Academic Press.
4 Suh, E.M., & Oishi, S. (2002). Subjective well-being across cultures. www.wwu. edu/psychology/~culture.

Study Questions

1 How may we consider a nation to be a culture?
2 What are some important features of national variation that have implications for the psychological functioning of a nation's citizenry?
3 How do nation-level phenomena exercise an impact on the social psychological functioning of individuals within that nation? Illustrate your thinking by using an example found in this chapter.

Part Two

Core Issues

5

The Making and Remaking of Cultures: A Developmental Perspective

The child is father of the man (William Wordsworth, *My heart leaps up*)

How does a developmental perspective help in understanding social behaviour across cultures? This question is addressed in this chapter, in which we present a developmental perspective on the family and self in their cultural context.

Why Do We Need a Developmental Perspective?

Social psychology is basically atemporal; that is, it focuses on social influence, social cognition and social behaviour, as manifested in interpersonal, group and intergroup interactions, social influences on the individual and the like, all occurring in the 'present' or at a given point in time, rather than searching for the antecedents of these phenomena in early experience. Thus, for example, one is more likely to find a chapter on 'social development' in developmental psychology textbooks or in separate social development texts than in social psychology textbooks. This situation has a parallel within cross-cultural psychology. Among cross-cultural researchers social psychologists are in the majority, and developmental psychology has not yet had much influence, even though cultural perspectives figure importantly in developmental psychology. In fact, as Keller and Greenfield (2000) note, culture has been more integrated into developmental psychology than into any other sub-field of psychology.

However, as mainstream social psychology has expanded to include the study of such topics as the self, moral judgement, and aggression, which challenge its present-oriented focus, it has started to take into consideration some developmental questions, even if marginally (see for example, Bond, 2004). This change in explanatory outlook promises to be beneficial for social psychology. Similarly, the low level of attention to human development in cross-cultural psychology needs to change, because a developmental perspective can provide us with insights into the dynamic relations between biology and culture, human universals, and cultural diversity.

Thus, a developmental perspective is called for by the cultural focus of this book. Social cognition and behaviour are not examined here with reference to the hypothetical 'non-cultural, universal human being' of mainstream social psychology, but rather with respect to a distinctively 'cultural' person. Consequently, the variance in human behaviour that we consider is much larger than is commonly confronted in social psychology texts because a global perspective involves considering a great deal of diversity. Therefore, together with common, possibly universal aspects of development, the varying, possibly indigenous aspects must also be considered. Generalizations from a study are not made automatically to all human beings. How does this make a difference in terms of a developmental perspective?

We can begin to answer this question by considering the ways in which persons describe themselves. Psychologists and philosophers have long debated how best to define the nature of the self. We shall not enter this debate directly, but will focus instead upon the way in which each person chooses to describe him or her self. Self-definition or self-construal as it is usually known has become a key element, both in social psychology and in cross-cultural psychology. It provides the central focus both of this chapter and of Chapter 6. A great deal of cross-cultural research in this area has pointed to the importance of the distinction between construing oneself as relatively **independent** of others or else as relatively **interdependent** with others (e.g., Markus & Kitayama, 1991). These two types of self-construal have generally been found to be more common in individualistic and in collectivistic cultural contexts, respectively. As we shall see in later chapters, most social psychological work focuses on how individuals with one or the other type of self-construal differ from each other in terms of their social cognitions and behaviour, ranging from person perception to emotions, and from communication styles to preferences for certain modes of resource allocation. These studies are basically descriptive and atemporal, dealing with the question, '*what?*'; that is, they ask what type of self-construal is associated with what types of behaviours at a given point in time.

If we are curious about *how* these variations in self come about, we need to go beyond the descriptive to a more basic, causal level of analysis. We would need to address the question of *how* one or the other type of self *develops*. Context-based developmental processes and child-rearing and socialization in the family need to be studied to understand how variations in self emerge in different cultural and socio-economic-familial contexts. This developmental consideration goes a lot further than merely associating different types of self-construal with individualistic and collectivistic cultures. It deals with the question, '*How?*'; that is, how does a certain type of self-construal develop?

An even more basic level of analysis is called for if we are curious about *why* a certain type of child socialization occurs in a particular familial, cultural and socio-economic context, and not in another. To deal with this type of a question, we need to delve into the functional bases of child socialization at the interface of family and society. In other words, we need to understand the reasons underlying different child-rearing patterns and their relative adaptiveness to different environments. By doing this, we can grasp how family interaction patterns and child socialization are influenced by the socio-economic and cultural context and in turn affect child-rearing.

Such an understanding can help address the '*Why?*', characterizing the observed diversity in human patterns. It would also help shed light on when to expect a change in these patterns, for any changes in contexts would have implications for changes in the chain of relationships. Box 5.1 gives this line of thinking in a schematic way. Level 1 refers to the eco-cultural issues, some of which we have discussed already in Chapter 4, while Level 3 is addressed in Chapter 6.

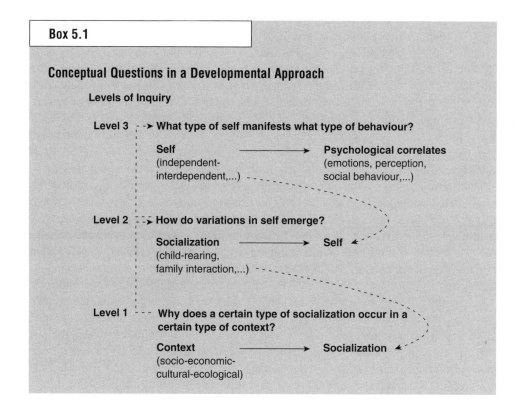

Box 5.1

Conceptual Questions in a Developmental Approach

Levels of Inquiry

Level 3 - -➤ What type of self manifests what type of behaviour?

Self ————————➤ Psychological correlates
(independent-   (emotions, perception,
interdependent,...) - - - - - - - - social behaviour,...)

Level 2 - -➤ How do variations in self emerge?

Socialization ———————➤ Self ◄
(child-rearing,
family interaction,...) - - - - -

Level 1 - - - Why does a certain type of socialization occur in a certain type of context?

Context ———————➤ Socialization ◄
(socio-economic-
cultural-ecological)

Thus, since we are interested in systematic variations among different socio-cultural groups or populations, going above and beyond possibly universal human social behaviour, it is important for us to address how those variations come about. Studying *how* these differences emerge and *why* would help us understand their function or adaptive value in varying socio-cultural contexts, thus in turn broadening our understanding of the observed variation in human social behaviour.

Life Stages and Culture

The way that we think about ourselves and the ways that we act are the result of life-long adaptations shaped to a large extent by cultural influences. Furthermore, these adaptations are ever changing and being reconstructed through continuing experience. This is the view introduced by lifespan perspectives in developmental psychology and is widely shared today. Continuous development is seen to span the whole spectrum from the prenatal period to old age and death. Nevertheless, through this lifelong process, infancy, childhood and adolescence are considered of special importance, as most growth, learning and change occur in the early periods of human development. The life-span developmental approach renders culture even more relevant, as the role of cultural factors shows variation in different phases of life, progressively increasing in their impact from infancy to adulthood.

The study of childhood in cultural context is seen not only in psychology, but has traditionally been a central topic for anthropologists (Whiting & Whiting, 1975; LeVine, 1989), for sociologists (Elder, 1974), and to some extent for social historians (Aries, 1962). In psychology, ecological perspectives (Bronfenbrenner, 1979; Super & Harkness, 1986) situate child development and parenting in socio-cultural context, the child being embedded within the proximal environment (family and immediate community) and the proximal environment being embedded within the distal environment (societal institutions, economy, cultural norms and conventions). The place of the child in family and society, in combination with parental values and orientations, give us important clues to understanding how socio-cultural variations come about in the development of the self, mind, behaviour, and values from a global perspective.

There is much commonality across cultures in the construal of infancy and early childhood, based on biological needs for care, nutrition, protection, etc. Accordingly, much infant care is based on biological/evolutionary functions, including universal 'intuitive parenting', which involves nursing and carrying infants in response to distress signals, mainly crying, smiling and talking a high pitched 'baby talk' (Keller, 1997). Keller, Lohaus, Volker, Cappenberg, & Chasiotis (1999) point to some basic components of parenting infants that have evolutionary bases and thus show commonality across cultures. These are the primary care system (especially nursing), the body contact system (especially carrying), the body motor stimulation system, and the face-to-face interaction system. However, Keller et al. also report that there are variations in the prevalence of the last three systems in particular, across different cultural contexts. Body contact and body stimulation are found to be more characteristic of the collectivistic agrarian traditional cultures in Africa, and the face-to-face system is more common in middle-class, urban Western contexts. They further claim that child-rearing characterized by close body contact is conducive to the development of relatedness with others, whereas face-to-face interaction with child-directed language is considered to lead to the child's development of a sense of independent agency. Box 5.2 shows how close attention to mothers' behaviour can reveal subtle but important cultural and historical differences.

Box 5.2

Child-rearing Varies even between Western Nations and Over Time

There can be variations in child-rearing even between educated urban populations within European societies that are quite similar in many respects. Comparing German and Greek urban middle-class mothers interacting with their 3-month-old babies, Keller, Papaligoura, Kuensemueller et al. (2003) found that both groups use

(Continued)

Box 5.2 Continued

face-to-face contact and object play, and less body contact and body stimulation. These are interactional strategies that are considered to lead to the development of a sense of independent agency in the child. However, Greek mothers expressed more interactional warmth by smiling during face-to-face interaction than German mothers, who responded with more contingency to babies' signals than the Greek mothers. Thus while both German and Greek mothers emphasized independence, Greek mothers also built relatedness through warmth. According to the researchers, the Greek pattern is conducive to the development of autonomous-related self-construal (Kağıtçıbaşı, 1996a, to be discussed later on).

Within a society significant changes can also occur over time. Keller and Lamm (2005) examined two comparable samples of German middle-class mothers over a 25-year period. They found a significant increase in face-to-face contact and object play, promoting independent agency and a significant decrease in body contact and warmth (expressed in smiling and tonal parameters of the voice), downplaying relatedness.

Thus, some developmental roots may be found in early mother–infant interactions that show variations across cultural contexts. Anthropological literature also points to the diversity of care practices based on different life styles and economies, as well as different customs and beliefs, called 'ethnotheories' (Harkness, 1992). Study of these early interaction patterns and care practices in different socio-economic-cultural contexts promises to provide us with clues to understanding *how* varying selves and behavioural repertoires develop and *why*, as we started out asking and as we will elaborate in the later sections of the chapter.

The above research shows that even in infancy with its common, basic survival needs there are cultural variations in parenting that may underpin different developmental pathways. Going beyond infancy, there is an even greater diversification with age in the definitions of children's roles and responsibilities in different societies. For example, early anthropological research (Mead, 1928) suggested that adolescence and gender roles in some preliterate societies were quite different from those in Western technological society. Although the validity of Mead's conclusions relating to Samoa were subsequently questioned, subsequent research from a global perspective shows that the familial roles of both children and adolescents do differ both between more and less affluent contexts and also between urban and rural contexts. We can take children's work as a case in point.

Studies find that children start early to assume responsibilities for household chores, care of younger siblings, and care of animals in agrarian societies with subsistence agriculture (Munroe, Munroe, & Shimmin, 1984). The complexity and amount of work increases with age, thus by middle childhood, most of children's waking hours are taken up by some sort of work. This is in contrast to children's lives in urban middle-class homes, particularly in Western societies, which include a preponderance of play. For example, in their classic early study of children in six cultures, Whiting and Whiting (1975) showed that among children aged between three and ten, 41% of Kenyan Nyansongo children's time was spent working, while only 2% of suburban American children's time was thus spent.

Child work contributes to the household economy, both in its own right, and also by freeing adults to put more time into economically productive work. According to an African psychologist, Nsamenang (1992), it is also an important way for children to learn their future social roles and responsibilities. Other work from Africa and similar socio-cultural contexts points to a similar picture (Dasen, 1988; Harkness, 1992). There are also variations in how children are taught and how they learn in everyday informal work contexts. Morelli, Rogoff and Angelillo (2003) compared how two- to three-year-old children spent their time in Congo, Guatemala and the USA. In Congo and Guatemala, children had frequent access to adults working, and quite often observed them doing so. Even at this young age, their play with one another sometimes emulated adult work behaviours. US children had much less opportunity to observe adults actually working and proportionally more of their playing time was spent playing with adults rather than each other. Studies thus point to different parental orientations toward child learning. Some of these appear 'traditional', others more 'modern'. Modifications over time are particularly notable, showing changes within the same societies with changing life styles (see Box 5.3).

Box 5.3

Changing Patterns of Childhood Socialization in the Maya

Greenfield and her colleagues reported the effects of economic changes in a weaving community of the Zinacantec Maya, located in Chiapas, Mexico. This community shifted from a subsistence economy to a commercial cash economy over a period of two decades. This shift influenced the way weaving was taught and carried out. In 1969 and 1970, mothers taught their daughters weaving through careful guidance with detail-oriented representation and imitation. The repetitiveness in weaving patterns reflected a conservative, compliant orientation. In 1991 and 1993, teaching and learning of weaving included a more independent apprenticeship. The weaving patterns also reflected this change in orientation in that there was a shift from traditional patterns maintained over generations to novel ones involving individual creativity, as indicated below:

	1969–1970		1991–1993
Economy:	Subsistence economy	⟶	Commercial cash economy
Weaving apprenticeship:	Careful guidance, detail-oriented representation, imitation	⟶	More independent activity
Independent weaving:	47.98 (mean) 34.12 (SD)	⟶	59.16 (mean) 30.64 (SD)

Sources: Greenfield, Maynard & Childs (2003); Greenfield & Childs (1977).

There is a current debate on the issue of when children's work stops being a positive social learning experience and starts to turn into child 'labour', even child 'abuse'. In particular, from a (Western) 'human rights' perspective, international agencies and children's rights advocates assail child labour that interferes with children's schooling. This is an example of the different cultural meanings that are assigned to the same behaviours in different settings, which can generate such debate. Cultural meanings associated with different life stages thus reflect lifestyles, social norms and values.

Old age is another life stage that is understood variously. While in Western techno-logical societies old people tend to get isolated from the family and community of young adults and lose social status, in many traditional societies they remain very much inte-grated within family and community, and do not experience status loss. They also tend to be active in important familial and communal roles, such as in transmission of values to the young, moderating disputes and the like. For example, a study of menopausal women in Singapore by Ward (1987) showed that in contrast to the commonly reported disturbances of mid-life crisis in Western societies, no mid-life crisis phenomenon is experienced by women in Singapore. The 'status' of women in the Western world tends to decrease with age, as youth and good looks are highly valued indicators of this status. In the traditional collectivistic societies, however, old age can be a period of increased status, especially for women, as they acquire more decision-making power and freedom of action in the familial and social spheres. Given the traditional gender roles in many patriarchal societies, young women are often under the protection and surveillance of family and male kin, but older women are freed from such constraints (see also Kağıtçıbaşı, 1982c). Another example of cultural differences in how aging is experienced is revealed by a study by Imamoglu, Kuller, Imamoglu and Kuller (1993), who found that elderly Turkish men had more frequent interpersonal contacts than elderly Swedish men. Nevertheless, the elderly Turkish men were less satisfied with their social relations because they wanted to be even more closely connected.

Thus, culturally informed lifespan perspectives show that different life stages are lived and understood variously in different socio-cultural contexts. Early patterns pave the way for later developments. Meanings vary across space and time. What appears to be universal is the inclination of all societies to use age as a basis for defining the individual and assigning certain roles and responsibilities to him or her.

The Value of Children and Family Change

Notwithstanding lifespan perspectives in studying human development in culture, childhood is given special attention both for its own sake and also because it is a key to understanding the dynamics of family and society in global context. For example, the above discussion of children working is a reflection of the particular place of the child in family and society and the values attributed to children by parents. Thus, to start our inquiry into the *how?* and *why?* of the variations in the development of self-construal, we need to look at the interface of societal values and lifestyles with family and human development. A concept that promises to shed light on this interface and which can serve as a mediating variable between the socio-cultural environmental factors and indi-vidual outcomes is the '**value of children**' (VOC). This is the value attached to children by parents; it underlies motivations for childbearing, that is, why people want to have children. It constitutes a determining aspect of childhood in every cultural setting.

A cross-cultural study on the value of children (the VOC Study) was conducted in the 1970s, surveying large, nationally representative samples of married respondents in Indonesia, Korea, the Philippines, Singapore, Taiwan, Thailand, Turkey, the USA, and a women's sample from Munich in Germany (Fawcett, 1983, Hoffman, 1987; Kağıtçıbaşı, 1982a, b). The value attributed by these parents to their children were found to vary significantly with the level of socio-economic development among the countries as well as within countries. A main finding of the comparative study was the greater salience of the economic/utilitarian value attached to children (especially sons) by parents in less developed contexts. This value decreased in importance at higher levels of socio-economic development and affluence. In contrast, the psychological value attached to children, such as the love, joy, companionship, and pride that children provide to their parents, either sustained their importance or were even found to be more important at higher levels of socio-economic development. Based on the VOC study findings, three different patterns of family relations in different socio-economic-cultural contexts have been proposed by Kağıtçıbaşı (1990, 1996b), comprising a Model of Family Change. Before examining the three different patterns, however, a *general model* of relations between families and their children is required, as presented in Box 5.4.

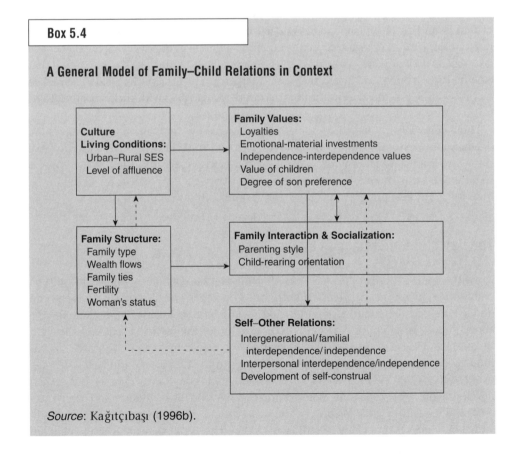

Box 5.4

A General Model of Family–Child Relations in Context

Culture
Living Conditions:
Urban–Rural SES
Level of affluence

Family Values:
Loyalties
Emotional-material investments
Independence-interdependence values
Value of children
Degree of son preference

Family Structure:
Family type
Wealth flows
Family ties
Fertility
Woman's status

Family Interaction & Socialization:
Parenting style
Child-rearing orientation

Self–Other Relations:
Intergenerational/familial
    interdependence/independence
Interpersonal interdependence/independence
Development of self-construal

Source: Kağıtçıbaşı (1996b).

This is a basic framework with three different manifestations that are elaborated below. It is a conceptualization of the embeddedness of the family in its context and of the development of the child's self-construal within the family context. Cultural values, beliefs, conventions, urban–rural lifestyles and variations in affluence are all important here. The family structure is mainly influenced by this context but also feeds back into it. It comprises several family characteristics that have been studied by sociologists and demographers. Context (culture, living conditions, and family structure) in turn affect the family system. This system comprises family values and family interactions and socialization, mutually influencing one another. Various factors that we have discussed up to now involve values and practices related to child-rearing and these constitute the family system in the model. Family values, family interaction and socialization lead to a certain type of self-construal and of self–other relations.

This basic model helps locate the family in context and sheds light on the first and second levels of the interrelated phenomena that we outlined in Box 5.1. In other words, here the conceptualizations addressing the queries 'Why does a certain type of socialization occur in a certain type of context?' and 'How do variations in self emerge?' can be dealt with. We examine next how this general model is manifested in three different family models in different socio-cultural economic contexts, and how these two queries are answered in each.

Three Models of the Family

In socio-economic contexts where children's contribution to their family's material well-being is significant, an economic/utilitarian value is associated with one's children, which is a value derived from their material contributions. This is the case especially in societies with low levels of affluence, particularly with rural agrarian people or low-income groups in urban or semi-urban areas, where children working both in and out of the home is common and contributes to the family economy. These children, when they grow up, also provide old-age security benefits to their parents, who usually lack other resources such as old-age pensions, insurance and retirement income. Thus, there is a dependence on children for family-of-origin livelihood, both while children are young and when they grow up to be adults. This is **the family model of interdependence** (Kağıtçıbaşı, 1990, 1996b). This model highlights what Arnett (1992) has categorized as 'narrow' socialization, since it emphasizes the induction of conformity and obedience.

This is also the context where fertility is highest, because more children mean more material benefits and old-age security, as material contributions are additive. If one has five or six children, and each one contributes some benefit to their elderly parents, this cumulation of inputs gives greater security than depending on only one or two. Furthermore, in the context of poverty, child mortality is high, underscoring the importance of bearing many children to make sure that enough survive into adulthood to support the now-aged parents. Thus, the monograph reporting the Indonesian VOC Study was entitled, 'Two are not enough' (Darroch, Meyer, & Singarimbun, 1981). Box 5.5 gives a schematic representation of the value of children as a mediator between the background socio-economic factors and the resultant fertility behaviour.

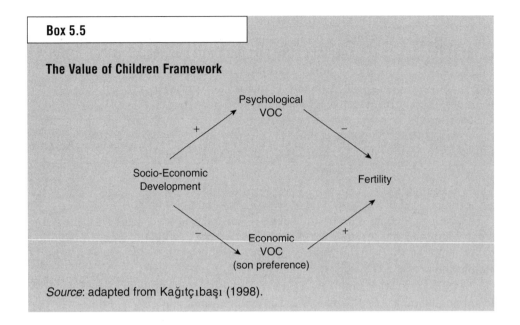

Box 5.5

The Value of Children Framework

Source: adapted from Kağıtçıbaşı (1998).

In the contrasting context of urban middle-class families living in more affluent contexts, children tend to be in school, rather than at work. They become economic costs rather than assets for the family. Since children's economic value is negligible, their psychological value becomes salient for parents as a reason for having children, often as the only reason. The psychological needs satisfied by children do not necessitate having many children, since their costs to the parents quickly come to outweigh their benefits. Parents can derive all the joy, love, and pride they need from only a few children and do not need more. This is **the family model of independence** (Kağıtçıbaşı, 1990, 1996b), since there is little or no dependence on the material contributions of children. Arnett (1992) categorizes the processes occurring within this model as 'broad' socialization, since it seeks to foster autonomy and initiative.

The implications of the value attributed to children and the corresponding family dynamics are important for child-rearing and for the resultant development of self-construal. In the **family model of interdependence**, there tends to be obedience-oriented child-rearing, which does not promote the development of independence and autonomy. This is because an autonomous child is likely to develop into a separate independent adult, who might look after his/her own interests rather than those of the family. Thus, independence is not valued and may even be seen as a threat to family integrity and livelihood. Intergenerational interdependence is manifested through the family life cycle, first in terms of the desired dependence of the child. This dependence is reversed later on, as the dependence of the elderly parents who in the course of the life cycle come to depend on their now-mature children for support.

The contrasting pattern within the **family model of independence** engenders self-reliance and independence in the growing child, as affluence and institutional welfare systems such as old age pensions render family interdependence less necessary. Together with the objective conditions of life that support independence go cultural values that also foster independence and separation and normatize it as a requisite for 'healthy' human development. For example, in North America and Northern Europe, it is expected that late adolescents/young adults move out of their parents' home to live on their own, whereas in most of the rest of the world, they remain in the parental home until they get married. Some stay on even after marriage. Indeed separation from family is not considered necessary for personal growth and maturity in non-Western cultures (Kağıtçıbaşı, 1982c).

It is commonly assumed that as societies modernize and get more affluent with increasing levels of education, there is a simple shift from the **family model of interdependence** to that of **independence**. Recent research shows, however, that rather than a simple shift, a more complex change takes place, associated with socio-economic development and especially with urbanization, which involves changes in lifestyles from traditional agrarian ones to urban ones (see Box 1.3 in Chapter 1). Especially in collectivistic cultural contexts with closely knit human/family relations, connectedness appears to continue in the realm of emotional interdependencies, while material interdependencies weaken due to increased affluence and alternative old-age security resources. A third pattern, **the family model of psychological interdependence**, is proposed to characterize this change (Kağıtçıbaşı, 1990, 1996b). This produces socialized outcomes that differ from both the traditional (rural) family of total interdependence and the individualistic urban (Western middle-class) family of independence.

Here, child-rearing involves control, rather than permissiveness, because the goal is not separated, individualistic independence. Together with control, however, there is also room for autonomy in child-rearing in the **family model of psychological interdependence**, for two main reasons. First, autonomy of the growing child is no longer seen as a threat to family livelihood, given decreased material interdependencies – elderly parents have alternative sources of support in old age. Secondly, the autonomy of the growing child, rather than submissive obedience, becomes adaptive to urban lifestyles, for example, for independent decision-making in school and obtaining of specialized jobs (see also Kohn et al., 1990). The effects of schooling appear particularly strong in promoting autonomy. This is reflected in a weakening of the economic value of children and a strengthening of the psychological value of children for parents. The utilitarian/economic value of children reflects material interdependencies between generations in the family; the psychological value of children, on the other hand, reflects psychological (emotional) interdependencies.

Evidence for this model of cultural change has been provided by a recent replication of the **Value of Children** Study in Turkey in 2003 (Kağıtçıbaşı & Ataca, 2005), as a part of a 15-country study, led by Trommsdorff and Nauck. When compared with the original Turkish VOC results from 1975, a notable decline in the economic/utilitarian VOC and an equally notable increase in the psychological VOC were found over this period of almost three decades. This change reflects the currently higher levels of education, urbanization and affluence, that is, socio-economic change and development, around the world. Urban–rural comparisons in 2003 further reveal, as expected, the highest endorsement of the economic/utilitarian VOC in rural areas, followed by urban low income groups, with the least importance attached to it by the upper middle-class urban groups. In psychological VOC, however, there is not much difference between the different groups. Furthermore, the endorsement of obedience in children follows closely the emphasis put on economic/ utilitarian VOC, with less educated/less affluent respondents valuing it more (see Box 5.5).

Thus, both the original VOC Study and its recent replication shed light on the interface between socio-economic context and family dynamics, which contributes to the development of different types of self-construal. This type of analysis provides an understanding into *how* a certain type of self-construal is fostered in a certain type of familial and societal environment and *why*. A functional perspective regarding adaptation to the environment and change in both the environment and the individual outcome underlies this theoretical perspective. It may be claimed that these different family patterns underlie collectivistic and individualistic cultures. Both the **family model of interdependence** and the **family model of psychological interdependence** appear to underlie collectivistic cultures, each deriving from collectivism and also contributing toward the further evolution of such cultures. The **family pattern of independence**, on the other hand, appears to be an integral aspect of individualistic cultures. Thus the developmental routes leading to these cultural world-views are **mediated** by family cultures and by family dynamics. As Box 5.6 illustrates, similar differences can be seen in child-rearing orientations even within developed economies.

Box 5.6

Mothers and Children in Advanced Industrial Nations

Dennis, Cole, Zahn-Waxler and Mizuta (2002) observed mother-child interactions among Japanese temporarily residing in the United States, and US mothers and their pre-schoolers. US mothers had more conversations that emphasized individual experiences, more often acted as playmates, maintained more physical distance, showed more positive emotions and more positive responses to the child's accomplishments. In contrast, Japanese mothers had more conversations that emphasized shared experiences, and maintained social role distinctions (between mother and child, not between playmates). The findings suggested an emphasis on autonomy in US dyads, and an emphasis on relatedness in Japanese dyads, but in a free play situation US mothers showed greater relational focus and Japanese mothers showed increased autonomous focus. Thus, autonomy and relatedness are relevant in both cultures.

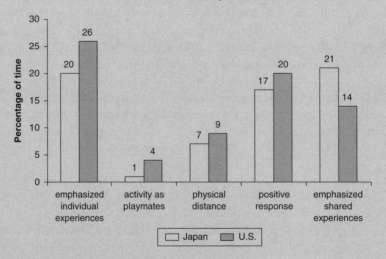

Maternal Actions and Speech Codes

Source: Dennis, Cole, Zahn-Waxler, & Mizuta (2002).

Autonomous-relational Self-construal

As we have seen above, the type of individual self-construal that is fostered within the **family model of interdependence** emphasizes relatedness and independence. This is because in obedience-oriented child-rearing there is no encouragement of autonomy. Instead, a 'heteronomous' self-construal emerges, characteristic of a person who is dependent on others and lacks volitional agency (autonomy). In contrast, the self-construal fostered by the **family model of independence** is characteristic of a person who becomes autonomous and separate. Separation is often believed to be a requisite of autonomy. The self-construal that is fostered within the **family model of psychological interdependence** can be defined as **autonomous-relational self-construal** (Kağıtçıbaşı, 1996a, b; 2005). This may be considered as an integrative synthesis of independent and interdependent self-construals. As mentioned above, the child-rearing orientation that contributes to the emergence of this type of self involves autonomy, but there is also parental control, rather than permissiveness, as the goal is not separation of the growing child. Thus a related self that is also autonomous is the outcome. This might be seen as a new type of interdependence. It has more to do with interpersonal connectedness than with adherence to values or norms endorsing hierarchy and subordination of the individual to the group; the latter is usually assumed to be found frequently among persons from collectivist, high power distance cultures (Hofstede, 1980; Triandis, 1995). Kağıtçıbaşı (1997a) has referred to the former as 'relational' collectivism and to the latter as 'normative' collectivism.

The coexistence of autonomy and connectedness within **autonomous-relational self-construal** is important. Note, for example, that Dennis, Cole, Zahn-Waxler and Mizuta (2002) in their work with Japanese and US mother–child pairs (Box 5.7) found coexistence of autonomy and relatedness, even though there were cultural differences in the relative emphasis put on each. Nevertheless, such a combination has not been readily recognized in mainstream Western personality theory, as it is often assumed that, to be autonomous, one has to separate from others. Particularly from the psychoanalytic perspective, as understood by 'object relations theory' and its 'separation-individuation hypothesis', separation has been considered a requisite of autonomy from early infancy onwards (Blos, 1979; Mahler, 1972). Its proponents claim that connected selves cannot be adequately autonomous. While this claim has been strongly challenged even within mainstream psychology (Guisinger & Blatt, 1994), the implications are even more far reaching for non-Western collectivistic 'cultures of relatedness' with closely-knit human relations. The concept of **autonomous-relational self-construal** supports challenges to this claim.

This is also a central debate in understanding adolescence. The psychoanalytically informed, individualistic perspective considers adolescence as a period of second separation-individuation, where separation or detachment from parents is regarded as a prerequisite for the development of autonomy (Steinberg & Silverberg, 1986). More recently this view has been challenged by a contrasting perspective that conceives of a close relationship with parents as nourishing the development of healthy autonomy in adolescence (Grotevant & Cooper, 1986; Kağıtçıbaşı, 1996b; Ryan & Deci, 2000; Ryan & Lynch, 1989). Nevertheless, there is a tenaciously held view in both academic and popular psychology that associates adolescent 'individuation' with separation.

To resolve this issue, Kağıtçıbaşı (1996a; 2005) has proposed that two dimensions underlie self-construal and self–other relations, namely interpersonal distance and agency. The interpersonal distance dimension extends from separateness to connectedness, reflecting the degree of connectedness of self to other. The agency dimension has to do with the degree of autonomous functioning, extending from autonomy to heteronomy. Autonomy refers to volitional agency, i.e., being a self-governing agent; heteronomy is the state of being governed from outside (see also Bloom, 1977). The construct of heteronomy was first used by Piaget (1948) as the initial stage of moral development, with heteronomous morality referring to being subject to another's rule, followed by the stage of autonomous morality, which is being subject to one's own rule. As the interpersonal distance and agency dimensions are distinct, it is quite possible for the different poles of each to coexist. Therefore, autonomy and relatedness can be compatible just as autonomy and separateness can, though only the latter combination is recognized by those who uphold an individualistic construal of autonomy.

Putting together the two underlying dimensions, the different family models, and the resultant selves that we have examined up to now, we can put forward a general integrative model, as presented in Box 5.7. This is a heuristic model to help relate variables at the different levels of analysis that we presented in Box 5.1. In other words,

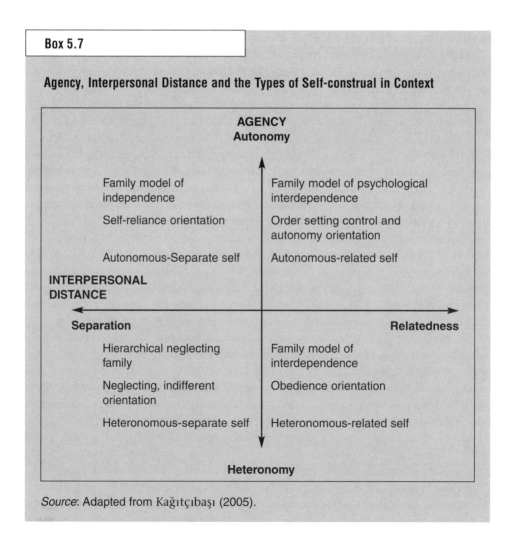

Box 5.7

Agency, Interpersonal Distance and the Types of Self-construal in Context

AGENCY
Autonomy

Family model of independence

Self-reliance orientation

Autonomous-Separate self

Family model of psychological interdependence

Order setting control and autonomy orientation

Autonomous-related self

INTERPERSONAL DISTANCE

Separation   **Relatedness**

Hierarchical neglecting family

Neglecting, indifferent orientation

Heteronomous-separate self

Family model of interdependence

Obedience orientation

Heteronomous-related self

Heteronomy

Source: Adapted from Kağıtçıbaşı (2005).

we can appreciate here how family models and child-rearing orientations link with different types of self-construal, along the basic underlying dimensions of agency and interpersonal distance. The two dimensions of interpersonal distance and agency are presented as orthogonal in the model. This is in order to make the point that they are distinct dimensions. It is possible that they may be related to some degree in some cultural contexts but not in others, although the integration of these two axes of social behaviour by Wiggins and Trapnell (1996) suggests they are orthogonal across many domains of behaviour and contexts of assessment.

We have discussed the patterns of self-construal represented in three quadrants of the model. The fourth one, characterized by separation and heteronomy, with the resultant heteronomous-separate self has not been dealt with, and it is not proposed that it prevails in any particular region of the world. At the individual-level, heteronomy and separation may point to an unhealthy situation of parental neglect or indifference (Maccoby & Martin, 1983). It has been observed in families with rejecting and autocratic parenting, instilling in the child a separate but heteronomous self (Fisek, 1991). This pattern is not common, as it reflects family pathology, and may be characteristic of children who manifest acting-out disorders in school and anti-social behaviour afterwards (Deater-Deckard & Dodge, 1997).

A growing body of cross-cultural research provides support for the existence of **autonomous-relational self-construal**. Close ties and attachment with parents, rather than detachment, are found to be associated with adolescent health and well-being in the USA, Russia, Korea, and Turkey (Chirkov, Kim, Ryan, & Kaplan, 2003) as well as in Germany (Grossman, Grossman, & Zimmerman, 1999), and a more positive relationship is found between autonomy and relatedness than between autonomy and separateness in the USA and in Korea (Kim, Butzel, & Ryan, 1998; Ryan & Lynch, 1989). Similarly, Jose, Huntsinger, Huntsinger, and Liaw's (2000) comparison of Taiwanese, Chinese American and Euro-American parents found that the two groups of Chinese parents endorsed both relatedness and autonomy.

These studies point to the separateness of the agency and interpersonal distance dimensions in a variety of different cultural contexts and support the utility of advancing the concept of **autonomous-relational self-construal**. Furthermore, Chou (2000) found the two components of 'emotional autonomy' (Steinberg & Silverberg, 1986), that is, individuation (separation) and de-idealization of parents, to be associated with depression in Chinese adolescents, and Aydin and Oztutuncu (2001) showed depression to be associated with separateness, but not with strong parental control in Turkish adolescents. Thus, especially in the collectivistic cultures, where family relatedness is highly valued, close adolescent–parent relations appear to provide a healthy developmental pathway.

It is important to note, however, that the above research suggests that **autonomous-relational self-construal** is associated with healthy outcomes even in the individualistic USA. This is because this type of self-construal integrates the two basic human needs, the need for relatedness and the need for autonomy that much psychological theorizing has put forward. Thus, even though Kağıtçıbaşı's work (1996a, b) on **autonomous-relational self-construal** was based on the urbanized, developed contexts in the Majority (that is, non-Western) World, which have collectivistic cultures, this construct promises to have universal validity. This provides one of several examples noted in this book where concepts originally thought useful only to cross-cultural psychologists have now been proven to have universal relevance. By studying phenomena in contexts within which they are particularly salient, we can formulate concepts that have been overlooked by mainstream researchers but which can enrich mainstream psychology.

In a similar way, the **family model of psychological interdependence** (Kağıtçıbaşı, 1990, 1996b) also promises to have universal validity. Some of the above research findings support this view. It is further evidenced by research on family control to which we next turn.

Family Control

An examination of the different family models points to family control as a key variable. It is ingrained in the **family model of psychological interdependence**, which engenders the autonomous-related self. A number of studies demonstrate the coexistence of parental control, relatedness, and autonomy orientation in this family model. For example, Stewart, Bond, Deeds, and Chung (1999) found family interdependency and parental control to be high despite modern individualistic values among affluent families in Hong Kong. Similarly, Lin and Fu (1990), comparing Chinese, immigrant Chinese, and Euro-American parents, found the Chinese to be higher on both parental control and encouragement of independence than the Euro-Americans. These findings contrast with American findings referring to an emphasis on separateness and permissive parenting, especially with parents of higher social class, reflecting adherence to the dominant individualistic ideology (Hoffman & Youngblade, 1998; Solomon, 1993).

Of essence here is the meaning of parental control. It is often assumed that strict parental control is a sign of parental hostility. In other words, no differentiation is made between the control and warmth dimensions of parenting, but a single bipolar dimension of parenting is envisioned, extending from (strong) control at one pole to warmth at the other. Warmth is thus seen to be incompatible with strong parental control, the latter being labelled 'authoritarian parenting'. This view originates from the psychoanalytic perspective that also underlies the 'authoritarian personality theory' (Adorno, Frenkel-Brunswik, Levinson, & Sanford, 1950). It reflects the individualistic, Western, middle-class family ideology which involves relatively permissive parental discipline, providing children with a great deal of freedom and independence, especially in adolescence. In this context strong discipline is a deviant (rather than normative) parenting pattern and therefore seen as 'not normal'.

One of the first studies challenging this view was conducted by Kağıtçıbaşı (1970), comparing the retrospective parenting experiences of Turkish and American late adolescents. While a difference in perceived parental control was found, with Turks reporting stronger control, no difference was obtained between the two national groups in perceived parental affection. Thus, Turkish adolescents reported having experienced controlling and warm parenting. This was an empirical demonstration of the independence of the warmth and control dimensions of parenting. Since then, other researchers, in particular Rohner and his collaborators (Rohner & Pettengill, 1985; Trommsdorff, 1985) have come up with similar findings. They found that for Korean and Japanese adolescents perceived parental control was associated with parental acceptance (warmth), but not for American and German adolescents, for whom parental control was associated with parental rejection. Trommsdorff even reported that Japanese adolescents felt rejected by their parents when they experienced only little parental control. Interestingly, when Korean-American adolescents were studied, the findings were more similar to the Euro-American findings than to the Korean ones. This apparent paradox again points to the variation in meaning of parental control in a society and to the social comparison process that is involved in defining what is 'normal' and what is not. Korean-American children and adolescents, comparing themselves to their Euro-American friends, find their own experience to be deviant and thus conclude that their controlling parents must be rejecting.

In general, higher levels of parental control are found in socio-cultural contexts where child-rearing is not oriented towards promoting individualistic independence of the adolescent from the family. Thus, a great deal of research has pointed to compliance-oriented child rearing in more closely knit collectivistic familial/societal contexts (Barry, Child, & Bacon, 1959; Berry, 1979; Bond, 1986; Dekovic, Pels & Model, 2004; Greenfield, Keller, Fuligni & Maynard, 2003; Kağıtçıbaşı, 1982a). This is particularly the case in low affluence contexts where families' material interdependence between generations is strong, as discussed before. However, even where intergenerational material interdependence weakens with urbanization and socio-economic development, parental control persists in child-rearing because the goal of child socialization is not separation, but psychological closeness and interdependence, as explained in the **family model of psychological interdependence** (Kağıtçıbaşı, 1990, 1996b).

A further distinction has been made by Lau and his colleagues between 'dominating control' and 'order-setting control' (Lau & Cheung, 1987; Lau, Lew, Hau, Cheung, & Berndt, 1990). Working with Chinese adolescents and adults, they found dominating parental control to be associated negatively with perceived parental warmth, but 'order-keeping' and caring control to be positively associated with it. This is in line with Moos' earlier distinction between functional and dysfunctional control (Moos & Moos, 1981). In both conceptualizations there is a distinction between a rather positively-oriented, caring control and a rather negatively-oriented, domineering control. Thus, the type of parental control and in particular the intention underlying it is important, and furthermore, the meaning attributed to this parenting behaviour is often culturally defined.

The Jose et al. study (2000) mentioned above also found Chinese parents to show both control and connectedness to their children, displaying more control than Euro-American parents but equal warmth. Among African-American families strong parental control is also common. This is often associated with parental stress and the need to gain the child's compliance and to protect children from negative influences in unsafe environments (McLoyd, 1990). Physical discipline, as a form of strong parental control, is more common among African-American families than among Euro-American families, even after controlling for socio-economic status (Day, Peterson & McCracken, 1998; Lansford, Deater-Deckard, Dodge, Bates, & Pettit, 2003). Thus, it appears to have a culturally accepted place, a normative status, in child-rearing. Its meaning for African-American children, therefore, should be more positive than for Euro-American children. Indeed, research shows a positive link between early physical discipline and later adolescent problem behaviours among Euro-American children, but a negative link among African-American children (Lansford et al. 2003). Similarly, Deater-Deckard and Dodge (1997) showed that links between parent behaviour and child behaviour, such as the association between parental physical discipline and child aggression, vary across cultural groups, depending on how prevalent and acceptable physical discipline is in a culture.

Thus, the meaning and general acceptability of physical discipline can vary across ethnic groups. Nonetheless, these studies do not endorse harsh physical punishment or physical abuse. Degrees of strictness in parental control and discipline also need to be taken into consideration. All the above research shows that the categorical assumption that strong parental control and physical discipline are bad and reflect parental hostility may not be valid outside of middle-class, American (Western) populations. Norms about proper ways of child-rearing, discipline, and the like vary across cultures, even within the same countries. On the basis of this research and other related work, it may be claimed that parental warmth and affection is a candidate for a human universal, reflecting an evolutionary process involving protection and care of the young for the continuation of the species. Parental control, on the other hand, appears more closely related to cultural conventions and shows variation through time and across cultures. A key factor underlying this variation is the desired level of dependence–independence upon which child socialization is focused.

The Immigration Context

We have seen that family patterns, including intergenerational dependencies, child-rearing orientations and the emergence of self-construal show variations according to cultures and lifestyles. For example, as we go from less affluent contexts to urban and higher socio-economic status contexts, family patterns change and adjust to changing environmental demands, as shown by the **value of children** study that we examined. Furthermore, as we compare more collectivistic cultures with more individualistic cultures, we find that family patterns vary. Such variation is particularly noticeable in international immigration contexts because immigrants frequently originate from Majority World countries with collectivistic cultures and then move to the individualistic cultures of Western Europe and North America.

Recently Kwak (2003) reviewed the mass of research into family relations carried out among ethnic migrants to the USA. Compared with the dominant US middle-class culture, she noted higher levels of family embeddedness (relatedness) in ethnic minorities, both within the core (nuclear) family and also within their kin/ethnic network. She also reported that, in general, studies find good adolescent–family relations and agreement between immigrant adolescents and parents with regard to family embeddedness, but disagreement with regard to issues of autonomy. This apparently inconsistent situation is explicable from the perspective of **autonomous-relational self-construal**. In US society, autonomy is adaptive for getting ahead. Adolescents adjust to the new lifestyles requiring autonomy and also identify with their host society peers. Therefore, they aspire to greater autonomy than their parents are willing to grant. While on the one hand adolescents want more autonomy, on the other hand they are also content with close family ties and relatedness, thus endorsing and developing an **autonomous-related self-construal**. Nevertheless, some adjustments are also made so that, for example, immigrant adolescents tend to pursue autonomy later than Euro-American adolescents do. Thus, immigration contexts involve a rich interface and stimulus for change in family and self-construal.

European societies constitute another target for international immigration, with an increasing number of countries in Northern Europe becoming immigration destinations. A team of researchers have recently studied Surinamese, Moroccan, Turkish, Somali, and Chinese ethnic groups in the Netherlands together with the native Dutch, focusing on family life and child-rearing patterns (Dekovic, Pels, & Model, 2004). A common finding across the immigrant ethnic groups is that many parents who use strong (authoritarian) control in child discipline are also warm and supportive with their children. This is in line with the results of the family control studies discussed earlier and points to the different meanings that parental control can have. In the context of immigration, such different meanings can create misunderstandings between the ethnic minority families and the dominant host society, especially for the host professionals who work with these families. These professionals are informed by mainstream psychological views, which claim that strong parental control is a sign of authoritarian, domineering hostility; they therefore try to instil permissive discipline in ethnic minority families. Yet, another finding of this work is that ethnic minorities consider Dutch permissive child discipline to be too lenient and not conducive to the 'proper' development of children. For example, they consider Dutch children to be 'disrespectful' – 'on top of their mother's heads', as one Surinamese respondent put it. The immigrants naturally resist this **imposed-etic** approach to child-rearing.

Thus what we see here are different cultural definitions of parental control and proper human development. The ethnic minority views in this study are reminiscent of findings from ethnic minorities in North America. For example, Chao (1994) suggested that what psychologists and other professionals term authoritarian parenting may be an ethnocentric interpretation of Chinese parents' goal of 'training' in child-rearing. Similarly, Stewart, Bond, Kennard, Ho, & Zaman (2002) in a retrospective parenting study with young adults in the USA, Hong Kong and Pakistan found this training goal (*guan* in Chinese) to be common in the Asian samples. Thus the parental goal of training their children is not unique to the Chinese, but appears to be common in families with closely-knit relatedness, in the collectivistic Majority World. It may also be relevant at least to some extent for other immigrant groups, for example Puerto Rican families in the USA (Harwood, Handwerker, Schoelmerich & Leyendecker, 2001).

Where family relatedness values are emphasized, a certain degree of respect for parents and the elderly is seen as inherent to a sense of decency and morality. The downside of this position becomes evident when taken to the extreme, and the stress on respect for parents changes from decency into hierarchical suppression of the young. Here again the **family model of psychological interdependence** may be the more healthy model for human development because it allows for autonomy together with control, leading to the development of **autonomous-relational self-construal**. The **family model of interdependence** offers less tolerance for the autonomy of the growing child, leading to the development of a more heteronomous self-construal.

Self-construal, Autonomy and Developmental Pathways

Up to now, we have examined a number of interrelated factors underlying culture, family patterns, and the development of self-construal. The dynamics of the development of autonomy within the context of relatedness has emerged as important, particularly within collectivistic cultures and in culture contact situations such as immigration contexts. In the last section of this chapter we pursue further the implications of individual autonomy and the varying extent to which it contributes to the person's developmental pathway. We will see that the degree to which individual's autonomy impacts the person's developmental pathway is influenced by the cultural and socio-economic environment to a greater extent than is readily recognized by Western psychology. This is particularly the case for adolescents living in disadvantaged environments.

Looking generally at the pathways of human development, the embeddedness of the individual in their socio-cultural context is crucial. Particularly during adolescence the developing individual's environment expands, as she or he moves into more encounters with people playing many roles, within the various societal institutions characterizing different ecological contexts (Bronfenbrenner, 1979). Political, economic, and institutional factors in the 'macro' (distal) ecological context have an impact on the 'micro' (proximal) ecology of the individual. In advantageous environments, this developmental press can be an enabling influence, while in disadvantageous environments it can be a suppressing and constraining influence. Thus developmental pathways show much diversity across socio-economic-political contexts as well as across individuals within similar contexts.

An ongoing question here is the relative role of the individual vis-à-vis the environmental influences in charting his or her developmental pathway. In current lifespan perspectives on the psychology and sociology of human development, there is an emphasis on the agency of individual adolescents in building their own lives (see Crockett & Silbereisen, 2000). This view is based on the recognition of the active role of the individual in the interplay between the individual, family/group based factors and social structures. It is a widely accepted perspective despite the recognition that economic, political and social factors can constrain opportunity structures and limit the pathways of some individuals and groups. For example, Flanagan (2000) has referred to adolescents as 'agents of change, as creators of history' (p. 195), since they played a role in civil protests in Eastern Europe over the decades preceding the collapse of the Soviet regime. Though civil protests, particularly by environmental groups, were important, they were hardly the reason for the collapse of the Soviet empire. The much more pervasive influences came from economic, socio-political, and institutional structures.

The principle of human agency is a positive, optimistic concept, stressing individual potential. It is a recognition of the capacity of the individual to take charge of his or her own life and carry the responsibility for what she or he makes of it. As such, this is in line with an individualistic world-view and with the psychological thinking that derives from it. For example, such a view is apparent in the social psychological construct of 'belief in internal locus of control of reinforcement' (I-E Control) (Rotter, 1966), which is a belief that individuals are responsible for what happens to them, rather than other people, fate, chance, and so on. It also underlies the so-called

correspondence bias, that is, the assumption that others' behaviour is caused by their individual dispositions (Ross, 1977). Thus, much of mainstream social psychology and personality theory, as well as humanistic and positive psychology perspectives uphold individual agency.

This outlook can be problematic when taken to its logical extreme, in other words when the assertion that individuals are the sole responsible agents for what happens to them means neglecting, even rejecting, environmental causes. The individualistic view that individuals build their own lives assumes initial equal opportunity, an obvious distortion of social reality. In fact, inequality of opportunities is possibly the most serious problem globally, even in affluent societies. In the context of poverty, the available pathways for child and adolescent development are more limited than in the context of affluence (Kağıtçıbaşı, 2002).

There are important implications for the outlook of youth, as well. For example, a study with inner-city minority youth in the USA (Flanagan, 2000) found that the youth tended to make dispositional attributions, holding individuals responsible for their successes or failures. On the one hand, this provides encouragement to try harder; otherwise these youth would give up in the face of hardship. On the other hand, given the worsening income distribution (Takanishi, 2000) and decreasing social mobility and job ceilings facing African-Americans (Flanagan, 2000), likely failure would result in negative psychological outcomes, such as self-blame and lowered self-esteem, unless alloyed with a belief in fate control (Leung & Bond, 2004).

A more balanced view recognizes the dynamic interface between macro- and the micro-level variables; that is, characteristics of both the environment and the individual are to be taken into consideration for a better understanding of developmental pathways. The interaction appears to be such that the relative contribution of individual agency to developmental outcomes increases with supportive environments and decreases with constraining environments. Accordingly, from a global perspective the role of individual agency may in general be less than it is in affluent societies (Kağıtçıbaşı, 2002). Indeed, a survey of perceived self-efficacy among more than 19,000 respondents from 25 nations supports this view (Scholz, Gutiérrez-Doña, Sud, & Schwarzer, 2002). Beyond affluence, provision of autonomy to the child and the adolescent may further increase the relative contribution of individual agency to developmental outcomes. Thus Euro-American societies, which combine affluence with endorsement of individual agency, are also the ones that provide the conditions that make such agency somewhat more possible. A more global glance reveals much diversity in both outlooks and objective conditions.

The above discussion has looked at environmental supports and constraints mainly in terms of the provision of opportunities. What are the implications for individualistic and collectivistic societies? As we noted earlier, it is generally assumed that there is less individual agency in collectivistic societies with closely-knit human ties. We have questioned this assumption by distinguishing 'interpersonal distance' and 'agency' dimensions and in proposing the concept of **autonomous-relational self-construal**. We further showed that there is growing empirical evidence supporting these constructs.

If, as we propose, autonomy is compatible with relatedness, a collectivistic culture should not be different from an individualistic culture with regard to an individual making an impact on his or her developmental pathway, as long as objective support conditions are the same. In other words, within similar levels of affluence, there should not be a significant difference in the effect of individual autonomy on a person's development. Separateness and relatedness can be equally agentic. However, this would be the case within the **family model of psychological interdependence** that nourishes autonomy, but not within the **family model of interdependence** that nourishes heteronomy.

In contrast to the above view are some cultural perspectives that question the importance, even existence, of autonomy in collectivistic contexts (Iyengar & Lepper, 1999; Miller, 1997; Oishi, 2000; Rothbaum, Pott, Azuma, Miyake & Weise, 2000). The reasoning here is that in collectivistic contexts individuals prefer guidance or choice by close others, and meeting others' expectations is experienced as satisfying. From such a perspective, the individual's relative contribution to the charting of his or her own developmental pathway would be rather small, since individual autonomy is limited in collectivistic cultural contexts.

A more balanced view, in line with the perspective we have put forward in this chapter, has been recently proposed by Bandura (2002), in a reformulation which places his social cognitive theory into a cultural context. He notes that agentic capacity rooted in perceived self-efficacy (either at the *personal* or the *group* level) is common in both individualistic and collectivistic cultures. He therefore opposes conceptualizations associating self-efficacy with individualism and lack of it with collectivism and claims that human agency can be exercised individually or collectively in all societies.

Autonomy, as we have used it in this chapter is very similar to agency. It is agency that includes volition, in other words acting willingly and without coercion. On the basis of our discussion above, what we can conclude is that interpersonal connectedness, as such, is not a barrier to autonomy. In both individualistic and collectivistic cultural contexts there can be autonomy, coupled with different degrees of separateness or relatedness. However, in environments that constrain autonomy, either in terms of objective limitations such as socio-economic disadvantage or in terms of child socialization with dominating control, the person's relative agentic contribution to the charting of his or her own developmental pathway would be relatively small.

Summary

A developmental perspective helps us understand better the systematic relationships between the individual, society and culture. It examines *how* the different types of self, with their concomitant behavioural repertoires, are fostered within particular socio-cultural contexts and *why* they do so. The role of parenting and the family is of key importance in this process of human development in context. Child-rearing reflects cultural values and thus ensures the making and the continuity of culture; however, it can also be an agent of change in the remaking of culture in the context of socio-economic change, as seen in urbanization and immigration. Variations in the value attributed to children, in family patterns and in the emergent self reflect the global human diversity which we need to keep in mind in studying social behaviour across cultures.

Further Reading

1 Chen, C., & Farruggia, S. (2002). Culture and adolescent development. www.wwu.edu/~culture

2 Eyetsemitan, F. (2002). Life span developmental psychology: Midlife and later years in Western and Non-Western societies. www.wwu.edu/~culture

3 Kağıtçıbaşı, Ç. (1996). *Family and human development across cultures: A view from the other side*. Hillsdale, NJ: Erlbaum.

4 Kağıtçıbaşı, Ç. (2002). A model of family change in cultural context. www.wwu.edu/~culture

5 Keller, H. (2002). Culture and development: Developmental pathways to individualism and interrelatedness. www.wwu.edu/~culture

6 Rohner, R.R., & Khaleque, A. (2002). Parental acceptance-rejection and life span development: A universalist perspective. www.wwu.edu/~culture

7 Seginer, R. (2004). Adolescent future orientation: An integrated cultural and eco-logical perspective. www.wwu.edu/~culture

8 Trommsdorff, G. (2002). An eco-cultural and interpersonal relations approach to development over the life span. www.wwu.edu/~culture

9 Vandermaas-Peeler, M. (2002). Cultural variations in parental support of children's play. www.wwu.edu/~culture

Study Questions

1 How is a developmental perspective helpful in studying social behaviour across cultures?

2 Point to some possibly universal and some culturally bounded aspects of life stages.

3 What is the importance of the value of children in understanding family dynamics and change in the context of socio-economic development?

4 What are the three different family models? Which one of these would you say is the most prevalent in the society/community where you live? Do you detect variations in these across time and space?

5 Discuss the construct of the autonomous-related self.

6 Give some examples of how family control is culturally constructed.

7 Discuss the view expressed in this chapter that the relative contribution of individual agency to determining the person's developmental pathway is higher in more favourable environments.

6 Making Sense of One's World

A full understanding of human adaptation and change requires an integrated causal structure in which sociostructural influences operate through mechanisms of the self system to produce behavioural effects (Bandura, 2002, p. 278)

In the two preceding chapters, we have explored the ways in which individuals are moulded by the cultural contexts into which they are born. The distal environment, the institutions of a society, our personal upbringing and our immediate interpersonal and social contexts all contribute to the creation of recognizably different profiles of citizens within a nation. Psychologists' relative neglect of these factors has permitted an implicit assumption to flourish that we as individuals are free agents whose beliefs, values and actions can be studied without reference to their origins. In the next four chapters, we return to the level of analysis at which most psychologists feel most comfortable. We will focus on individuals, but we do so in a way that still differs from the conventional approach: we assume that context is relevant; we will take account of where studies are done and will especially seek out studies in which researchers have included measures tapping the **cultural orientation** of the participants. The reasons for highlighting cultural context are central to the whole intent of this book.

Many studies are now available in which researchers have compared samples of individuals from two or more nations and reported mean differences on some measure. These differences are then typically attributed to the fact that one nation scored higher than the other on Hofstede's measures of **individualism-collectivism**. However, this type of explanation is weak and scientifically unhelpful. Firstly, the particular persons in the sample may not actually have differed in terms of individualism and collectivism. It is unwise to assume that they do differ simply because they come from nations that differed on a **nation-level** measure of individualism or collectivism in some prior study. By doing so, one commits the **ecological fallacy** by applying **nation-level** findings to an individual-level study and would be similar to an experimental psychologist failing to check whether an experimental manipulation was actually interpreted in the intended way by participants in a study. Secondly, as we have noted in Chapters 3 and 4, nations differ in many ways other than their levels of individualism and collectivism. The differences that are found could be due to any of the other factors that the researcher had ignored. We need to **unpackage** the different elements of cultures and determine which elements within them can best explain the phenomena that we are studying (Whiting, 1976).

One way to address these difficulties is to use some measure of the participants' **cultural orientation**, such as **independent** or **interdependent self-construal**. Where a study contains one or more measures of this type, it becomes possible to determine their effect on the results that are obtained. Two effects are possible: **moderation and mediation**. **Moderation and mediation** are often confused. Box 6.1 illustrates the difference, as applied to cross-cultural studies.

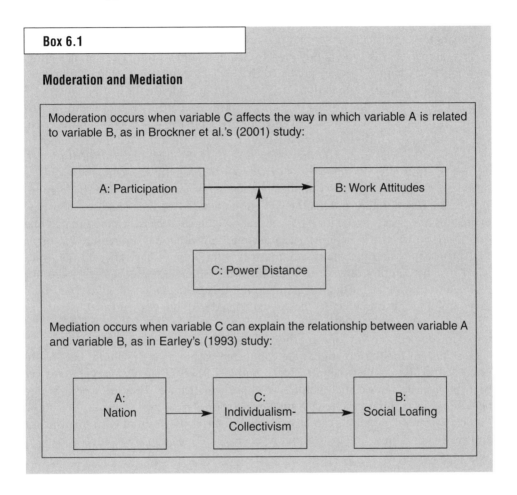

Box 6.1

Moderation and Mediation

Moderation occurs when variable C affects the way in which variable A is related to variable B, as in Brockner et al.'s (2001) study:

A: Participation → B: Work Attitudes

C: Power Distance

Mediation occurs when variable C can explain the relationship between variable A and variable B, as in Earley's (1993) study:

A: Nation → C: Individualism-Collectivism → B: Social Loafing

As an example of **moderation**, we can use a study by Brockner, Ackerman, Greenberg, et al. (2001). These authors were interested in whether the work attitudes of employees were influenced by degree of 'voice', in other words their participation in decision-making. In a series of studies, they obtained data from students in Hong Kong, China, Germany, the USA and Mexico, including a measure of respondents' orientation towards power distance. In two studies, the students responded to scenarios, and in the other two they made ratings of events that they had actually experienced at work. The results indicated that commitment to the organization and participation were more positively linked when respondents endorsed low power distance than when they endorsed high power distance. Putting this finding technically, a person's score on power distance was shown to **moderate** the relation between work attitudes and participation.

We have emphasized earlier the difficulties attending our assumption that nations have unified cultures, and can therefore be treated as coherent categories. **Moderation** effects illustrate the manner in which we can **unpackage** some of the numerous variables that contribute to national differences in social psychological outcomes. **Mediation** analyses are more ambitious, in the sense that they attempt to show whether a chosen theoretical concept can partially or even completely replace nation or culture as an explanation of a particular cultural difference.

An example of this type is provided by Earley's (1993) studies of social loafing, mentioned in Chapter 2. Earley predicted that social loafing occurs where individuals have an individualistic orientation. He found strong evidence for loafing among US respondents – those who worked in teams worked less hard than those who worked alone. In Israel this effect was weakened and in China it was completely reversed. Using a measure of **individualism-collectivism**, Earley then showed that the amount of social loafing was almost entirely dependent on the individualism of the participants in the study, regardless of whether their nationality was Chinese, Israeli or American. To put this finding in more technical terms, Earley found that the relationship between nationality and loafing was 98% **mediated** by individualism. This type of analysis has great promise for cross-cultural psychology because it shows that all the other ways in which Chinese, Israelis and Americans differ are not required in order to explain Earley's results. Many other factors will no doubt have affected the likelihood that his samples differed in individualism and collectivism, but they are not required to provide an adequate explanation of this particular result. Of course, there may turn out to be other factors that are correlated with our chosen variable that can explain the effect equally well. When such factors are identified, their effects can be tested in competition with one another, to see which is preferable.

Most current **mediation** studies are conducted within a single nation, but we are interested in those which sample several nations. Few studies of this type have yet been published, but we shall emphasize those which have. They provide a bridge between cross-cultural psychology and mainstream psychology, because they show that cross-cultural variations can be explained in terms drawn from both mainstream and cross-cultural psychology, without resort to ill-defined constructs such as nationality (Brockner, 2003).

Individual-level Self-representations

To undertake studies like those by Earley and by Brockner et al. individual-level indicators of **cultural orientation** are required. As we reported in Chapter 3, an increasing range of validly measured scores is becoming available, and can be used for this purpose. Dependent upon the particular focus of a research project, Schwartz's (1992) individual-level value types or his broader value dimensions may be suitable. So also may be citizen scores on the five individual-level dimensions derived from social axioms (Leung & Bond, 2004). However, the major impetus to the field has so far mostly been provided by Hofstede's **nation-level** dimensions. In the two studies so far examined in this chapter, Earley created a measure tapping each respondent's individualist and collectivist attitudes, while Brockner et al. did the same for power distance. Hofstede's analysis provided the inspiration; these researchers provided their own tailor-made measures for individuals.

The past two decades have been marked by the development of many further **individual-level** measures of **cultural orientation**. Several factors have influenced the way in which this blossoming has occurred. Following the publication of Hofstede's (1980) research, Triandis, Leung, Villareal, and Clack (1985) were among the first to develop **individual-level** measures related to **individualism-collectivism**. They used items developed in the USA by Hui (1988), describing aspects of one's relations with different groups (the 'INDCOL' scale). In order to reduce confusion between measures at different levels, they named their measures as idiocentric (individualistic) and allocentric (collectivistic). Unfortunately, this terminology has not been adopted by others, so that the terms individualism and collectivism are frequently used to refer both to **individual-level** concepts and **nation-level** concepts.

The INDCOL scale was subsequently modified to reflect not only the cultural contrast between individualism and collectivism, but also the contrast between high and low power distance (Singelis, Triandis, Bhawuk, & Gelfand, 1995). Separate scales were provided tapping individuals' preference for horizontal collectivism (collectivism + low power distance), vertical collectivism (collectivism + high power distance), horizontal individualism (individualism + low power distance) and vertical individualism (individualism + high power distance). In a further version, each item specifies a situation, and provides a choice between four responses, for example, 'Happiness is attained by: a) gaining a lot of status in the community; b) linking with a lot of friendly people; c) keeping one's privacy; d) winning in competitions' (Triandis, Chen & Chan, 1998, p. 280). These types of measure are essentially a blending of attitude statements and self-described behaviours. Many of the items refer to specific circumstances or events, and there is a consequent risk that they will be more readily applicable to some cultural contexts than to others.

Self-construals

In an attempt to produce measures that were **emic** rather than **imposed-etic**, several groups of researchers have asked respondents to describe themselves using the open-ended 'Twenty Statements Test' (TST), first devised by Kuhn and McPartland (1954), in which respondents complete 20 sentences each of which begins with 'I am ...' (Bochner, 1994; Bond & Cheung, 1983; Triandis, McCusker, & Hui, 1990). Content analysis has generally shown that members of individualist cultures more frequently use traits to describe themselves, whereas responses from members of collectivist nations contain a higher proportion of references to the social roles that they occupied.

However, it appears that the TST is not necessarily any more **emic** than other methods that ask respondents to describe themselves. Cousins (1989) investigated the possibility that members of collectivist nations might find it difficult to describe themselves without specifying a particular social context. If one's behaviour is strongly influenced by the requirements of different settings, then one could only say what one is like with regard to each type of setting. He found that when responding to contextualized TST statements, for example, 'When at home, I am ...', Japanese respondents used more trait descriptions than did Americans. On the other hand, Americans were more inclined to qualify their responses to the contextualized version of the TST, implying that although they behaved in a certain way in that setting, this was not an accurate portrayal of themselves *as a whole*. Kanagawa, Cross, and Markus (2001) compared Japanese and American self-descriptions on the TST relating to four separate social settings. Japanese descriptions varied more between situations than did American descriptions. Tafarodi, Lo, Yamaguchi, et al. (2004) confirmed these contrasts by simply asking students in Canada, Japan and Hong Kong a series of direct questions about their 'inner self'. Very large differences in response were found. For instance, asked whether their inner self remained the same across different activities, 72% of Canadians said that it did, but only 36% of Japanese and 28% of Chinese did so.

This rather basic distinction between those who attend to context and those who do not leads to a difficulty in defining what is a valid way to measure self-construal. Haberstroh, Oyserman, Schwarz, Kuhnen and Ji (2002) showed that attention to context does not just affect persons' descriptions of their own or others' behaviours, it also affects how they respond to questionnaires. Chinese students' answers differed, depending on the order in which the questions were asked, whereas German students' answers did not. In other words, Chinese responses were more context-sensitive, being affected by how they had responded to earlier questions. Furthermore, Ji, Schwarz, and Nisbett (2000) found that Chinese were also better than Americans at accurately recalling frequency of their previous behaviours. Ji et al. conclude that the preoccupation of Chinese with preserving social harmony leads them to remember past events, since these past events may help define the meanings that are applied by them and others to present events. They see Americans as more likely to treat each event as independent. These problems remind us of the discussion of how best to define culture in Chapter 3. Gaining comparable self-reports of behaviours may be more problematic than obtaining statements of values or beliefs.

An increasingly popular approach has been to focus on structured measures of self-construal, rather than the open-ended TST measures. Both Singelis (1994) and Gudykunst, Matsumoto, Ting-Toomey, et al. (1996) created scales for **independent** and **interdependent self-construal**. These terms are taken from Markus and Kitayama's (1991) review of contrasts between Japan and the USA. This influential paper did not discuss individualism and collectivism, but the authors did characterize American cultural dynamics as focused upon the self as independent of others and Japanese cultural dynamics as focused upon the self as interdependent with others. This selection of contrasting exemplars of the two cultural traditions has encouraged a tendency for many to think of the USA as the prototypical individualist nation and Japan as the prototypical collectivist nation. As we have seen in Chapter 3, data indicate that this characterization is not the case. In terms of **nation-level** characteristics, the data in Box 3.5 indicate that the USA is lower on autonomy than many European nations and Japan is lower on embeddedness than almost half of all the nations in Schwartz's survey. We shall return to the impact of the conceptualization provided by Markus and Kitayama, but for the moment the focus is on measures of self-construal.

The measures developed by Singelis (1994) have been used in many recent cross-cultural studies. The Singelis items include some that are descriptive of oneself and some that are closer to attitude statements. Gudykunst et al. (1996) attempted to create scales in which all items were self-descriptive, but some attitude items remain. The Gudykunst scales are reproduced as Box 6.2. Note that, as is also the case with the Singelis scales, all items are phrased in a positive direction, raising the possibility of culturally shaped **acquiescent response bias**.

Box 6.2

How do I see myself?

Independent self-construal	Interdependent self-construal
I should be judged on my own merit.	I consult with others before making important decisions.
Being able to take care of myself is a primary concern for me.	I consult with co-workers on work-related matters.
My personal identity is very important to me.	I will sacrifice my self-interest for the benefit of my group.
I prefer to be self-reliant rather than to depend on others.	I stick with my group even through difficulties.
I am a unique person separate from others.	I respect decisions made by my group.
If there is a conflict between my values and the values of groups of which I am a member, I follow my values.	I will stay in a group if they need me, even when I am not happy with the group.
I try not to depend on others.	I maintain harmony in the groups of which I am a member.
I take responsibility for my own actions.	I respect the majority's wishes in groups of which I am a member.
It is important for me to act as an independent person.	I remain in the groups of which I am a member if they need me, even though I am dissatisfied with them.
I should decide my future on my own.	I try to abide by customs and conventions at work.
What happens to me is my own doing.	I give special consideration to others' personal situations so I can be efficient at work.
I enjoy being unique and different from others.	It is better to consult with others and get their opinions before doing anything.
I am comfortable being singled out for praise and rewards.	It is important to consult close friends and get their ideas before making a decision.
I don't support a group decision when it is wrong.	My relationships with others are more important than my accomplishments.

Source: Gudykunst & Lee (2003).

Slowing Down the Runaway Horse

Research fields are just as vulnerable to the ebb and flow of a fashion as other areas of human endeavour. Over the past decade, focus on **individualism-collectivism** as represented at the level of individuals has escalated rapidly. A decade ago in the predecessor to this book, Smith and Bond (1998) were able to applaud the value of individualism and collectivism in providing a conceptual integration for cross-cultural studies. To choose a metaphor from the horse-racing world, it now appears that with the stable door once opened, the horse has galloped off so fast that we cannot always see where we are going! We identify three ways in which we would do well to slow down and think things through more carefully.

Uses and Abuses of Individual-level Measures

The measures described by Singelis (1994), Singelis et al. (1995) and Gudykunst et al. (1996) have become the most frequently employed **individual-level** measures employed by researchers with an interest in culture. Many other lesser known measures have also been devised, but all have in common the intention of tapping differences that derive from Hofstede's (1980) **nation-level** distinction between **individualism-collectivism**. A major first step in evaluating this development was achieved by Oyserman, Coon, and Kemmelmeier (2002), who undertook a series of **meta-analyses** of studies that had used any one of 27 of these measures. Oyserman et al. investigated whether scores differed between the USA and elsewhere, whether scores differed between different ethnic communities in the USA and whether scores were found to predict variations in other dependent variables. Levine, Bresnahan, Park, et al. (2003) performed a similar **meta-analysis**, but focused solely on those measures that tapped self-construal.

Oyserman et al.'s (2002) comparisons of effect sizes for different nations yielded some startling conclusions. While representatives of some nations scored higher than the Americans on both individualism and collectivism, others scored lower on both. Egyptians scored lowest on both forms of self-construal and Peruvians scored highest on both. Convergence across levels with Hofstede's nation scores was minimal. Oyserman et al.'s paper was published in *Psychological Bulletin*, with a series of accompanying commentaries, most of which suggested either that Hofstede's characterization of nations was outdated or else that other quite different approaches to cross-cultural study would now be more fruitful. However, if you have read closely the methodological precepts advanced in earlier chapters of this book, a study of Oyserman et al.'s paper will reveal two weaknesses, both of which threaten the conclusions that they drew. The same two flaws are present in the study by Levine et al. (2003).

Firstly, none of the measures included in these **meta-analyses** was corrected for cultural differences in **acquiescent response bias**. Since these differences are known to be substantial across national groups (Smith, 2004b; see also Chapter 2), drawing comparisons from uncorrected means is invalid. Schimmack, Oishi, and Diener (2005) utilized data from a 40-nation student survey to question this aspect of Oyserman et al.'s conclusions. They showed that their scores, uncorrected for bias, correlated positively with those derived by Oyserman et al. Furthermore, their estimate of bias correlated strongly with Oyserman et al.'s effect sizes for both individualism and collectivism. However, when Schimmack et al.'s scores were corrected for bias, they then correlated substantially with **nation-level** scores derived from Hofstede's work. So, correcting for cross-national differences in **acquiescent response bias** is essential when comparing nations' levels of individualism or collectivism.

The second weakness in the two meta-analyses is that their effect sizes for nations were essentially **citizen scores**. As we discussed extensively in Chapter 3, the ways in which variables relate to one another at different levels of analysis is not necessarily the same. It is not surprising that data analysed at the **national-** and at the **individual-level** yield different conclusions. The first step in slowing down the 'runaway horse' should be to restrict the use of individual-level data to the analysis of individual-level phenomena. That level of analysis was the focus of the latter part of Oyserman et al.'s (2002) integration of research results, and is also the major focus of this chapter. It is unfortunate that it has been the early parts of their analysis that attracted substantial attention. As Bond (2002) pointed out in his commentary on Oyserman et al. our field needs to move on, to develop cross-culturally equivalent measures for individual variations in the many aspects of collectivism and individualism, and then link these measures to the outcomes whose variation across cultural groups we want to explain.

Are We Measuring the Right Aspects of Self-construal?

The parentage of current self-construal measures is clear. The items are derived from Hofstede's **nation-level** contrasts between individualism and collectivism, plus power distance in the case of Singelis et al.'s (1995) vertical and horizontal dimensions. However, the items that different authors have included in their scales vary greatly, depending on how they interpret the meaning of Hofstede's concepts. Oyserman et al. (2002) identified five domains of independent items and eight domains of interdependent items. Reported reliabilities of the Singelis (1994) scales are typically rather lower than the accepted level of 0.70. Scale structures also vary between samples and between groups from different nations (Levine, Bresnahan, Park, et al., 2003; Hardin, Leong, & Bhagwat, 2004). One reason for this may be that these measures combine interpersonal distance (relatedness-separateness) and agency (autonomy-heteronomy). Independence is seen and measured as entailing both autonomy and separateness and interdependence as entailing both heteronomy (dependency) and relatedness. As we noted in Chapter 5, there are strong arguments for a different combination, such as the **autonomous-relational self**, which is not recognized or measured by these scales. Such a combination may be valid particularly for individuals in the more developed socio-economic contexts within collectivistic cultures.

It appears that more work is required to determine the dimensions along which individual-level self-construals vary, and to instrument these dimensions accordingly. One source of help in overcoming this problem is provided by recent research into the self-concept by researchers whose main focus is not on culture. Sedikides and Brewer (2001) present evidence in favour of a tripartite classification of self-construal. They propose that people may think of themselves as an individual self, as a relational self, or as a collective self. Their conception of individual self is equivalent to **independent self-construal**. Defining oneself relationally involves defining oneself in terms of interpersonal bonds or attachments to specific others, such as family members or a romantic partner. Defining oneself collectively involves seeing oneself as part of a larger entity and does not necessarily entail personal bonds with members of that entity. It appears that in creating measures of interdependence, cross-cultural researchers may have confused aspects of relational and collective identity. For instance, among the items in Box 6.2, 'I stick with my group even through difficulties' refers to the group as a collective identity, whereas 'It is important to consult close friends and get their ideas before making a decision' is more relational. Indeed, it might make a good item in a measure of **autonomous-relational self-construal** (Kağıtçıbaşı, 1996a).

Consistent with this line of reasoning, Yuki (2003) proposed that Japanese collectivism is primarily relational rather than collective. He showed that among Japanese students his measures of in-group identification and loyalty to their group and to their nation were predicted by their knowledge of relationships in the group. In contrast, among US students, identification and loyalty were also predicted by the group's status in relation to other groups. Thus the US respondents drew on both collective and relational criteria, whereas the Japanese used only relational criteria. A scale that does distinguish between individual, relational and collective self-construal has been developed recently in Australia, and has shown convergent validity with other self-construal measures (Kashima & Hardie, 2000).

Kashima, Kashima, Chiu, et al. (2005) have provided a further step in refining our understanding of cultural differences in self-construal. Students from eight nations provided self-construals as well as ratings of the extent to which individuals, family, friends and society as a whole possess qualities of 'agency', in other words the extent to which each of these entities has the ability to initiate actions. **Citizen scores** for self-construal and agency were compared across nations. Respondents from all nations perceived individuals as having more fixed and unchangeable qualities than groups. However, while respondents from the five more individualist nations also saw individuals as having greater agency than groups, respondents from the three East Asian nations saw individuals and groups as having equal amounts of agency. Thus, measures that focus simply on the interdependence of an individual's self-construal would fail to detect the extent to which the respondent attributes agency both to him- or herself and to the groups to which he or she belongs. As Bandura (2002) acknowledged, collective efficacy can be just as important as self-efficacy. A pattern of beliefs that includes both self-efficacy and collective efficacy would be more characteristic of **autonomous-relational self-construal** than of **interdependent self-construal**.

Mascolo, Misra, and Rapisardi (2004) used content analysis of interviews to provide some initial indications of contrasts in how independent, relational and collective selves are understood in India and the USA. Further tests of the relational-collective distinction are required in additional locations. We also need fuller information on the extent to which the different existing measures of self-construal and measures of values overlap with one another. Bresnahan, Levine, Shearman, et al. (2005) showed that Singelis self-construal scores and TST scores did not correlate well with one another among samples from Japan, Korea and the USA. This may be because self-construal is a relatively stable trait-like quality, whereas TST responses reflect the respondent's state or context at the time of responding. Consistent with this, in their earlier study, the same group of researchers found that self-construal scores were not influenced by experimental priming, whereas TST scores were (Levine, Bresnahan, Park, et al., 2003).

The interweaving of collective and relational identities in self-construal measures may stem from a misreading of Hofstede's dimensions. Although the measures that we are discussing are derived largely from **individualism-collectivism**, his masculinity-femininity dimension contrasts nations that value achievement with those that value quality of relationships. Be that as it may, there are unresolved questions as to whether the *current* popularity of the distinction between just two types of self-construal gives an adequately rich description of the ways in which individuals' **cultural orientation** varies. We have a more securely established set of **individual-level** measures of values available from Schwartz's studies or from Leung and Bond's measures of social axioms, and we may require self-construal measures that reflect the full range of these values and axioms. Cukur, Guzman, and Carlo (2004) have found consistently positive but modest correlations between Schwartz's values and Singelis et al.'s (1995) measures of horizontal and vertical self-construal among students from Turkey, the Philippines and the USA.

Where Should We Study Self-construals?

A further contribution to recent developments has been the explosion of studies triggered by Markus and Kitayama's (1991) discussion of **independent** and **interdependent** **self-construal**. The central element in their proposal was that if one thinks of oneself as either independent or interdependent, this self-conceptualization has profound consequences for all other aspects of social cognition. Persons who construe themselves as interdependent (or benevolent, traditional, and conformist, in terms of Schwartz's analysis of values) will scan their environment for cues as to how they should behave in order to optimize relations with those who are their primary point of reference. In Markus and Kitayama's view, this basic orientation towards the world will lead them to think in ways that differ from those who construe themselves as independent, to experience a different range of emotions, and to be differently motivated.

We will evaluate each of these propositions later. Firstly, we should reiterate a little caution about identifying causes and effects. Hofstede (1980) attracted some criticism for entitling his book **Culture's Consequences**, but at the **individual-level**, we are on slightly safer ground. We explored in Chapter 5 the processes by which children are socialized in ways that progressively lead them towards thinking of themselves as more independent or as more interdependent. Childhood socialization certainly precedes adult social processes, but adult life entails numerous additional socialization pressures. In a series of studies, Kitayama, Markus, Matsumoto, and Norasakkunkit (1997) have explored the social contexts of US and Japanese society. They find that in the USA, there is a greater frequency of settings that have the likely effect of inducing individuals to feel good about themselves, whereas in Japan there are more occasions that are conducive to self-criticism. The frequency of these types of situations provides encouragement for Americans to think of themselves as independent and not needing the support of others, while Japanese would be more aware of their need to accommodate and fit in with others. Thus, the frequency of different types of social interactions may cause us to construe ourselves in one way or another, just as much as our self-construals may lead us towards engaging in different types of experiences.

The following sections of this chapter concern some of the issues that were identified by Markus and Kitayama (1991). In reviewing these studies it is important to note that they almost all focus upon contrasts between North America (in most cases, the USA) and Pacific Asia (in most cases, Japan). The reasons for this limited focus are not hard to find. They include the growing affluence of the 'Asian tiger' nations, migration in both directions of key individual researchers between Pacific Asia and North America, and journal editors' preference for papers reporting clear and significant contrasts between samples stereotypically regarded as different. From the perspective of cross-cultural psychology, we should note that both Japan and the USA are relatively distinctive and unusual nations, in terms of how they score on many of the cultural dimensions explored in Chapter 3. In comparing them, we do not exhaust the range of global variations in values or in self-construal. Neither do we test fully the difference between individualism and collectivism or between independence and interdependence. Nonetheless, these studies provide an impetus and a challenge to cross-cultural researchers from other parts of the world to enlarge their data base and their conceptualization of how the self is construed in different cultural contexts (Lehman, Chiu, & Schaller, 2004).

Interdependence and Cognition

Markus and Kitayama (1991) proposed that **interdependent self-construal** is an aspect of a distinctive way of thinking, a mode of comprehending the world which refers not just to oneself but to all other aspects of one's ecological niche. Nisbett, Peng, Choi, and Norenzayan (2000) were able to summarize a broad range of evidence indicating that East Asians tend to think holistically, while North Americans tend to think analytically. Similar distinctions have also been drawn between North Americans and Africans (Nsamenang, 1992) and even between Caucasian-Americans and African-Americans, as well as between genders.

This proposition recalls much earlier research by cross-cultural psychologists, such as Berry's (1976) **eco-cultural** framework, which proposed that survival in different types of environment calls for differing perceptual and cognitive skills. In particular, socialization into more relational roles promotes more context dependency and holistic thinking. Supportive evidence was obtained using Witkin's (1950) theory of perceptual differentiation and one of its key instrumentations, the Embedded Figures Test. Respondents to this test are asked to identify a series of shapes, each of which is hidden within a larger background. An example is shown in Box 6.3. Respondents from groups whose survival requires individual action, such as the Inuit, showed **field independence**, that is to say they were better able to pick out targeted figures from the confusing background. Respondents from groups whose survival required collective action, such as the Temne of West Africa, showed greater **field dependence** and had trouble disembedding the targeted figures. The early studies showed substantial variations in **field dependence** among samples from many parts of the world (Witkin & Berry, 1975).

Box 6.3

Embedded Figures Test

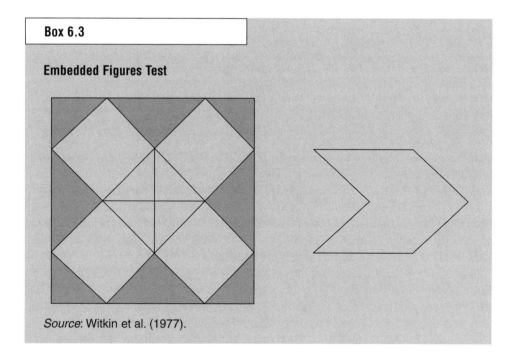

Source: Witkin et al. (1977).

The more recent studies enable us to explore more fully the contrast between **field dependent** or holistic thinking and **field independent** or analytic thinking. Ji, Peng, and Nisbett (2000) found East Asian students studying in the USA to be more **field dependent** than US students, while Kuhnen, Hannover, Roeder, et al. (2001) found Malay and Russian students more **field dependent** than German and US students. Masuda and Nisbett (2001) showed Japanese and US students animated vignettes of underwater scenes and photographs of wildlife. The Japanese recalled the context in which they had been shown the animals better. The Japanese were also better at recognizing whether they had been shown particular animals before, if they were shown again in the same context, but not if they were shown in new contexts. Kitayama, Duffy, Kawamura, and Larsen (2003) showed Japanese and US students a series of vertical lines, each of which appeared within a square frame. In each trial, they were then shown a second square frame of different size. The task was to reproduce the line from the first square, either in the same absolute size as it had first been seen, or in proportion to the dimensions of the second square. Americans were better at reproducing the absolute length and Japanese were better at producing a new version whose length was relative to the new square.

Evidently, Pacific Asians, who are from more collectivistic backgrounds, attend more to the context in processing perceptual stimuli. Further studies have focused on the context of social stimuli. Ishii, Reyes, and Kitayama (2003) tested whether Japanese and US students were more distracted in completing tasks by the verbal content of speech or by the tone of voice of the speaker. Americans were more distracted by verbal content and Japanese were more distracted by the emotional tone in which the words were embedded. Ishii et al. consider tone to be more contextual than words. These results might be due to the differences between the English and the Japanese languages, so Ishii et al. did a second study using bilingual Filipinos. The Filipinos were more distracted by verbal tone than by words, regardless of whether the speech was in English or in Tagalog. Thus, the effect appears to be cultural rather than linguistic.

Thinking in holistic ways also involves an awareness of complexity, whereby many causal factors impinge on one another. Thinking holistically gives less reason to expect the identification of direct causal links between what is happening now and what may come next. Ji, Nisbett, and Su (2001) showed Chinese and US students a series of shapes and asked them to predict whether each ensuing shape would be similar or different to the last. Americans predicted greater continuity, Chinese more change. Choi and Nisbett (2000) presented descriptions of an individual's behaviour to Korean and US students. After being asked to predict what the individual would do next, they were then told what had actually occurred. When their predictions were proved false, Koreans expressed less surprise, and were more likely to use hindsight to explain what happened, perhaps because they are more tolerant of uncertainty.

Because of the limited applicability of causal logic to complex systems, a focus on the interdependence of the elements in a social system or in an abstract problem is likely to lead to a preference for intuitive problem-solving. Norenzayan, Smith, Kim, and Nisbett (2002) compared preferences for formal reasoning versus intuitive reasoning among Chinese, Korean and US students. Problems were presented to them in a way that created a conflict between the two styles of reasoning. Faced with this conflict, the Chinese and Koreans used intuitive reasoning and the US students used more formal reasoning. However, when no conflict was created between reasoning styles, no cultural differences were found.

In understanding the nature of these differences in cognitive style, it is important to be clear that these are not differences in ability. As the Norenzayan et al. (2002) study indicates, holistic and analytic thinking are better thought of as culturally socialized habits. Most of us can reason in either way, but over time we may learn from the cultural context within which we are located to rely more on reasoning in one way than in another. We can, however, revert to the other style if primed by a social situation to do so. As a further instance, Choi, Nisbett, and Smith (1997) showed that Americans made stronger inductive inferences when presented with sets of premises concerning animals, whereas Koreans made stronger inferences when presented with premises referring to persons. Choi et al. suggest that cognitive categories referring to persons are more accessible to Koreans because of their greater interdependence.

Further illustrations of the ability to switch between one cognitive style and the other can be found in studies of **correspondence bias**. Before considering these, we should pause to note that none of the studies of differences in cognitive style that we have discussed actually tested whether these differences are actually related to self-construals. They are simply presented as a series of contrasts between North Americans and East Asians. There is no reason to suggest that self-construal is any more basic than the aspects of cognition discussed in this section. Indeed, it is probably less basic. However, it would help to consolidate our view of cultural aspects of cognition if the measures and concepts used by researchers in this field could be shown to correlate with one another, and hence to **unpackage** these cultural effects.

Correspondence Bias

Numerous studies have been reported in which US respondents who are asked to explain an individual's behaviour where either dispositional or situational explanations are possible are found to attribute the cause to the individual, rather than to contextual determinants. In other words, they see a correspondence between the individual's actions and their personality, attitude or intentions. This tendency has often been referred to as the Fundamental Attribution Error. However, we follow those authors who refer to the phenomenon as **correspondence bias** because, as we shall see, cross-cultural studies have shown the phenomenon to be less fundamental than was first thought. Interestingly, while North American theorists have portrayed **correspondence bias** in terms of individual cognitive processes, French social psychologists study the same process in terms of the social context in which it is presumed to be embedded, preferring to refer to it as the internality *norm* (Beauvois & Dubois, 1988), emphasizing its social origins.

Shweder and Bourne (1982) asked Indian and US adults to describe their peers. They found that 72% of the qualities attributed by US respondents were context-free personality traits. Only 50% of the qualities attributed to Indians fell into this category. In a more detailed study, Miller (1984) found that Indian students gave many more situational explanations and fewer trait-based explanations than did US students for events in a series of scenarios that she provided. Given the greater weight that Asians attach to the individual's context, it is not surprising that **correspondence bias** has been found to be much less evident in studies from this region (Choi, Nisbett, & Norenzayan, 1999).

However, Norenzayan, Choi, and Nisbett (2002) tested the proposition that whether or not **correspondence bias** is found will depend upon the type of information provided to respondents. When Koreans and Americans were provided only with information about individuals, both were equally willing to make predictions as to how the individual would behave in future. In contrast, when situational information was also provided, Koreans drew upon it in making predictions much more than did the Americans. In a similar way, Miyamoto and Kitayama (2002) found that when respondents were told that an individual's behaviour had been constrained by situational role requirements, Americans still showed a **correspondence bias**, but Japanese did not. However, when respondents were told that although the individual had been constrained by role requirements, his actions might nonetheless give some indication of future actions, both Japanese and Americans showed equally strong **correspondence bias**. Thus cultural differences in correspondence can be induced or eliminated under experimental conditions.

Miyamoto and Kitayama (2002) also obtained on-line evidence of respondents' reasoning styles while they were making their judgements. Codings were made of the extent to which respondents referred to situational rather than to personal information. The degree of situational thought was found to **mediate** whether **correspondence bias** occurred. Among all the cross-cultural studies of cognition in relation to independence and interdependence that we have discussed, this is the only one that has attempted an explanation of the results obtained on a more precise basis than simply stating the nationality of respondents and then speculating on what might underlie the observed difference. One study conducted in the USA did show that **independent self-construal** was a significant predictor of **correspondence bias** (Newman, 1993). Thus, it is possible that self-construal provides the best explanation for the effects that are found, but we cannot yet be sure. It may do, but until we perform the **unpackaging** studies necessary to support this argument, it remains an intriguing possibility. For the moment, we turn to the second major topic explored by Markus and Kitayama (1991).

Interdependence and Emotion

Markus and Kitayama (1991) proposed that while some types of emotion may be universal, there would also be differences in those that were most frequently experienced in those contexts in which independence is salient and those in which interdependence is salient. In independent contexts, emotions that serve to sustain one's independence from others will be functional and therefore more frequently experienced. For instance, we should expect more frequent experience of pride; in interdependent contexts, friendly feelings will be more functional. Kitayama, Markus, and Kurokawa (1995) found initial support for these propositions. Students were asked to keep diaries. Among US students, feeling good was associated with episodes in which respondents reported pride, whereas among Japanese students feeling good was associated with episodes in which friendliness was reported.

In evaluating Markus and Kitayama's (1991) propositions, two basic issues have to be addressed, each of which was touched on in our discussion of cognition. Firstly, are there absolute differences in the emotions that are experienced by members of different cultures, or is it more the case that the emotions that humans can experience are universal, but occur more frequently in some contexts than others? Secondly, if we do find cultural differences in the frequency of reported emotions, are these differences 'real', or are they better interpreted in terms of differing cultural norms about the appropriateness of emotional expression? In the case of cognition, we concluded that differences in thinking in holistic or analytic ways were not absolute, but something more akin to culturally socialized habits of varying strength. The evidence relating to emotion can be evaluated in the same way.

The Universality of Emotions

An extensive series of studies has focused upon the ability of respondents to identify emotions portrayed in photographs of faces. Ekman (1972) found high percentages of correct recognition of faces portraying anger, joy, sadness, disgust, surprise, and fear among respondents in Brazil, Chile, Argentina, Japan and the US. The stimuli used in early studies were all American, so that the design was **imposed-etic**. However, Ekman, Friesen, O'Sullivan, et al. (1987) used faces taken from all nations and found a continuing high proportion of correct identifications. Furthermore, Ekman, Sorenson, and Friesen (1969) had earlier reported a study in which US faces were shown to respondents from West Irian in New Guinea, who had minimal previous contact with modern societies. To balance their research design, they also showed New Guinean faces to US respondents. Even in this case, there was a high proportion of correctly identified emotions.

The implications of studies of this type have been much debated. The accuracy rates may be boosted by the fact that respondents are provided with the names of the emotions to be fitted to the faces, and by the fact that the faces portray emotions that are posed rather than natural. Verbal labels for emotions may not exactly correspond with the labels that are used in English. In everyday life, numerous cues are available that are not provided by static photographs. In most languages, the number of words used to describe distinct emotions is very much larger than six. Russell (1994) concludes that emotions may be categorized somewhat differently in different cultures, with the boundaries between the major emotions drawn in different ways. Some more finely differentiated emotions may also be indigenous to a particular culture or to a range of related cultures. For instance, Samoans differentiate between anger that is expressed toward different categories of person (Steele & McGarvey, 1996), while the Ifaluk islanders (also in the Pacific) distinguish *song* (translated as justifiable anger) from other types of anger (Lutz, 1988). Box 6.4 explores evidence for two emotions said to be indigenous to Korea.

Box 6.4

How does one Test whether or not an Emotion is Indigenous?

Schmidt-Atzert and Park (1999) tested the hypothesis that the emotions described in the Korean language as *uulhada* and *dapdaphada* could not be adequately translated into equivalent emotions within the German language. To test their hypothesis, they asked Korean and German students what feelings they would experience in each of a series of 10 one-paragraph scenarios. Responses to scenarios eliciting joy, happiness, anger, love, hate, loneliness, and fear did not differ between Koreans and Germans. 64% of Koreans reported feeling *uulhada* in response to the first scenario reproduced below and 62% reported *dapdaphada* in response to the second scenario. Germans showed much more varied responses. For the first scenario, the most frequent responses were depression (36%) and a non-emotional response (22%). For the second scenario, the frequent responses were helplessness (38%) and a non-emotional response (18%). To determine whether these emotions could be considered indigenous to Korean culture, much wider sampling would be required, but it is clear that Germans were much less well agreed as to how to label their reactions to the two key scenarios.

- *The uulhada scenario*
  'I feel bad for no reason. Perhaps I do know the reason why I feel bad, but I prefer not to become aware of the reason. I do the necessary work without any enthusiasm, I do not do any extra work and I have no intention of doing anything while I am in this emotional state. Laughing is the last thing I feel like doing, and no joyful smile is touching me. Nevertheless, I do not weep because I have no reason for doing this. There seems to be nothing but rain all around me and a gloomy atmosphere seems to be in total control of me.'

(Continued)

Box 6.4 Continued

- *The dapdaphada scenario*
  'I have been living abroad for a considerable length of time now, and I have to communicate in a foreign language. My language skills are improving. Nevertheless, I have problems expressing exactly what I want to say. Just when I think "I am sure that my conversation partner has understood what I want to say", I recognize that there is a misunderstanding. After a few vain attempts, I find that I must accept that I cannot communicate successfully with my partner. In my mother tongue I would easily be able to express what I want to say.'

Despite these limitations, it is apparent that the sequence of studies initiated by Ekman does provide evidence for the cultural generality of a set of basic emotions. Broadening the support of this conclusion, Scherer, Banse, and Wallbott (2001) showed high levels of correct identification of anger, fear, joy, and sadness by students from nine nations, when listening to actors' verbal expression of nonsensical phrases. Debate concerning the realism of emotional recognition studies has triggered several recent improvements in research methods. Some researchers have tried to determine ways in which the intensity with which emotions are portrayed affects judgements. In their 11-nation study, Ekman et al. (1987) already reported strong agreement as to which portrayed emotions were most intense. However these judgements were solely concerned with the actual intensity of emotional display. Because of cultural differences in display rules, Matsumoto, Consolacion, Yamada, et al. (2002) expected that Japanese would make stronger inferences than Americans about the internal feelings of those who were portraying the emotions. They, therefore, asked respondents to rate separately how intense was the actual portrayal of each emotion and how intense was the subjective experience of the person portraying that emotion. Results for low intensity faces showed much stronger cultural differences, with Japanese rating subjective experience as more intense. Matsumoto et al.'s study also included a measure of self-construal, which was found to **mediate** almost all of the differences that were found between Japanese and US responses. More **interdependent self-construal** predicted stronger ratings of subjective experience. This is thus the first of the studies that we have discussed concerning emotion that satisfies the criteria that we laid out at the start of this chapter for valid tests of explanations of cross-cultural differences.

A second attempt to extend our understanding of emotional recognition was made by focusing not simply upon the overall accuracy with which emotions were identified, but by taking greater account of interactions between who was perceiver and whose face was being perceived. Elfenbein and Ambady (2002) conducted a **meta-analysis** of all previous studies and reported that there was an 'in-group advantage', in other words that accuracy was greatest when emotions were portrayed and perceived by persons from the same national or ethnic group. In a further analysis, they then tested alternative explanations for the in-group advantage (Elfenbein & Ambady, 2003). Drawing on the four largest studies of visual and vocal emotion recognition, they showed that accurate recognition was significantly predicted by the overall *difference* between Hofstede scores for the nation of the perceiver and the nation of the person portraying the emotions. Larger differences in individualism, power distance and uncertainty avoidance each predicted decreased accuracy. We should note that this is a **nation-level** analysis, not an **individual-level** analysis, so it gives us no clues as to what it is about the similarity between persons from different nations that permits their more accurate decoding of emotions.

One possibility is that even when the posed emotions refer to the more basic and universal emotions, there are non-verbal 'accents' in the way that they are portrayed. Marsh, Ambady, and Elfenbein (2003) subtly modified a series of photographs of emotion portrayals by Japanese and by Japanese-Americans so as to standardize their muscle contractions. Japanese-Americans were used because they are visually similar to Japanese, but have been socialized within US culture. Respondents were then asked to guess whether the person in each photograph was Japanese or American. When the poser was showing a neutral expression, accuracy was at chance levels. However, when a specific emotion was being portrayed, accuracy became significant. There must therefore be distinctive non-verbal accompaniments to facial portrayals of emotion that US judges can detect, even though they cannot say what these cues are. We can speculate that more interdependent persons would be better able to detect these subtle cultural differences, but a direct test has yet to be made.

Putting Emotions Back into their Context

The entire sequence of studies of emotional expression that we have reviewed extracts emotional expression from the context within which emotions normally occur. Given that Markus and Kitayama (1991) stressed the way in which context was of particular importance to those who favour **interdependent self-construal**, it is not likely that this type of study can give a full picture of the relation between emotion and culture. Requirements as to how one should behave vary from one setting to another, and this may influence the extent to which one will express whatever emotions one is experiencing. Even within mainstream theories, the experience of emotion is no longer seen simply as something that is either present or absent. What is known as the componential theory of emotion identifies a whole series of stages, comprising the appraisal and labelling of inner states and subsequent processing of choices as to how those states should be represented within a given social context. Each of these stages is potentially subject to cultural variation (Mesquita & Frijda, 1992).

An early illustration of these processes was provided by Friesen (1972). Friesen showed Japanese and US adults a short film depicting bodily mutilation. They watched the film either on their own or in the presence of others. While watching the film, their facial expressions were videoed and later coded. It was found that when US participants watched the film their faces registered disgust, although not when they watched a neutral film. On the other hand, the Japanese showed disgust when watching the mutilation film alone, but not when being observed while they watched. Friesen concluded that Japanese display rules inhibited the direct expression of disgust, but the details of his study are often described incorrectly, and it appears that the US watchers also changed their expressions when watching mutilation scenes, though not in the same way as the Japanese (Fridlund & Duchaine, 1996). Matsumoto and Kupperbusch (2001) replicated

Friesen's study, using only Caucasian-American women as participants, but also including a measure of self-construal. They found that interdependence was associated with greater smiling and less expressions of negative emotion when watching the unpleasant film than was the case for independence. Thus an effect originally described as cross-cultural can be reproduced within a US sample, when applying concepts and measures derived from cross-cultural studies. A multicultural perspective can enrich mainstream research and help contextualize its possibly indigenous results.

The rules concerning the extent to which emotions may be expressed publicly and in what settings vary between nations. Argyle, Henderson, Bond, et al. (1986) identified more rules restraining expression of anger and distress in Japan and Hong Kong than they did in Italy and the UK. Mandal, Bryden, and Bulman-Fleming (1996) found that Indians reacted more negatively than Canadians to expressions of negative emotion. Appropriate locations for emotional expression may also vary by situation. Redford and Smith (2004) showed that Greek and Turkish students expressed more anger to strangers than within the family, whereas students from the UK expressed more anger to their family than to strangers. These effects were **mediated** by **interdependent self-construal**, so we may conclude that in the case of the Greeks and the Turks, it was more important to sustain harmony within the family than it was for the British respondents.

An extensive database that permits further analyses of emotion in natural contexts is provided by the International Study on Emotional Antecedents and Reactions (ISEAR), which included 37 nations (Wallbott & Scherer, 1986). Students were asked to keep a diary for one week, describing recent episodes when they had experienced joy, sadness, fear, anger, disgust, shame and guilt, what happened before and after and who was present. Scherer (1997) later analysed the data in terms of the 'appraisal' stage within the componential model of emotion (Mesquita & Frijda, 1992). In other words, he tested whether there was consistency in the ways in which the circumstances were appraised that led to each type of emotion. The dimensions of appraisal were novelty, unpleasantness, obstruction of one's goal, external causation, one's ability to cope with the situation, immorality and self-consistency. Scherer concluded that each emotion had a distinctive pattern of appraisal conditions that was equally applicable to the data derived from almost all nations. Of course, this does not mean that equal amounts of each emotion occur everywhere, because the eliciting circumstances will occur more often at some locations than at others. The principal divergence from these culture-general conclusions was found among African nations, especially Malawi and Botswana. In the data from these nations, appraisal of immorality, unfairness and external causation had stronger effects on any of the emotions that were elicited.

Wong and Bond (2002) used the ISEAR data to determine the extent to which there are some elements common to emotionality, regardless of the specific emotion being experienced. They found consistency across emotions in their reported recency, intensity, and duration. This enabled them to analyse the extent to which **citizen scores** for nations represented in the sample differed in these aspects of emotionality. Nations whose citizens reported longer-lasting emotions were shown to be lower on Schwartz's (1994) intellectual autonomy, suggesting a regulatory function of cognitive activity on emotional experience (Wong & Bond, 2005).

The ISEAR data did not include self-construal measures, so we cannot be sure that greater emotionality is associated with independence rather than interdependence in all cultural contexts, but it appears likely. Many kinds of emotional expression serve to define one's individuality and may therefore have greater utility within individualist cultural contexts. Other dimensions of culture will also be relevant to what happens when emotions are expressed. Becht and Vingerhoets (2002) surveyed how students in 30 nations felt after they had cried. Most people felt better. However, four factors were found to explain the extent to which people felt better: Hofstede's **nation-level** score for femininity, low feeling of shame, being from an affluent nation and from a nation where crying was relatively frequent. Among these, the strongest predictor was Hofstede's femininity score. Crying works best in Finland and least well in Switzerland!

Interdependence and Motivation

Markus and Kitayama (1991) proposed that a cultural emphasis on interdependence would have a series of consequences for the types of individual motivation that would be most functional. The concern for harmony with one's group can be expected to lead to modest self-presentation, a motivation to achieve on behalf of the group rather than for oneself and a lesser need for consistency across settings.

Self-enhancement and Modesty

Kitayama et al. (1997) observed the way in which Japanese contrast with Americans in their emphasis on adjustment to others' requirements and their more modest self-presentation. Morling, Kitayama, and Miyamoto (2002) extended this analysis by asking respondents to recall occasions when they had influenced others and occasions when they had adjusted their behaviour to the requirements of others. Americans remembered more influence episodes and the episodes were more recent. Americans reported that the influence episodes had made them feel efficacious. On the other hand, Japanese recalled more situations when they had adjusted to others and these episodes were more recent. Adjustment episodes had made them feel more closely related to others.

   Persistent findings that the Japanese favour modesty over self-enhancement challenge the widespread assumption that some degree of positive self-evaluation is a universal requirement for effective social functioning (Heine, Lehman, Markus, & Kitayama, 1999). There has been extensive recent debate as to whether Japanese persons are 'really' modest, whether it is merely the case that interdependence requires a more modest self-presentation, or whether the results obtained are an artefactual consequence of the research methods that are used. Brown and Kobayashi (2002) proposed that Japanese only rate themselves low when they are evaluating themselves on qualities that are valued in individualist nations. They showed that when rating themselves on their most highly valued qualities, such as friendliness and modesty, the Japanese rated themselves as highly as Americans did on their mostly highly valued qualities. Sedikides, Gaertner, and Toguchi (2003) obtained similar results when comparing US students and Japanese students studying in the USA. However, findings from studies in which self-enhancement was measured by ratings of whether one is better than average are discounted by Heine (2003). Ratings of this type have been shown to yield some spurious effects, since even a randomly chosen other person is found to be rated better than average, and it would not be surprising if this type of effect was found only on favoured qualities.

Heine and his colleagues report that other measures yield results confirming Japanese modesty. Discrepancies between ratings of self and ideal self were shown to be larger for Japanese than for Canadians (Heine & Lehman, 1999). These discrepancies were greatest for attributes that were rated the most important. In a laboratory experiment, Canadians were found reluctant to believe that they had performed worse than average. Japanese were reluctant to believe that they had done better than average (Heine, Takata, & Lehman, 2000). Heine and Renshaw (2002) had school club members in the USA and Japan rate themselves and each other. Japanese respondents rated themselves lower than the ratings they received from their peers; Americans rated themselves higher. This study also included a measure of independent and **interdependent self-construal**, and **independent self-construal** was found to **moderate** these effects both among Japanese and among Americans.

The consistent modesty of Japanese responses is by now clearly established. Is this modesty 'real' or is it a matter of self-presentation? Muramoto (2003) asked Japanese students to reflect on past successes and failures. As expected, they were found to attribute successes to others and failures to themselves. However, Muramoto also asked her respondents to rate how their friends and family would evaluate these successes and failures. Here she found that her respondents believed that friends and family would give them credit for successes and blame them less for failures. This suggests that modesty is primarily a matter of self-presentation in different social contexts. Kurman (2003) obtained several types of measure of self-enhancement from high school students in Israel and Singapore and also asked her respondents to rate how important it was to be modest. High ratings of the importance attached to modesty were found to **mediate** (low) self-enhancement in both nations.

Although the debate about modesty continues, it appears that although they certainly want to meet with others' approval, Japanese as well as members of some other collectivist nations, either do not self-enhance, or do so much less than is done elsewhere (Heine, in press). This self-effacement has to do with their greater interdependence with others. There are numerous other aspects of relations with others which are interwoven with modest self-presentation, and we shall consider these connections in Chapter 8.

Socially-oriented Achievement

Early research into the motivation to achieve assumed that achievement was something that brought credit to the individual. An individual's motivation was assessed by coding references to individual achievement and recognition produced by the person in describing a series of pictures. McClelland (1961) sought to apply this kind of thinking in accounting for the greater economic success of some nations over others. He reasoned that by encouraging individual achievement, a generation of entrepreneurs could be created who would find ways to foster economic development. However, this type of thinking can now be seen to rest on an **imposed-etic** conceptualization. More interdependent persons are not likely to think of achievement solely in terms of individual gain and recognition. Indeed, McClelland did not succeed in getting Indian managers to compete against fellow managers on an individual basis. Yu (1996) developed separate measures of individually- and socially-oriented achievement motivation and found them to be largely independent of one another among Chinese respondents. Those who score high on socially-oriented achievement motivation look to others in their group to define targets, to work towards those targets and to evaluate how well those targets are achieved. Similar conceptualizations of socially-oriented achievement motivation have emerged from research in India (Agarwal & Misra, 1986) and from a comparative study of Turkish and Belgian adolescents (Phalet & Claeys, 1993).

Consistent with this analysis, Redding (1990) studied Chinese entrepreneurs. He found that the economic success of Chinese family firms was strongly dependent upon collaborative links between networks of interrelated family members. Church and Katigbak (1992) compared work motivations of US and Filipino students. The Americans stressed getting good grades and personal achievement, while the Filipinos stressed preparation for getting a good job and receiving approval from others. This differentiation of different types of achievement motivation parallels Bandura's (2002) acknowledgement that personal efficacy and group efficacy can have equally strong effects on human action.

There are further consequences of socially- rather than individually-oriented motivation. An independent person who fails may experience self-doubt in his or her abilities. Yu (1996) notes that failure among Chinese is more often attributed to poor connections with others, fate, bad luck or one's socially undesirable attributes. Chang, Arkin, Leong, et al. (1994) asked students in the USA, Hong Kong and Singapore to rate their concern for high performance, doubt in oneself, doubt in one's perseverance, and doubt in one's social connections. As expected, among US respondents concern for performance was linked to self-doubt and to **independent self-construal**. However, in the Chinese samples these effects were absent, and in Singaporeans concern for performance was linked to doubt in one's social connections. So, the focus of one's achievement motivation appears to have broad-reaching implications for how one makes sense of positive and negative outcomes. Such attributions about the causes of one's own success or failure provide a special case of the more general issues of **correspondence bias** and modesty, which we discussed earlier.

In common with many of the sections of this chapter, the studies of achievement that we have reviewed comprise contrasts between North American and East Asian respondents, assumed to exemplify the distinction between those who construe themselves as independent and those who construe themselves as interdependent. However, particularly in Chapter 5, we noted the need to distinguish a third type of self-construal, **autonomous-relational** (Kağıtçıbaşı, 1996a, 2005). Ryan's (1993) self-determination theory proposes that adolescents will develop strong intrinsic motivation if their parents and teachers support their autonomy, in other words, if their autonomy is relationally supported. Support for this theory has been found among Russian and US schoolchildren (Chirkov & Ryan, 2001). From a different perspective, Nelson and Shavitt (2002) compared endorsement of achievement values in Denmark and the USA with measures of vertical and horizontal self-construal. In both nations, achievement values were associated with vertical individualism. Studies that incorporate a fuller range of self-construal measures will be needed before we can integrate these separate types of findings, but the present evidence underlines the need for broader sampling of nations and of measures tapping different types of self-construal.

Consistency

If I construe myself as an independent entity, it will be important to me to see myself as a unified locus of action. If I construe myself as interdependent, however, my actions will be driven by the need to respond appropriately to those who are important to me. Consequently, it may be necessary for me to behave inconsistently in different settings, especially where those different settings involve different actors. However we construe ourselves, the exigencies of life will most probably cause us to act in ways that are inconsistent for at least some of the time. An important question concerns how these inconsistencies shall be handled.

Fu, Lee, Cameron, and Xu (2001) compared Canadian and Chinese students', teachers' and parents' evaluations of stories that included the telling of lies about pro- or anti-social behaviours. Canadians evaluated truth telling positively, but Chinese did so only in relation to anti-social behaviours. They evaluated a person who had performed a pro-social behaviour but denied having done so more positively than a person who admitted that they had performed the pro-social behaviour. Furthermore, nearly half of the Chinese respondents stated that in their view the person whose lying was described in the scenario did not in fact lie. Fu et al. interpret these results in terms of the Chinese need for modest self-presentation. To speak the truth about having done a good deed would be boasting. So, an apparent inconsistency is handled by referring to the higher-order value of modesty, a value whose preeminence is probably related to one's level of **interdependent self-construal**. We have touched on other studies earlier in this chapter that imply a greater use of tact and diplomacy in Pacific Asian nations. For instance, Tafarodi et al. (2004) found much lower reported consistency of one's 'inner self' across situations for persons from Japan and Hong Kong, where we would expect **interdependent self-construals** to be generally higher. This particular result suggests not just an expedient use of tact or diplomacy that varies between settings, but that respondents actually sense that they are different persons in each setting.

Culture as a Set of Persistent Primes

In Chapter 2, we discussed several steps in the process whereby psychologists interested in culture have sought to link their studies to the development of the mainstream of psychological research. Substantial progress has been achieved in making these links. However, until recently, one of the largest impediments has been the reluctance of cross-cultural researchers to use the experimental methods that provide the bedrock in many areas of psychological research. How could it ever be possible, they argue, to manipulate culture experimentally? For their part, mainstream colleagues have doubted that studies based upon field surveys could ever give clear tests of causal hypotheses.

The development of the **individual-level** constructs of independence and interdependence has encouraged some researchers to propose a way to overcome this problem. If self-construals are thought of not as wholly fixed personality-like traits, but as also entailing a focusing of one's attention on to certain priorities at a particular time, then it may be possible to manipulate them experimentally. Maybe we can all be independent some of the time and interdependent at other times, an argument consistent with the orthogonal relationship of **independent** and **interdependent self-construals** (Singelis, Bond, Sharkey, & Lai, 1999). In a first attempt at experimental manipulation, Trafimow, Triandis, and Goto (1991) simply asked Caucasian and Chinese students in the USA to sit for two minutes and visualize either all their links with the family, or all the things that make them different from others. They then completed the Twenty Statements Test. The experimental manipulation had a substantial effect on how members of each group described themselves. When asked to think about links with their family, their TST scores showed greater interdependence. When asked to think about their separateness, their TST scores showed greater independence.

If one can cause people to think of themselves in independent or interdependent ways, then it becomes possible to test what other aspects of social cognition are associated with this experimentally induced change. Over the past decade an increasing number of studies has been published that use this type of experimental priming to test hypotheses relating to individualism and collectivism. Among North American bi-culturals, reference to **ethnic identity**, exposure to flags and other icons and presentation of materials in different languages all achieve significant priming effects (Oyserman, Sakamoto, & Lauffer, 1998; Morris, Menon, & Ames, 2001; Ross, Xun, & Wilson, 2002). Protagonists of this approach argue that it provides a way in which studies of cultural differences can be brought within the ambit of the experimental method (Hong & Chiu, 2001; Hong, Morris, Chiu, & Benet-Martınez, 2000).

So far, most cross-cultural studies using cultural primes have sampled bi-cultural persons, among whom alternative cognitive frames can be presumed to be more readily present and accessible. Furthermore, although priming does cause significant effects, it does not eliminate pre-existing differences. In Trafimow et al.'s study, the Chinese-Americans continued to report more interdependent cognitions than the Caucasians in all experimental conditions, and the Caucasians were consistently more independent. As we noted earlier in the chapter, Levine et al. (2003) found that priming affected TST responses, but not self-construal responses. Finally, it is sometimes the case that cultural priming produces effects opposed to the primed culture. For instance, in Hong Kong, a Chinese experimenter speaking in English evoked an increased proportion of responses from Chinese respondents affirming their cultural heritage (Yang & Bond, 1980; Bond & Cheung, 1984; see also Box 7.4 in Chapter 7).

In order to strengthen the bridge between these kinds of experimental study and the ways in which we have suggested that individuals are culturally socialized, we need to argue that short-term life experiences are constantly priming us to attend to certain aspects of ourselves and our environment and to ignore others. Some examples have already come to light of how this flexibility in attention might occur. For instance, Kashima and Kashima (1998) showed that most languages spoken within collectivist nations permit the dropping of the personal pronoun 'I', whereas those that are most spoken in individualist nations do not permit pronoun drop. By speaking in certain ways, we may be constantly priming a particular **cultural orientation** in ourselves and in those around us. It would be much too great a simplification to suggest that priming causes cultural differences, but it may well serve to reinforce and sustain them. Priming studies provide an additional path towards our understanding of cultural differences, especially those differences that relate to social cognition.

Summary

The distinction between **independent** and **interdependent self-construal** helps us to test the degree to which the basic psychological processes inherent in cognition, emotion and motivation are universal. There are continuing problems in defining how best to measure self-construal and sampling of an adequately broad range of cultures has not yet been achieved. The evidence to date indicates that processes that are fundamentally universal are channelled in different directions by those who construe themselves in particular ways. This leads us to think differently, to interpret the behaviour of those around us in different ways, to experience and express emotions differently and to strive for different types of social relationship with others.

Further Reading

1 Altarriba, J., Basnight, D.M., & Canary, T.M. (2004). Emotion representation and perception across cultures. www.wwu.edu/~culture
2 Kitayama, S., Markus, H.R., Matsumoto, H., & Norasakkunkit, V. (1997). Individual and collective processes in the construction of the self: Self-enhancement in the United States and self-criticism in Japan. *Journal of Personality and Social Psychology*, *72*, 1245–67.
3 Markus, H.R., & Kitayama, S. (1991). Culture and the self: Implications for cognition, emotion, and motivation. *Psychological Review*, *98*, 224–53.
4 Nisbett, R.E., Peng, K.P., Choi, I., & Norenzayan, A. (2000). Culture and systems of thought: Holistic versus analytic cognition. *Psychological Review*, *108*, 291–310.
5 Oyserman, D., Coon, H.M., & Kemmelmeier, M. (2002). Rethinking individualism and collectivism: Evaluation of theoretical assumptions and meta-analyses. *Psychological Bulletin*, *128*, 3–72.

Study Questions

1 How do you construe yourself? Either describe yourself using a Twenty Statements Test format, or rate your agreement with the items in Box 6.2.
2 How is self-construal measured and how do you think it might be better measured?
3 What aspects of cultural differences would be detected if other regions of the world were studied as intensively as North America and Pacific Asia have been?
4 What are the strengths and weaknesses of using photographs and diaries to study culture-general and culture-specific aspects of emotion?
5 Identify aspects of your own culture that encourage modest or assertive self-presentations.

7 Personality in Cross-cultural Perspective

You will find, as a general rule, that the constitutions and the habits of a people follow the nature of the land where they live (Hippocrates, Precepts)

In the preceding chapters we have seen how motivations, values, beliefs and self-construals are associated with cultural differences in various social psychological processes. Each of these aspects of personal dispositions represents an aspect of personality, so we next consider the sources of the variation in these dispositions and the extent to which personality differences may account for the evident differences in behaviour around the world. In fact, it was the kaleidoscopic diversity in observable behaviours that led to our seeking explanations for cultural differences in the first place.

Early anthropologists encountered especially dramatic differences in behavioural patterns during their residence in exotic places far removed from their cultures of origin. For instance, Bronislaw Malinowski (1927) in the Trobriand Islands, Laura Bohannon (Bowen, 1964) in Nigeria, and Clifford Geertz (1975) in Bali encountered an extraordinary range of behavioural differences in the societies that they studied and subsequently reported to an often-amazed readership. As we noted in Chapter 2, some social scientists, many of them trained in psychoanalysis, turned to personality to explain these observed differences in behaviour, creating the '**culture and personality**' school (e.g., Kardiner & Linton, 1945). 'Their main thesis was that individual persons living in the same cultural environment and having gone through a similar socialization history ... develop the same personality' (Poortinga & van Hemert, 2001, p. 1035). Thus, Muensterberger, a member of the Chinese group for Research in Contemporary Cultures, founded by Ruth Benedict at Columbia University wrote:

> The Southern Chinese chooses ways of channelization and sublimation of drives which appear, on first sight, strange to us. To a greater extent than among Westerners, his pregenital impulses and fantasy systems continue to find expression directly together with his reality adjustments. In avoidance of Oedipal conflicts it is culturally permitted to resolve inhibitions and tensions in daydreams, ideals, hallucinations, and pseudo activity. The dependence on each other is a culturally determined defence mechanism against instinctual demands. As a result of this psychic constellation the Chinese have created their art and philosophy and contribute so much to human civilization. (Muensterberger, 1969, p. 329)

This analysis was tightly grounded on close observation of daily life in a dramatically different cultural system, and constitutes a creative extension of Freudian constructs and dynamics into an alien reality. It is typical of early analyses by the culture and personality school in its assertion that:

the primary institutions (like subsistence and family organization) of a society, through socialization practices, lead to a certain basic personality structure, consisting of aspects common to all or most members. This personality structure, in turn, forms the basis of the secondary institutions of the society (including religious beliefs, myths and style of artistic expression). (Poortinga & van Hemert, 2001, p. 1036)

In the period after the Second World War, anthropologists drew on psychoanalytic theory in analysing ethnographic records from a great number of pre-industrial societies (Whiting and Child, 1953), and also carried out in-depth studies in six cultures (Whiting & Whiting, 1975). These studies pointed to the central role of child-rearing as the link between the ecology/economy and maintenance systems of cultures on the one hand and child personality leading to adult personality and cultural products on the other. Thus a developmental perspective was used, but one that was rather narrowly construed in terms of psychoanalytic theory.

Three significant positions characterize the approach to culture that was taken by members of the **culture and personality** school: the tendency to perceive considerable similarity in the personalities of a culture's members; the presumption that this modal personality system exerts a pervasive influence on all aspects of social life; and the treating of 'cultural' productions of a distinctive group as 'secondary' extensions of the 'primary' institutional influences acting through the basic personality type that characterizes that cultural group. As we now appreciate, each of these positions may be questioned.

Mapping the Personality of Individuals and their Cultural Groups

As McCrae (2000) has pointed out, the **culture and personality** school made little impact upon personality psychologists in part because of the poor psychometric properties of the instruments that they used to measure personality, most of which were derived from psychoanalysis. Inter-judge reliabilities of the measures used to tap constructs like ego strength and projected anger were low. Furthermore, the Freudian theory underlying these measures has been replaced over time by social-learning and trait theories of personality. These theories encouraged the development of new personality measures, mostly written responses to written questions, which were amenable to **factor analysis** and yielded multi-faceted structures of constructs. These complex measures, like Cattell's 16 PF or Eysenck's EPN, could be used to compare individuals on a variety of dimensions. Their high test–retest reliabilities reassured psychologists that something consistent about individuals' character was being tapped. Their written nature and standardized response categories ensured that inter-judge reliabilities in their scoring were very high, indeed usually perfect. The days of scoring Rorschach 'inkblot' responses to assess cross-cultural difference (e.g., Abel & Hsu, 1949) were behind us.

Comparing Personality across Cultures

After the Second World War, psychological research was initially restricted to just a few nations. Some psychologists, for example McClelland (1961), had a broader, multi-cultural vision. He was fascinated by the issue of socio-economic development, and tried to link the economic advancement of a society to the socialization practices in schools. Specifically, he scored primary school textbooks across many nations for their density of achievement themes, using Murray's (1938) theory of motives to link the inculcation of achievement motivation to a nation's subsequent economic growth. This was a **nation-level** analysis, of course, and he required the orchestration of huge resources at that time to accomplish his project.

Most cross-cultural psychologists were less ambitious, and preferred to work at the individual level of analysis. Their **imposed-etic** research method typically involved taking a personality test with established theoretical linkages and empirical track record in one nation, usually the USA, and then comparing American responses to this instrument with those from respondents in another nation. For example, Bond and Tornatsky (1973) administered Rotter's (1966) measure of internal versus external locus of control to Japanese and American respondents. Using the available theoretical assumptions of the time (e.g., Nakane's, 1973, portrayal of Japan as a 'vertical' society), they argued that Japanese, well socialized into such a vertical system, should describe themselves as more external than an equivalent sample of Americans.

Given that Rotter's (1966) test had never been administered in Japan, the researchers took the precaution of using **factor analysis** to check whether the presumed unidimensionality ascribed to locus of control was in fact found among Japanese respondents. Consistent with some emerging US results (Collins, 1974), Bond and Tornatsky (1973) found not one, but two, factors underlying the 23-item instrument. These factors were similarly constituted by both Japanese and Americans, thereby meeting the requirement for equivalence of factors across cultures before valid comparison could proceed. On both the factor of personal control and of system modifiability, the Japanese respondents indicated greater externality of control, confirming the original hypothesis.

With a more ambitious aim of theory testing, though again using a two-culture comparison, Kağıtçıbaşı (1970) subjected the 'authoritarian personality' theory to a cross-cultural test in a comparative study of Turkish and American youth. She found that some of the characteristics assumed to constitute the so-called authoritarian *personality* syndrome, such as respect for authority, were social norms in Turkey and thus uniformly high in the respondents. The overall internal coherence of this personality syndrome was therefore much weaker in Turkey than in the USA. This finding was a challenge to a psychoanalytically based personality theory assumed to be universally valid. It was also an early examination of personality versus culture as determinants of attitudinal orientations.

The cross-cultural psychology literature is filled with many such two-culture comparisons of scores on imported personality tests. Sometimes a basis for comparison is established by doing either exploratory or confirmatory **factor analysis**, followed by assessment of equivalence for the identified factors as constructs; sometimes not. Even when such equivalence has been established, however, such research is at best preliminary. No two-culture comparison of means on a construct, however intriguing that construct, can provide any definitive proof of the societal characteristics that might have given rise to those average differences. Early on, Campbell (1970) warned against the uninterpretability of simple two-group comparisons, suggesting instead a 'triangulation' of cross-cultural research methods to ensure greater certainty in the conclusions being drawn. Triangulation would involve the use of several different types of research measures, not just the use of quicker paper and pencil tests. Today we suggest that a minimum of twenty or so cultural groups, ideally from widely different geographical locations, economic conditions and philosophical traditions, would be a necessary minimum of nations to pinpoint possible antecedents.

A further problem is that a specific personality measure is often nested within a hierarchy of broader personality dimensions. In characterizing cultural differences, it may make more sense to compare broader rather than narrower constructs. Internal versus external locus of control, for example, is a focused belief system that relates to the broader belief dimensions now identified as fate control and cynicism in Leung and Bond's (2004) comprehensive measure of social axioms (Singelis, Hubbard, Her, & An, 2003). Not only is locus of control a more specific construct, it also appears to be many-faceted with respect to the more comprehensive system that Leung and Bond have now found to characterize beliefs. This may not be a problem if one is testing a focused hypothesis derived from theorizing about locus of control, but if one is examining the wider influence of culture on variations in personality, a more comprehensive measure of personality structure will be the tool of choice.

Pan-cultural Similarity in the Organization of Personality?

The Lexically Derived Big Five

Building upon earlier work by Fiske (1949), Norman (1963) identified five robust dimensions of variation in the rated personality of acquaintances in fraternities at the University of Michigan. What made this work 'universal', to use Norman's word, was its diligent attempt to be comprehensive in the range of personality variation that was included in the assessment of people. The work was based upon personality descriptors originally culled from the English lexicon by Allport and Odbert (1936) and reduced by Norman to the five distinct or independent dimensions of personality variation that he labelled as Extraversion, Good-naturedness, Conscientiousness or will to achieve, Emotional stability, and Culture. Norman called these the 'Big Five' because of their robustness across the various samples from which they had been extracted.

The Norman (1963) personality descriptors were applied as an **imposed-etic** measure in the Philippines by Guthrie and Bennett (1971), in Japan by Bond, Nakazato, and Shiraiishi (1975) and in Hong Kong by Bond (1979). It was clearly possible to identify the first four dimensions of personality in these new locations, though the fifth dimension, 'culture' was often poorly and inconsistently defined. Of course, these were English language descriptors imported into foreign cultures whose languages were quite different. It is entirely possible that many indigenously important descriptors of personality were missing, and could have helped define a replacement for the dimension of 'culture' or even to define further dimensions of personality variation in nations that use different languages.

Goldberg's 'lexical' hypothesis states that, 'the most important individual differences in human transactions will come to be encoded as single terms in some or all of the world's languages' (Goldberg, 1990, p. 1216). This influential hypothesis has inspired considerable within-nation exploration of local languages, so as to identify indigenously derived structures for personality. From Chinese (Yang & Lee, 1971) and Japanese (Nagashima, Fujiwara, Harano, Saito, & Hori, 1967) to Polish (Szarota, 1996) and Tagalog (Church, Kagitbak, & Reyes, 1996), local lexicons of personality terms, usually adjectives, have been analysed in terms of how they function in that culture as descriptors of either oneself or others. As always with **factor analysis** and other multivariate techniques, there is some arbitrariness about the decision on how many factors are to be extracted.

Integrating across some of this plethora of studies, De Raad, Perugini, Hrebickova, and Szarota (1998) concluded that 'using the American English solution as a target ... the congruences show replicability of the first four American English Big Five factors in the other languages' (p. 212). However, confirmation of a consistent fifth factor was not found in several languages. Nonetheless, they argue that the Big Five model should be retained, since a fifth factor is usually identified in all language traditions. In their view, lack of congruence across language systems occurs in part because only adjectives, rather than also nouns and verbs, are typically used, and ability terms, especially those related to intelligence, have not been consistently included in the various lexicons used for the ratings of personality. The fifth factor is now referred to by researchers as 'Openness to Experience', rather than 'Culture', while Good-naturedness is now referred to as Agreeableness, and Emotional Stability is now referred to as its opposite, Neuroticism.

Thus it appears that variants of the Big Five do exist in all languages. What is important for present purposes is that these five have been extracted from the language-system-in-use wherever it has been studied. This universality in use suggests that there is a strong functional basis for the emergence and use of the Big Five factors in daily discourse to describe ourselves and others. Hogan (1982) argues that these dimensions of personality description arise because they help people identify those persons who are capable of meeting the functional prerequisites of social integration and task coordination that all social systems must address because of our evolutionary heritage. As he argues:

> The problems of achieving status and maintaining peer popularity are biologically mandated. ... status ... provides the opportunity for preferential breeding and reproductive success ... popularity ... has considerable survival value .... The core of human nature consists of certain fixed, insistent, and largely unconscious biological motives ... three of them give a distinctive style to human social behaviour: (a) ... needs for social approval, and at the same time they find criticism and disapprobation highly aversive ... (b) ... needs to succeed at the expense of others, modified ... by the genetic relationships between them ... (c) ... needs for structure, predictability and order in their social environment. (pp. 56–7)

More recently, Hogan (1996) has summarized the ways in which these basic needs can be related to the Big Five dimensions that first arose from lexical studies:

> The Adjustment dimension [Neuroticism] concerns how well a person will perform under pressure and how emotionally stable he or she is on a daily basis. The Sociability/Ambition dimension [Extraversion] concerns leadership potential. The Prudence dimension [Conscientiousness] concerns trustworthiness and dependability. The Likeability dimension [Agreeableness] concerns how much others enjoy a person's company. The Intellectance dimension [Openness to Experience] concerns the degree to which a person will be a resource for solving technical problems confronting the group ... the dimensions of the FFM

(Five Factor Model) resemble Jungian archetypes; they are innate categories of human perception used to evaluate the potential contribution of others to the success of one's family, tribe, corporation or combat unit. (pp. 173–4)

The names applied to these dimensions vary from test developer to test developer, but seem to share a basic functional similarity that Hogan believes arises from the requirements of human living anywhere, any time. As such, the Big Five are transcultural, transhistorical universals. Hogan's conclusions show an interesting and reassuring convergence with the major dimensions of values identified by Schwartz (1994), which we discussed in Chapter 3. Just as we noted in the case of values, the structure may be universal, but individual people will vary in the strength of their social needs and in their capacity to meet those needs in their particular social environment. An individual earns a distinctive reputation in his or her community based on how and how well he or she addresses the community's profile of needs. A person's profile on the local variant of the Big Five system identifies him or her as a resource configuration, shaping expectations for future performance and guiding perceivers' behaviour towards the person so described. So, for example, Bond and Forgas (1984) presented Australian and Hong Kong Chinese perceivers with descriptions of persons varying across four of the Big Five dimensions used in their culture to characterize others. In both cultural groups, perceivers indicated that they would be more likely to associate with a target described using terms indicating high extraversion and high agreeableness. People in both, and probably all, cultural systems prefer to interact with someone who is generally enthusiastic and broadly accommodating towards others. However, culture-specific dynamics are also involved in this process of interpersonal regulation. Hong Kong Chinese attached much greater weight to a target person's agreeableness in choosing whom they wished to spend time with than did Australians. This difference in the value placed on agreeableness may characterize any comparison between an individualistic and a collectivist nation.

Box 7.1

Investigating a Person's Sense of Superiority using Lexical Measures of Personality

Regarding oneself as better than others is disapproved of to varying degrees in all cultures, as doing so invites interpersonal hostility and is socially divisive. So, it will be difficult to measure a person's sense of superiority over others by asking that person directly to compare his or her merit relative to others, important as a sense of one's superiority may be for social functioning.

Trait words, like 'friendly' or 'argumentative', are easy-to-use measures of personality, one's own or others'. Osgood, May and Miron (1975) have shown cross-culturally that such trait words all have an evaluative component, though the strength of favourability indicated by a given trait label may vary somewhat from culture to culture. Could this characteristic of trait labels be used within a particular cultural group to assess a given person's sense of superiority over others in his or her social world?

Box 7.1 Continued

The researcher could ask the respondent to rate himself or herself across the lexical markers for the Big Five in local use. The evaluative strength attached to the self could be calculated by summing the level of favourability associated with the person's self-ratings. Then, the respondent could rate a group of acquaintances using the same lexical markers, and the average level of favourability associated with this group of acquaintances could be calculated. A difference in the favourability scores for self versus others could be calculated, yielding a simple, unobtrusive measure of that person's sense of superiority over others in his or her social world.

Bond, Kwan, and Li (2000) followed this procedure with Chinese students working with fellow students in project groups. They discovered that a respondent's rating of self-favourability (self-regard) was independent of his or her rating of other-favourability (regard for others). Additionally, they found that respondents high in self-regard were perceived by their other group members as more extraverted, assertive, and open; respondents with high regard for others were liked more and perceived by other group members as higher in helpfulness and restraint. Possibly, then, a person's sense of superiority is communicated to others interpersonally through his or her tendency to do good things, i.e., being 'helpful' and to avoid doing bad things to others, i.e., being 'restrained'. It has nothing to do with how he or she regards him or herself. Instead, self-regard predicts aspects of one's social performance that are unrelated to offending others. These conclusions are relevant to the studies of modesty versus self-enhancement discussed in Chapter 6, and must be tested in other cultures, especially those with differing levels of hierarchy. Such testing can best be done by using lexical measures of indigenous dimensions of personality.

The Big Five in Personality Inventories

The lexical tradition and the questionnaire tradition in the study of personality have converged with the development of the Revised NEO Personality Inventory (NEO-PI-R) by Costa and McCrae (1992). In their Professional Manual for this widely used test of personality, these authors claim that their instrument:

> is a concise measure of the five major dimensions, or domains, of personality and some of the more important traits or facets that define each domain. Together, the five domain scales and 30 facet scales of the NEO-PI-R allow a comprehensive assessment of adult personality ... The NEO-PI-R embodies a conceptual model that distils decades of factor analytic research on the structure of personality. The scales themselves were developed and refined by a combination of rational and factor analytic methods and have been the subject of intensive research conducted for 15 years on both clinical and normal adult samples. (p. 1)

Given the extensive use of this instrument throughout the discipline, along with its demonstrated **reliability** and **validity**, it becomes an ideal starting point for addressing the earlier challenges to the culture and personality school that its methods were faulty and without empirical foundation.

Starting with an early case study of Chinese culture (McCrae, Costa, & Yik, 1996), followed by Filipino and French surveys (McCrae, Costa, Pilar, Roland, & Parker, 1998),

Box 7.2

Dimensions and Facets in the Five-Factor Model of Personality

Costa and McCrae's Five Factor Model provides a synthesis of broad overarching dimensions, each of which is defined by a series of more specific facets that are in turn made up of items reflecting individual traits. We may expect evidence for cultural generality to be strongest at the level of dimensions, with greater cultural specificity attending the meaning of individual facets and especially of individual items. The facets making up each dimension give some indication of its meaning:

Agreeableness	Conscientiousness	Neuroticism	Extraversion	Openness to Experience
Trust	Competence	Anxiety	Warmth	Fantasy
Straightforwardness	Order	Angry hostility	Gregariousness	Aesthetics
Altruism	Dutifulness	Depression	Assertiveness	Feelings
Compliance	Achievement striving	Self-consciousness	Activity	Actions
Modesty	Self-discipline	Impulsiveness	Excitement seeking	Ideas
Tendermindedness	Deliberation	Vulnerability	Positive emotions	Values

McCrae and his collaborators gradually extended their investigation of personality into 36 nations (Allik & McCrae, 2004). The coverage has now expanded to 42 nations, with the respondents typically being college students with occasional adult samples (McCrae, Terracciano, et al., 2005). **Individual-level factor analyses** of NEO-PI-R data have demonstrated equivalence in the pattern of its facet groupings across all nations examined. Further, the balance between positively worded and negatively worded items in each facet has enabled these investigators to overcome the problem of **acquiescent response bias** that might distort the meaningfulness of the resulting comparisons. Following the techniques that we have discussed in earlier chapters, Allik and McCrae (2004) were next able to conduct a **nation-level factor analysis**. Their analysis revealed the important finding that the same five factors emerged at the **nation-level** as are consistently found at the **individual-level**. This parallelism enabled them to calculate the modal personality profile for each nation, yielding a 'geography of personality traits'. This 'psychography' for social scientists replaces the scattered conclusions of the **culture and personality** school, and rests on a defensible empirical basis.

Conducting secondary analyses based on these scores, Allik and McCrae (2004) conclude that:

> cluster analysis showed that geographically proximate cultures often have similar profiles, and multidimensional scaling showed a clear contrast of European and American cultures with Asian and African cultures. The former were higher in extraversion and openness to experience and lower in agreeableness. A second dimension reflected differences in psychological adjustment. (p. 13)

These conclusions are drawn from statistical associations with the two-dimensional mapping of the personality profiles of typical cultural group members that are given in Box 7.3.

This type of scaling represents the positioning of nations on all five personality dimensions simultaneously. However, we have labelled the dimensions in terms of

Box 7.3

Multidimensional Scaling Plot of 36 Cultural Groups

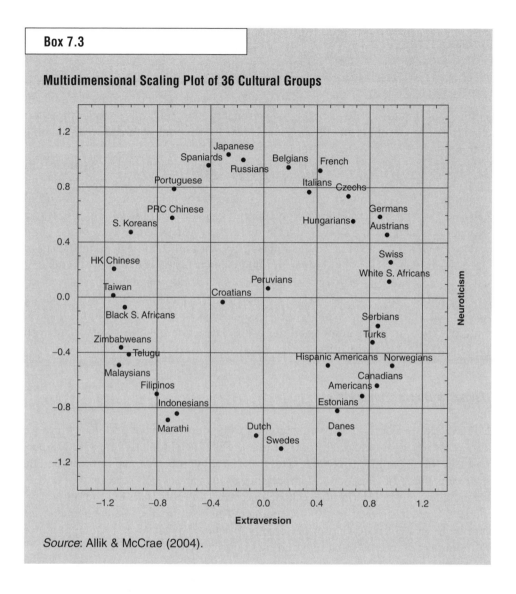

Source: Allik & McCrae (2004).

neuroticism and extraversion, because these are the two dimensions that correlate most strongly with the model. As the authors point out:

> the horizontal axis ... is positively associated with extraversion and openness to experience and negatively associated with agreeableness. People from European and American cultures thus appear to be outgoing, open to new experience, and antagonistic, whereas people from East Asian and African cultures are introverted, traditional, and compliant. Euro-American cultures are lower in power distance (i.e., they reject status hierarchies) and higher in individualism (i.e., they put self-interest before group interest); there is a trend ($p < .10$) for Euro-American cultures to be higher in post-materialist values, such as self-actualization. They also are generally wealthier, the income is more evenly distributed ..., the quality of life is higher, and people are more satisfied with their lives.

> ... cultures (and their typical members) towards the top of the figure are high in neuroticism and low in conscientiousness; (these cultures) are also high in uncertainty avoidance ... They are also low in interpersonal trust and subjective well-being. (pp. 21–2)

This approach to research on culture and personality demonstrates the possibilities of linking societal variations to the typical profiles of individual members of different nations. The results so far do not all accord with expectation. Note for instance the representation in Box 7.3 of Japan as a nation characterized by unhappiness, suspiciousness, neuroticism and low conscientiousness. Future work will increase the comprehensiveness and representative sampling of personality mapping and 'provide important clues to the origin of personality traits and their interactions with culture in shaping both individual behaviour and the collective ethos' (p. 25).

As an example of how the Big Five may be used to explain cultural differences in individual behaviour, Kwan, Bond and Singelis (1997) reported data indicating that respondent extraversion and agreeableness predicted the achievement of relationship harmony in both US and Hong Kong samples, but that conscientiousness was a stronger predictor for the Hong Kong Chinese. This result is reminiscent of the Bond and Forgas (1984) finding that Hong Kongese responded much more than Australians to variations in target conscientiousness in undertaking trusting behaviours towards that target. Variations in aspects of conscientiousness – self-restraint, planfulness, achievement-striving and diligence – all seem relatively more crucial in guiding choices about whom to seek out and whom to avoid within a collectivist compared to an individualistic culture. Where in-group responsibilities are heavier, one chooses to associate with those who are more trustworthy.

Ratings of Others' Personalities

Not only do we assess our own attributes by using dimensions of personality, but we also assess others in our social worlds. Language is a social tool, serving practical purposes. In this regard, Hogan (1982) takes the lexical hypothesis a step further when he maintains that, 'the presence and importance of the various trait terms will be lawful, not random, and will mirror the relative importance of those traits in promoting individual and group survival' (p. 59). According to this position, the relative frequency of trait terms in a given domain of personality functioning will suggest the importance of this aspect of interpersonal functioning in one culture compared to another.

Church's work on lexical representation of traits, however, suggests that cultural dynamics are *not* revealed in the relative availability of terms for each of the Big Five dimensions. In examining the Filipino lexicon, Church et al. (1996) found that the agreeableness domain had the largest representation of trait terms. One might conclude that such a relative preponderance reflects the interdependent press of the collectivist Filipino culture. However, Church also points out that, 'studies in English and Dutch at least also show the most terms in the Agreeableness domain ... The Extraversion/Surgency domain also seems to be second largest in these languages, while the Emotional Stability and Intellect domains tend to be smallest across languages. This suggests that the size of the domain may be less a function of underlying cultural values, but of other more universal factors' (personal communication), for instance the universal, functional concerns identified by Hogan (1982).

Does the size of the trait domain in natural languages parallel their social importance? Church et al. (1996) point out:

> Thus, the relative sizes of these domains may indicate their relative importance in person perception and trait attribution in a number of cultures. For example, the many facets and nuances of agreeable versus disagreeable interpersonal behaviour apparently require more elaborate encoding than the characteristics used to describe an individual's emotional stability or intellect. (p. 21)

Williams, Satterwhite, and Saiz (1998) directly measured the importance of the Big Five domains in 20 nations, concluding that across all these countries extraversion and agreeableness were the most important, emotional stability and openness to experience, the least, with conscientiousness falling in between. There were, however, exceptions to this pattern with Singaporeans, for example, rating emotional stability as most important. The authors conclude that, 'sufficient variability was observed to warrant the further exploration of between-country differences in the qualities associated with psychological importance' (pp. 126–7). Presumably these variations in importance relate to the political and economic priorities of the societies involved.

So, culture does not appear to affect the relative frequency of Big Five trait terms available in the language. Instead, culture may exercise its impact in the relative weight attached to a given dimension of personality in guiding certain social behaviours, as we saw earlier in the Bond and Forgas (1984) study. In one of the few other tests of this hypothesis, Zhang, Kohnstamm, Slotboom, Elphick, & Cheung (2002) compared free descriptions of children by their parents in Dutch and Mainland Chinese. The authors conclude that, 'Chinese parents of school-age children generated many more descriptors, mostly critical, in the domain of conscientiousness. The findings reflect the Chinese high achievement orientation and show that the classification system [*for trait descriptions*] … is sensitive to cultural differences' (p. 165, our emphasis). Parental descriptions of their children are more numerous in the conscientiousness domain because academic achievement by children of school age is so crucial to the family at that point, relative to other life concerns. This emphasis on conscientiousness-related trait terms reflects the Chinese pre-occupation with inculcating self-discipline in school-age children and maintaining social order throughout the rest of their lives. The point here is that the salience of language terms for describing personality is responsive to cultural concerns-in-context, and that these concerns may be detected by comparing the relative frequencies of words-in-use across cultural systems.

Trait terms are available for descriptions of others and as well as of the self. This availability is important for building a social psychology around personality. Of course, we believe that the personality of the actor is one factor underpinning interpersonal behaviour. When the actor's personality is considered without reference to context, however, we know from Mischel's (1968) challenge that only a small proportion of the outcome variance is explained. This is not surprising. As Hogan puts it, 'Personality is stable, but behaviour varies; it varies largely because, in order to be consistent, people must change their actions when they deal with different people' (p. 85); that is, the personality of one's interaction partner is also a key factor eliciting one's behaviour. It would seem that by pitching one's behaviour to the character of the other, for instance their reputation, status or role, one's interpersonal behaviour would be more effective, even if apparently inconsistent across different target persons.

These issues have been debated in social psychology for some time, for example within the so-called personality versus situationism controversy. Self-monitoring (Snyder, 1987) is a construct that is relevant here in pointing to individual differences. Those persons who monitor themselves are more attuned to the evaluations and expectations of others than those who do not monitor themselves. The former are therefore more likely to be affected by social situational variations. Beyond individual differences, there tend also to be cultural variations. People in collectivistic cultures tend to be more attuned to others, especially in-groups, and tend to show greater variation in behaviour across different social situations. In contrast to Hogan's claim above, some anthropologists and **cultural psychologists** propose that the variation is not only at the surface level of *behaviour*, but that even the *person*(ality) itself is being constantly reconstructed, in accordance with the roles enacted in interaction with varying others (Geertz, 1975; Shweder & Bourne, 1982). Their formulation would require that one thinks of personality not as a predisposition to behave in certain ways, but as a predisposition to respond to situational demands. These situational demands change, and in some cultures they change more than in others.

Ratings of a target person by others in terms of traits provide a way of testing just how strong are these situational effects on social behaviour. One's social behaviour is a function of one's personal motivations in combination with the characteristics of one's interaction partners and other situational factors. Ratings of target persons' traits are found to be not merely projections of the rater's own personality, but show high levels of similarity when members of a social group rate a given target person (see e.g. S.K. Leung & Bond, 2001). Furthermore, these trait ratings are organized into the Big Five dimensions that also emerge from self-ratings (Goldberg, 1981). Given the replicability of such trait taxonomies from nation to nation, the Big Five dimensions of personality can be used to summarize the personality inputs of both an actor and his or her partner in an equation predicting the actor's social behaviour.

McCrae, Terracciano and their collaborators (2005) have examined the factor structure of other-rated personality traits, using the NEO-PI-R questionnaire measure of personality. To do so, they asked college students in 42 nations to rate the personality of a man or woman whom they knew well. Within-nation factor analyses of the 30 facets constituting the NEO-PI-R replicated the organization of the normative American self-report structure in most nations; in the remaining nations, this familiar five-factor structure was still clearly recognizable. Thus, the organization of other-rated personality into the basic dimensions of extraversion, agreeableness, conscientiousness, neuroticism, and openness to experience paralleled the organization of self-ratings using questionnaire items, just as the structure of trait terms used to describe others parallels the structure of trait terms used to describe the self.

Using these other-rated personality profiles, McCrae, Terracciano, et al. (2005) were also able to compare ratings of males and females across nations. They conclude that women are rated somewhat higher on all five dimensions, just as Allik and McCrae (2004) found for self-ratings. Examining the specific facets that make up each of the dimensions, they note that, 'men are rated as being higher than women in E3: Assertiveness, E5: Excitement Seeking, O5: Ideas, and C1: Competence. Women are rated as higher on many traits, especially N1: Anxiety, N6: Vulnerability, O3: Feelings, and A6: Tender-Mindedness. Most of these effects, however, are small, with only a single instance of more than .5 SD difference' (p. 16). These gender differences in other-ratings are consistent in direction but vary in size by nation: 'As in self-report data, Asian and African cultures generally show the smallest sex differences, whereas European and American cultures show the largest' (p. 17).

In explaining the reduction in the size of gender differences in more traditional nations, McCrae et al. (2005) refer to the work of Costa, Terracciano, and McCrae (2001) and conclude:

> that the most plausible reason for cultural variability in the magnitude of sex differences was attribution of characteristics to roles. In cultures with traditional gender stereotypes, sex-typical behaviour is perceived as a reflection of role requirements rather than individual traits, and correspondingly discounted in forming an impression of the individual. This argument presumes that most or all cultures share the same gender stereotypes, an assumption that appears to be warranted. (Williams & Best, 1990, p. 557)

Other explanations are possible. For example, as we saw in Chapter 5, both males and females are socialized to develop more relational selves in more collectivist cultures. It is possible that this effect is stronger for men than for women, thus increasing the similarities between them. However, the important point here is that the use of other-ratings across so wide a range of samples not only enables researchers to assess the convergence with results using self-ratings, but also to address social psychological issues distinctive to this focus in personality assessment. For example, McCrae, Terracciano, et al. (2005) were able to compare male and females as raters, rather than as targets. Their first finding was that the differences due to rater gender were low, rarely more than .10 standard deviation of difference. When differences were found, women raters were more 'lenient' than men, especially when rating women. As the authors point out:

> When rating men, female raters described them as more straightforward and altruistic than did male raters. When rating women, female raters described them as being less anxious, self-conscious, and vulnerable, and more warm, gregarious, open to ideas and values, and competent than did male raters. All these findings are consistent with the observation that women in general are more agreeable than men, and that agreeable raters make more lenient ratings of others ... (p. 18)

These effects did not vary by nation. However, it is difficult to disentangle personal and situational effects in these results. Women may rate others more leniently because women are more agreeable, but they might also do so because others behave more agreeably towards them. Either way, if the other's personality is a factor influencing one's behaviour towards that other, then the rater's gender will have to be included as a factor in predicting that behaviour more precisely, regardless of one's culture.

Is the Five-Factor Model of Personality Complete?

The Big Five dimensions of personality variation are found in almost all nations where its factor structure has been tested against the American norms for the structure of the NEO-PI-R (Allik & McCrae, 2004). These five distinct features of personality functioning are surely useful starting points for developing a pan-cultural model for social behaviour, involving both the characteristics of the actor and those of his or her interaction partner. Each of the five has a functional basis and provides information about a person's standing on socially important concerns. But are they complete?

It is possible that additional functional concerns are salient in different cultures than those that spawned the Big Five. By sampling those cultures, investigators may adduce items that define supplementary dimensions of personality. To prove the distinctiveness of these possibly unique dimensions, indigenous personality questionnaires must first be developed (see e.g., Cheung, Cheung, Wada, & Zhang, 2003, on indigenous test development in Asian countries). Then the indigenous questionnaire should be given along with the imported measure of the Big Five, and a joint **factor analysis** of the two instruments conducted in the indigenous culture. If a distinct dimension appears over and above the Big Five, then an **emic** local dimension has been isolated (see Yang & Bond, 1990, for the earliest example of this approach). Work can then proceed to establish its local utility, and whether that indigenous dimension can also be identified in other cultural populations. If so, this sixth dimension becomes a candidate for universal status as a 'Big Sixth' dimension of personality variation.

This is a demanding research undertaking, and understandably rare. It has been attempted by Church and his colleagues in the Philippines and by Cheung in China. Katigbak, Church, Guanzon-Lapena, Carlota, & del Pilar (2002) administered three indigenously developed Filipino personality inventories along with the Filipino translation of the NEO-PI-R to students in the Philippines. They concluded that:

> (a) most Philippine dimensions are well encompassed by the FFM and thus may not be very culture specific; (b) a few indigenous constructs are less well accounted for by the FFM; these constructs are not unknown in Western cultures, but they may be particularly salient or composed somewhat differently in the Philippines; (c) the structure of the NEO-PI-R FFM replicates well in the Philippines; and (d) Philippine inventories add modest incremental validity beyond the FFM in predicting selected culture-relevant criteria. (p. 89)

Thus, there seems to have been only a modest yield from an extensive, meticulous programme of research aimed at discovering whether there are distinctive indigenous constructs of personality when placed in a head-to-head comparison with the standard Western measure of the Five-Factor Model (see also Yang & Bond, 1990). On this basis, the Filipino inventories were not translated and tested in non-Filipino cultural groups.

Working within China, however, Cheung, Leung, Zhang, et al. (2001) found clear evidence for the existence of an indigenous dimension of personality variation when respondents completed both the NEO-PI-R and the Chinese Personality Assessment Inventory in three separate studies (Cheung, Leung, Fan, Song, Zhang, & Zhang (1996). They labelled their additional dimension, Interpersonal Relatedness:

> This factor, which was originally labeled as the Chinese Tradition factor, consists of the indigenous personality scales developed specifically for the CPAI, including *Ren Qing* (relationship orientation), Harmony, and face. In addition, this factor is loaded negatively by Flexibility. The characteristics associated with these personality scales reflect a strong orientation toward instrumental relationships; emphasis on occupying one's proper place and in engaging in appropriate action; avoidance of internal, external, and interpersonal conflict; and adherence to norms and traditions. (p. 425)

There is a strongly hierarchical and collectivist logic to this dimension. Particularly noteworthy is the authors' highlighting of 'adherence to norms'. Any theory of social behaviour that gives a role to the actor's responsiveness to the normative requirements of the situation would benefit by assessing such a disposition in that actor. Combined with a knowledge of what the appropriate norms might be, the psychologist would have a ready recipe for predicting the actor's behaviour.

The next issue of importance is to determine whether the Interpersonal Relatedness factor could also be isolated as a dimension of personality among non-Chinese, especially Western respondents. Cheung, Cheung, Leung, Ward, and Leong (2003) have provided such evidence by administering the NEO-FFI (a shorter measure of the Big Five) and an English-language translation of the CPAI both to Singaporeans and to Caucasian-Americans. Their results replicate the earlier Chinese results: a sixth independent dimension of personality identified as Interpersonal Relatedness emerges from the joint **factor analyses**. As the authors suggest, 'the absence of Interpersonal Relatedness in a Western instrument may "point to a blind spot" in Western personality theories, specifically the interdependent domains that receive relatively less attention in Western personality theories' (p. 450). Again, such a dimension is crucially important for theories of social psychology. The social situation itself has been neglected by most contemporary theorists of social behaviour. Indeed few such theories have focused on social behaviour rather than cognitive processes. If we wish to explain behaviour, then a personality measure of responsiveness to interpersonal influence and normative situational force will be most helpful. Cheung et al. signal this way forward by concluding, 'In future studies, we will validate the functional equivalence of Interpersonal Relatedness by examining its external behavioural correlates in different cultural contexts' (p. 450).

Box 7.4

Do Bilinguals have Two Personalities?

In assessing the structure of personality across cultures, any inventory of personality must be translated from its language of origin into the language of the receiving culture. The accuracy of this translation procedure is usually ensured by having competent bilinguals translate and back-translate the questionnaire, then resolve any discrepancies. The original and the translated versions of these questionnaires may then be given to a separate set of bilinguals to further check on the accuracy of the translation (e.g., McCrae, Yik, Trapnell, Bond, & Paulhus, 1998). Differences in the facet or dimension scores would then be used to adjust scores from the two language groups when comparisons are made.

An alternative way to conceptualize these differences is to use the shift in bilinguals' profile across their two languages as revealing their dual personalities – one learned for use in each language. This logic was first applied by Ervin (1964) when she administered Thematic Apperception Test pictures to French-English bilinguals and asked, 'Do these findings [of content differences across languages] mean that our subjects have two personalities? The answer seems to be yes, at least to the extent that personality involves verbal behaviour … ' (p. 506). The initial stimulus for exploring personality shift as a function of language was the linguistic relativity hypothesis of Whorf (1956), who argued that different languages provided different worldviews, so that a language shift would entail a personality shift. More recently researchers have framed the 'personality shift' in terms of what they call the 'culture framing hypothesis' (Hong, Morris, Chiu, & Benet-Martinez, 2000). The argument is that

(Continued)

Box 7.4 Continued

bilinguals are bi-culturals who have acquired two internalized cultures with personalities consistent with the two cultural systems. The language of the personality question-naire cues the culturally appropriate personality, so that the bilingual's apparent personality shifts towards the modal personality found among native speakers of the bilingual's second-language. For example, Ramirez-Esparza, Gosling, Pennebaker, and Benet-Martínez (2004) compared the responses of Spanish-English bilinguals to the Big Five Inventory (Benet-Martínez & John, 1998). When responding in their second language of English, Spanish-English bilinguals 'were more extraverted, agreeable and conscientious in English than in Spanish and these differences were consistent [though not as strongly] with the personality displayed in each culture' (p. 19).

Such shifts in responses towards the position of a cultural group when using one's second language as a first language has been called 'cross-cultural accommoda-tion' (Bond & Yang, 1982), and observed in many studies (e.g., Harzing & Maznevski, 2002). Occasionally, however, the opposite pattern of 'ethnic affirmation' occurs, i.e., the bilingual shifts away from the position of their second-language culture and gives responses even stronger than those produced by typical members of their first-language culture (Yang & Bond, 1980; Bond & Cheung, 1984). A given language shift can thus produce personality shifts in either direction. But, how can bilinguals have such flexible personalities? Instead, it would seem more sensible to regard questionnaire responses of bilinguals in their second language as being unconscious self-presentations directed towards the audience that typically uses that language. The more familiar the bilingual is with that second culture, the greater the accommodative shift they may be expected to show. In cases of cultural conflict, however, they will affirm their ethic identity by overreacting, with the strength of that reaction dependent on the strength of the identification they wish to claim with their first-language culture.

Cross-cultural versus Intra-cultural Variation in Personality

In discussing the average scores for the Big Five dimensions in their 36 nations, Allik and McCrae (2004) remind us that, 'These mean values do not, of course, characterize each individual, but they do provide a sense of the typical personality that could facil-itate cross-cultural interactions' (p. 25). When considering these validly computed **citizen scores** we must always remember their origin from individual responses that themselves show considerable variation from nation to nation, cultural group to cultural group.

As Poortinga and van Hemert (2001) point out, a matrix of individual scores on a given personality test provided by persons from many nations produces a matrix of scores whose variability may be expressed as between-nation variance and between-person variance for individuals nested within nations. The between-nation variance refers to the variance of what we have been calling **citizen scores** or national averages on a given aspect of personality; between-person variance refers to the average within-nation variance of scores on that aspect of personality. The between-nation variance may be expressed as a proportion of the total variance in the matrix of scores, yielding some surprising results:

> From a data set containing scores on the four scales of the Eysenck Personality Questionnaire, including 153 studies from 38 countries, estimates of (this proportion) were derived: .14 for Psychoticism, .17 for Extraversion, .16 for Neuroticism, and .25 for the Lie scale ... Similar computations for the 10 types of Schwartz's value scale (Schwartz, 1992), based on samples of teachers and samples of students from 38 countries showed (proportions) ranging from .06 for stimulation to .21 for conformity. (p. 1045)

These results are surprising and important, because cross-cultural psychologists tend to highlight cultural differences at the expense of individual variability. They may forget that the mean scores used to claim difference themselves derive from distributions of individual scores. Cultural differences are simply one way of pulling apart the full range of individual difference across the pan-cultural array of data. On personality and on values, intra-cultural variation is substantially greater than inter-cultural variation. There is a clear implication of this finding: it will more often be fruitful to do cross-cultural studies at the **individual-level**, using measures that are known to be valid cross-culturally than to do studies that compare mean scores at the level of nations. In Chapter 6, we reviewed some studies that '**unpackaged**' culture in this way, using measures of self-construal and values. The Big Five studies make it possible to do similar studies using personality scores.

Intriguing questions are provoked when the size of cross-cultural variation is compared against that of individual variation: for which variables is cross-cultural variation relatively stronger? Why, for example, is the cross-national proportion of variance for conformity so much higher than that for stimulation in the Poortinga and van Hemert (2001) results? What is it about the nations involved that render the value of conformity to be more responsive to societal variation? In particular, what is the role of social norms and traditions? Does the value attached to stimulation derive from temperamental characteristics of a population that are more evenly distributed across the cultures of the world? Does the value attached to conformity derive from the degree of hierarchy in social relations that is very differently distributed across the cultures of the world? What features of personality are more resistant to societal influence, and if so why? More generally, how should we now conceptualize the way that personality and culture influence one another? Box 7.5 provides two contrasting viewpoints.

Box 7.5

Personality and Cultural Values

The availability of nation-level scores both for personality and for values, makes it easy to test the correlations between them. All four Hofstede dimensions are significantly associated with scores on one or more Big Five personality dimensions:

(Continued)

Box 7.5   Continued

Big Five Dimensions	Power Distance	Uncertainty Avoidance	Individualism (versus Collectivism)	Masculinity (versus Femininity)
Extraversion	−.57		.64	
Conscientiousness	.52			
Openness to Experience	−.39			.40
Neuroticism		.58		.57
Agreeableness		−.55		−.36

Note: The direction of these correlations refers to the variables that are not placed in brackets.

Hofstede and McCrae (2004) debate how best to interpret the meaning of these correlations. McCrae sees personality as having a strong genetic component. Consequently, he expects that the predominance of a particular profile of genes in a given nation will encourage the development of cultural adaptations to whichever personality type prevails locally. Over centuries, those whose personalities do not fit well may also be more likely to emigrate. Hofstede concedes that there may be some genetic basis to personality, but points out that the variation of personality types and of differing ethnic origins within large nations indicates that other causes for cultural difference must be sought. For instance, we can expect that those who grow up within a given cultural context will be socialized to express their personality in culturally appropriate ways.

Source: Hofstede & McCrae (2004).

Future Directions

Progress over the past decade in establishing valid ways of comparing personality across cultures has opened the way to a broader range of investigations. We next explore several such growth points.

Personality as a Relational Orientation   Fiske (1991) proposed a 'relational models' theory, based initially on an analysis of ethnographic field studies in West Africa. 'The theory proposes that there are four fundamental models that people use to interpret, construct and evaluate relationships. These models are understood to be universal cognitive structures with which people coordinate their interpersonal lives, according to implementation rules and parameters supplied by their local cultures' (Caralis & Haslam, 2004, p. 398). The four models are:

> Communal sharing (CS) relationships are based on an understanding that relational partners are equivalent and undifferentiated and have a shared identity, and are common within romantic couples, families and sporting teams. Equality matching (EM) relationships, which

are common among friends, are based on a sense of egalitarian balance: people keep track of favors and obligations and maintain balance by in-kind reciprocity, equal divisions of labor, and turn-taking. Authority ranking (AR) relationships, common in hierarchical organizations and between parents and children, are based on status asymmetries: one person leads and takes precedence and the other follows and defers. Market pricing (MP) relationships follow a principle of proportional equity, each person seeking to gain a suitable rate of return for their investment of time, money or effort, and are common within work groups. (Caralis & Haslam, 2004, p. 398)

The authors have shown that within the USA, these four relational tendencies are associated with different personality profiles using the Big Five dimensions. It is, however, possible to argue that personality lies precisely in one's interpersonal style and that an interpersonally oriented social psychology should be assessing such relational orientations as a point of departure. Extending such work cross-culturally would be logical, since many of the typologies of nations we have examined use dimensions that seem to map closely onto these relational styles. For example, one would expect that a preference for authority ranking in one's interpersonal motivations and behaviour would be more frequent in persons from nations higher in Schwartz's (1994) hierarchy or Bond et al's (2004) societal cynicism. Cross-cultural comparisons using Haslam and Fiske's (1999) Modes of Relationship Questionnaire and Haslam, Reichert, and Fiske's (2002) Relationship Profile Scale would be revealing and encourage a more social approach to social psychology across cultures.

Using Implicit Measures of Personality   Some personality researchers have recently been extending the range of constructs assessed by implicit measures of personality. For instance they assess motives for intimacy using the Thematic Apperception Test (TAT) or implicit self-esteem using the association of positive and negative valences to the self (Greenwald & Farnham, 2000). These measures can add power to our typically used explicit measures of values, beliefs or self-construals in predicting important outcomes. So, for example, McAuley, Bond, and Ng (2004) found that the prediction of life satisfaction in working Hong Kong adults was improved beyond that provided by measures of traits, values and strivings by an implicit TAT measure of affiliative motive. Hofer and Chasiotis (2003) used congruence between implicit and explicit measures of achievement and affiliation/intimacy motives to improve their prediction of life satisfaction in Zambian male adolescents.

   Given the additional value of implicit personality measures, there is a clear incentive for cross-cultural psychologists to begin incorporating them into their toolkit of tests. Additional support for this initiative comes from Cohen (1997), who has reminded us that many cultural differences in behaviour may be driven by automatic processes. His rationale for this judgement is that:

because they are either so over-learned (or were never explicitly taught in the first place), they may bypass conscious processing altogether. Our verbal reports and judgments are most clearly tied to conscious levels of processing, and so they may never get connected with the cultural rules embedded in our preconscious. (p. 126)

In consequence, it may well be crucial for cross-cultural social psychologists to begin tapping these unconscious processes guiding behaviour by returning to the use of implicit measures.

The use of implicit measures is demanding on the experimenter, since considerable training is often required to score the respondent's protocols with adequate inter-rater reliability, as was the case when researchers in the psychoanalytic tradition originally developed these types of test. There is an additional problem when implicit measures are brought to the cross-cultural arena: the **imposed-etic** materials and tasks required to extract the respondent's score on the relevant construct are often unfamiliar, even intimidating, to respondents in new locations. Hofer and Chasiotis (2003) administered TAT cards to Zambian adolescent males and discovered that the 'cue strength' (that is, the amount of imagery) elicited by each card differed, as was to be expected, but that each card's cue strength also varied from that found in their German sample. Apparently, the 'same' situation depicted on each TAT card had different elicitation power for the three basic motives measured, exactly as one would expect if culture operates by shaping the meaning of any given situation.

Direct cross-cultural comparisons require that cards have equivalent 'cue strength'. In response to this frustration with traditional TAT test stimuli, Hofer and Chasiotis (2004) have been seeking to develop 'bias-free' picture sets for both the TAT and their more recent Operant Motives Test (Friedlmeier, Hofer, Chasiotis, Campos, & Nsamenang, 2004), by trying to equate their cue strength. Should they solve this problem of equivalence, the way is open to discover what can be done to improve our predictive reach with such tests of implicit processes, especially in conjunction with explicit tests.

Developing If-then Models for Social Behaviour   The logic that personality variations drive behaviour may not be as simple as we proposed at the outset of this chapter. Since Mischel's (1968) classic text, the discipline has been struggling to develop models of behaviour that predict a higher percentage of the variance in observed behaviour than is provided by information about actor personality alone. In line with our previous discussion, the obvious solution is to incorporate measures of the situation into the predictive equation. Hogan (1982) believes that the crucial element in the situation is other persons, be they interaction partners or imagined reference groups. These others may be characterized in terms of their perceived personalities (Bond & Forgas, 1984) or the interpersonal norms they are expected to apply during the interaction (Ohbuchi et al., 2004), or the norms surrounding the behavioural expression itself (Heise & Calhan, 1995).

In terms of the issues that we are exploring in this book, the key situational variation is the cultural context. To what extent would an individual who is high on extraversion behave in the same way in different parts of the world? We have seen that cultures vary in the extent to which they foster individual autonomy. So, extraverted behaviour needs to be expressed within the limits that a particular culture specifies. Role theory provides a framework that can help us to identify the ways in which culture funnels the expression of personality: behaviour could be more completely explained by incorporating the actor's assessment of the interaction episode (Forgas & Bond, 1985), or the role relationship characterizing that interaction (McAuley, Bond & Kashima, 2002), or the actor's belief system about the world in which he or she must function (Leung & Bond, 2004). Each of these potential supplements to our prediction of social behaviour has been shown to vary across national groups, and so may be an important adjunct to our explanations of social process across cultures. Regardless of which situational factors are considered important, our predictive models will need to become more complex than the simplistic formula: personality predicts behaviour. Instead, the field will begin fleshing out Shoda and Mischel's (1996) 'if-then' models for explaining behaviour, where the 'ifs' refer to the personality of the actor in conjunction with some aspect of the situation he or she faces.

As a first instance, we can consider what happens when a relatively introverted child goes to school in different nations. Chen and his colleagues compared the school experiences of 2,000 9- to 12-year-old children in China, Brazil, Italy and Canada (Chen, He, De Oliveira, et al., 2004; Chen, Zapulla, Lo Coco, et al., 2004). They were particularly interested in the experience of 'shy-sensitive' children, compared to other children. The sampled nations were selected to illustrate the range from a strongly collectivist nation to a strongly individualist nation. Children reported their self-perceived competence and loneliness, while information on social behaviours was assessed by peer nominations and teacher ratings. Shyness-sensitivity was found to be positively associated with reported loneliness and negatively related with self-perceived social competence most strongly in Canada, less strongly in Brazil and Italy and not at all in China. The lonely children in China were the aggressive ones, not the shy ones. Overall levels of loneliness did not differ between nations after **acquiescent response bias** had been discounted. Thus, it is just as possible for a child to be lonely at school in a collectivist nation, but shyness and sensitivity are not the handicap that they are within schools in more individualistic nations.

Friesen's (1972) work on emotional display in public versus private situations by Japanese and Americans also showed a probable difference in responsiveness to situational variation across nations. When this situational variation is combined with personality variation, we expect that cultural dynamics will be revealed in the different interactions between personality and situation found from culture to culture. There are very few studies that provide more direct evidence in the cross-cultural literature. In Chapter 6 we discussed Matsumoto et al.'s (2002) findings concerning situational effects on emotional expression. More recently, Oishi, Diener, Napa Scollon, and Biwas-Diener (2004) surveyed reports of positive and negative affect among students in Japan, the USA and India, when they were in each of five different everyday settings. Their interesting findings include further instances of culture-driven situational effects. For instance, respondents from the more collectivist samples showed a larger increase in positive feelings when they were with others rather than alone than did respondents from the more individualist samples. This study relied on reported affect rather than a personality measure, but it makes clear how cultural effects can be **unpackaged** not by using personality alone, but by using personality–situation interactions.

Summary

Psychologists have attempted to explain the differences in typical behaviours of persons from different cultures by assessing the typical personalities of individuals from those cultures. Early attempts to do so were frustrated by the unreliable and unfamiliar instruments available for personality measurement. Psychometric progress in the last three decades has enabled psychologists to export translated versions of extensive personality questionnaires to many countries. Because the structure of these questionnaires has proven to be equivalent across cultures, personality psychologists can now compare the profiles of persons across cultural groups, i.e., their **citizen scores**.

The results of this work have combined with those emerging from lexical studies of various languages around the world to indicate that personality may be described across five basic dimensions – extraversion, agreeableness, conscientiousness, emotional stability and openness to experience. These features of individual variation appear to be grounded in pan-cultural issues of interpersonal and societal functioning, so that the typical profile of individuals from a given nation represents that nation's solution to the challenge presented by its particular ecological-historical legacy. Nations can now be compared in terms of how they position their typical members' personality across the Big Five dimensions.

Indigenous study of Chinese personality indicates that the Big Five are an incomplete representation of personality variation. A sixth dimension named interpersonal relatedness has been found and replicated in other, non-Chinese cultural groups, and constitutes an important addition to the basic five. It may be especially relevant in more collectivist cultures. Implicit measures of personality have also been refined for use across cultures and shown to add power to the explicit measures in predicting outcomes of interest, like life satisfaction. These refinements to the personality approach are being supplemented with information about the social situations facing individuals, so as to produce more accurate predictions of their social behaviours.

Further Reading

1 Cheung, F.M., & Cheung, S.F. (2004). Measuring personality and values across cultures: Imported versus indigenous measures. www.wwu.edu/psychology/~culture
2 Church, A.T. (2001). Personality measurement in cross-cultural perspective. *Journal of Personality, 69*, 979–1006.
3 Church, A.T., & Katigbak, M.S. (2002). Studying personality traits across cultures: Philippine examples. www.wwu.edu/psychology/~culture
4 Hofstede, G., & McCrae, R.R. (2004). Personality and culture revisited: Linking traits and dimensions of culture. *Cross-Cultural Research, 38*, 52–88.
5 Hogan, R., & Roberts, B.W. (2000). A socioanalytic perspective on person/environment interaction. In W.B. Walsh, K.H. Craik, & R.H. Price (Eds.), *New directions in person-environment psychology* (pp. 1–24). Hillsdale, NJ: Lawrence Erlbaum.
6 McCrae, R.R. (2002). Cross-cultural research on the five-factor model of personality. www.wwu.edu/psychology/~culture
7 Triandis, H.C., & Suh, E.M. (2002). Cultural influences on personality. *Annual Review of Psychology, 53*, 133–160.

Study Questions

1 What sorts of variation in personality are observed across the nations of the world?
2 What does the variation in personality observed across the nations of the world tell us about the national factors that affect this variation?
3 If most of the variation in personality occurs at the individual-level, how scientifically useful is it to characterize the 'personality' of nations?
4 How would you explain the finding that gender differences are greater in European and North American nations than they are in the rest of the world?

8 Communicating and Relating with Others

> 'When I use a word', Humpty Dumpty said, in a rather scornful tone,
> 'it means just what I choose it to mean – neither more nor less.'
> 'The question is', said Alice, 'whether you can make words mean so many
> different things.'
>
> (Lewis Carroll, *Through the looking glass*)

In the preceding chapters, we have identified several ways to characterize individuals that take account of cultural differences. We have cross-culturally valid measures of values, beliefs, self-construals, personality and aspects of emotional experience, what one might call 'the psychological software'. It is time to move the focus away from the psychological interior and towards the ways in which individuals conduct their relations with one another. In doing so, we shall again emphasize studies in which researchers have used one or other of these earlier measures of **cultural orientation**, since this will enable us to emphasize the need for theory involving individual differences in **unpackaging** variations in interpersonal relationships in different cultural contexts.

Styles of Communication

Verbal Communication

We can expect that people's **cultural orientation** will be reflected in the ways that they communicate with one another, both verbally and non-verbally. Growing up within a given cultural context will provide socialization as to what aspects of others' communications to attend to as well as what it is worthwhile for oneself to speak about, when to speak about it, and how to do so. Perhaps the most basic way in which this complex set of considerations is accomplished is through the usages that have become integrated into different language systems. We have noted already Kashima and Kashima's (1998) finding that use of the personal pronoun 'I' is more strongly required in languages spoken within individualist nations.

For a long time the relationship between language and culture has been studied in terms of the different ways languages classify items of experience. For example, as is well known by now, Inuits have many words for types of snow, which they apparently experience in more finely distinguished ways than is the case for most other people.

Classification of kinship terms has been of great interest to anthropologists in reflecting the variations in the importance attributed to distinctions in kinship relationships. For example, in Turkish there are three words for aunt and three words for uncle, referring to whether the relationship is through the paternal or the maternal side or through marriage. In a similar way, some languages have more extensive provision for expressions of deference and hierarchy than do others. For instance, Japanese has three separate levels of formality and also requires men and women to speak in different ways.

No study is yet available that has determined whether there is any systematic relation between these types of language features and nation scores on dimensions of culture, such as power distance. Interestingly, Munroe, Munroe, and Winters (1996) have shown that words within languages spoken in hot countries differ from those spoken in cooler parts of the world. Languages originating in hot countries contain many words with alternating vowels and consonants (Malawi, Malaya, Panama), whereas cold country speech has many more consonants (e.g., in English – awkward, screech, stretch). Hot country languages are easier to decode because of their regularity, and Munroe et al. suggest that they evolved to permit easier communication over longer distances outdoors. Cold country languages were more likely to be spoken in sheltered or indoor settings. However, the locations in which the world's most widely spoken languages are spoken now bear little relation to the places in which they originated.

Languages also differ in the relative proportion of different parts of speech. Semin, Gorts, Nandram, and Semin-Goossens (2002) predicted that in cultures where relationships and interdependence are salient, emotions serve as relationship markers and will be more often expressed concretely as verbs. Conversely, they predicted that in cultures where emotions serve to identify the self, emotions will more often be represented abstractly as nouns and adjectives. As predicted, they found verbs more frequent in Hindi and Turkish, but nouns and adjectives more frequent in Dutch. Since verbs are cognitively more accessible than nouns and adjectives, different languages may prime different ways of thinking. More evidence is required of the ways in which such effects may occur, and there is a long history of controversy concerning linguistic effects on cognition, as illustrated in Box 8.1.

Box 8.1

Does Language affect Cognition?

In 1956, Lenneberg and Roberts reported a link between language and cognition. They compared memory for colours of monolingual speakers of the Native American language Zuni and of Harvard undergraduates. Zuni has a single word for yellow and orange. Shown a series of colours, Zunis were unable to recall which were orange and which were yellow. Similar effects were later obtained by various researchers sampling cultural groups from hot countries that also lacked words for some colours. These studies are often cited as evidence for the Whorfian hypothesis, which states that language constrains the way that we are able to think.

(Continued)

Box 8.1 Continued

More recently it has been established that chronic high levels of ultraviolet radiation (UV-B) in tropical latitudes leads to a loss of sensitivity to blue and green. Lindsey and Brown (2002) showed that native English speakers viewing colours through lenses simulating these effects had a similar inability to name colours. This suggests that lack of colour names in some languages of cultural groups is a *consequence* of their inability to identify and remember certain colours, not a cause of it. However, loss of sensitivity cannot explain all the studies of language effects. Turkish has two words for blue, *mavi* (blue) and *lacivert* (dark blue). Turkish speakers have been found better able to discriminate differing shades of blue than English speakers. Moreover, it has also been shown that training improves the ability of English speakers to discriminate between shades of blue (Özgen & Davies 2004). This finding suggests that the existence of an additional colour term in Turkish does over time encourage the development of greater colour sensitivity.

Sources: Au (2004); Özgen & Davies (2004)

Given that one is speaking a particular language, there are choices to be made as to how to express oneself. Kim (1994) developed a theory of what she called conversational constraints. These are ways in which one might wish to limit the effects of what one says. Kim proposed that speakers within collectivist cultures would constrain themselves not to hurt the hearer's feelings and not to impose themselves on others. Within individualist nations on the other hand, she predicted a constraint favouring clarity of expression. Initial evidence showed support for the predictions among samples from Korea and the USA. In a further study, Kim, Hunter, Miyahara et al. (1996) included measures of self-construal and increased the range of specified constraints. Respondents in Korea, Japan, Hawaii and mainland USA were asked how important each of five constraints would be in a series of imaginary scenarios. Constraints favouring the task outcome of the scenario were rated more important in the USA and this effect was **mediated** by the respondent's level of **independent self-construal**. Constraints favouring relationship harmony were rated more important in the Pacific Asian samples, and this effect was **mediated** by the respondent's level of **interdependent self-construal**.

Service encounters of various sorts, such as getting a technician to repair a 'frozen' computer, obtaining a room for a night at a hotel, ordering coffee at a café, are occasions when the interdependency of conversation becomes highlighted. Persons wishing to be served are dependent on the service provider to deliver the desired service. They will want to obtain the service as quickly and fully as possible without offending the service provider, thus maintaining the relationship for possible future use. Chan, Bond, Spencer-Oatey, and Roja-Laurilla (2004) examined how the concern of persons seeking service to protect and promote their relationship with the service providers varied for Filipinos and Hong Kong Chinese, using scenarios involving five different types of service delivery. They found strong differences across the five situations, with those seeking service more concerned to promote a relationship when the service provider had discretionary authority in delivering that service. Filipinos were more concerned than Chinese about relationship promotion in only one of the five scenarios, and this was a request for computer repair, where the conditions of service delivery in the Philippines put them into a more dependent position than it did in Hong Kong. However, endorsement of Schwartz's (1992) dimension of self-transcendence **mediated** concern, regardless of nationality. Those who valued interpersonal harmony and peacefulness more were generally more eager to nurture and promote the relationship with the service provider by communicating in face-saving and non-conflictual ways.

The models of Kim and of Bond et al. are formulated in terms of individuals' desire to constrain their behaviour to attain relationship goals. However, the process shaping the conversational results on which they focus could equally well be considered in terms of cultural norms. Although systematic studies of cultural differences in norms are few, there are qualitative accounts from many collectivist cultures of the prevalence of norms favouring harmony. For instance, persons from Hispanic cultures are said to endorse *simpatía* (Triandis, Lisansky, Marin, & Betancourt, 1984), Greeks give value to *philotimo* (Vassiliou & Vassiliou, 1973), which stresses the importance of the in-group, Indonesians favour *rukun* (Oerter, Oerter, Agostiani et al. 1996) and *kapwa* is a key concept to Filipinos (Enriquez, 1993). Studies could easily be conducted where respondents are asked for their perceptions of the operative norms in communication exchanges, and these normative impressions related to the respondent's communication content and style.

The contrast between communication styles that are preferred within individualist and collectivist cultures was discussed by Hall as long ago as 1966. Hall proposed a contrast between low-context and high-context cultures, by which he implied that in individualistic cultures a communication is treated as a relatively separate event, without much reference to the particular interpersonal context within which it occurs. In contrast, in collectivist cultures he proposed that communications are treated as integrally linked to the context of relationships within which they occur, including the history of the interactants, their common ground of shared understandings, and the setting of their interaction. This contrast has consequences for the ways in which communication is likely to be expressed. For instance, if one's relationships with others are already well established and there is high priority given to maintaining the existing state of harmony, communication is likely to be less explicit and more indirect, since context carries meaning that does not need to be verbalized. There will be no need to spell out those aspects of the relationship that are unchanging. Conversely, in a low-context communication, we can expect greater directness and less ambiguity.

Holtgraves (1997) developed a self-report measure of conversational indirectness. Separate scales assessed whether one speaks indirectly and whether one looks for indirect meanings in what others say. Koreans scored higher than Americans on both scales. Using Holtgraves' measure, Sanchez-Burks, Lee, Choi, et al. (2003) showed that Korean and Chinese business students took more account of indirect messages than Americans and that this effect was **mediated** by a measure of **interdependent self-construal**. Similar **mediation** effects were also obtained among students in Hawaii (Hara & Kim, 2004).

Gudykunst, Matsumoto, Ting-Toomey, Nishida, Kim, and Heyman (1996) drew on Hall's concepts to develop a broader range of measures of high- versus low-context communication styles, and to relate these measures to self-construal. Among students from the USA, Japan, Korea, Hawaii and Australia, **independent self-construal** was associated with use of dramatic, feeling-oriented, precise and open communication, as well as ability to interpret indirect messages. **Interdependent self-construal** predicted greater sensitivity and negative attitudes toward silence. As Gudykunst et al.'s results illustrate, the contrast between high- and low-context nations has broader applicability than Kim's model of constraints, because it focuses upon receiving communications as much as on sending communications. Furthermore, drawing on the contrast between high and low context, Kitayama and Ishii (2002) compared the attention given to passages of emotional speech by Japanese and US listeners. Using a task where emotional tone and the words used were inconsistent with one another, they were able to show that Japanese attended more to the vocal emotion that was expressed, while the Americans attended more to the content of the words that were used.

The results of the studies that we have discussed in the preceding paragraphs need to be evaluated cautiously, for a reason that is important in relation to the issues that are discussed throughout this book. If collectivist cultures are high-context cultures, then the way that persons within those cultures choose to communicate with others will depend upon whom they are communicating with. Of course, communication style will also vary between contexts in low-context cultures. One speaks to one's partner in a different manner than to how one speaks to a teacher, a bank manager, or a stranger. However, the variation should be greater in high-context cultures. The in-group/out-group distinction is important here. In general there is greater difference between behaviours and communication within one's in-groups and with out-groups in collectivist societies than in individualistic societies. We have seen already that **interdependent self-construal** is associated with seeing oneself or other persons differently in different contexts. Consequently, conclusions about differences in communication style that hold across all contexts are open to challenge. We may find that communication in high-context cultures is direct in some settings and indirect in others. The distinction between communication with known in-group members and out-group members is likely to be a particularly important one.

In Chapter 6, we reported the findings of Redford and Smith (2004) that cultural differences in anger expression towards different targets were **mediated** by self-construal. Extending this analysis, it would be possible to explore individual difference variables not only as **mediators** of the communication process but as **moderators** of it. So, for example, more interdependent persons should show greater variation in their communication activities across social contexts than less interdependent persons. While all persons show variation in their social performance across social contexts, certain individuals will show this variability to a greater degree. These individuals may be more typical of a given cultural group compared to another, giving each cultural group its distinctive communication style. This use of personality as a **moderator** of effects across social contexts is becoming more widely used to help resolve the person-situation debate (Fleeson, 2004). Research of this kind is more demanding, because it requires that each participant be observed across a number of situations, but the extra work will yield otherwise unavailable scientific benefits.

Gudykunst, Gao, Schmidt, et al. (1992) compared in- and out-group communication among students in Hong Kong, Japan, Australia and the USA. When ratings for in-group and out-group persons were compared, several significant differences were found among the more collectivist samples from Japan and Hong Kong. Respondents reported more questioning of each other, more feelings of similarity, more shared networks, and more feeling that they could understand the others' feelings without their being explicit in in-group communication. US and Australian respondents did not show any significant differences between in- and out-group communication. As suggested above, this difference between in-group and out-group communication outcomes may well be predicted by respondents' level of **interdependent self-construal**, and different strengths of this self-construal in each cultural group may **mediate** the observed cultural differences.

Much remains to be learned about cultural differences in communication style. Self-report measures may have limited validity, particularly when they do not specify whom one is interacting with. Studies that sample actual dialogue may give us a richer understanding. Nelson, al Batal, and el Bakary (2002) analysed Egyptian and US spoken refusals to requests said to have been made by someone of high, equal or low status. Egyptian men were the most direct, but the greater deference toward persons of higher status did not differ between the two nations. In a similar, earlier study, Nelson, el Bakary, and al Batal (1993) focused upon the giving of compliments. Here too, they found the Egyptians at least as direct as Americans. Egyptian compliments were more elaborated, often using metaphors.

The finding that Egyptians favour direct communication styles is important. It points to the risks of generalizing findings obtained in some collectivistic nations, mainly in East Asia, to all collectivistic nations. It may be that the indirect forms of communication commonly found in research with East Asian respondents are due more to East Asian tact or modesty or face-saving than to collectivism, as such. There may be other ways of communicating that maintain the integrity of collectivist in-groups.

Non-verbal Communication

One could argue that an excessive focus on the verbal content of communication is itself culturally biased. At least in high-context cultures, the evidence that we have already discussed indicates that we may learn more by broadening our focus to include the various non-verbal aspects of the communication process. These include facial expressions, gestures, proximity and touch. Research studies in this area have only rarely drawn upon cross-cultural theory and mostly provide us with simple descriptive contrasts. The difficulty in this field of study may stem from some of the definitional issues that we discussed in Chapter 3. Non-verbal communication is most typically studied by observation of behaviours. However, as we noted in Chapter 3, behaviours can have different meanings in different contexts, and consequently, although some attempts have been made (Andersen, Hecht, Hoobler, & Smallwood, 2002), it is difficult to integrate these observations with conceptualizations of culture that stem from the meanings that are given to what goes on around us. For instance, someone who spends a high proportion of time looking at another person may be judged in one part of the world by that other person to be communicating friendliness, but in another to be showing insufficient deference, or even hostility. Li (2004) analysed video recordings of Canadian and Chinese students role-playing a doctor–patient interview. Canadian same-gender pairs showed more than twice as much mutual gaze as same-gender Chinese pairs. How should we understand this dramatic difference?

Proximity The greatest amount of data on non-verbal communication concerns preference for proximity. Watson (1970) asked pairs of students from 31 nations attending the University of Colorado to sit at a comfortable distance and converse with one another. Arabs and South Asians sat closest, followed by Latin Americans and South Europeans. Next most distant were East Asians and finally 'North Europeans' (who included North Americans and Australians). Although this study has some weaknesses, such as small sample size and variations in how well the partners said they liked each other, the range of nations sampled is unusually broad and entirely apt when studying this question. Sussman and Rosenfeld (1982) found that previously unacquainted Venezuelan negotiators sat closer than did US negotiators, who in turn sat closer than the Japanese negotiators. The particular interest of these studies is that they array national samples in a different way to that implied by studies of **independent** and **interdependent self-construals**. Despite strong interdependence, persons in East Asian nations prefer to keep their physical distance from one another. One possibility, at least among Europeans, was indicated by Holland, Roeder, van Baaren, Brandt, and Hannover (2004), who found **independent self-construal** to predict greater actual spatial distance during seated conversations between German students. Similar distance effects were found by priming independence among Dutch students.

In the Sussman and Rosenfeld study as in Nelson et al.'s Egyptian studies, gender effects were as large as the differences found between nations. We would similarly expect differences for different gender pairings across cultures, but at present we have few explanations of the way in which the meaning of proximity varies between nations that would help us explain the differences.

Spatial positioning Aside from simple distance, the positioning of people in relation to one another can convey different meanings in different locations. Marriott (1993) provided evidence concerning spatial positioning within Japanese business firms. Through observing meetings in Japan, she noted that seating position represented the relative seniority of each person present. In contrast, Australian managers took no account of status in determining where to sit. Thus, they failed to read contextual cues that would have enabled them to relate more effectively with the Japanese managers with whom they were meeting. The Japanese were probably also confused in their judgements of seniority among the Australians.

Touch Together with his differentiation of high and low context cultures, Hall (1966) also proposed a parallel contrast between contact and non-contact cultures, referring to variations in the amount of touching. Proximity makes both touching and maintaining eye contact easier, and Watson (1970) also found that those who sat closer touched one another more frequently. Shuter (1976) also observed close proximity and frequent touching among Latin Americans. Remland, Jones, and Brinkman (1995) surreptitiously videoed people talking to one another while standing in public places in six European nations. Greeks and Italians showed more touching than did the French, Dutch, British and Irish. However, overall touching rates are unlikely to be useful because different types of touch most probably have different meanings. Illustrating this difference in meaning, Dibiase and Gunnoe (2004) observed couples in nightclubs in Boston, Prague and Rome, distinguishing between hand touches and non-hand touches. Overall, men did more hand touches and women did more non-hand touches. Touching was more frequent in Italy and the Czech Republic than in the USA, with hand touches more frequent among the Czechs and non-hand touches among the Italians. However, hand touches were more frequent by Czech men but by Italian women, suggesting that the meanings of different types of touch can be quite culture-specific. Nevertheless, the overall amount of touching, particularly between same-sex persons, may illustrate Kağıtçıbaşı's (1996a) relatedness-separateness dimension.

Gestures The frequency of use of 20 different hand gestures across 40 locations in Western Europe has been documented (Morris, Collett, March, & O'Shaughnessy, 1979). Some were more widespread across nations than others. However, there are well-known variations in the meanings of many gestures, for instance 'V' signs and the 'A-OK' gesture, as well as head nodding and shaking. We lack a theory to explain the way in which such meanings have evolved. There is also substantially more gesturing in some nations than others. Graham and Argyle (1975) found that gesturing in Italy enhanced the effectiveness of communication more than in other locations. Low gesture rates are thought to be associated with greater formality and gesturing may therefore be less frequent in high power distance cultures. On the other hand, bowing may be largely restricted to hierarchical cultures, although it is not found in all such cultures, since relative status can also be signalled in many other ways, including variations in proximity, gazing and spatial positioning.

Facial Expressions In Chapter 6 we discussed evidence for universal *recognition* of expressions of emotions. However, we may also make additional inferences from facial expressions. Matsumoto and Kudoh (1993) showed photographs of smiling and neutral faces to Japanese and Americans. Smiling faces conveyed sociability to all respondents, but Americans also judged smiling faces as more intelligent. In a similar study, Albright, Malloy, Qi, et al. (1997) compared Chinese and Americans. Both saw smiling faces as more sociable, but the Chinese also saw them as lacking in self-control and calmness. Thus, there is evidence for both universality and cultural distinctiveness in reactions to smiling and therefore in the meanings attributed to it.

Silence It is often said that Japanese make extensive use of silence, for instance to signal disagreement without the need for direct contradiction. Hasegawa and Gudykunst (1998) compared American and Japanese attitudes toward silence. They proposed that silence can be thought of as an extreme example of high-context communication, which should therefore be more frequent in Japan than in the USA. Their study also included the important distinction between communicating with close friends and with strangers. Two dimensions were identified: using silence strategically and viewing silence negatively. As expected, Japanese reported being silent more frequently. Their reactions to silence varied, depending on whether they were with friends or strangers. They were more uncomfortable being silent with strangers, whereas for Americans it made no difference whether they were with friends or strangers. Americans reported more strategic use of silence than did the Japanese, which contradicts the stereotypic belief that it is Japanese who use silence strategically. This stereotype may have arisen because American observers of the Japanese scene projected their own cultural logic about silence onto the Japanese. However, Hasegawa and Gudykunst propose that their result is plausible, because low-context Americans will be more self-conscious during silences, whereas Japanese will be less self-conscious and will therefore see the use of silence as natural rather than strategic.

Giles, Coupland, and Wiemann (1992) found a similar contrast between American and Chinese attitudes toward silence, although they found the Finnish to be even more comfortable than the Chinese with silence. There are sayings in many societies, for example in Turkish, 'if speech is silver, silence is gold', which reflect traditional values upholding reflection and caution before acting or speaking and frowning upon verbosity. Speech is so basic an element in all social life that one wonders what cultural dynamic could be responsible for the different meanings of silence across cultural groups.

Emotional Display Non-verbal expressions are often associated with the experience of various emotions, with each emotion having its distinctive profile of observable behaviours. Wong and Bond (2005) examined display profiles for the experience of joy and anger across the 30 national groups in the ISEAR database created by Walbott and Scherer (1986). Emotional reactions were measured by verbal, non-verbal, and movement responses. Across nations, they found that joy elicited more verbal reactions, more non-verbal reactions, and more moving towards the other than did anger. For joy and for anger, both the felt intensity of the emotion and the desire to control its emotional expression influenced the degree and type of emotional reaction. Although the strength of the linkage between intensity, desire to control expression and its associated emotional reaction was relatively constant across the 30 nations, there were also variations between desire to control and the expression of anger, depending on the type of display involved. It thus seems that we cannot simply say that some nations are more expressive than others; expression depends on emotional intensity and on socialization for control of expressing that emotion using any particular channel.

Success and Failure in Communication

The preceding sections have reviewed verbal and non-verbal aspects of communication, and found the relevant literatures to lack coherence because the majority of studies have not been built upon a cumulative development of theory. An alternative approach to communication has been to develop and test theories that focus on successful and unsuccessful aspects of communication. Specific theories of this type that focus upon processes such as leadership and negotiation will be discussed in Chapter 9. Here we discuss a more general approach, which explores the related phenomena of face, politeness and embarrassment. The parties to any communication process have a shared interest in achieving its purposes. As Goody (1978) puts it:

> The basic constraints on effective interaction appear to be essentially the same across cultures and languages; everywhere a person must secure the co-operation of his interlocutor if he is to accomplish his goals. To secure cooperation, he must avoid antagonizing his hearer. (p. 6)

Politeness An initial step toward achieving and sustaining cooperation is to be achieved by addressing the other party in a manner that will be judged appropriately polite.

Holtgraves and Yang (1990, 1992) compared judgements of how polite were various ways of phrasing requests (e.g., 'Go, get the mail', 'Would you mind getting the mail?') by US and Korean students, in relation to status differences and closeness of relationship. Americans showed a stronger preference for the more polite forms of address and were more likely to use them. Holtgraves and Yang explain this by noting that US respondents rated themselves as more distant from the person of whom they were making the request than the Koreans did. Greater distance required greater politeness. The effects of status and of closeness were relatively similar in each sample. However, as we would expect, Koreans took more account than Americans of variations in context when choosing which degree of politeness to use. Ambady, Koo, Lee, and Rosenthal (1996) coded videotapes of interactions, also sampling Korean and US respondents. By comparing codings of audio and video versions of the same interactions, they found variations in non-verbal 'circumspection' as well as in verbal behaviours, depending upon the degree of politeness that a particular context required. Consistent with studies reviewed earlier in this chapter, Koreans' politeness strategies were again more affected by the relational aspects of the setting, whereas Americans were more affected by the politeness of the actual words that had been addressed to them.

Of course, not all communicators wish to be polite. What is found to be insulting is likely to vary in different cultural contexts. In particular we may expect that, in individualist nations, insults will tend to be targeted at the individual who has given offence, whereas in collectivist nations insults could also focus on the group to which that individual belongs. Uskul and Semin (2004) compared insults that are available in the Dutch and Turkish languages. While most insults in both languages are addressed to the individual, there are more 'relational' insults in Turkish, which is presumed to be the more collectivist cultural context. Turkish insults more frequently refer to others who were close to the person who was insulted, especially that person's mother (e.g., various imagined sexual acts directed towards the mother) and are more frequently relational (e.g., that she is ill-mannered or unreliable). Dutch insults more frequently refer to illness or to membership of outgroups (e.g. you are old, ugly, belong to an ethnic minority). Furthermore, when asked how offended they would be if someone insulted their mother, Turks reacted more strongly.

Face   Politeness strategies may or may not succeed. If they fail, there will be some loss of face to the parties involved. In individualistic cultures, if it is my strategy that fails, it is I who will risk losing face, unless I can engage in some form of defensive facework that alleviates the problem. Facework was first analysed in Western settings by Goffman (1959), who identified a range of actions through which one might discount or redress a loss of face. In collectivistic settings the situation becomes more complex. Ting-Toomey (1988) formulated a theory of face negotiation that takes account of collectivist issues. Her theory emphasizes that if my identity is defined by my group rather than by myself as an individual, then *my* loss of face will also cause *you* to lose face. You and I therefore have a shared interest in avoiding loss of face. The preference for harmony in collectivist groups is focused around anticipating and forestalling any loss of face within one's dyad or group. The focus upon context and upon indirect styles of communication can therefore be seen as forms of preventive facework.

Languages spoken in collectivist cultures reflect concerns with face. For instance, Chinese has two characters, *lian* and *mianzi*. *Lian* refers to personal or moral integrity, whereas *mianzi* refers to the social face that one displays in relation to others (Ho, 1976). *Mianzi* has parallels with *chemyon* in Korean and *mentsu* in Japanese (Choi & Lee, 2002). In studies where Ting-Toomey and her colleagues have tested face negotiation theory cross-culturally, these concepts are referred to as self-face and other-face, and a third concept of mutual-face was also required. The need to invent new English phrases in order adequately to represent these concepts provides a timely reminder of the way in which any one language cannot necessarily capture important aspects of another culture. In this case the language of an individualistic cultural tradition, English, cannot encompass the complexities of collectivist relational concerns except by creating tailor-made words and links among these new words.

Oetzel, Ting-Toomey, Masumoto, et al. (2001) compared self-construals, face concerns and facework strategies employed during interpersonal conflicts in China, Germany, Japan, and the USA. As would be expected, they found that **independent self-construal** was associated with self-face concerns, while **interdependent self-construal** was associated with other- and mutual-face concerns in all cultural groups. A further analysis by Oetzel and Ting-Toomey (2003) showed that concern with self-face wholly **mediated** national differences in a form of facework referred to as dominating. In other words, the threat to one's own face was averted by seeking to shift the blame to the other party. In contrast, other-face concern partially **mediated** national differences in types of facework referred to as avoiding and integrating. In other words, the threat to other-face was averted by downplaying the conflict or by seeking joint solutions, and persons with higher levels of other-concern were more likely to use these harmonizing facework strategies.

Embarrassment When facework fails, some degree of embarrassment is likely to occur. Singelis, Bond, Sharkey, and Lai (1999) administered an embarrassability scale to students in Hong Kong, Hawaii, and mainland USA. In all samples, two factors were identified, self-embarrassability and empathetic embarrassability, defined as the shame that one feels for others who violate social expectations. This distinction parallels Ting-Toomey's definitions of self- and other-face, providing a further illustration of the way in which concepts that derive originally from studies in collectivist cultures may nonetheless be applicable and useful in individualist cultures. As expected, the Caucasian-Americans scored lower on the embarrassment measures than did the Asian-Americans and the Hong Kong Chinese. Singelis et al. also obtained measures of independence and interdependence and showed that group differences in self-embarrassability and empathetic embarrassability were partially **mediated** by low independence and high interdependence, respectively.

Face and embarrassability need also to be understood from a developmental perspective, since they are ingrained in the socialization of children in any culture. Ridiculing and shaming are some of the socialization strategies designed to develop a sense of embarrassment and face-concern towards others over time. It appears that shaming is used more readily in collectivistic cultures, where others' evaluations are very important, and blaming (to instill a feeling of guilt) is more central in individualistic cultures. For instance, Conroy, Hess, Azuma, and Kashiwagi (1980) compared the words that Japanese and US mothers said they would use to respond to a series of child misbehaviours. Japanese mothers stressed the feelings that misbehaviours would cause and the consequences for others, using phrases such as, 'It will be annoying to them if you misbehave'. US mothers much more often referred to infractions of rules and authority that the child is supposed to have internalized, using phrases such as 'You know better than that'. The former input emphasizes interdependence and concern for others; the latter, independence and responsibility.

Relating to Others

The processes of communication that we have considered in this chapter lead over time to the establishment of a rich variety of different types of social relationship. These may be conceptualized in terms of closeness and separation, in other words the interpersonal distance dimension that we have discussed already in Chapter 5. We should also expect that distinguishing in-group and out-group relations will shed further light on the observed variations in relating to others. Before giving detailed attention to issues that are salient within the various types of in-group relationship, we give some consideration to cultural differences in the ways in which we relate to strangers.

Strangers

Early studies provided some confirmation of travellers' subjective impressions that people are much more helpful to strangers in some parts of the world than in others. For instance, Feldman (1968) reported a higher percentage of helpful responses to a request for help in Athens than he did in Paris or London. However, to understand such differences, we need careful matching of locations and request procedures along with the inclusion of a broader sample of nations. Such a study was completed by Levine, Norenzayan, and Philbrick (2001). Three separate measures of helping were collected in the largest city within each of 23 nations. In the first task, a trained accomplice accidentally dropped a pen while walking past a single pedestrian. In the second task, as a pedestrian approached, an accomplice who appeared to have hurt his leg dropped a pile of magazines and struggled to pick them up. In the third task, the accomplice, dressed as a blind person, waited at a pedestrian crossing as the light went green to see who might help.

Percentages of helpful response in the three scenarios were moderately and positively correlated across the 31 nations, yielding an overall index of helpfulness. Helpfulness varied between 93% in Brazil and 91% in Costa Rica to 40% in Malaysia and 45% in New York. In seeking nation-level explanations for these large differences, Levine et al. found no support for links with **individualism-collectivism**. However, helpfulness was moderately predicted by low walking speed (Levine & Norenzayan, 1999) and by lesser affluence. Levine et al. also predicted that the endorsement of *simpatía* in Hispanic cultures would lead to greater helpfulness. The five Hispanic nations in their sample were indeed significantly more helpful, but the study did not include any measure of *simpatía*. Nor are plausible measures of this interpersonal disposition available from other cross-national studies, so it is not yet possible to confirm Levine et al's speculation about the psychological processes involved in such helping behaviour. Some caution is also needed in interpreting these results, since the experimental accomplice was a different person, albeit a local, in each country sampled. Nonetheless, the study focuses on an important social behaviour, and underlines the need for a richer theory in explaining cultural differences.

Several constructs might be involved as underlying mechanisms here, such as the in-group/out-group distinction, traditional hospitality norms, and differing understandings of what is moral behaviour. For example, in a comparison of Indian and US respondents' moral reasoning, Miller, Bersoff, and Harwood (1990) found that morality for Indians was focused particularly on beneficence and social responsibility, whereas for Americans the moral code was defined more in terms of justice and freedom (individual choice). There are clear implications of such variations for the incidence of helping behaviours.

While Levine et al's study stands alone as an exemplar of cultural aspects of pro-social behaviours towards strangers, there are of course many studies of *un*helpfulness to strangers. We consider studies of prejudice and intergroup relations in Chapter 11.

Approaches to Understanding Interpersonal Closeness

The current predominance of concepts derived from individualism and collectivism in cross-cultural research highlights the need to distinguish between in-groups and out-groups, especially if we are to understand the behaviours of members of collectivist cultures. But how shall the boundaries be drawn between in- and out-group membership, and do they differ between cultures? In traditional Chinese culture, a distinction has been made between *jia-jen* (family members), *shou-jen* (relatives outside the family, neighbours, friends, classmates and colleagues), and *sheng-jen* (strangers) (Goodwin and Tang, 1996). In Japan, a *shin-yu* relationship (lifelong confiding friendship) was reported to have characteristics more akin to marriage relationship in Germany (Salamon, 1977). Brazilians distinguish friends (*colegas*) from very close friends (*amigos*). Box 8.2 gives details of another aspect of relationship style that may be distinctive to Japan: *amae*.

Box 8.2

Amae – A Relationship Style Indigenous to Japan?

Japanese persons quite frequently relate to one another in a distinctive manner referred to in Japanese as *amae*. In a first attempt to explain the phenomenon to a wider audience, Doi (1973) translated this term as 'indulgent dependence'. An *amae* episode typically occurs between two persons, and involves one relatively junior person making what would in most circumstances be considered an unreasonable demand on a more senior person. Furthermore, this demand is made with the presumption that the demand will in fact be accepted, as indeed it often is.

(Continued)

Box 8.2 Continued

Yamaguchi (2004) has made a series of studies of *amae*. Initial surveys among the Japanese population indicated that a high percentage of respondents agreed that they do engage in *amae*-type relations, either in the family, at work, or among friends. Although *amae* relations most probably originate in childhood, *amae* episodes are also reported as frequent among adults. In an attempt to define what are the essential components of an *amae* relationship, Yamaguchi next asked participants to evaluate whether *amae* was present in each of a series of scenarios describing situations in which inappropriate demands or behaviours occurred. 87% reported that *amae* was present when the protagonists were described as presuming that their demands would be met, with lower percentages when no presumption was made. However, the scenarios did not yield direct evidence of how presumption is actually communicated between the two parties.

Yamaguchi argues that *amae* provides an effective means for upward influence within Japan and possibly other collectivist cultures because of the nature of attachment within collectivism. The presumption that the demand will be met affirms the strength of attachment. To test his interpretation, adults were presented with descriptions of children's behaviour in the 'strange situation' that has been much used to study the attachment of infants to their caregivers. In this procedure, the caregiver leaves the child with a stranger temporarily, and the child's behaviour is noted during separation and after the caregiver's return. Cross-cultural studies have shown substantial variations in infant response (Harwood, Miller, & Izarry, 1995). Yamaguchi found that infants described in ways that characterize the 'secure-attachment' response were the ones that his respondents predicted would show most *amae* behaviour. In contrast, *amae*-type behaviour by a child within a Western nation might be expected to be more typical of insecurity. (Rothbaum, Weisz, Pott, et al., 2000)

Though initially assumed to be uniquely Japanese, *amae* may be relevant in other collectivistic societies as well. For example, there are terms in Turkish and Persian with rather similar meanings.

A long time ago, Kurt Lewin, the pioneer of modern social psychology, already commented on differences in the meaning of friendship in Germany and the USA (Lewin, 1936). He perceived German friendships to start more slowly but to be deeper and more permanent than their American variant. Current findings referring to a lesser number of friends but greater closeness to one's best friend in collectivistic societies (e.g., Verkuyten & Masson, 1996, to be taken up later; Wheeler, Reis, & Bond, 1989) seem to point in the same direction, though Germany appears to be much more individualistic today than in the 1930s (Keller & Lamm, 2005). In individualistic societies, especially in the USA, being sociable and having many friends is a good thing. Initiating contact with new people appears to come easily, as a part of being 'friendly', for example saying 'Hi!' to passers-by on a university campus. Thus, the 'outer' layer of the self is more open or penetrable, but then there is a rather less penetrable inner layer, the 'private' inner self. In collectivist contexts on the other hand, the outer layer appears to be more impenetrable, but once the other person is accepted as a 'friend', there tends to be more disclosure to him or her (Kağıtçıbaşı, 1996b). Relationship formation may thus have different tempo and rhythm in different cultural contexts.

In contrast to these categorical distinctions between relationship types, some researchers have recently used **imposed-etic** measures that assume that relationships can be arrayed along a dimension of closeness. Fijneman, Willemsen, and Poortinga et al. (1996) asked students in Greece, Turkey, Hong Kong, the Netherlands, and the USA to rate how close they were to each of six types of family member, a close friend, a neighbour, an acquaintance, and a stranger. Closely similar rank orders of the ratings were found in all samples, with parents rated closest. Closeness ratings were found to correlate strongly with the degree to which respondents would be willing to support each person and how much they would expect support from them.

Fijneman et al. (1996) argue that these results negate **individualism-collectivism** theory because no differences are found between samples, even though they span nations said to be both individualist and collectivist. However, this conclusion is debatable. The strength of the correlations between closeness and support is likely to rest primarily on the inclusion of numerous family members and the contrast between them on the one hand and neighbours and strangers on the other hand. **Individualism-collectivism** theory does not assert that families are unimportant to members of individualist nations, nor does it negate the fact that more emotional and material investments would be made to those closer to oneself than to those distant from oneself (Kağıtçıbaşı, 1999). We must look in more detail at what 'closeness' is.

Aron, Aron, and Smollan (1992) provide a similar conceptualization and operationalization of closeness. They developed an 'Inclusion of Others in the Self' (IOS) scale in Canada. Respondents are asked to portray their closeness to various others by choosing between seven pairs of circles that vary between overlapping with one another to increasing degrees of separation. Uleman, Rhee, Bardoliwalla, Semin, and Toyama (2000) compared ratings on the IOS scales relating to family, relatives and friends by students from the USA, Japan, Netherlands, and Turkey. Ratings were repeated using a series of different criteria for closeness, such as similarity, harmony and reputation. Across cultural groups, family and friends were rated closer than relatives. However, the basis of closeness varied between nations. Among Dutch and Caucasian-American respondents, closeness rested most on supportiveness and least on similarity with others and on their reputation. Among Turks and Asian-Americans, closeness was distinctively associated with reputation and with harmony. For the Japanese, harmony alone was the strongest basis for closeness and similarity the weakest. So, although the outcomes may be similar across cultural groups, the rationales for that outcome may vary and do so in ways consistent with the logic of individualism and collectivism.

Li (2002) compared IOS responses of Chinese and Canadian students. Chinese reported greater closeness to their families. Using a different measure, Claes (1998) found Italian and Belgian adolescents to report greater closeness to their families than Canadian adolescents. Uskul, Hymie, and Lalonde (2004) compared IOS scores from Canadian and Turkish students for family members, romantic partners, friends and acquaintances. Ratings were completed once for actual closeness and a second time for desired closeness. Turkish respondents scored higher on both actual and ideal closeness. Both samples placed romantic partner ahead of family, then friends and then acquaintances. This study also included self-construal measures, and interdependence was found to partially **mediate** the effects of nation on both actual and desired closeness.

The IOS studies do help to clarify which relationships are most salient to respondents and the extent to which they may rest on different bases within different cultural contexts. However, more specific forms of measurement can help to pin down these differences. Verkuyten and Masson (1996) surveyed same-sex friendships among the various ethnic groups living in the Netherlands, while also measuring **independent** and **interdependent self-construal**. Moroccans and Turks showed higher interdependence than Dutch and Southern Europeans. Interdependence was found to be associated with greater closeness with one's best friend, but a lesser number of other friends. Interdependence also predicted having more rules about how to represent one's best friend in dealing with third parties. These findings recall the description of *shin-yu* friendship in Japan, as well as observations of the contrast between friendship in Hong Kong and the USA (Wheeler, Reis, & Bond, 1989), and as we noted earlier, even perhaps Lewin's contrast between German and American friendship. Within collectivist societies, friendship appears to be more intense, more focused, and more exclusive.

We can see just how important this type of friendship is, by reflecting on the study of life satisfaction by Kwan, Bond, and Singelis (1997). These authors developed a measure of reported levels of harmony in one's relationships. As one would expect, some of the variance in life satisfaction was explained by respondents' self-esteem. In addition, relationship harmony was **mediated** by **interdependent self-construal** in predicting additional variance in life satisfaction. Furthermore, the amount of life satisfaction explained by relationship harmony relative to self-esteem was greater in Hong Kong than it was in the USA. In a similar way, a measure of family cohesion was a stronger predictor of low emotional distress in Japan than in the USA, even after controlling for self-esteem (Abe, 2004).

Family Relations

Many of the types of interpersonal relations studied cross-culturally refer to relations with family members. Some studies are exclusively psychological, tapping intimate relations and attachment (to be dealt with in the next sections), while some build upon anthropological work on the family spanning many decades. In Chapter 5 we presented a general model of the family in a socio-cultural context (summarized as Box 5.4), which involves family interactions as one of its components. Family interactions have both interpersonal and intergenerational aspects, each of which varies systematically in families built upon the models of **interdependence, independence,** and **psychological interdependence**. These variations are the outcomes of different socio-cultural-economic contexts that entail different lifestyles (Kağıtçıbaşı, 1990, 1996b).

Similarly, Georgas, Berry, van de Vijver, Kağıtçıbaşı, & Poortinga (2006) have recently studied family relations in 27 countries, using Berry's (1976, 1979) **eco-cultural** framework. Across these countries, Kağıtçıbaşı's distinction between psychological and material family interdependencies is supported. Affluence is found to be the most powerful predictor of psychological rather than material family interdependence. Going beyond affluence, religion also explains some of the variance in family values, roles and relations. This type of **eco-cultural** research is valuable in looking into both similarities and differences in family relations across cultures.

Intimate Relations

Seki, Matsumoto, and Imahori (2002) asked Japanese and US students to rate the intimacy level of their relations with mother, father, lover and same-sex best friend, and to rate the frequency of various intimacy-related actions and feelings. Japanese intimacy was found to be more strongly associated with feelings such as appreciation, ease and 'bond', whereas American intimacy was more strongly associated with engaging in physical contact. However, there were differences dependent on relationship type. Japanese preferred direct communication with their same-sex, presumably *shin-yu*, best friend and indirect communication with others, whereas Americans preferred direct communication with lovers and indirect communication with parents and same-sex best friend.

While Seki et al. (2002) chose to apply the concept of intimacy to a wider range of one's relationships, the remainder of this section is focused upon relationships that

---

Box 8.3

Finding a Partner

United Kingdom	India
Professional Male Brown haired, blue-eyed male, 28, 5 feet 9 inches seeks female, 24–34 for friendship and more. **Smart, Petite** Fun-loving female, 27, seeks genuine male for friendship, maybe more. **Smooth Operator** Gay male, 41, 6 feet, 14 stone, smooth, likes pubs, clubs and cinema. Seeks male for fun and friendship. **Laugh a Lot** Warm and witty individual and independent female seeks interesting bloke 25–35 to laugh and love with. **Don't Sweat, It's Easy from Here** Attractive male, 60s, looks 50s, professional, slim, 5 feet 6 inches, very good sense of humour, likes skiing, music, eating and entertaining would like to meet caring, petite, slim, attractive female, on/off piste for lovely long run.	**Father** ISRQ executive seeks alliance for son, 26, 5 feet 11 inches, BE MS, employed in USA, visiting India in December from North Indian Brahmin girl. **Pune-based** Keralite Christian parents Marthomite invite proposal for their employed son, M.Com, first class CA, fair, clean, God-fearing, financially sound, from parents of professionally qualified Christian girls above 5 foot 2 inches. **Horoscope** With biodata invited from professionally qualified boys for Palakkad Iyer girl BDS (Dentist) currently doing internship in Bombay. **Physician** 186, 29, MD, employed hospital Delhi. Caste no bar, professional preferred.

Sources: *Independent on Sunday* (London), 6 June 2004; *Times of India* (Mumbai), *Sunday Matrimonials*, 16 December 2001.

have an explicitly sexual element. The major studies in this field have been conducted from the perspective of evolutionary theory. Researchers have therefore been particularly interested in identifying those universal aspects of male–female relationships that may contribute to the survival of the species. In discussing these studies, we give equal attention to the search for universals, and to the potential of cross-cultural theories for explaining aspects of the findings that are culturally variable. Box 8.3 provides an illustration of some rather striking contrasts in the qualities sought in partners within contemporary UK and India.

Gender Differences Buss (1989) surveyed gender differences in preferred qualities of a heterosexual partner among more than 9,500 students from 37 nations. Across the entire sample, men were found to prefer partners who are young, healthy and beautiful, whereas women preferred partners who are ambitious, industrious and have high earning potential. In a further analysis of the same data, Buss, Shackelford, and Leblanc (2000) found evidence that among men, the greater the preferred difference between their own age and that of their (younger) partner, the larger is their preferred number of children. As they had predicted, no such effect was found among women. Using samples from Korea, Japan, and the USA, Buss, Shackelford, Kirkpatrick, et al. (1999) found that men were more threatened by the sexual aspect of infidelity, whereas women were more threatened by the emotional aspect of infidelity. In a 62-nation survey discussed more fully below, Schmitt and 120 co-authors (2003) found men to report greater desire for a variety of sexual partners than women. Men were also found more frequently to report having seduced a partner from another relationship or to have allowed themselves to be seduced from their current relationship (Schmitt, 2004). The results of each of these studies are presented as evidence that men's behaviour is interpretable in terms of their biological mandate to father as many children as possible, while women's behaviour is interpreted in terms of their stronger priority to ensure the survival of their own genes by nurturing the children that they have already borne and to sustain a relationship with a male who will provide for them.

While each of these surveys has found the predicted gender effects, the very large samples employed have ensured that effects which explain only a modest amount of variance do achieve statistical significance. In Buss's (1989) survey, gender differences accounted for just 2.4% of variance. In contrast, further analyses of the same dataset yielded differences between the results from different nations that accounted for an average of 14% of variance (Buss and 49 co-authors, 1990). The greatest variation was in preferences as to whether one's partner should be chaste or sexually experienced, which accounted for 37% of variance. Buss et al. used multidimensional scaling to cluster the nations within which desired mate characteristics were most similar. The principal contrast that they identified was between nations that they described as traditional and modern, but their data included no measures of **cultural orientation** of those whom they had sampled. It is rather ironic that even though much greater variance was explained by culture than by gender, this study is extensively cited as demonstrating the significance of evolutionary/biological determinants of partner preferences.

The Buss data have been re-examined more recently. Shackelford, Schmitt and Buss (2005) factor analysed the 18 characteristics of a potential partner and identified four individual-level factors. These were labelled as love versus status, dependable/stable versus good looks and health, education and intelligence versus desire for home and children, and sociability versus similar religion. Chan (2004) tested hypotheses about **nation-level** predictors of scores on these factors. She found that on average persons from more affluent nations had a stronger preference for love, dependability, education and sociability in their partner than had those from less affluent nations. These correlations were strong to moderate, suggesting a powerful background role for economic development in shaping the basis by which the marriage bond is established. This result is reminiscent of the Georgas et al. (2006) finding of the powerful role of affluence in influencing family relations across cultures. Gender is important, but so, too, is culture, in particular the priorities that result from economic development and the associated prevalence of individualistic rather collectivist values.

Researchers favouring evolutionary theory have the benefit of a coherent theory against which to test their hypotheses. However, even here care is needed in evaluating whether some of the abstract qualities that are specified by evolutionary theory have similar meanings in different settings. Box 8.4 illustrates this issue in relation to physical attractiveness. In accounting for the much stronger cultural effects on partner choice, firmer theoretical bridges are required than are yet available. We explore some additional studies that may help us forward.

Box 8.4

Physical Attractiveness

Are the same attributes seen as attractive in different cultures? Evolutionary theorists have emphasized that features which convey youthfulness make an individual attractive, especially among women. For instance, McArthur and Berry (1987) found that 'baby-faced' women, that is to say those with large eyes, full lips, smooth skin, small noses and round faces were judged more attractive in both Korea and the USA. However, Wheeler and Kim (1997) showed that while physically attractive persons in the USA are judged to be more potent, in Korea they are judged to be more sensitive. Thus attractiveness can have different meanings in different contexts. It is also possible that whatever proportions are average within a particular cultural group are judged the most attractive. Sampling in Brazil, Paraguay and the USA, Jones and Hill (1993) found both young age and 'averageness' significantly affected attractiveness for both genders, but that baby-faced features were also important for perceptions of attractiveness of women.

Slender physique is currently rated as most attractive in Western nations, although it appears that this was not the case historically. Furthermore, there is evidence that slender physique is not seen as most attractive within all contemporary cultures. Hodes, Jones, and Davis (1996) found that Anglo mothers in the UK found slimmer girls more attractive, while mothers in the UK originating from South Asia, Mediterranean nations, the Caribbean and Africa did not. Cogan, Bhalla, Safadedeh and Rothblum (1996) found that larger body sizes for both men and women were rated as more attractive in Ghana, but not in the USA. Furnham, Moutafi, and Baguma (2002) found that both men and women students preferred slender female body shapes in the UK and Greece, but a heavier shape was preferred in Uganda. These results indicate that wider sampling casts some doubt on the predictions derived from evolutionary theory that youthful appearance always maximizes female attractiveness.

Attachment and Culture   In Chapter 5, we explored the manner in which different family structures have evolved within differing cultural environments. Family structure has a twofold linkage with intimate relationships, in the sense that families are at the same time built around a relationship that is sexually intimate and to varying degrees relationally intimate between the parents, and also socializing their offspring towards particular styles of attachment, which will in due course colour their later preferences for an adult partner. Models of family thus predict varying bases of interpersonal attachment. Families built upon the **model of interdependence** are likely to favour attachments for their offspring that are based upon the needs of the family as a whole. Marriages are likely to be arranged on behalf of offspring rather than by individual initiative. Families built upon the **model of independence** will encourage the autonomy and self-reliance of their offspring, and this autonomy will extend to partner choice. Romantic attachment will be the norm. Families built upon the **model of psychological interdependence** will favour partner choice that takes account of the preferences of both the individual and the family.

Consistent with these predictions, it is often stated that romantic love is characteristic of individualist nations, while 'companionate' love is more frequent within collectivist nations (Dion & Dion, 1995; Hatfield & Rapson, 1996). Levine, Sato, Hashimoto, and Verma (1995) provided a preliminary test of such a hypothesis. Students in 11 nations were asked, 'If a man (woman) had all the other qualities that you desired but you were not in love with them, would you marry them?' Substantial percentages of respondents from India, Pakistan and Thailand answered that they would. The percentage who agreed that they would across the 11 nations correlated +0.56 with Hofstede's collectivism scores for these nations. However, such a simple equation of romantic love with individualism is not convincing. Without any more specific definition, respondents may understand 'love' in different ways. Indeed, a study offering respondents a variety of definitions of love did detect significant differences across eight nations in favoured 'love styles' (Neto, Mullet, Deschamps, Barros, et al., 2000). In Levine et al's study, willingness to marry without love was almost as low in some samples said to be collectivist, such as Hong Kong and Brazil, as it was in the individualist nations that were sampled. The affluence of nations was a better predictor of unwillingness to marry without love, correlating at +0.70 for this sample of nations. This result is consistent with Chan's (2004) findings.

The 62-nation data analyses referred to above formed part of the recent International Sexuality Description project (Schmitt et al., 2003, 2004). Respondents numbered nearly 18,000, most of whom were students. Respondents were asked a series of simple questions intended to tap their style of attachment to those with whom they had close relations. They rated whether the extent to which they had a positive view of self and a positive view of others. These items are **imposed-etic**, being derived from earlier studies in the USA (Bartholomew & Horowitz, 1991). Combinations of responses to questions of this type yield scores on four types of attachment: secure (positive view of both self and others), dismissive (positive view of self and negative view of others), preoccupied (negative view of self and positive view of others), and fearful (negative view of both self and others). Having presented some evidence favouring the cross-cultural validity of their measures, Schmitt et al. (2004) then report that in most nations the secure type of attachment is endorsed more strongly than the other types of attachment. While this might be interpreted as evidence of a universal attachment style, Schmitt, et al. note that respondents from nine Asian nations, ranging from India to Japan, all report a more positive view of others than of themselves. This result is consistent with our earlier discussion of the self-effacement tendency in many East Asian cultures, and may well reflect different styles of relating oneself to others. Bond et al. (2000) have found that other-enhancement in personality ratings correlates with an **interdependent self-construal** and with a social reputation as being both helpful and restrained. These results connect Schmitt et al.'s attachment results to the more general body of theory concerning collectivism and suggest that there are observable social consequences to such self-effacement.

In a separate analysis of their data, Schmitt et al. (2003) compared the responses of men and women to their measure of attachment styles. Expectations based on earlier research that men would favour dismissive styles more than women were not fully upheld. Gender differences were small and differed by nation. Men were more dismissive than women only within the more affluent nations in the sample. The results of this large scale survey thus found some evidence for universality for gender effects in attachment style, but also some evidence for cultural **moderation** of this effect. However, the measures that were used do not provide the type of adequately rich characterization that would be required to detect the attachment styles to be expected on the basis of Kağıtçıbaşı's (1996b) typology of family relations. Furthermore, since most persons sampled were students, respondents living within fully interdependent families would be underrepresented, because they are less likely to enter university.

Rothbaum, Pott, Azuma, et al. (2000) argue persuasively that if Western models of attachment are used as the basis for theorizing about relations in Japan, we fail to gain a full understanding of Japanese attachment styles. This proposition has much broader applicability. Studies using an **emic** approach may give us some indication of what can be gained from studies that use a broader brush. For instance, Rothbaum and Tsang (1998) have analysed the content of popular romantic songs in China and the USA. American songs focus more frequently on the present positive qualities of the loved one, while Chinese songs have more references to sadness, the future and the context where love occurs. Romance may be universal, but the manner in which it is expressed may vary, dependent upon the broader context of interpersonal relations within different cultures. We need better measures before studies in this field can be linked adequately with cross-cultural theory.

We also need to bear in mind that romantic relations are not always harmonious. Archer (in press) compared rates of physical aggression between partners in 12 nations. He found that within Western nations, physical aggression by women towards men was as frequent as physical aggression by men towards women, especially among student samples. However, physical aggression by men towards women predominated in India, Jordan, Japan, Nigeria, Korea and especially in Papua New Guinea. Predominance of aggression by men was strongly and negatively correlated with an index of gender empowerment. These results are not consistent with the types of evolutionary theory that have guided many researchers in this field, and suggest that gender roles evolve in response to changes in social power.

Summary

The way in which we communicate with others is constrained by the way in which we think about ourselves and the degree to which this self-construal causes us to take account of our social context. Successful communication rests on shared assumptions about politeness, how to handle threats to face and the transience or permanence of particular relationships. Cultures differ in respect of non-verbal behaviours, but we do not yet have clear explanations of the way in which these variations relate to values, beliefs or self-construals. There is a greater difference between communication with in-group and out-group members in collectivist cultures than there is in individualist cultures. Friendships are more focused, more intense, and more permanent within collectivist cultures, whereas in individualist cultures intimacy is more strongly associated with romantic love. Some aspects of gender relations are universal, but cultural variations in the preferred basis of gender relations outweigh these effects. The extent to which attachment processes vary between national groups shows promising connections to theorizing about collectivism and individualism, but more culturally responsive measures are needed along with extensions of this work into less modernized social systems and their populations.

Further Reading

1 R. Goodwin (1999). *Personal relationships across cultures*. London: Routledge.
2 R.V. Levine (2004). Measuring helping behaviour across cultures. www.wwu.edu/~culture
3 Schmitt, D.P., & 110 co-authors (2004). Patterns and universals of adult romantic attachment across 62 cultural regions: Are models of self and of other pancultural constructs? *Journal of Cross-Cultural Psychology, 35*, 367–402.
4 Singelis, T.M., Bond, M.H., Sharkey, W.F., & Lai, S.Y. (1999). Unpackaging culture's influence on self-esteem and embarrassability. *Journal of Cross-Cultural Psychology, 30*, 315–41.

Study Questions

1 How would you characterize your non-verbal behaviours? In what way are your preferences in relation to proximity, touch, eye contact and use of silence distinctive to your culture of origin?
2 Discuss the extent to which researchers have succeeded in making a convincing case that cultural differences in communication are different from gender differences in communication.
3 How would you communicate to someone from a collectivist culture in a way that preserved face?
4 In what circumstances is it permissible to tell lies in your culture?
5 How can the concept of attachment be applied validly to all cultures?

9 Working Together

Management processes basically have changed little over time ... and this will remain so. They differ less from period to period than from part of the world to part of the world, and even from country to country (Geert Hofstede, 2004, p. 30)

Japanese and American management is 95% the same, and different in all important respects (T. Fujisawa, co-founder, Honda)

The contrasting quotations above illustrate the way that the same observations can be used to justify quite different conclusions, depending upon where the emphasis is placed. It would be possible to make a similar pair of comments concerning whether social and organizational psychology are similar or different to one another. Almost all of the processes discussed in the preceding chapter on relating to others also take place within organizations. Conversely, most of the processes to be discussed in this chapter also occur within families and in interpersonal relationships. Cross-cultural psychologists have been particularly active in studying aspects of organizational behaviour, and many of the more general issues that we have discussed in earlier chapters find application in this area. While the divisions that are drawn between social and organizational psychology are no more than a matter of convenience, the processes we discuss here are those that are generally thought to be most central to the effective functioning of organizations. Although much of our discussion to this point has concerned concepts derived from individualism and collectivism, in this chapter we shall also consider the distinctive relevance of hierarchy and power distance to an understanding of organizational behaviour.

Work Motivation

Two of the four dimensions of national culture identified in Hofstede's (1980) classic study (**individualism-collectivism** and masculinity-femininity) were based on ratings made by employees as to which aspects of their job situation were most important to them. Thus, we have long-standing evidence that work motivations vary across nations. Of course, Hofstede's measures were **imposed-etic**, and in evaluating more recent studies, we need to consider whether measures have been devised that take greater account of cultural differences in the type and meaning of different motives, such as the distinction between individual achievement and socially-oriented achievement (Yu, 1996).

The Meaning of Working International Research Team (1987) surveyed samples of employees in eight industrialized nations. When asked to divide 100 points between work, family, hobbies, religion and other interests, the Japanese gave more points to work than did those from the other nations. More Japanese also stated that they would continue working, even if they won the lottery. Schwartz (1999) predicted that work centrality scores for nations would be predictable on the basis of his **nation-level** scores for mastery and hierarchy. His predictions were supported, but the sample of nations was small. However, knowing that work has more importance for people in some nations than others provides only a small step towards understanding what is universal and what is distinctive about organizational behaviour. We need to examine more specific aspects of employee work experiences.

Job Satisfaction

Some more recent studies have drawn on data that has become available from databanks derived from representative surveys conducted in many nations. Using multi-level analyses, tests can be made of specific predictors for **individual-level** and **nation-level** correlates of job satisfaction. Huang and van de Vliert (2004) analysed responses of nearly 130,000 employees from 39 nations, all of whom worked for the same multinational company. In individualistic nations, white collar employees were more satisfied than blue collar employees, especially if their job provided challenging opportunities to use their skills and abilities. However in collectivist nations, job satisfaction did not vary with type of job. Furthermore, where opportunities to use one's skills were low, blue collar employees were the most satisfied. These effects were obtained after controlling statistically for differences in national wealth. This study provides strong evidence of differing work motivations between nations classified as individualistic and collectivistic by Hofstede (1980). However, it provides no direct evidence as to whether the motivators that are more salient in collectivist nations, such as socially-oriented achievement, which we introduced in Chapter 6, could account for more variance in job satisfaction for persons from the more collectivist nations.

In a similar study that drew on a different sample of 58,000 work employees from 42 nations, Hui, Au, and Fock (2004) found that job satisfaction was predicted by greater **individual-level** job autonomy and by lower **nation-level** power distance. Furthermore, the **national-level** of power distance **moderated** the effects of job autonomy, a finding which would parallel Huang and van de Vliert's conclusions, if we assume that job autonomy gives opportunities for more challenging work. Hui et al.'s use of Hofstede's scores for power distance rather than collectivism serves to remind us that every **nation-level** effect that is attributed to collectivism could as well be attributed to power distance, since the two sets of Hofstede scores are strongly correlated with one another. We must thus decide which is the relevant cultural factor, on the basis of theoretical considerations and the plausibility of the author's argument.

Job autonomy and opportunities for challenging work are both instances of motivations that are intrinsic to the job. Researchers in this field frequently contrast the effects of intrinsic motivators with more extrinsic factors, such as pay. Sweeney and McFarlin (2004) tested the extent to which satisfaction with pay could be explained in terms of comparisons with others' pay. Representative samples were drawn from twelve nations, ten of them European. Pay was just as strong a predictor of satisfaction in richer nations as it was in the less rich nations. Consistent with this uniform effect, significant variance in pay satisfaction was predicted by comparisons with 'other people in my country' in all nations. In another large scale study, Huang and van de Vliert (2003) contrasted intrinsic and extrinsic work motivations. They found that the strength of the positive link between intrinsic aspects of the job (for instance, chances to use one's skills) and job satisfaction was **moderated** by **nation-level** individualism and low power distance. In contrast, positive ratings of extrinsic job characteristics (for instance, pay) were associated with higher job satisfaction in all nations.

While pay may thus be a relatively universal extrinsic motivator, inclusion of **individual-level** measures of **cultural orientation** make it possible to examine more specific ways in which pay achieves its motivational effects. Bordia and Blau (2003) obtained measures of satisfaction with pay, and of independence and interdependence from public sector employees in India. Pay satisfaction was predicted by perceptions of the cost of living for the total sample. However, for interdependent respondents, the pay level of others in one's family was a significant predictor of satisfaction, whereas for independent respondents it was not.

Including measures of intrinsic motivators in a study also makes it possible to contrast the effects of pay and other potential incentives. For instance, Fey (2005) compared work motivation of Swedish and Russian managers. Levels of pay and of bonus were significant predictors for the Russians, but for the Swedes it was being treated fairly, having interesting work and a good work environment that were the significant predictors. Fey speculated that these differences arose because of lower rates of pay in Russia, but data from more countries would be required to place confidence in this conclusion.

Although job satisfaction has been studied extensively, the results are not as useful as they might be because knowing the extent to which someone is or is not satisfied does not necessarily tell us the extent to which they will contribute to organizational performance. Alternative concepts such as the psychological contract, organizational commitment and organizational citizenship address this gap. We discuss these in turn.

The Psychological Contract

While there is usually some form of explicit contract between employer and employee, the psychological contract refers to the implicit understandings that employees have as to what their employer has the right to ask of them and what they are obliged to contribute in return. Rousseau and Schalk (2000) outline several ways in which psychological contracts may vary across cultures. For instance, cultural understandings of procedural justice may mean that promises are more binding in some cultures than others, and in some locations their firmness may vary depending on the in-group or out-group membership of the employer vis-à-vis the employee.

We can gain insight into work motivations by studying perceived breaches of the psychological contract. Kickul, Lester, and Belgio (2004) compared ratings of the extent to which Hong Kong and US managers judged that their employers had breached their contracts on a range of specific aspects of work. They found that US managers reacted more negatively to breaches of intrinsic aspects of the contract (for instance, freedom to be creative and receiving honest communication), whereas Hong Kong managers reacted more negatively to breaches of extrinsic aspects (for instance, training opportunities and health care benefits). Kickul et al. also found that breach of contract predicted lesser commitment to the organization, greater intention to leave and lower reported performance. The samples in this study were not well matched, but the results are consistent with the conclusions of the studies cited earlier indicating that intrinsic motivation is a stronger predictor of satisfaction in individualistic nations. Lo and Aryee (2003) also studied contract breach in Hong Kong. They found that the link between contract breach and negative effects, such as intention to leave, was partially **mediated** by whether the employee still trusted the employer. We lack evidence as to whether contract breach leads to loss of trust in other nations. We expect that attributions made by the employee for the breach of contract are decisive in this process.

Organizational Commitment

Commitment to the organization may often have elements of job satisfaction, but its central component is an intention to remain with the organization and to contribute towards its goals. The measures devised by Meyer and Allen (1997) in the USA are found to comprise three somewhat interrelated elements: affective commitment, normative commitment, and continuance commitment. These refer respectively to involvement with the organization because it gives satisfaction, because of obligations to the organization, and because of a lack of alternatives. The distinction between these types of involvement provides opportunities to investigate possible differences in the basis on which employees in different cultures feel attached to their organizations. Following our previous discussions, we should expect normative commitment to be a stronger predictor in collectivist, high power distance nations, because behaviour is believed to be more governed by roles and norms in these settings. On the other hand, affective commitment should be a stronger predictor in individualist, low power distance nations, because individuals' feelings in those settings are more likely to govern their choices to stay in a job or to quit. The first step in testing these ideas must be to determine whether Meyer and Allen's **imposed-etic** measures can be validly used in other cultural contexts.

Ko, Price, and Mueller (1997) reported particular difficulty in using the unmodified measure of continuance commitment in Korea. However, Lee, Allen, Meyer, and Rhee (2001) argue that all three concepts are applicable cross-nationally. They developed and validated modified measures for use in Korea. Normative commitment was more strongly correlated with intention not to quit than is typically found in the USA. Sommer, Bae, and Luthans (1996) also sampled employees in Korea and found that a generalized measure of commitment was higher where the organization climate was more employee-focused. Fischer and Mansell (2004) made a **meta-analysis** of the levels of commitment that had been reported by other researchers in studies that spanned 49 nations overall. Some studies had used scales that differentiated types of commitment, while others had used a single overall measure. Commitment was found to be significantly higher in less wealthy nations and in nations whose economies are growing more slowly. Across a smaller sample that had the necessary information, Fischer and Mansell found evidence suggesting that the relationship between low commitment and intention to quit is stronger in more collectivist nations. These data do not yet allow us to determine whether normative commitment has the stronger effects in collectivist nations that we would expect.

A promising alternative is to test directly the influence of cultural determinants on different types of commitment. In a study of this type, Wasti (2003a) explored the relation between **individual-level** measures of independence and interdependence and the three types of organizational commitment among employees in Turkey. Among those scoring high on independence, satisfaction with the work itself was a significant predictor of all three types of commitment. Promotion opportunities also contributed to affective commitment. In contrast, among those high on interdependence, satisfaction with one's supervisor was a significant predictor of all three types of commitment. Promotion opportunities and satisfaction with the work itself also contributed to normative commitment. Furthermore, the association between intention to quit one's job and family approval of quitting was stronger for those higher in interdependence (Wasti, 2003b).

Wasti's results confirm that at least for those who are relatively interdependent within the high power distance context of Turkey, relations with one's supervisor are a more potent motivator than the intrinsic aspects of the work itself. Yao and Wang (2004) also examined cultural determinants of commitment. Among a sample of Chinese employees, affective commitment predicted job satisfaction, **moderated** positively by interdependence. In contrast, both affective and normative commitment were linked to fewer previous job changes, **moderated** positively by interdependence. The contrast between the Turkish and the Chinese results may be due to the different measures that were used. Intention to quit may not equate with frequency of actually changing one's job. Nonetheless, we should be on our guard against the naïve assumption that all collectivist nations are equivalent to one another in the organizational processes that they socialize. Studies are needed that extend the types of analysis made by Wasti and by Yao and Wang, to include respondents from more culturally different nations, especially some that are more individualistic.

Andolšek and Štebe (2004) surveyed affective and continuance commitment among nationally representative samples from East and West Germany, the UK, Hungary, Slovenia, Japan and the USA, but they did not include any measure of **cultural orientation**. Separate **individual-level** analyses were conducted for each nation. After controlling for demographic variables, commitment was found in all samples to be predicted by high job satisfaction, good relations with superiors and colleagues and by reportedly working hard. However, differences were also found. For instance, in the UK and the USA opportunity to work independently was a significant predictor of commitment, whereas performance-related payment predicted high commitment in Japan but low commitment in Hungary. In a study of workers in the Netherlands, Hungary and Bulgaria, Roe, Zinovieva, Dienes, and ten Horn (2003) found intrinsic factors more predictive of satisfaction and commitment in the Netherlands, but extrinsic factors were more important in Hungary and Bulgaria, perhaps because pay was lower there. Explanations for these types of variation in results from different nations must await the inclusion of theory-based predictors, so that we can move from description into understanding.

Organizational Citizenship Researchers in the USA have also formulated a concept of organizational 'citizenship'. This refers to behaviours of an individual who acts in ways that benefit the organization over and above that which is required on the basis of their psychological contract. In this case also, some caution is needed before assuming that organizational citizenship is a concept with broad applicability. We need first to be sure whether the boundaries as to what defines the psychological contract are the same in different nations. Would the expectations of good behaviour by an organizational employee be the same in the context of collectivist cultural dynamics and the types of paternalistic leadership to be found in high power distance nations as they would in the individualistic USA? Lam, Hui, and Law (1999) asked supervisors and their subordinates whether each of a series of behaviours was part of what a subordinate could be expected to do. Their sample was drawn from four nations, but all respondents worked for the same company and all performed the same jobs. Lam et al. found that the boundaries of what is required of a subordinate were drawn more widely in Japan and Hong Kong than they were in Australia and the USA. Clearly, if the boundaries are drawn more widely in Pacific Asia, there is less scope for organizational citizenship. One cannot be given extra credit for doing something that is already a normative requirement.

It is likely that organizational citizenship in different nations will vary not only in extent, but in the nature of the contributions that good organizational citizens make, with both being dependent upon locally prevailing values and beliefs. Farh, Earley, and Lin (1997) developed a locally valid measure of organizational citizenship in Taiwan. Their measure included three types of behaviour derived from US measures (civic virtue, altruism, and conscientiousness) and two **emic** ones (interpersonal harmony and protecting company resources). They found that organizational commitment and perceived justice were better predictors of these **emic** measures than of the **imposed-etic** US scales. More recently, Farh, Zhong, and Organ (2004) collected descriptions of 726 instances of organizational citizenship behaviours by employees in Chinese enterprises. These were content analysed inductively, yielding ten types of organizational citizenship behaviour, only five of which resembled those found in the USA. Thus, even on the basis of samples from only two nations, there appear to be elements of organizational citizenship that are relatively culture-general and others that are more culture-specific, as illustrated in Box 9.1. However, it is notable that the citizenship behaviours in the Box that are recorded as culture-specific to China are by no means unknown within Western organizations. Their claim to be considered as culture-specific derives from the relative frequency of their occurrence and the beliefs of respondents that these behaviours fall outside their psychological contract.

Our exploration of work motivation has progressed from the very abstract level of work centrality to much more specific instances of behaviours exhibited by those who are motivated to benefit their organization. Of course, employees are not always motivated to benefit their organization. Munene (1995) discusses a culture-specific phenomenon from Nigeria known locally as 'not-on-seat' behaviour. This phrase describes the action of a manager who arrives for work on time, hangs his jacket in his office and then

Box 9.1

Types of Organizational Citizenship across Cultures

China only	Both China and USA	USA only
Self Training (Initiative to improve one's own skills)	Civic virtue (Group activity participation)	Courtesy
Social Welfare Participation (Participation in company leisure activities)	Altruism (Helping co-workers)	Sportsmanship (Tolerating adverse circumstances)
Protecting or Saving Resources	Conscientiousness (Taking initiatives)	Advocacy Participation (Encouraging others to speak up)
Keeping the Workplace Clean	Loyalty (Promoting company image)	
Interpersonal Harmony	Voice	

Source: Farh, Zhong, & Organ (2004).

leaves for up to several hours, during which time he does no work. Munene showed that managers who were punctual in their arrivals and departures at the beginning and end of the day were nonetheless rated high on conscientiousness by their superiors.

As we have noted in earlier chapters, as soon as one starts to discuss specific behaviours, diversity of meanings become apparent. Concepts such as organizational commitment and organizational citizenship do have value, but studies based upon them need to ensure local validity of measurement. Once this has been achieved, a fuller picture can be obtained of the ways in which locally valid measures are interrelated. For instance, Hui, Lee, and Rousseau (2004) examined whether support from the organization and good relations with one's supervisor could predict levels of affective commitment and organizational citizenship in a state-owned Chinese enterprise. Organizational support correlated only with affective commitment, but good relations with the supervisor predicted both affective commitment and organizational citizenship behaviours. As was the case with Wasti's Turkish study, relations with the supervisor proved crucial. Hui et al. also found that this effect was **moderated** by whether or not respondents were oriented towards tradition. In the rapidly changing context of Chinese organizational life, they found that more traditional employees engaged in organizational citizenship behaviours regardless of their relation to supervisor, whereas less traditional employees did so only when their relations to the supervisor were good. We consider later some other instances of relationships between organizational variables that change in response to increasing modernity.

It is important to examine not only the consequences of high levels of satisfaction and commitment, but also what happens when satisfaction and commitment are low. Rusbult, Farrell, Rogers, and Mainous (1988) identified four possible responses, named as Exit, Voice, Loyalty, and Neglect. Thomas and Au (2002) predicted that within the more emotionally expressive individualist nations, employees are more likely to complain and seek redress (Voice), whereas in collectivist nations they would be more likely to favour avoidance, as reflected in the remaining options (Exit, Loyalty and Neglect). For practical reasons, exit is typically measured as intention to leave, rather than actual departure. Using samples from New Zealand and Hong Kong, Thomas and Au used Singelis et al.'s (1995) measures of vertical and horizontal self-construal to test their hypotheses. As predicted, the measure of horizontal individualism, which taps independence, predicted greater voice. Furthermore, it **moderated** positively the effect of job dissatisfaction and of good job alternatives on exit. Vertical collectivism, which is more akin to **interdependent self-construal**, predicted greater neglect and decreased loyalty. Contrary to prediction it also **moderated** positively the effect of good job alternatives on exit. In a similar further study, low satisfaction in New Zealanders correlated with increased exit and neglect and decreased loyalty more than it did among Indonesians (Thomas & Pekerti, 2003). Thus, while self-construals may affect choices between exit and voice in individualistic nations, organizational norms are likely to be more influential in collectivist nations. Supporting this view, Abrams, Ando, and Hinkle (1998) found employees' perceptions of norms about leaving one's job to be a significant predictor of their intention to leave in Japan, but not in the UK.

In discussing some of the effects of motivated behaviour, we have touched briefly upon several other interrelated aspects of organizational behaviour, such as perceived justice, teamwork and leadership. We shall take up each of these areas of organizational life in the following sections.

Theories of Justice

In this chapter, the focus so far has been upon the individual employee's motives, commitment, and consequent behaviours. Looking at individuals in isolation has only limited value because the ways in which their motives find expression will be heavily dependent upon the ways in which they perceive the organizational context in which they act. One key issue has to do with the degree to which they judge that they have been fairly treated by their organization and by those in their immediate surroundings. Many years ago, Deutsch (1975) proposed a distinction between three different bases for distributive justice, in other words the way that rewards are allocated among employees, and suggested that each would be more prevalent in a particular type of organization. In organizations whose first priority is economic profit, he predicted a preference for equity, in other words an allocation of rewards that is proportional to the contributions made by each individual. In organizations where the development and maintenance of harmonious relations is the priority, he predicted a preference for the egalitarian sharing of rewards. Finally, in settings where personal welfare is the priority, he predicted a preference for allocation of resources based on need.

Employees may also have concerns about the means that are used to decide the amounts of reward to be allocated, an issue called procedural justice (Lind, Tyler, & Huo, 1997). A third concept, interactional justice, which refers to the ways these decisions are transmitted to employees, has also been proposed and this too has been included in some cross-cultural studies. The extent of overlap between these three conceptualizations of justice is unclear, even within the North American literature (Colquitt, Conlon, Wesson, Porter, & Ng, 2001).

Reward Allocation

Cross-cultural studies of reward allocation are quite numerous and have spanned a wider range of nations than has been the case in other research fields. However, the results have not been easy to interpret because of inconsistencies in how the various studies have been conducted. Leung (1997) argued that it was important to distinguish studies in which participants are asked to allocate rewards between themselves and someone else from studies in which participants choose how to distribute rewards between two or more others. Since this second type of study approximates more closely to everyday organizational experience, we first consider studies of this type.

Distributive Justice   Fischer and Smith (2003) made a **meta-analysis** of 25 cross-cultural comparisons of distributive justice effects, 21 of which involved comparison between persons from the USA and another nation. Overall, respondents from 14 nations were involved in these studies. Fischer and Smith found a significantly stronger preference for equity over equality in samples from nations with high power distance scores; **individualism-collectivism** was not a significant predictor, although several earlier researchers have used this concept to interpret their results. By drawing on a full range of studies, **meta-analysis** can give a more precise interpretation of factors affecting the results of individual studies. Fischer and Smith examined several factors of this type. Firstly, they found that there was a significant difference between the results of studies in which students had been asked to allocate hypothetical rewards and those few studies that actually sampled business employees. We are likely to obtain the most valid understanding by focusing on the two studies of business employees. Chinese managers were found to favour allocations based upon equity more strongly than US employees (Chen, 1995). Russian managers also favoured equity, but they nonetheless distributed rewards more equally than did US managers (Giacobbe-Miller, Miller, & Victorov, 1998).

Russia is thought to score highly on power distance so allocations by Russians based on equality do not support the findings of the overall **meta-analysis**. This suggests that there are further uncontrolled variables affecting the results that have so far been obtained. Firstly, it is important to note that Chen (1995) was the only one among the 25 studies that included measures of individuals' **cultural orientation**. Participants in the particular samples surveyed may have had values that did not accord with the Hofstede scores for their nation. Secondly, none of these studies included measures of the extent to which the persons receiving allocations were perceived as members of the allocator's in-group. As we noted when discussing studies of emotional expression, persons with **interdependent self-construal** make a much sharper distinction between the ways in which they behave toward in-group and out-group members than do those who construe themselves as independent. Variations in the results could have occurred dependent on how respondents construed their closeness to the recipients of their allocations.

More recent studies have attempted to overcome some of these problems. He, Chen, and Zhang (2004) surveyed preferences for reward allocation among business employees in China. Using the horizontal and vertical self-construal measures of Singelis et al. (1995), they found that those who endorsed vertical collectivism favoured differential reward allocation, in other words allocation based upon job performance. In contrast, those who endorsed horizontal collectivism favoured more equal allocations. A direct link is thus established for the first time between reward allocation and self-construal, but the study is still unclear as to the in-group/out-group status of those to whom allocations would be made. Fischer (2004a) asked business employees in East and West Germany and in the UK to describe and evaluate the ways in which rewards had been allocated in their organizations. Since ratings referred to recent events in the respondent's organization as a whole, ratings would have concerned out-groups rather than immediate associates. Allocations based on equity, equality and need were all seen as having been more frequently employed in the UK, whereas allocations based on seniority were more frequent in Germany. In a further analysis, Fischer and Smith (2004) found that respondents' scores on the Schwartz value measure of self-enhancement predicted favourable evaluation of reliance on equity and unfavourable evaluation of reliance on seniority in both nations. Further studies will be required to clarify the interactions between the attributes of allocators and the targets to whom allocations are directed before we can fully understand cultural effects on distributive justice.

Procedural Justice   Some of the researchers into the procedures that are used in allocating rewards have also given attention to the measurement of their respondents' **cultural orientations**. Lind, Tyler, and Huo (1997) proposed that decisions on allocations and other matters are perceived as fair when procedures are perceived as unbiased and honest, decision-makers are seen as benevolent and trustworthy, and the recipients of decisions are treated with dignity and respect. Presuming these effects to have some universality, they then suggested that members of nations high in power distance are more accepting of interpersonal differentials and may therefore have lesser concerns about these aspects of procedure. Consistent with this reasoning, they found that in describing dyadic conflicts that they had experienced, US respondents reported having more concerns about their standing in a group than did Japanese respondents. This line of reasoning was also supported in the study by Lam, Schaubroeck, and Aryee (2002), who surveyed the reactions of employees in Hong Kong and the USA to workplace decisions. Perceptions of just procedure augmented evaluations of outcomes more in the USA than they did in Hong Kong. **Individual-level** measures of power distance were found to **moderate** these effects. For those low in power distance, perceived justice was a stronger predictor of job satisfaction, job performance and low absenteeism.

In Chapter 6, we already discussed as an example of **moderation**, a related study by Brockner et al. (2001). These authors found that lower **individual-level** scores on power distance predicted more positive reactions to having voice among respondents in a series of studies including samples from China, Mexico, Hong Kong, Germany and the USA. Finally, Farh, Earley, and Lin (1997) showed that in Taiwan, among those with less traditional and more 'modern' values, perceived justice (in this case, both procedural and distributive justice) predicted increased organizational citizenship. Thus we have four studies, three of which included **individual-level** measures, and each of which found support for the proposition that high **individual-level** power distance (equated here with traditional values) is associated with lesser concern about justice.

A further series of studies by Brockner and his colleagues (Brockner, Chen, Mannix, Leung, & Skarlicki, 2000) appears at first sight to contradict these findings. Sampling from Taiwan, Canada, China and the USA, Brockner et al. found that among his student samples, **interdependent self-construal** enhanced rather than diminished the effect of procedural justice on ratings of the favourability of outcomes. We noted earlier that justice studies using students tend to give different results from those that use managers (Fischer & Smith, 2003), and this may have contributed in some way to this apparent contradiction. Another difference between the studies by Brockner et al. (2000) and those reviewed above is the nature of the tasks for which respondents were asked to evaluate outcome fairness. Brockner et al.'s studies referred to situations involving those outside the organization, such as buyer–seller negotiations and the hiring of new employees. Thus, these studies concern fairness judgements about the outcome of events involving out-group members, whereas the other studies that we have considered are focused upon fairness in relation to in-group events. Once again, it appears that the distinction between in-group and out-group may be a key determinant of the results obtained. To test this view, we need investigations that make direct comparisons between in-group and out-group effects. Some studies of this type are considered when we discuss conflict and negotiation, later in this chapter.

Interactional Justice   Procedural justice in organizational life thus appears to be of especial concern to those endorsing egalitarian social relations. In a similar way, it appears that concern for interactional justice (how decisions are transmitted) may increase with modernity. The study by Farh, Earley, and Lin (1997) in Taiwan also included measures of interactional justice, and these measures showed significant effects on organizational citizenship among those who endorsed modern values, but not among those who did not. In a study of Chinese managers working in joint venture hotels in China, Leung, Smith, Wang, and Sun (1996) found that perceptions of distributive justice and procedural justice, but not interactional justice, predicted job satisfaction. However, three years later, distributive justice was no longer a significant predictor, while interactional justice had become predictive (Leung, Wang, & Smith, 2001). The authors explained these changes by showing that at the earlier time respondents compared their outcomes favourably with Chinese managers working in state-owned enterprises. Three years later, respondents believed that their increased level of expertise permitted them to make comparisons with the expatriate managers with whom they were working; in other words, the group with which they believe it is fair to compare themselves, their 'reference group' (Kelley, 1952), had changed.

The bulk of our discussion of reward allocation has concerned the allocation of rewards between two or more other parties. Once one considers the allocation of rewards and resources between oneself and others, it is more appropriate to think in terms of conflict and negotiation, which we next examine.

Conflict and Negotiation

In considering studies of conflict, it is more than ever important to specify the party with whom the conflict is occurring. Even within individualist nations, conflicts are unlikely to be handled in the same manner between these who are close and those who are strangers to one another. It is central to the concepts of collectivism and power distance that these differences will be larger in collectivist, high power distance contexts. The field of conflict research is also particularly interesting because theorists working in different parts of the world have formulated separate models of conflict and negotiation, which produce predictions that are sometimes mutually contradictory.

Researchers in North America have mostly conceptualized conflict in terms of a series of 'dual-concern' models. Negotiation styles are seen as a product of how strong is the concern for one's own outcomes and how strong is the concern for the other party's outcomes (e.g., Pruitt & Carnevale, 1993). If concern for self outweighs concern for others, a tough competitive stance is predicted, whereas if concern for others is high, a more accommodating or yielding approach is thought likely. Where concern for both self and others is high, a more integrative or 'problem-solving' approach is predicted. Finally, low concern for both self and others is expected to lead to avoidance of the conflict situation.

As an example of a contrasting East Asian model, we can consider Leung's (1997) approach. Leung identifies two principal concerns relating to conflict, which he labels as animosity reduction and disintegration avoidance. He hypothesizes that the strength of these two motives will vary, dependent upon whether the conflict is with an in-group or an out-group party. Within the in-group, a primary concern will be to avoid disintegration of the relationship, since the group is central to one's own identity. Consequently, all kinds of tactical avoidance and face-saving behaviours will be engaged. With the out-group, concern for others is lower, but the risk of animosity is much higher. Leung therefore predicts greater use of compromising and collaborative behaviours in this kind of interaction.

The point of contention between these two models lies in their conceptualization of avoidance. Western models see avoidance as occurring when the parties are indifferent to one another. In the East Asian model, avoidance is maximal where concerns for self and other are highest. No studies have been reported that have directly tested these predictions against one another. However, existing studies have tested the range of nations within which each model can account for the effects obtained.

Tests of the Dual-concern Model

First indications are provided by a series of studies in which business persons participated in an hour-long simulation of a buyer–seller negotiation. The simulation permits an objective evaluation of negotiators' success in achieving an optimal outcome. Data from 16 nations showed that a problem-solving approach was employed more frequently by negotiators from collectivist nations, such as Japan, Korea and Taiwan, whereas European and North American negotiators were more competitive (Graham, Mintu, & Rodgers, 1994). However, the studies also yielded effects indicating that pre-diction of negotiation style is a poor guide to eventual outcome (Graham & Mintu Wimsat, 1997). Although US negotiators were less inclined to use a problem-solving approach, best outcomes were achieved when they did so, provided the other party reciprocated. In Spain on the other hand, a problem-solving approach led to a less positive outcome. In Japan, buyers invariably obtained a better bargain than sellers regardless of approach because sellers owe deference to buyers.

Encouragement to examine more than simple East–West contrasts is also provided by van Oudenhoven, Mechelse, and de Dreu (1998), who asked managers from five European nations to describe episodes of conflict with their superiors and their col-leagues. Dutch, British and Danish managers reported more problem-solving behaviours than did Belgian and Spanish managers. Dutch managers reported giving more consid-eration to the other party's viewpoint. There are thus strong behavioural differences in conflict management even within the more culturally homogeneous area of Europe.

Morris, Williams, Leung, et al. (1998) moved the field forward by making a direct test of whether negotiation style is predicted by the individual negotiator's **cultural orientation**. Their samples comprised business students in India, Hong Kong, the Philippines and the USA. Using Schwartz's value measures, they confirmed that achievement values partially **mediated** national differences in competitive bargain-ing, while conservation values wholly **mediated** national differences in avoidance behaviours. Since conservation values represent protection of the status quo rather than concern for others, this study does not directly test cross-cultural validity of the dual-concern model. However, it does indicate that across several nations, avoidance is predicted by variables other than those specified in the dual-concern model. The Morris et al. study did not include a distinction between in- and out-group negotia-tions, so there is some uncertainty as to whether the effects that were found are equally applicable to both types of setting.

Pearson and Stephan (1998) compared student ratings of how they would negotiate with strangers and with friends in Brazil and the USA. As predicted, Brazilians scored higher on measures of **interdependent self-construal** than Americans, and preferred non-competitive ways of handling conflict. Furthermore, they differentiated more sharply than US respondents between the in-group and out-group scenarios. In a further study comparing Mexicans and Americans, Gabrielidis, Stephan, Ybarra, Pearson, and Villareal (1997) obtained similar results, but they also reported correlations between their self-construal measures and their measures of negotiation style. Contrary to the dual-concern model, they found significant positive correlations in both nations between a measure of **interdependent self-construal** and preference for avoidance.

These two studies contrasting negotiation with in- and out-group members are con-sistent with earlier work on reward allocation towards in- and out-group members. Many studies have shown that students prefer in-group allocations based on equality, but prefer out-group allocations to be based on equity. Part of the explanation for these preferences may have to do with one's reason for being in a particular type of group. Leung and Park (1986) tested the hypothesis that equality would be preferred where the group goal is harmony, whereas equity would be preferred where the goal is task accomplishment. This hypothesis was supported among both Korean and US students, but it was still the case that Koreans had a greater preference for equality. In collectivist nations the preference for in-group harmony will be stronger, whereas working on a task can foster more impersonal ways of relating. Few studies have directly compared in- and out-group allocations. In a scenario study, Leung and Bond (1984) found that among Hong Kong students rewards were shared equally among friends, but that allocation based on equity was favoured when rewards were allocated to strangers. US students did not differentiate allocations in this way. In a similar study, also in Hong Kong and the USA, Hui, Triandis, and Yee (1991) showed that differentiation in reward allocation between in-group and out-group was partially **mediated** by an individual-level measure of collectivism, which should reflect **interdependent self-construal**.

Tests of the Leung Model

The Leung model differs from the dual-concern model in that it specifies the *reasons* why negotiators would behave in particular ways in a given context. Consequently, tests of the model require not just choices between equity and equality but also measures of preference for animosity reduction or disintegration avoidance. Leung (1987) obtained ratings of the extent to which Hong Kong and US students favoured various procedures for conflict resolution, such as negotiation, mediation and adjudication. He found that the preferred procedures were those rated as most likely to reduce animosity, across both samples. Gire and Carment (1993) conducted a similar study with Canadian and Nigerian students. In this case, both groups favoured negotiation. However, while Canadians rated negotiation as most likely to reduce animosity, Nigerians also perceived that the issuing of threats would do so. This distinctive result from Nigeria is one of the few in this book drawn from African respondents, and it would be valuable to understand more fully how the Nigerian respondents conceptualized the negotiation process.

Bond, Leung, and Schwartz (1992) used a similar research design, sampling Hong Kong and Israeli students. Israelis were more likely to make threats than were those in Hong Kong. In this case, the Israeli preference for threats was predicted in part by their lower concern about the animosity reduction it would generate. Additionally, however, Israelis preferred arbitration. This preference arose because of the stronger Israeli belief that arbitration would result in greater animosity reduction. So, both the preference for animosity reduction and the expectation that using a given negotiation tactic will lead to greater animosity reduction are involved in predicting the choice of negotiation tactics. Cross-cultural differences arise because each of these factors, values and beliefs, varies between nations. These studies do not provide a full test of the Leung model, but they illustrate once more the various ways in which specific behaviours may vary between cultures, but may be linked by common explanatory concepts, in this case their perceived utility in reducing animosity and the value of animosity reduction itself. No studies have yet been reported in which measures of disintegration avoidance were included.

There is thus some evidence in favour of both the dual-concern model and the Leung model, but neither has been extensively tested. Some more recent studies have attempted to describe cultural understandings of conflicts in a way that captures the complexity of most conflict situations in additional detail. Gelfand, Nishii, Holcombe, et al. (2001) analysed descriptions of conflict episodes provided by US and Japanese students. Respondents from both nations assessed the conflicts in terms of compromising versus winning. However, Americans also construed the situations in terms of threats to their preferred individual identity, whereas the Japanese saw situations in terms of meeting their relational obligations to others. Ohbuchi, Fukushima, and Tedeschi (1999) obtained ratings of conflict experiences of Japanese and American students. Americans saw assertion as a way of achieving justice. Japanese saw avoidance as a way of preserving harmony. Understanding the nature of contracts also varies across nations. Levinson, Peng and Wang (2004) contrasted US emphasis on instrumental concerns with Chinese emphasis on relational concerns. Respondents rated scenarios in which various types of offers to sell goods had not been fulfilled by the vendor. Americans interpreted the scenarios much more in terms of legal responsibility, whereas Chinese evaluations were couched much more in terms of morality and personality judgements about the delinquent vendors.

The results from the studies with students that have just been cited differ somewhat from those that have been studied by managers. Tinsley (2001) observed pairs of German, Japanese and US managers negotiating in an intra-cultural simulation. She predicted that Americans would prefer to seek ways of integrating their own and their opponents' preferences, in other words to satisfy both negotiators rather than simply optimizing one's own preference. Japanese were predicted to emphasize power, and Germans to emphasize adherence to rules. Her predictions were upheld and she found that her results were wholly **mediated** by individual-level measures of individualism, hierarchy and directness, respectively. The predicted linkage between German directness and their focus on rules is based upon her expectation that Germans would challenge rule deviations. In a similar study of pairs of Hong Kong and US business students negotiating intra-culturally, Tinsley and Brett (2001) again found that Americans more often achieved outcomes that integrated the preferences of both parties. They also more frequently achieved agreements that involved trade-offs between the different elements in a negotiation, rather than negotiating each issue separately. More frequent Hong Kong outcomes were referring decisions to the supervisor or leaving the situation unresolved. Hong Kong respondents endorsed collectivism and respect for authority more, but in this case these measures did not predict outcome. Van de Vliert, Ohbuchi, van Rossum, Hayashi, and van der Vegt (in press) obtained ratings from Japanese business employees of how well they had handled disputes with their superiors. A combination of having 'contended with' (i.e. disputed) and accommodated to the superior's wishes predicted effectiveness. Van de Vliert et al. contrasted this finding with earlier results showing that for Dutch employees a combination of contending and integrating of their own and their superior's wishes was most effective.

We may expect that other aspects of interpersonal relations that we have discussed in earlier sections will also be operative in conflict settings. For instance, Brew and Cairns (2004) compared Anglo-Australian and Chinese students' responses to conflict scenarios that involved threats to their own face and to others' face. Type of face threat accounted for more variance than did nationality of the respondents. Both groups favoured direct communication in relation to threats to own face. The Chinese responded more strongly to threats to other face, primarily by using more cautious styles of communication.

Cross-national Negotiation   All the factors that are operative in intra-cultural negotiation are likely to be operative in inter-cultural negotiations, rendering their outcome that much more unpredictable. Using a complex negotiation simulation, Brett and Okumura (1998) confirmed that Japanese–US negotiations had less successful outcomes than either Japanese–Japanese or US–US negotiations. Drawing on the same study, Adair, Okumura, and Brett (2001) showed that Japanese negotiating intra-culturally used indirect information exchange and direct influence attempts more than Americans did. When negotiating cross-culturally, the Japanese modified their approach, moving towards the US style of direct information exchange and fewer direct influence attempts. The US negotiators did not modify their style. Although no actual measure of interdependence was obtained, these results are consistent with the view that interdependent negotiators will be more willing to adapt their actions to a change in context. Situational factors would be of greater importance to their behavioural outcomes (see also Chapter 6). It will be important in future work to test explanations for why one party moves towards the other party, and to what extent, especially if their acts of accommodation are not reciprocated.

Culture and Ethics

The great majority of cross-cultural studies of negotiation has been concerned with the relatively ordered world within which organization members use legitimate procedures to seek influence over one another, with consequences that we have shown to be somewhat predictable. The growing internationalization of business has heightened awareness that there are also cultural differences as to the propriety or impropriety of exchanging various other kinds of inducements, such as offering or receiving bribes, theft of company property, and collusion between employer and employee to cheat on tax returns. Cullen, Parboteeah, and Hoegl (2004) drew on data contained with the World Values Survey databank to compare the willingness of 3,450 managers from 28 nations to justify ethically suspect behaviours, such as cheating on taxes or accepting bribes in the course of duty. **Factor analysis** of seven suspect behaviours indicated a single factor solution: respondents were consistent in their level of acceptance or rejection of all the various suspect behaviours. Cullen et al. then used a multi-level analysis to determine what factors predicted acceptance of suspect behaviours. At the **individual-level**, young age and rejection of religion were the strongest predictors; at the **nation-level**, low access to schooling and high industrialization were the strongest predictors. The measure of industrialization reflected the proportion of the population living in cities and not employed in agriculture. Hofstede (2001) also correlated his **nation-level** scores with the 1998 version of the Corruption Perception Index. This index is updated annually and published on a website (Transparency International, 2004). Perceived corruption was greatest in less wealthy nations that score high on power distance.

Triandis, Carnevale, Gelfand, et al. (2001) used a simulation of a contract negotiation to test **individual-** and **nation-level** hypotheses about the willingness to bribe or to lie. Participants were students from eight nations. Respondents from more collectivist nations were found more willing to offer bribes and tell lies. However, at the **individual-level**, those with more **independent self-construal** were the ones that favoured unethical behaviour. One cannot be sure that the results of this simulation would reflect actual managerial behaviours, but the study provides a further instance of an investigation that gives results that differ between levels, but are nonetheless plausible at each level of analysis. At least in the short run, it might be easier for an individualist to cheat within a collectivist context.

Van Nimwegen, Soeters, and van Luijk (2004) illustrate the practical difficulties that multinational organizations face in this field. Employees of the Dutch bank ABN-AMRO, from 17 nations were asked to indicate how they would react to each of 17 ethical dilemmas, three of which are illustrated in Box 9.2. Scores were assigned by the researchers representing the answers that the organization considers 'correct'. However, the authors do acknowledge that differences, for instance in power distance, might affect the appropriateness of particular responses in different settings. Unsurprisingly, the responses of Dutch employees accorded most closely with the responses that the bank was seeking to encourage. For the three dilemmas in the box, the desired responses that are said by the authors to be appropriate were a, a, and b.

Box 9.2

Dilemmas in the Banking Industry

1 Your family owns shares in a certain company and one day at work you hear from colleagues who are involved with the company that the share price will probably drop because of a bad financial situation. What do you do?

   (a) I do not do anything.
   (b) I advise my family to analyse the company.
   (c) I advise my family to sell.
   (d) I ask my boss what to do.

2 A client sends you a beautiful and expensive watch as a present for the good relationship. What do you do?

   (a) I send it back.
   (b) I accept it and take it home after work.
   (c) I ask my boss what to do.
   (d) I also send my client a nice present.

3 You work in the back office and have to pay a reimbursement for a colleague that had a dinner one night with clients. You remember that you saw that colleague that night with his family in a restaurant. What do you do?

   (a) I do not do anything, and make the reimbursement.
   (b) I do not make the reimbursement yet, but I will first talk to my colleague.
   (c) I ask my boss what to do.
   (d) I tell the boss of my colleague what had happened.

Source: Van Nimwegen et al. (2004).

Working in Teams

Work very frequently requires the establishment of collaborative relations with others. While collaborative working does not necessarily exclude some of the elements of conflict and negotiation discussed in the preceding sections, Smith, Peterson, Leung, and Dugan (1998) found that across 23 nations, conflict in business organizations was reported more frequently between departments than within departments. To the extent that they are relatively permanent, teams have a shared interest in the development of a collaborative culture. Within certain types of organization, such as small family businesses, the team and the organization are likely to be synonymous and relatively permanent. While businesses based upon families are found in all parts of the world, they have been particularly characteristic of ethnic Chinese in South East Asia and Indians in many locations. Redding (1990) has delineated the way in which collaborative family linkages have contributed to the particular economic success of Chinese entrepreneurs.

Within larger organizations, the creation of collaborative linkages within teams becomes the primary responsibility of appointed managers, and we will discuss research into leadership shortly. However, the emergent culture of a work team is not simply a product of leadership: it is also a product of prevailing cultural values and of organizational procedures. In earlier sections, we have explored Earley's (1993) pioneering studies of social loafing. Team members with **interdependent self-construal** actually work harder when they are collaborating with others. A key issue for teams is how to optimize performance without jeopardizing cohesion, and we should be cautious about assuming that teams with interdependent members always accomplish this best. Man and Lam (2003) surveyed 471 work teams located in Hong Kong and the USA, all of whom were working for the same multinational bank. Teams that faced more complex tasks and were more autonomous from the overall organization were more cohesive and performed better. As they had predicted, Man and Lam found that these effects were **moderated** positively by a measure of individualist attitudes that had been aggregated to the team level. They argued that autonomy and task complexity require more differentiation of individual roles and that individualists are better able to make the individually distinctive contributions that are required in this type of setting than are collectivists.

Kirkman and Shapiro (2001) tested for cross-cultural influences on the effectiveness of 81 self-managed work teams in Belgium, Finland, the Philippines and the USA. They reasoned that the collaborative work procedures used by self-managed work teams would be congenial to those with collectivist values, but that the lack of formal leadership would be threatening to those who favour high power distance. Since power distance and collectivism are strongly allied at the **nation-level**, this may appear to be a challenging pair of hypotheses. However, as we continue to emphasize, variables may relate to one another in different ways at different levels of analysis. Kirkman and Shapiro used **individual-level** measures of collectivism and power distance, aggregated to the team level. At this level, the two cultural predictors were not significantly related to one another, and both hypotheses received significant support, using independent ratings of team effectiveness provided by more senior management.

Teams are also likely to vary in the extent to which they draw upon the contributions of different team members. Earley (1999) tested the effect of status on contribution to a team decision task among managers attending training programmes in the UK,

France, Thailand and the USA. Senior members, defined by age, had a greater impact within teams that scored higher on an aggregated measure of **individual-level** power distance. Regardless of nation, teams with more hierarchically oriented members deferred more to their team leaders.

Feedback Processes

Whatever the specific dynamics occurring within them, individuals and their teams will require feedback on their individual or collective performance in order to be effective. If the feedback is not to jeopardize cohesion, it will need to be given in a form that is compatible with the prevailing culture. Earley, Gibson, and Chen (1999) used a managerial simulation to study differences in the response to feedback of managers from China, the US and the Czech Republic. Feedback indicating that task performance had been either above average or below average was provided, either individually or to groups. Individual positive feedback yielded the strongest effect on personal efficacy among those who scored high on a measure of individualistic values, regardless of their nationality. However, those endorsing collectivist values showed enhanced efficacy from both individual and group positive feedback.

In a similar study, van de Vliert, Shi, Sanders, Wang, & Huang (2004) compared the reactions of Dutch and Chinese students to various types of feedback. **Interdependent self-construal** predicted a significantly more favourable response to feedback that was concerned with the work of the whole team, particularly when it was delivered to the team as a whole, but much greater variance was explained simply by whether the feedback was positive or negative. Those who received positive feedback, in this case praise and encouragement, reported more positive affect and less destructive intentions. As is the case with many of the findings reported in this book, caution is required in assuming that the results obtained in a few intensively researched locations would necessarily prove applicable in other locations. Gausden (2003) studied feedback processes among Albanian staff employed by the BBC's world service. She noted that feedback was often expressed in forceful and negative ways, and that her respondents believed that solely positive feedback had no value.

Morrison, Chen, and Salgado (2004) compared the extent to which students from Hong Kong and the USA had actually sought feedback from their superiors while in a former job. As predicted, US employees sought more feedback than Hong Kong employees and this difference in feedback-seeking was positively and wholly **mediated** by **individual-level** measures of power distance and independence. Morrison et al. did not investigate how the Hong Kong employees had obtained necessary guidance in their jobs, but we may expect it was accomplished through peers and through more indirect forms of communication, such as comparisons against established standards. An illustration of this type of contrast is provided by Tinsley and Weldon (2003), who asked Chinese and American managers how they would react to a colleague who had taken credit for work that had actually been done by the respondent. Americans stated that they would give feedback to the colleague by confronting them directly, while the Chinese said they would speak to others, in an attempt to shame the delinquent or to teach them a moral lesson.

Multicultural Teams

It is now an everyday occurrence that work teams comprise members from different nations, often from many different nations. Such teams may meet face-to-face, but frequently they work together as virtual teams, through electronic mail. Both the differing cultural expectations of what is required for effective teamwork and the lack of face-to-face contact can pose problems to such teams (Earley & Gibson, 2002).

Studies of multicultural student work teams have the advantage that they more readily permit collection of longitudinal data. Several researchers have hypothesized that a homogeneous team faces lesser problems and in the short run will prove more effective. However, they propose also that a heterogeneous team has greater potential, if it is able to create a team culture that draws upon the diverse skills and perspectives that are available. Watson, Kumar, and Michaelsen (1993) found culturally heterogeneous student teams in the USA had surpassed homogeneous teams in problem identification and generation of alternative solutions after 17 weeks during which course tutors provided consultation on team dynamics and development. This result proved replicable by Watson, Johnson, and Zgourides (2002) also in the USA, but not by Thomas (1999) over ten weeks in New Zealand. These contrasting results could be due to the different tasks involved or to the lesser time period or to differences in amount of interventions by tutors. A further possibility is that we need clearer theorizing about ways in which cultural diversity achieves its effects. Van der Zee, Atsam, and Brodbeck (2004) explored the interaction of personality variables and team diversity among 43 culturally diverse student teams in the UK over ten weeks. A multi-level analysis showed that more diverse team membership and individuals' flexibility interacted to predict final grades. Team diversity and individuals' emotional stability also interacted to predict ratings of members' well-being.

An alternative way forward is provided by the work of Earley and Mosakowski (2000), who proposed that a simple contrast between homogeneity and heterogeneity is too limited. If the requirement is for a multicultural team to develop an effective team culture of its own, this may be easier to achieve if members come from many different nations, rather than just from two. Both these types of team would be considered heterogeneous, but a team derived from just two nations risks a polarization that is much less likely in a team drawn from multiple nations. Earley and Mosakowski confirmed their predictions using four-person business school teams in the UK, with team members drawn from many nations. Their result suggests that intra-team divisiveness around culturally defined blocs of members can undercut the accommodation and flexibility needed to make multicultural teams effective.

None of the studies of multicultural student teams that we have discussed had formally appointed leaders. Within less temporary types of teams, such an unstructured situation is less likely and it would be important to take account also of the manner in which leaders address the multicultural issues faced by their teams. Fewer studies are available of teams in the workplace. Elron (1997) surveyed 22 top management teams in multinational corporations. Members of the more culturally diverse teams felt less satisfied with their performance, but their teams were nonetheless shown to be more effective than the more homogeneous teams.

Leaders and Leadership

Leadership has long been a major focus of interest in organizational behaviour, and cross-cultural researchers in this field have succeeded in including respondents from a broader range of nations. Most leadership studies both cross-nationally and within single nations have targeted formally appointed leaders. However, if leadership is defined in terms of the exercise of influence, it is more appropriate to consider first those studies that have examined the actual process of influence, whether that is exercised by those who are formally appointed or by others.

Influence Processes

Ralston, Vollmer, Srinvasan, et al. (2003) asked managers from six nations to evaluate the utility of six methods of influencing one's seniors. After standardizing the measures to eliminate **acquiescent response bias**, it was found that US and Dutch managers favoured 'soft' tactics such as rational persuasion and willingness to put in extra work. Mexican and Hong Kong managers were more willing to entertain 'hard' tactics such as withholding information or using information to manipulate others. German and Indian managers fell in between these two patterns. A series of scenario studies conducted by Yukl and his colleagues also initially considered upward influence styles. Yukl, Fu, and McDonald (2003) found that US and Swiss managers favoured rational persuasion and inspirational appeals to persuade others and oral objections to resist others. Chinese managers reported that informal approaches and avoidance of confrontation were more effective. Hong Kong managers were intermediate between these positions.

Kennedy, Fu, and Yukl (2003) broadened their focus to include scenarios that referred to upward, lateral and downward attempts. Managers from 12 nations were asked to identify which of 16 influence styles would be effective in each scenario. Rational persuasion, consultation and collaboration were rated effective in all samples. Gift-giving, socializing, use of informal settings and pressure were universally rated as relatively ineffective. After clustering the influence styles, it was found that **nation-level** means for effectiveness of a cluster containing consultation and collaboration were significantly higher in low power distance, individualist nations.

Fu, Kennedy, Tata, Yukl et al. (2004) made a multi-level analysis of the same responses, including in addition data on Leung and Bond's (2004) measures of individuals' social axioms (beliefs). The 16 influence styles yielded three factors that were named 'persuasive', 'assertive', and 'relationship-based'. At the **individual-level**, persuasive tactics were rated more effective by those who endorsed Leung and Bond's measure of belief in reward for application. Assertive and relationship-based tactics were both rated more effective by those who endorsed social cynicism, fate control, and religiosity. At the **nation-level**, several significant **moderations** of these effects were found, using **nation-level** scores derived from House et al.'s (2004) 62-nation survey (to be described shortly). For example, belief in the effectiveness of assertive and relationship-based tactics was more strongly linked with fate control in nations that were low on uncertainty avoidance. The strength of this series of studies is that respondents were asked for ratings of effective influence in specific settings and towards specific types of person, rather than in general. Responses of this type are more likely to have cross-cultural validity, provided that the settings are representative. By measuring responses in a number of nations, the investigators were able to examine whether **individual-level** connections between beliefs and ways of influencing that are perceived to be effective were pan-cultural or were **moderated** by features of the nations in question.

Contextualizing Leadership

A further series of studies has also emphasized the relations between leaders and the full network of others with whom they interact. Smith, Peterson, Schwartz, et al. (2002) surveyed the extent to which around 7,000 managers in 43 nations reported that they relied on each of eight different sources of guidance in handling each of eight frequently occurring work events, for example, the appointment of a new subordinate. In most nations, the most frequent sources of guidance were found to be one's own experience and training, one's superior, and formal rules and procedures. Nonetheless, the extent of reliance on each source varied across nations. An index of reliance on 'vertical' sources was constructed, weighting positively reliance on one's superior and on formal rules and procedures and weighting negatively reliance on oneself and one's subordinates. **Nation-level** means for this index correlated strongly with Hofstede scores for collectivism and power distance, and Schwartz's scores for hierarchy. A multi-level analysis showed that the rated effectiveness of relying on different sources in introducing changes to work procedures was significantly **moderated** by Hofstede scores for different nations. Reliance on one's own experience was rated as more effective in more masculine, lower power distance nations. Reliance on one's peers was rated as more effective in more collectivist nations (Smith, Peterson, et al., 2005). The ways in which managers process critical situations in everyday working life thus relate in understandable ways to known types of cultural variation.

The GLOBE Project

The studies by the Yukl group and the Smith–Peterson group have each emphasized the need to understand leadership in relation to the social and cultural context within which it occurs. This places their studies somewhat outside the mainstream research tradition in leadership, which continues to emphasize the distinctive qualities of effective leaders. Among cross-national studies, the major recent contributor to the mainstream tradition has been the GLOBE project, directed by Robert House and involving nearly 200 collaborators from 62 nations (House et al., 2004). Over the past decade, the GLOBE (Global Leadership and Organizational Behaviour Effectiveness) researchers have surveyed more than 17,000 managers, drawn from the telecommunication, financial services, and food supply industries within each nation. Respondents were asked to select from a list those traits that they perceived to characterize an effective leader. With further ratings, they also described in terms of nine dimensions their nation and their organization, both as they saw it (in other words, a measure of current practices) and as they would like it to be (in other words, a measure of values). The nine dimensions were derived from the earlier conceptualizations of Hofstede and others.

Den Hartog, House, Hanges, Dorfman, and Ruiz-Qintanilla (1999) reported the initial GLOBE results for effective leader traits. Substantial worldwide consensus was found, favouring charismatic leaders seen as trustworthy, dynamic, motive-arousing and intelligent, and rejecting those seen as non-cooperative, egocentric and irritable. These and other traits were first summarized in terms of 21 clusters, and these in turn were represented in terms of six styles of leadership. In order to summarize their complex findings most clearly, the GLOBE researchers also formed ten clusters of those nations in their sample that were judged to be relatively similar to one another with respect to values. The leader styles identified as charismatic and team-oriented were most positively endorsed in all clusters, while the self-protective and autonomous were least favoured. However, there were variations in endorsement across clusters for four of the six styles. The most crucial findings of this study concern the extent to which the differences in the styles of leadership perceived to be effective in each cluster of nations could be explained in terms of the values that prevailed in those clusters. The results were found to vary significantly at both the organization- and the **nation-level**. Box 9.3 summarizes the organization- and

---

Box 9.3

National- and Organizational-level Predictors of Desired Leader Styles

Leader style	Clusters where this style is seen as more effective	Values that predict endorsement of this style
Charismatic	Anglo Germanic Nordic Southern Asia Latin Europe Latin America	High Performance Orientation (O) High In-Group Collectivism (N, O) High Gender Egalitarianism (N)
Team-oriented	No difference between clusters	High Uncertainty Avoidance (N, O) High In-Group Collectivism (O)
Participative	Germanic Anglo Nordic	Low Uncertainty Avoidance (N, O) High Performance Orientation (O) High Gender Egalitarianism (N, O)
Humane	Southern Asia Anglo Sub-Saharan Africa Confucian Asia	High Humane Orientation (O) High Uncertainty Avoidance (N, O)
Autonomous	No difference between clusters	High Performance Orientation (O) Low Institutional Collectivism (N, O)
Self-protective	Middle East Confucian Asia Southern Asia Eastern Europe Latin America	High Power Distance (N, O) High Uncertainty Avoidance (N, O)

N = Nation-level; O = Organization-level.

Source: House et al. (2004).

nation-level results for each of the leadership styles. Although all of the effects shown in the box are statistically significant, the majority of effects are not strong. At these levels of aggregation, clusters are necessarily somewhat heterogeneous. We should expect to find stronger effects at the level of single nations, industries and organizations.

An indication of the type of results that we may expect from more specifically-targeted samples is provided by Spreitzer, Perttula, & Xin (2005). Spreitzer et al. tested the impact of traditional values on the effectiveness of 'transformational' leadership in two organizations in Taiwan and the USA. Transformational leadership (Bass, 1997) is similar in conception to the charismatic style identified by the GLOBE researchers and some evidence supports the claim that it is effective in many contexts (Bass, 1997). Spreitzer et al. showed that a measure of traditional Chinese values **moderated** the impact of transformational leadership on performance negatively, in other words transformational leaders were less effective with more traditional employees.

Overall, leadership researchers concur with one another that there are elements of effective leadership that are universal and other elements that are more specific to certain cultures. There is less agreement as to whether it is the universal or the specific elements that are more important. The GLOBE project was originally conceptualized in terms of the models of charismatic or value-based leadership that have been espoused by many recent US leadership researchers, and it was expected that some universal effects would be obtained. The use of an initially unstructured listing of traits has permitted the additional emergence of some quite marked culture-specific results. However, a listing of traits is itself an **imposed-etic** approach because we know that persons from many parts of the world think in terms that are more situation-specific. Leadership in high power distance, collectivist contexts may have more to do with role obligations than with traits or styles. Leaders may actually have to work harder to achieve influence in low power distance nations because those around them are less responsive to normative obligations and more responsive to the influence styles that leaders employ. Studies that detect aspects of leadership specific to high power distance nations would need to start not with traits but with situations. We have noted earlier some very specific instances of influence such as Japanese *amae* (see Chapter 8) and another instance is provided by studies of Chinese *guanxi* (see Box 9.4).

Box 9.4

Guanxi Relationships: Help or Hindrance?

Considerable attention has been given recently to the importance of *guanxi* relations in Chinese society. A *guanxi* relationship is a relationship that entails mutual obligations between two persons who are in some way linked. Links can be based upon being a relative, sharing of ancestors, being neighbours, attending the same school, having the same family name or working together. The linkage is based upon the connection of linked roles, not on personality. Persons engaged in *guanxi* relations are expected to remember and reciprocate favours given to one another over long periods of time. Typically, each party will seek to grant the other more favours than they receive, thereby enjoying a positive 'bank-balance' of favours to draw upon in future transactions.

(Continued)

Box 9.4   Continued

Farh, Tsui, Xin, and Cheng (1998) surveyed 560 pairs of superiors and subordinates in Taiwan. 100 pairs concurred that they had a *guanxi* relationship with one another. Trust in the superior was found to be significantly higher among those who had *guanxi* relations based upon being a relative or upon being a former neighbour, but not for those with other types of *guanxi* relations. Farh et al. next surveyed a smaller sample of 32 managers in China who reported a total of 212 lateral business connections. Thirty-seven of these were identified as *guanxi* relations, based upon being former classmates, relatives or those with shared ancestry. Trust in *guanxi* relations was again significantly higher than in the remainder of the sample.

Chen, Chen, and Xin (2004) used a scenario study to investigate reactions to *guanxi* relations. Chinese business students were asked to rate how much trust in their supervisor they would have if he (or occasionally she) appointed someone to a job on the basis of a *guanxi* relationship. A large decrease in trust was found where the *guanxi* was based on being a relation or on coming from the same town. A lesser and non-significant decrease was found where the *guanxi* was based on being a former schoolmate or a close friend. Chen et al. suggest that this result occurred because respondents may have reasoned that the supervisor would know more about the actual abilities of the friend or schoolmate. Thus, there may be some forms of *guanxi* that are more compatible than others with the conduct of effective business relationships in China's contemporary emerging economy.

Guanxi relations are interesting to cross-cultural psychologists for three reasons. First, are they an **emic** aspect of Chinese culture, or are parallel phenomena present in other cultures? Second, how is this phenomenon responding to current rapid social change in China? Third, how might *guanxi* relationships best be handled by expatriate business persons, whose own value system may lead them to see some aspects of *guanxi* as nepotism?

Paternalism

A somewhat more general approach, but one that does take its starting point within non-Western cultures, is provided by a ten-nation study of paternalism (Aycan, Kanungo, Mendonca, et al., 2000). Paternalism is defined as a hierarchical relationship in which the superior provides guidance, nurturance, protection and care, and in return the subordinate is loyal and deferent. After standardization to eliminate **acquiescent response bias**, Aycan et al. found paternalism to be highest in India, Pakistan, Turkey and China and lowest in Israel and Germany. Multiple regression indicated that in seven nations, endorsement of paternalism was associated with a heightened sense of obligation toward others, and in five nations it predicted an expectation of employee participation. Thus, the consequences of paternalism differ depending on one's culture, suggesting that the role played by paternalism in some nations is replaced by other ways of handling hierarchical relationships in those cultural systems where paternalism has negative connotations.

Consistent with this evaluation, an **individual-level** measure of low power distance also used by Ayçan et al. had no effect on sense of obligation or expectation of participation, but it did significantly predict subordinate proactivity. This result is consistent with those discussed earlier that found low **individual-level** power distance to enhance perceptions of justice (Lam, Schaubroeck, & Aryee, 2002) and to give more positive reactions to voice (Brockner, Ackerman, Greenberg, et al., 2001). The results obtained by Ayçan et al. indicate that development of concepts and measures additional to those derived from the original Hofstede dimensions may open up aspects of leadership that have so far been neglected.

Organizations as Cultures

The preceding sections have discussed separately various phenomena that are characteristic of organizational behaviour. To do so is to neglect the interrelatedness of these phenomena. Leadership can be thought of as a type of negotiation. Negotiations result in feelings of justice and injustice. Each of these processes is both a cause and a consequence of work motivations. Another way of putting these statements would be to say that organizations (like nations) are social systems. Just as nations have cultures, so too do organizations. Organizations within the same nation may have cultures that reflect a common national culture, but the same environmental contingencies that lead nations to develop different cultures will often also lead different organizations to develop different cultures.

Hofstede, Neuyen, Ohayv, and Sanders (1990) proposed that national cultures differ primarily in terms of the sets of values that they share, but that organizational cultures differ more in terms of shared practices. Thus members of different organizations within the same nation may share values but work for organizations that have evolved different ways of implementing those values in practice. Hofstede et al. studied 20 public and private organizations, ten in Denmark and ten in the Netherlands, identifying seven dimensions characterizing types of organizational practices within them. Having first discounted **nation-level** differences in scores, they were able to use these seven dimensions of practice to characterize the culture of each organization, regardless of the nation in which it functioned. The dimensions included, for instance, orientation towards processes or results, employee focus versus job focus and open versus closed systems. Significant relations were found between the types of organization culture that emerged and structural indices, such as organization size, type of ownership, percentage of budget spent on labour costs and proportion of women employees.

As we emphasized in Chapter 3, even when data are collected from individuals, analysing that data at different levels of aggregation will yield different structures, each of which is appropriate to its own level of analysis. In this chapter we reported several studies of teams, in which the researchers had taken care to aggregate their data to the team-level before testing their hypotheses. Hofstede, Bond, and Luk (1993) underlined this point by taking the data collected by Hofstede et al. (1990) and **factor analysing** it at the individual-level. As we would expect, this analysis yielded a different factor structure. In contrast to the dimensions of organization-level practices discussed above, six dimensions were found. These refer to the ways in which organizations were perceived to vary by their individual employees, namely, professionalism, distance from management, trust in colleagues, orderliness, hostility, and integration. Irrespective of organizational type or nation of the respondents, women perceived more trust, more orderliness, and less hostility than men, and those lower in the organizational hierarchy perceived more distance from management and less integration than those higher in the organizational hierarchy.

Cross-cultural studies can also contribute to the understanding of organizational culture. Dickson et al. (in press) used a subset of the GLOBE data to test the hypothesis that preferred leader style will vary between organizations with a mechanistic culture and organizations with an organic culture. The distinction between mechanistic and organic cultures originated with Burns and Stalker (1961) and refers to the degree to which they are structured and formalized versus flexible and constantly changing. To test this hypothesis, the researchers made a **nation-level** standardization, so that cultural influences were eliminated, and processes within different types of organization could be detected. It was then found that autocratic and bureaucratic leadership styles were judged as more effective in mechanistic organizational cultures, and transformational and considerate styles were judged as more effective in organic organizational cultures.

National culture may also influence the type of local organizational cultures that evolve. Van der Vegt, van de Vliert and Huang (in press) investigated whether **nation-level** scores for power distance would **moderate** the effect of employee diversity on the emergence of a climate of innovation. Two hundred and forty eight 'locations' of employees working for the same multinational firm were surveyed. They found that the diversity of departments existing at each location and the diversity of respondents' tenure with the organization were significant predictors. In low power distance nations, diversity on these factors was associated with an innovative climate. However, in high power distance nations this relationship was significantly reversed: diversity was linked with a less innovative climate.

Managements of large organizations currently often devote considerable resources in attempting to mould the culture of their organizations. Indeed, one reason why IBM might have been reluctant to make public that the Hofstede (1980) study was done within that company was because his results emphasized that IBM had not succeeded in its goal at the time of creating a global organizational culture. Organizations differ from nations in that they have rather more precise control over whom they employ than nations do over whom they include within their borders. This can enable them to recruit those they expect to create and sustain the required organization culture. Against this, current economic pressures give strong inducement to organizations to do business globally and to employ a multinational workforce whose values, loyalties and language skills may diverge from what is desired.

The difficulties of creating a unified company culture are perhaps most acute in the instance of joint ventures. Where an economic partnership is established between two or more organizations, each of which is often based in different nations, substantial resources will be required if emergent inter-cultural problems are to be identified and resolved effectively. Some of the personal and organizational issues that arise within such challenging operations are discussed in Chapter 10.

Summary

Collectivism, power distance and national wealth are significant predictors of work motivations and the consequent work satisfaction of employees. The psychological contract within collectivist nations lays more stress on relations with the supervisor, on normative commitment, and on extrinsic aspects of the job. Components of organizational citizenship vary depending on local circumstances. Distributive justice according to the equity principle is favoured in high power distance nations, but perceptions of procedural justice have stronger effects in low power distance nations. Eastern and Western models of effective negotiation each capture important elements of the process, but both are incomplete, and insufficient attention has been given to the in-group/out-group status of those with whom negotiations are conducted. The predictors of effective teamwork are also culture-specific. Some aspects of effective influence by leaders are culture-general, but more contextualized models of leadership and their effectiveness are required.

In general, greater numbers of studies including individual-level measures of **cultural orientation** are now available, permitting sharper tests of the psychological reasons for the differences that are found. Individual and **nation-level** measures of power distance are rather more successful predictors of the cultural differences than have been found to be the case in other areas of psychology. While many of the studies that were discussed in this chapter did find differences between samples, few of them give us an estimate of the magnitude of these differences. We cannot yet therefore evaluate how true is the characteristically trenchant assertion by Geert Hofstede with which this chapter began. Culture does matter, but just *how much* does it matter in the organizational domain?

Further Reading

1 Earley, P.C., & Gibson, C.B. (2002). *Multinational work teams: A new perspective.* Mahwah, NJ: Erlbaum.
2 House, R.J., Hanges, P.J., Javidan, M., Dorfman, P.W., Gupta, V. & GLOBE associates (2004). *Leadership, culture and organizations: The GLOBE study of 62 nations.* Thousand Oaks, CA: Sage.
3 Leung, K. (1997). Negotiation and reward allocation across cultures. In P.C. Earley & M. Erez (Eds.), *New perspectives on international industrial organizational psychology* (pp. 640–75). San Francisco, CA: New Lexington.
4 Pearson, V.M.S., & Stephan, W.G. (1998). Preferences for styles of negotiation: A comparison of Brazil and the US. *International Journal of Intercultural Relations, 22,* 67–83.
5 Rousseau, D.M., & Schalk, R. (2000). *Psychological contracts in employment: Cross-national perspectives.* Thousand Oaks, CA: Sage.

Study Questions

1 How would you describe the satisfying and dissatisfying aspects of any work that you have undertaken? What expectations did you have of your employer?

2 On what basis would you say that rewards should be allocated to a work team in your country? Distribute 100 points to show what priority you would give to allocations based on performance, equality, need, and seniority.

3 What considerations should be taken into account when preparing to negotiate a business deal with a party from another culture?

4 Should multinational organizations seek to create global organization cultures? Why and why not? What problems will need to be overcome if they do?

5 Is it more useful to focus on culture-general or culture-specific aspects of organizational behaviour? How does each focus assist our understanding?

6 Which of the styles of leadership identified by the GLOBE project researchers would prove most effective in two different types of organization with which you are familiar?

7 In what ways could van Nimwegen et al.'s study of ethics, illustrated in Box 9.2, be made more valid?

10   Coping with Difference

> The words I learn now don't stand for things in the same unquestioned way they did in my native tongue (Eva Hoffman, *Lost in translation*, 1989, p. 106)

Most of the studies that we have reviewed in the preceding chapters have been concerned with describing and attempting to explain the differences in various psychological phenomena that occur in different parts of the world. In the remaining chapters of this book, we give more direct attention to the processes that occur during the increasingly frequent occasions when persons who have been socialized in different cultural contexts interact with one another. Intercultural interactions can be studied at each of the levels of analysis that we have distinguished. At the most basic level, we can consider what happens when one individual meets another individual, and this will provide the focus for the present chapter. However, when two individuals interact, the outcome will be determined not just by the attributes of those two individuals, but also by the nature of relations between the larger groupings with which they are affiliated. Cross-cultural aspects of intergroup relations are examined in Chapter 11. Finally, the myriads of intercultural interactions that have been occurring over recent decades have the potential to influence the global changes that are currently underway, and these are explored in Chapter 12.

A fictitious example of a particularly unsuccessful intercultural interaction is given in Box 10.1. As you read though this case study, note the numerous bases for misunderstanding. Perhaps the most striking is the way in which Mrs Robertson, a language teacher, nonetheless fails to express herself with English words that are simple, unambiguous and well known, choosing instead many complex idiomatic phrases, including some that would be understood only in her native Scotland. However, there are many other ways in which communication is hindered by the socialization of Mr Chan and Mrs Robertson into their respective cultural backgrounds. Mrs Robertson's background is one characterized by individualism and low power distance, whereas Mr Chan has grown up in the cultural context of collectivism and high power distance. Based on what you have read in earlier chapters, how many of these cultural differences can you identify for yourself? You will find our own analysis of the case in Box 10.2. Many of the key issues contributing to this failure of communication have been explored in earlier chapters and here we shall mostly emphasize difficulties relating to language use.

Box 10.1

Learning a Language and Learning a Culture

Chan Chi Lok, a Chinese freshman at a Hong Kong university, has taken a course in Business English from Mrs Jean Robertson, a divorced British teacher recently arrived from Scotland. Mr Chan has failed his final exam and Mrs Robertson has made an appointment to meet him at 12 o'clock to discuss his poor performance. She has a 12.30 p.m. lunch date with the department chair, George Davis.

Chan arrives with a friend at 12.20, knocks on Mrs Robertson's door and they both enter without waiting for a response. Mrs Robertson looks up in surprise. Chan and his friend approach her chair and stand right beside her.

Chan smiles and asks, 'Have you had your lunch yet, teacher?'

Mrs Robertson replies sternly, 'Chan, sit y'rsel doon over there,' pointing to a chair positioned about two metres from her desk. 'I doubt you are 20 minutes late', she complains, 'and we had best speak alone.' She points at Chan's friend. 'Ye can wait outwith the door.'

'Huh?' Chan asks, his mouth remaining open.

Mrs Robertson repeats herself slowly and Chan's friend leaves.

'We all feel you very good … teacher.' Mrs Robertson's mouth drops. 'We all like to invite you to class party tomorrow. You contribute your precious time, yes?'

Mrs Robertson stares at Chan in astonishment. 'I cannae do that; I book well ahead,' she retorts, with furrowed eyebrows.

'Don't you like books, teacher?' asks Chan smiling and gazing attentively.

'Chan, ye must realize that we have serious matters to discuss. Ye have yet to explain your lateness.' Chan looks at his teacher blankly and waits. 'Chan, why were ye late?'

Chan laughs and then pauses. 'Well, ah, the train was delayed,' he lies, looking down, 'and the school bus was crowded, so I walk all the way to your office,' he explains, telling the truth.

'Did anyone ever tell ye that ye are a wee bit slippery, Mr Chan?'

'Huh?'

(Continued)

Box 10.1   Continued

'Mr Chan, it's impolite to say 'huh'. Ye should say, 'I beg your pardon'.'

'Sorry, teacher,' mutters Chan, eyes downcast.

'Never bother,' she continues, 'your exam mark was none too good. What way have ye done so poorly?' Chan sneezes twice.

'D'ye have a cold?' asks Mrs Robertson.

'No, teacher – you stink,' replies Chan, referring to her perfume.

Mrs Robertson's eyes widen.

Chan responds to her apparent distress by switching back to her earlier question and explains, 'It's very difficult. But I tried very hard and reread the b-b-b-book f-f-four times before the exam,' Chan stammers. 'All we found your test very difficult and ...' Chan continues, referring to his classmates, 'and...'

'It's nae good hiding behind the others. Ye must stand on your own two feet,' interrupts Mrs Robertson, 'and effort is nae enough for a pass.'

'But my English has improved so much from you. Your teachings are so good. I have to pass out from this course for being promoted'.

'I'm not caring about any of that, Mr Chan. What is at issue is your ability at English. And it was nae helped by your frequent absence from class.'

'My mother was in the hospital during this term times. 'I had to . ...' (Chan pauses lengthily while he searches for the word) '...visited her every day.'

'Your first responsibility is your studies, Mr Chan. Ye could well have visited your mother fine in the evenings.'

'But who watches after my younger sister?' Chan retorts.

'Ye dinna get it, do ye?' Mrs Robertson sighs.

'Yes,' answers Chan, puzzling his teacher still more.

'Mr Chan, I'm away now, as I have a previous appointment.'

'Couldn't you just give me a compassionate pass, teacher? I really need to pass out of your course.'

'What?! A *compassionate* pass? I've never heard of the like! Anyway, I've got to run. Phone me for an appointment if ye want to have a wee word about retaking the exam.'

Mrs Robertson then goes to the door and holds it open as Mr Chan walks out to find his friend, eyes downcast.

'Don't be late next time, Chan. If ye canna get here on time, you'll never get anywhere.'

Source: adapted from Smith & Bond (1998).

Box 10.2

A Failure to Meet – Mrs Robertson and Mr Chan

Mrs Robertson	Mr Chan
Values prompt timekeeping.	Sees harmonious interpersonal relations as more important than promptness.
Is monochronous – she wants only to discuss one issue at a time.	Is polychronous – he sees passing the exam, getting a job and caring for family as interrelated.
Values her personal space.	Feels comfortable approaching closer.
Keeps her door closed and expects others to enter only when she invites them in.	Does not understand the need for this type of deference.
Sees Chan's exam failure as the failure of him as an individual.	Sees no reason to exclude his friend from the meeting and prefers having her support when dealing with his teacher.
Feels insulted by Chan's apparent lack of acceptance of her control of the interaction and asserts her status by using only Chan's family name.	Defers to Mrs Robertson by using the honorific 'teacher'.
Judges Chan as trying to ingratiate himself.	Seeks to give Mrs Robertson status by reporting the class's favourable evaluation of her teaching, and referring to her time as 'precious'.
Believes that exams measure performance and ability.	Believes that evidence of effort is of equal importance to evidence of ability.
Considers her professional role to be one of upholding an absolute standard of quality, in this case the quality of written English.	Considers it appropriate to ask his teacher to use her discretion, by referring to family problems, giving her praise and referring to his career needs.
Is critical of the telling of lies.	Uses lying and indirectness as ways of trying to restore harmony.
Seeks to take control of the interaction by determining the only topic to be discussed, but fails to achieve what she wants in the time remaining.	Finds all of his preferred ways of handling the situation ineffective.
Asks a negative question, which in English requires a negative response to indicate agreement.	Indicates agreement to a negative question by saying 'yes', as is the way in Cantonese.
Takes offence at unintended language errors.	Refers to Mrs Robertson as 'stinking' because of her perfume, rarely used in Cantonese culture.

Language Issues

If we consider first the situation where two strangers meet, many of the issues that arise are equally applicable to meetings between strangers from within the same culture and meetings between those from different cultures. In both cases, a process of first impression formation will occur, as a way of coping with the inherent uncertainty of the situation. These first impressions will be strongly influenced by the physical appearance of each party, by whatever is knowable about their group memberships and by the circumstances under which they meet. However, in cross-national encounters, an additional issue very frequently arises: what language shall be spoken? The two parties may share a single language, more than one language, or of course, no spoken languages at all. We consider these situations in turn.

The Single Language Option

Where only one language is shared, there is little choice in how to converse. Once interaction commences, a process of communication accommodation is inevitable. In other words, a pressure arises on both parties to align their speech patterns (vocabulary, accent, style of speaking) with one another (Giles, Coupland, & Coupland, 1991). Most typically, the chosen language is the first language of one speaker but a second language of the second speaker. This entails a series of consequences for both parties. First language speakers are provided with affirmation of their identity, through speaking their natural language, but are under pressure to communicate in ways that differ from their normal speech. Their vested interest in being understood argues in favour of simplified speech, avoidance of idioms and slower speaking with more pauses. Gass and Varonis (1985) identify these effects as 'foreigner talk'. Some studies confirm that first language speakers do accommodate in these ways more when speaking to second language speakers than with other first language speakers (Pierson & Bond, 1982).

However, this helpful accommodation does not always occur, as there may be factors in the situation that encourage first language speakers to resist accommodation, for instance if the speakers see themselves as representing groups that are in conflict with one another. It is also notable that in addition to 'underaccommodating' to their partners, first language speakers may 'overaccommodate'. In other words, they may use 'foreigner talk' needlessly or excessively, in a way that is similar to persons who use 'babytalk' when addressing persons who are very old (Williams, Garrett & Tennant, 2004).

Studies of simulated and naturalistic conversations between Chinese students in Australia and native Australians showed that first language speakers who did accommodate were better liked (Jones, Barker, Gallois, & Callan, 1994). This series of studies also illustrated the rich variety of ways in which accommodation can be achieved by first language speakers (Gallois, Giles, Jones, Cargile, & Ota, 1995). In speaking with Chinese students, female Australian students responded more slowly and paused more often, whereas male Australian students asked more questions to check on their interlocutor's comprehension, and Australian faculty members steered the conversation towards topics with which their interlocutors would be more familiar. Which strategy is used by whom under which social circumstances is an important future topic of research.

The situation of second language speakers is somewhat different. To speak or write in a language other than one's own may cause one to think in different ways. Depending upon the context of the interaction, one might think of oneself as less identified with one's language community, or as even more identified with it. Harzing and Maznevski (2002) showed that in seven different nations, their respondents described their values differently when responding to a survey in English than when responding in their local language. When responding in English, their reported values became more similar to those reported by native English speakers, an outcome known as cross-linguistic accommodation.

However fluent second language speakers may be in their second language, it is rare that their speech cannot be discriminated from that of a first language speaker, either by vocabulary, accent or by distinctive language usage. For instance, Al Issa (2003) asked US and Jordanian students to refuse requests while speaking in English. Even though speaking in English, the Jordanians used an Arab style of speaking, indicated by more frequent references to the defining of one's relationship with the other, more emphasis upon the reciprocation of favours, more requests for understanding and more emphasis on removing negative feelings. In a further study of accommodation between Chinese students and Australians, Chinese who accommodated were judged more positively by Australians. This was particularly true for accommodation involving markers of one's group membership, such as language use, accent and voice register, rather than for markers of one's individual attributes, such as gaze and gestures (Hornsey & Gallois, 1998).

Because of the various distinguishing features of their speech, second language speakers are likely to be rated lower in competence by first language speakers, even where their competence for a given task is equally high (Hui & Cheng, 1987; Cargile & Bradac, 2001). Many unfortunate consequences can stem from misperceptions of this type and conscious strategies are required on the part of first language speakers to eliminate or at least minimize them. The problem is compounded by the fact that although English is not the most widely spoken first language in the world, it is the most widely used language of international communication. The current profile of cross-national contacts means that the first language speaker is rather often a speaker of English. Consequently, the first language speaker is often also from a nation that is economically or politically more powerful, thereby introducing considerations of relative power into the conversational dynamic. Considerations of relative power may be handled differently by persons from cultures varying in their degree of hierarchy or power distance.

The Language Choice Option

Where the parties share more than one language, a separate set of issues becomes relevant. The choice of language in which to converse is likely to be guided by the 'ethnolinguistic vitality' of the languages in question. The concept of ethnolinguistic vitality refers to the relative numbers of speakers of a language in a given community, its prestige and its use within relevant local institutions. Ethnolinguistic vitality can be assessed objectively, but in many circumstances the subjective perceptions of speakers of a particular language as to its vitality are more important in predicting their actions. In Canada, perceived vitality positively predicts preference for speaking a language and negatively predicts willingness to learn a second language (Harwood, Giles & Bourhis, 1994). Noels, Clément, and Gaudet (2004) asked French Canadian students to imagine themselves speaking with someone from a particular ethnolinguistic group. Evidence for accommodation was found: in speaking with an English language interlocutor, their English identity was raised and their French identity lowered. Noels et al. also had respondents rate their confidence in speaking English, the vitality of the English and French languages, and how much they identified with the English and French communities in Canada. Where English language confidence was low, identification with the French community was consistently high. However, among those with increased confidence, vitality was associated with enhanced French identity in intimate settings and enhanced English identity in public settings. Indeed the primacy of the mother tongue in the private realm is probably a universal pattern. Thus, the ethnolinguistic vitality of one's first language can be a protective factor against the predominance of English and other widely spoken languages.

A further option where conversation partners share two languages is code-switching. This term refers to the use of single words or longer utterances from the shared second language, when conversing in the first. Scheu (2002) studied a group of bilingual students in a school in Spain. Conversations occurred in both German and Spanish, but code-switching within sentences was most often used for emphasis, for instance when swearing. More generally, code-switching serves to define one's identity in relation to those with whom one is conversing. Lawson and Sachdev (2000) sampled code-switching between French and Arabic by Tunisians, using both diaries and field observation of street conversations. They concluded that code-switching defines more informal discourse between in-group members and was much less frequent when Tunisians spoke with their teachers and with non-Arabs.

Code-switching can also have a valuable function in immigrant families. Ng and He (2004) studied Chinese families in New Zealand. Grandparents tended to switch the conversation from English to Chinese and children tended to switch from Chinese to English. The middle parental generation more frequently switched within an utterance, rather than between utterances. Their code-switching often served to aid grandparents' understanding of English and children's understanding of Chinese, so the middle generation was serving as linguistic mediators.

No Common Language

Circumstances also arise when it is necessary that persons communicate with one another when they do not have a shared language. In these situations, a third party interpreter is essential to effective communication, but the use of a third party introduces a host of further difficulties. How should interpreters represent each party to the other? Should they provide literal translations of what is said, or should they also use their own knowledge of either culture to interpret and communicate what they believe to be the intentions behind what either party says? It is often the case that an interpreter is of the same nationality as one of the parties, thus leaving the other party faced by not one but two protagonists, who can converse with one another in a private manner, dramatically changing the power balance in the conversation and often provoking suspicions by the excluded party.

Box 10.3

The Hazards of Translation

Business companies have to struggle with the difficulty of reproducing the meaning of their advertising slogans into other languages. They do not always succeed:

- In marketing their pens in Latin America, the Parker Pen company initially chose to use the word *bola* to refer to their ballpoint pen. This conveys the intended meaning at some locations, but in one nation *bola* refers to a revolution, in another it is an obscenity and in a third it describes a lie.
- A mistranslation meant that a US shirt manufacturer advertised its shirts in Mexico with the slogan, 'Until I used this shirt, I felt good', rather than the US version 'When I used this shirt I felt good'.
- Advertisements for face cream were markedly unsuccessful in some Arab countries. The advertisement featured photographs of a woman's face before and after using the cream. The text was correctly translated but the 'before' picture remained on the left hand side of the advertisement, with the 'after' picture on the right. Since Arabic is read from right to left, the photographs indicated that the cream made one's face worse, not better.
- Advertisement in a French clothing store: 'We sell dresses for street walking'.
- Advertisement for a Japanese garden: 'The Japanese garden is the mental home of the Japanese'.

Source: Ricks (1993).

In the field of diplomacy, achieving agreement may often rest upon the degree to which one or more crucial words can be translated in a manner that has equally acceptable connotations in two or more languages. In less public settings, the difficulties will be less exclusively focused on what is said and include also those aspects of the communication process that cannot be verbally translated. In medicine or psychotherapy, for instance, a therapist or other practitioner working with a patient from a different cultural background may be unable to rely on an accurate interpretation of non-verbal cues that would ordinarily be important sources of information. So, for example, Li-Ripac (1980) found Caucasian-American therapists compared to Chinese-American therapists 'over-diagnosing' depression in Chinese-American clients, and much of this 'misdiagnosis' probably arose from a culture-derived 'mis-reading' of non-verbal cues, for instance lack of gaze during conversation (Li, 2004). Levels of eye contact may also be impeded or misunderstood by the propensity of both therapist and client to address the interpreter (Hillier, Huq, Loshak, Marks & Rahman, 1994). Interpreters can find themselves engaged by the emotional intensity of the issues being addressed and in some danger of supplanting the therapist's central role. Non-professional interpreters may also be other members of a client's family, often younger ones, and this is likely to impose barriers on which issues can be spoken about openly (Rea, 2004). Going beyond issues of translation, independent or interdependent perspectives of the therapist and the patient regarding identities and loyalties may be quite different, presenting challenges to the therapeutic process (Pedersen, Draguns, Lonner, & Trimble, 1996).

Box 10.4

Cultural Issues in Counselling

During the late 1990s, the Milosevic regime in the former Yugoslavia orchestrated the attempted 'ethnic cleansing' of Albanians from the province of Kosovo. More than half a million refugees were forced to flee, as their homes were burnt to the ground; some family members were killed and many family members lost touch with one another. Within Western nations, it is expected that counselling would contribute towards more positive outcomes to post-traumatic circumstances of this kind. However, within a very traditional, strongly collectivist cultural community, individual counselling is unlikely to be the best form of intervention, particularly if it is provided by foreigners working through interpreters. Cavill (2000) describes how training of local group leaders from the refugee camps enabled them to conduct single-gender, single-clan group meetings that addressed the shared experience of trauma in culturally appropriate ways.

Similarly, Dwairy (1998) identifies distinctive challenges in conducting counselling among Palestinian Arabs. Arab identity is closely interwoven with one's family. Consequently, intervention is far more likely to be effective if conducted with the participation and approval of family members. Furthermore, therapeutic interventions must differ from Western styles of family therapy, giving respect to the hierarchical nature of Arab family relationships and the way in which true feelings are often hidden behind a positive, diplomatic face (*mosayara*). Less direct forms of therapeutic intervention can include the use of drawings and of metaphors.

Sources: Cavill (2000); Dwairy (1998).

Understanding Cross-cultural Interactions

In discussing the dilemmas faced by interpreters, we are touching on issues that have a more general importance. How can one 'read', i.e., accurately interpret, the words and actions of someone from a cultural background other than one's own? Conversely, how will the other party read one's own words and actions? Language fluency is a necessary but not a sufficient condition for effective interactions. One needs to know also how one's words will be interpreted within the context of the other party's cultural assumptions. In Box 10.1, when Chan asks Mrs Robertson whether she has had lunch, his English is correct, but he has misjudged the appropriateness of making that specific enquiry at that time. When a Dutch visitor uses his fluent Portuguese to ask his Brazilian host when he should really arrive for dinner, he has met his need to avoid uncertainty, but has violated Brazilian hospitality norms. When a Chinese professor states to a visiting Irish teacher that his wife (who is present) did not attend university because she is stupid, he is adhering to Chinese norms of modesty, but failing to give consideration to European norms about public criticism of one's family when those family members are present (Wei & Yue, 1996). They are all committing errors in socio-pragmatics.

We have some evidence on the extent to which persons understand that behaviours can have different meanings in different contexts. Pittam, Gallois, Iwawaki, and Kroonenberg (1995) asked Australian and Japanese students to rate the extent to which a series of non-verbal behaviours would be associated with each of eight different emotions, as expressed by both Australians and by Japanese. Some culture-general effects were found. For instance, smiling was said by both Japanese and Australians to be associated with love, respect, elation and relief, but not with anger, fear or grief, regardless of the nationality of the person observed. Other effects were ethnocentric. For instance, Japanese associated fast speech rate with anger and fear and slow speech rate with love, respect and relief, regardless of which nationality they observed. In contrast, Australians did not link speech rate with any particular emotions. Finally, a few instances of awareness of cross-cultural differences were also detected: Japanese perceived walking about as characteristic of anger and fear among Australians, but not among Japanese. Australians associated soft speech with love among Japanese, but not among Australians. Awareness of difference may have been low because the students sampled had little experience with persons of one another's nationality; such differences may well be more evident for persons with greater intercultural experience.

Albert and Ha (2004) asked Anglo and Latino 10–15-year-old students within the USA and their teachers to give their interpretation of twelve school-based scenarios that highlighted instances of various types of touching by Latino students and of silence and avoidance of touching by an Anglo teacher. Even though these respondents had much more day-to-day intercultural contact, the results indicated that the scenarios were mostly interpreted in ways that took no account of cultural differences in interpretation. Anglos tended to interpret behaviours in terms of personal qualities, whereas Latinos made more reference to context. For instance, Anglo teacher silence was perceived as meanness by Anglos, but as an attempt to punish a naughty boy by Latinos. The teacher's request that students remain at their desks rather than crowd around her was more often seen as a need for personal space by Anglos and as the exercise of authority by Latinos. Box 10.5 provides another instance of the way that classroom events can carry different meanings for those from different cultural backgrounds.

Box 10.5

Culture in the Classroom

A kindergarten class in Los Angeles contained mostly Latino children and the teacher was also a Latina. She had ensured that the class was provided with a series of cups containing red crayons, blue crayons, green crayons and so forth, for use when they were needed. A visiting Anglo supervisor suggested to the teacher that this arrangement was inappropriate. She argued that having the crayons grouped collectively in this way gave no opportunity for each child to experience having individual property and learning to care for it. Children could learn that if they took care of their own cup of pencils they would not be impeded by others who may have spoiled their crayons.

The teacher implemented the new system of individual cups advocated by the supervisor. However, this system contradicted the collectivist assumptions experienced every day at home by the Latino children in the class. They took little care to ensure that their crayons were placed in their own cups at the end of the day. After a while the teacher found that she needed to replace the crayons in each individual's cup at the end of each day. The innovation had failed.

Episodes such as this provided the basis for a series of 'bridging cultures' workshops in which teacher-researchers created and tested more effective ways of handling cultural issues in the classroom.

Source: Greenfield, Trumbull, & Rothstein-Fisch (2003).

If one understands that behaviours have different meanings in different cultural settings, it is likely that at least some of the time it will be necessary to modify one's own behaviours, so as not to be misunderstood by persons from the other culture. The extent to which respondents are found to have an understanding of this need no doubt rests on the experience and maturity of those who are sampled. Rao and Hashimoto (1996) surveyed 202 Japanese managers working in Canada. They assessed intercultural adaptation by comparing how the Japanese managers acted when seeking to influence Canadian managers or other Japanese managers who were also in Canada. It was found that when working with Canadians, the Japanese reported speaking more assertively, appealing more to reason, making more threats and appealing more to higher authorities. With fellow Japanese they communicated more indirectly, as would be the case back in Japan. Thomas and Ravlin (1995) played US managers a videotape of a Japanese manager who either had adapted his behaviour towards US styles of communication or had not done so. The culturally accommodating Japanese manager was judged as more trustworthy and more effective.

It is noteworthy that both these studies illustrate Japanese managers adapting their behaviour. We discussed in Chapter 6 the way that persons from collectivist nations are more inclined to adapt their behaviour to its context in their own cultures. Another example is provided by Li's (2004) study of eye contact (discussed in Chapter 8).

Canadians made eye contact with one another much more frequently than did Chinese. However, in mixed Canadian-Chinese pairings, the Chinese increased their level of eye contact to the Canadian level. This accommodation to others can be seen as an instance of 'self monitoring', a personality dimension along which there are individual differences (see Chapter 7). Further studies are required to determine how well and how frequently persons from individualist nations adapt their behaviours when interacting in a different cultural context. One early study indicated that US managers in Hong Kong did not do so (Black & Porter, 1991).

Stereotypes or Frameworks?

In deciding how to act toward a previously unknown person from another culture, we are faced with a choice of strategies. On the one hand, it is possible to approach that person from a 'culture-blind' perspective, in other words to assume that there is much in common between the ways in which people around the world communicate with one another. From this perspective, it makes sense to act normally until such time as one becomes aware that some miscommunication is occurring. This would be analogous to a researcher who uses an **imposed-etic** research strategy, modifying instruments only when it becomes clear that they are not functioning as expected. On the other hand, one could approach the previously unknown person in a way that is guided by the research studies that we have been examining. In other words, one could construct a set of expectations based upon the **nation-level** characterizations that have been provided by cross-cultural researchers (e.g., Bond, 1991a). Relevant expectations might include knowing how individualistic, how hierarchical, and how expressive are typical interpersonal interactions within the stranger's nation. In drawing upon these characterizations, we should be engaging in some initial stereotyping, and we might find that our stereotypic expectations did not fit the individual in question too well. On average, though, we should expect fewer misunderstandings to arise than with the culture-blind approach.

Stereotypes are often defined in ways that suggest that they involve prejudiced and negative perceptions of others. However, the generalizations about groups or nations with which we are here concerned are based upon empirical investigations rather than untested prejudices. Relatively accurate stereotypes may be derived from many sources other than the reading of this book, including direct experience, talking to other travellers, exposure to information in the media, and training programmes. Training programmes will be discussed later. Stereotypes often contain a 'kernel of truth' (Allport, 1954) and so long as they are treated as a *provisional* basis for one's interactions with others, they can assist intercultural effectiveness. For instance, Lee and Duenas (1995) made a study of meetings between Mexican and US business people. Each party had a stereotype of the other's orientation towards time. The Mexicans described the Americans as 'machines', referring to their preference for conducting business in a linear, ordered, 'monochronic' fashion. For their part the Americans referred to the Mexicans as 'banana people', referring to their more relaxed way of working on several issues concurrently without any strict time regulation. These stereotypic characterizations provided the basis on which both parties were able to negotiate how they could work effectively together, by accommodating on important aspects of interpersonal style.

Cross-cultural Skills

The process whereby awareness of difference is converted into effective handling of cross-national interactions is not yet well understood. Some researchers have recently attempted to systematize and develop earlier studies of the cross-cultural skills of individuals, now labelling the various possible components as 'cultural intelligence' (Earley, 2002; Thomas, & Inkson, 2004). However, it is not clear how much an individual's learning of skills in relating to others across a given cultural boundary can generalize across other cultural boundaries. If I develop some expertise in relating to persons from Latin America, am I likely also to be more skilled in relating to South Asians or East Europeans? Recent studies provide some relevant evidence.

Van der Zee and van Oudenhoven (2001) created a measure described as the Multicultural Personality Questionnaire (MPQ), which comprises scales of self-reported Cultural Empathy, Openmindedness, Emotional Stability, Social Initiative, and Flexibility. Self and peer ratings showed that Dutch students with prior international experience obtained higher MPQ scores than those who had not left the Netherlands. MPQ scores also predicted expatriates' personal, professional and social adjustment in Taiwan (van Oudenhoven, Mol, & van der Zee, 2003). However, since the MPQ taps qualities that are also likely to have value in relating to members of one's own nation, if it is to be judged as a valid measure of distinctively *cross-cultural* skills, it must be shown to predict the outcomes of cross-cultural experience better than a conventional measure of personality does. Van Oudenhoven and van der Zee (2002) reported that the MPQ was a better predictor of the adjustment of foreign students at a Dutch business school than was a measure of self-efficacy. In a similar way, Matsumoto, LeRoux, Bernhard, & Gray (2004) developed a scale of potential for intercultural adjustment. Scores on this scale measured before Japanese students' departure to the USA successfully predicted their subsequent self-rated adjustment, degree of culture shock, and life satisfaction in their host culture, even after variance explained by a Big Five personality measure had been discounted.

Thus we have some preliminary indications that it may be possible to measure cross-cultural skills, but the conclusions so far achieved mostly rest on self-reported skills and self-reported adjustment. Independent criteria of adjustment will be required before firm conclusions can be drawn. No studies are available that test the extent to which these generalized measures of cross-cultural skill compare with the acquisition of localized knowledge about the particular nation that is a traveller's specific destination. We also need more evidence about the extent to which cross-cultural intelligence differs, if at all, from the social intelligence required to function effectively in a mono-cultural environment.

Cross-cultural Training

Most of those who visit another culture experience no form of preparatory training for their encounter. However, one way of enhancing the prospects for successful cross-cultural interactions is to provide such training, particularly for those who will be spending extended periods of time abroad. The methods that are used can be divided into those that provide basic information, those that seek to enhance understanding of different nations, and those that give practice in behaving in more effective ways.

Provision of information by itself is unlikely to have a marked effect on successful outcomes because information rarely matches up with the specific circumstances that one encounters and may frequently be forgotten. However, it may usefully be combined with other types of training.

Programmes focused upon understanding attempt to sensitize trainees to the existence of cultural differences and to the consequent need to attend to the way that one's behaviour is interpreted by locals. This can be achieved through the use of simulations such as 'BaFa BaFa' (Shirts, 1995). Trainees are randomly assigned to one of two simulated cultures, in each of which trainees are required to behave in accordance with a set of rules provided by the trainers. Meetings between members of the two cultures typically lead to a series of misunderstandings, which are later used to illustrate the way in which we all tend to interpret the behaviours of others using the preconceptions of our own mother cultures. There is little evidence, however, as to whether the effects of this and similar simulations have a lasting impact on one's intercultural effectiveness (Ward, Bochner, & Furnham, 2001).

Skill-oriented programmes come much closer to the requirements for effective training intervention. This chapter has emphasized the crucial importance of language in cross-cultural interactions and there can be little doubt that the most effective form of cross-cultural training is to learn the local language. However, language learning takes a long time, and attempts have been made to provide briefer opportunities to develop relevant skills. These can be based upon meetings with members of a local culture prior to one's own departure, where such a possibility is available. Alternatively, trainees are presented with descriptions of one or more critical incidents that have occurred when others have visited the same destination. Through group discussion they can learn to interpret what went wrong and how the incidents could have been handled more effectively.

Collections of critical incidents have also been used to develop what are known as culture-assimilators. These comprise a series of brief descriptions of critical incidents, each of which is accompanied by four or more different interpretations, one of which is correct and the remainder incorrect. An example is given in Box 10.6. By working through an assimilator composed of varied descriptions of this type, trainees can increase their understanding of how to behave, particularly where the assimilator is focused on a particular target culture and based on accurate knowledge about that culture.

Box 10.6

The Culture Assimilator

OH SO PROPER!

The English class that Martha Anderson is helping to teach is going very well. The Vietnamese, Cambodian and Central American students seem to enjoy one another and are adjusting to each other well. The men and women frequently help one another. Having very little exposure to other cultures, Martha is amazed at their ease of interaction and often asks the instructor about the different behaviour she observes in the classroom. They are all very polite to each other even when they do not seem to be able to understand each other. They are also especially polite when

(Continued)

Box 10.6 Continued

they are talking to her or to the other instructors, always addressing them with very formal, polite titles.

Martha would like to develop relationships with some of the students and to make them feel more at home. In one particular instance she is in private talking with Vien Thuy Ng. She asks him to call her by her first name, saying, 'My name is Martha, please call me Martha!' Vien responds by acknowledging that he does indeed know her name but, 'Would it not be good to call you by your proper title?' She persists by saying that that is too formal and that they can just be good friends and go by first names. Vien just smiles and nods, but he does not return to the English class the next week.

What could explain this situation?

1 Vien Thuy Ng thought that Martha was too aggressive and forward to him, as women do not talk to men.
2 Martha should not have singled out one individual person. Vien did not like being singled out.
3 English class is too complicated for Vien and he does not really know what is going on.
4 Martha violated a rather intricate system of hierarchy that exists in South Asian countries.

Choose your answer before looking at Box 10.7.

Evaluations of the effectiveness of cross-cultural training have yielded modest but positive results. In a **meta-analysis**, Deshpande and Viswesvaran (1992) concluded that cross-cultural training for managers was effective. However, the indices of success in many of the studies were completed immediately after training, rather than when the trainee goes on assignment or after its completion. Gannon and Poon (1997) compared information-giving plus watching a video, watching several videos, and participation in BaFa BaFa. No differences were found in students' increased cultural awareness, but participation in BaFa BaFa was enjoyed more. Earley (1987) compared different versions of a three-day programme preparing 80 US managers for an assignment in Korea. As part of the programme, trainees either received documentary information on Korea followed by group discussion, or else they spent an afternoon visiting an Asian-American community, or both, with subsequent group discussion. Performance ratings by the trainees' managers in Korea showed that both forms of training were more effective than no training at all. However, those who received both forms of training did best of all.

The difficulty in reaching conclusions about the effectiveness of cross-cultural training is that the outcome is assessed in a multitude of different ways in different studies, each of which may be appropriate to a different type of intercultural contact. Thus, the best that we can say is that there is some evidence that training can be beneficial, if the training design is well adapted to trainees' needs. We need some clarification of which forms of training show improvement on which criteria of inter-cultural success.

Box 10.7

Explanations for Answers to the Culture Assimilator

1   In many Southeast Asian countries, the roles of women may be restricted in some ways, such as approaching men. However, this class is in the USA and there are some students from other countries as well as the instructors interacting together. The fact that the class is mixed and that the students seem to get along fairly well suggest that this is really not the reason for Vien's disappearance from class.

2   It is true that individuals from Asian societies do not like to be singled out. However, in this instance, this minor correction was not a singling out. Martha was talking with Vien alone, so there would be no great embarrassment involved, since others were not present.

3   This conclusion can hardly be drawn, as the scenario states that all seemed to be going well in the class.

4   This is the best answer. Southeast Asians have a very intricate system of status hierarchy. Martha violated it by trying to downplay her role or perceived status. Her attempt may not have been the total cause for Vien's not wanting to return, however. Probably if she had just suggested it and left it open for Vien to choose he may have felt more comfortable. Her persistence in the matter forced Vien into a situation where he had to relinquish a value that affected his whole worldview or lifestyle.

Source: Brislin, Cushner, Cherrie, & Yong (1986).

Psychological and Socio-cultural Adaptation

Terms such as 'adjustment', 'adaptation', 'acculturation' and 'effectiveness' have been much used in the analysis of the outcomes of intercultural contact. We shall see in the remainder of this chapter and in the next that care is needed in thinking through how these terms can be most usefully employed, just as has been the case in studying issues of stress, strain and adjustment in psychology more generally. Ward et al. (2001) distinguish three categories of response to spending time with members of another cultural group. Firstly, there will be affective reactions, ranging for instance from pleasure through confusion to anxiety or depression. Ward et al. define these types of reaction as '**psychological adaptation**'. Secondly, there will be a process of culture learning, which will include learning (or failing to learn) both how the other cultural group functions, and how to operate within that culture oneself. Ward et al. define these processes as '**socio-cultural adaptation**'. Finally, if cross-cultural contact is prolonged, issues will arise as to the extent to which one thinks of oneself as part of the local community or as separate from it. Ward et al. discuss these more cognitive processes in terms of '**acculturation**'. In this chapter, we are concerned only with the first two of these adaptations, since at this point our focus is upon individuals who stay for relatively brief periods of time.

Types of Contact

Those who spend time within a cultural group other than their own, but nonetheless expect to return home before long are usually referred to as sojourners, to distinguish them from migrants. We now consider in turn some studies relating to the three most frequent types of sojourners.

Tourists

Tourism is currently the largest single source of cross-national contact in the world. In 2003, 694 million cross-national tourist visits occurred (World Tourism Organization, 2004). Tourist visits are frequently of quite short duration and are often undertaken with groups of co-nationals. For these reasons, direct contact between tourists and those who live in the locations that they visit is quite often restricted to structured vis-itations and routines. Furthermore, contact is frequently buffered by representatives of the hospitality industry, whose task it is to guide, interpret for, and entertain tourists.

The impact of tourism on tourists themselves will vary widely depending upon the type of tourist motivation involved. Those engaging in beach holidays, skiing vaca-tions or sex tourism are least likely to be interested in the local populations of the areas that they visit. Heritage tourism, visits to locations in which films were shot, back-packer holidays and ecotourism all have greater potential to increase awareness of and appreciation of cultural differences (Ward et al., 2001). Despite this diversity, there are some elements common to all forms of tourism, namely absence from one's normal location, and the consequent increased likelihood of unfamiliar bacteria, unfamiliar foods, unfamiliar accommodation, and unfamiliar companions. Consequently, tourists do experience some degree of 'culture shock' in varying degrees (Pearce, 1981).

More importantly, the sheer scale of contemporary tourism ensures that it has a sub-stantial impact on host populations, particularly where the ratio of tourists to local population is high. The most immediate effect is a restructuring of the economy, so that an ever higher proportion of the population is engaged in servicing the needs of tourists, with the consequent loss of previous less profitable occupations and skills. These changes in turn cause a series of stresses and uncertainties that challenge pre-existing cultural values. Berno (1999) compared the impact of tourism on different destinations within the Cook Islands in the Pacific. Within the less visited islands, tourists were treated as guests. In Rarotonga, where tourist visits outnumbered locals by 3.6 to 1, traditional language and practices were lost and there was evidence of the local population adopting the behaviours demonstrated by tourists. Local, even national economies benefit from tourism; some sectors of the host population also benefit eco-nomically and welcome these changes. Host population attitudes have been surveyed in a wide variety of locations (Reisinger & Turner, 2002; Jurowski & Gursoy, 2004), with a balance that differs by location and by distance from major tourist destinations between those who applaud the economic benefits and those who regret the environ-mental and cultural effects.

Urry (1990) identified what he termed the 'tourist gaze', in other words the desire among tourists to emphasize the fact that they have travelled to somewhere different by looking at and photographing sites and spectacles that are exotic and different. In many cases, the very presence of so many tourists has led to the extinction of cultur-ally distinctive ceremonies, events and crafts, so that a pressure then arises to recreate them for the benefit of tourists. Although the revival of traditional skills has a positive aspect, the need to adapt ceremonies in directions that tourists will enjoy watching and to modify cultural artefacts in ways that enhance sales can often distort the very cultural processes being marketed. As Moscardo and Pearce (1999) note, 'ethnic tourism is in danger of consuming the commodity on which it is based' (p. 417).

Thus, the cultural impact of tourism is felt much more by host nations than by the tourists themselves. In some cases, the pressure of tourism has led to the development of cultural training for members of the host nation. For instance Bochner and Coulon (1997) developed culture assimilator training to help Australian hospitality workers respond more effectively to Japanese tourists. Members of the host culture with culture-specific skills then become valued resources as employees in businesses catering to tourists from relevant cultural groups.

Student Sojourners

There are currently estimated to be more than a million student sojourners, sometimes known as international students, at any one time. Since student sojourners tend to be away from their home country much longer than tourists, research has focused more upon the types of relations that they develop during their stay, and how these relationships contribute to their adjustment. It is useful to distinguish between relations with one's co-nationals, relations with host nationals, and relations with student sojourners from nations other than one's own. Rather consistent patterns of findings are reported, even though studies have been done in diverse settings, such as the USA, Australia, Israel, the UK and other European nations (Ward et al., 2001). Sojourners are most likely to report that their best friend during their visit is a co-national. Relations with host nationals are primarily instrumental, that is to say focused on fulfilling academic requirements and gaining help with language. Relations with non-compatriot sojourners, in other words fellow sojourners who are from nations other than one's own, mostly provide social support. Measures of **psychological adaptation** are predicted by better relations of student sojourners with host nationals and with co-nationals.

The difficulty in interpreting these types of results is that we have no way of determining causal relationships between the variables. Does forming relationships cause satisfaction, or are those who are more satisfied better able to form supportive relationships? Or is there a third component, a personality variable, like optimism or social intelligence, that drives both outcomes? Studies that have obtained pre-departure measures from student sojourners can help to clarify this confusion. They confirm that personality is indeed a significant predictor of later adjustment. Ying and Liese (1991) found that pre-departure level of depression predicted adjustment of Taiwanese students in the USA negatively. Ward, Leong, & Low (2004) found that among Australian and Singaporean sojourners, low neuroticism and high extraversion were associated with both **psychological** and **socio-cultural adaptation**.

However, it is not likely that personality attributes by themselves would be sufficient to predict adjustment. We must take account also of the type of culture to which the sojourner is moving. Oguri and Gudykunst (2002) predicted that the match between sojourners' self-construals and those favoured in the local culture would predict adjustment in the USA. **Independent self-construal** was found to predict **psychological adaptation. Socio-cultural adaptation** was predicted by use of more direct communication and greater acceptance of silences. This style was judged to accord with local US norms. Ward, Leong, and Low (2004) tested the 'cultural fit' hypothesis in a different way, comparing the Big Five personality of sojourners with average Big Five norms within the nations where they were sojourning. They found no indication that Australians with a personality more similar to Singaporeans or Singaporeans with a personality more similar to Australians achieved better **psychological adaptation**. The contrast between the results of these two studies may be caused by differences in the circumstances of sojourners in the locations studied, or by the different types of 'fit' that were tested.

Indeed, circumstances vary greatly, making for much diversity in sojourn experiences. Among the variables that appear important are the age of the sojourners, the duration of the sojourn, the degree of similarity between the home and the host culture, the opportunities for meaningful interpersonal relations with host nationals and the level of perceived acceptance–rejection by the host nationals. For example, if the sojourner sees that his or her country does not enjoy a positive image in the eyes of host country nationals, he or she may experience a 'loss of status'. In an early study, Kağıtçıbaşı (1978) examined some of these factors among two groups of Turkish high school students spending a school year in the USA, living with host families. She used both pre-departure and post-return measures of attitudes, self-concepts and world-views. Especially because they lived in accepting families, these sojourners showed positive growth and adjustment, involving greater belief in internal control, higher self-confidence, less authoritarianism, and more world-mindedness compared with matched control groups who spent the same period in Turkey. The sojourners also showed positive readjustment to the home country even one to two years after their return.

This study appears to have tapped a particularly optimal sojourner experience. There is some evidence that student sojourners also quite frequently have some difficulties in returning to their country of origin, experiencing 're-entry' problems. Recently, Ward, Berno, and Main (2002) showed that among Singaporean students returning from Australia, psychological adjustment in Australia predicted **psychological adaptation** back in Singapore. However, socio-cultural adjustment in Australia did not predict **socio-cultural adaptation** back in Singapore. This makes good sense, since **psychological adaptation** is strongly influenced by the personal attributes that travel with one, whereas **socio-cultural adaptation** has more to do with the quite different situational challenges that one would face in Australia and in Singapore.

Organizational Sojourners

Business travel has changed somewhat over the past two decades. In former times, the focus was largely upon expatriate managers, who undertook assignments of anything up to five years, working typically within a subsidiary of a multinational organization. While expatriation does continue, the advent of e-mail and improved travel facilities means that many business trips are very much shorter. As we noted in Chapter 9, much business may be conducted by multinational teams, who communicate by e-mail or by videoconference, and only rarely meet face-to-face. We focus here on employees of business and other types of organization, for example aid agencies and the diplomatic service, who continue to fit the more traditional expatriate role.

Some issues facing organizational sojourners parallel those faced by students. However, there are also additional, distinctive challenges. Being on average older, organizational sojourners are more frequently accompanied by spouses and by children. The adjustments achieved are necessarily tempered by the adjustment of all those who travel, not just the individual directly employed by the organization. Early reports that substantial percentages of business expatriates returned prematurely from their placements have proved to be untrue (Harzing, 1995). Nevertheless, it remains true that premature return is often associated with spouse dissatisfaction (Thomas, 2002). Although a spouse may provide support to an expatriate, there is also the risk that the spouse may not be able to find additional meaningful roles within the local community. Indeed, the spouse may discover quite a different and unwelcome set of role prescriptions for a spouse in the new culture! Among Japanese managers working in the USA, work–family relations were found to affect adjustment in both directions: work pressures affected spouse adjustment, and poor spouse adjustment predicted intention to return early to Japan (Takeuchi, Yun, & Tesluk, 2002). A second hazard faced by organizational sojourners is that they are at the same time required to perform satisfactorily as judged both locally and in their country of origin. Since criteria of success at home and in the new location often contradict one another, this new set of employment challenges can be problematic. For instance, locals may expect behaviours that are respectful of local cultural norms, while head offices will often apply global performance criteria. This problem is best handled through frequent appraisals that include feedback from both local and head office sources (Gregersen, Hite, & Black, 1996).

The distinction between **psychological adaptation** and **socio-cultural adaptation** has also proved fruitful in studies of organizational sojourners. In a study of aid workers in Nepal, identification with the sojourner's co-nationals predicted **psychological adaptation**, whereas identification with local Nepalese predicted **socio-cultural adaptation** (Ward & Rana-Deuba, 1999). Poor **psychological adaptation** was best predicted by personality as measured by external locus of control, low identification with Nepalese, and high reported loneliness (Ward & Rana-Deuba, 2000). However, as in the case of student sojourners, while high **socio-cultural adaptation** no doubt contributes to effectiveness during the placement, it is likely to be of no help to returning expatriates. Sussman (2002) found that among US teachers returning from Japan, those who had identified more strongly with Japanese were those who experienced greatest distress on returning to the USA.

The studies of different types of sojourners that we have reviewed indicate that all those who cross cultural boundaries are faced with varying degrees of role conflict. Some will find ways of handling this tension better than others, but the problem is inescapable. This occurs not just because of sojourners' individual attributes, but also because of the particular groups with whom they identify. We explore these processes more fully in the next chapter.

Summary

Although first language speakers of English frequently fail to appreciate it, language use is by far the most important influence on the outcome of cross-cultural interactions.

Language fluency determines power relations and influences the degree to which persons like one another. Language can be used to define one's identity in relation to others. The absence of a shared language severely constrains the success of a cross-cultural interaction. However, use of a shared language does not ensure that one understands the other party's goals or perspectives. Cross-cultural skill requires an awareness that others' assumptions may differ from one's own and the ability to adapt behaviours in ways that enhance mutual understanding. It is not yet clear whether cross-cultural skill is primarily general or more situation-specific; nor is it certain whether cross-cultural skill is a component skill of any socially intelligent person, or is a separate competency. Cross-cultural contacts are increasing through tourism, which has become a major component of cultural change. In evaluating the experiences of sojourners, who stay longer and interact more widely with locals than tourists, the distinction between **psychological adaptation** and **socio-cultural adaptation** has considerable promise.

Further Reading

1 Brislin, R. (2004). Encouraging depth rather than surface processing about cultural differences through critical incidents and role plays. www.wwu.edu/~culture
2 Bochner, S. (2004). Culture shock due to contact with unfamiliar cultures. www.wwu.edu/~culture
3 Reisinger, Y., & Turner, L.W. (2002). *Cross-cultural behaviour in tourism: Concepts and analysis*. Oxford, UK: Elsevier.
4 Scollon, R., & Scollon, S.W. (2001). *Intercultural communication: A discourse approach*. Malden, MA: Blackwell.
5 Thomas, D.C. (2002). *Essentials of international management: A cross-cultural perspective*. Thousand Oaks, CA: Sage.
6 Ward, C., Bochner, S., & Furnham, A. (2001). *The psychology of culture shock*. (2nd ed.) Hove, UK: Routledge.

Study Questions

1 If you are bilingual, how different does it feel to express yourself in one language rather than in the other? What are some of the things that you can say better in each of your two languages? Why?
2 If you are monolingual, how do you modify your behaviour when talking to those who are conversing with you in their second language, and what impact will these forms of accommodation have upon your relationship with the second-language user?
3 Is cross-cultural skill broadly applicable, or is it more important to know how to be effective in a particular cultural context? Why?
4 If you are a sojourner, what factors will help or hinder your adaptation?

11 Cultural Aspects of Intergroup Relations

... in your 50 groups, with your 50 languages and histories and your 50 blood hatreds and rivalries. But you won't be long like that, brothers, for these are the forces of God you've come to ... . Germans and Frenchmen, Irishmen and Englishmen, Jews and Russians – into the crucible with you all! God is making the American (Israel Zangwill, *The melting pot*, 1909, p. 33)

Almost a century ago, the character in Zangwill's play that speaks the forceful words above already had a potent image of the way in which migration would change the world and the culture of those participating in this evolutionary drama as it unfolds into the twenty-first century. In this chapter, we shall examine whether the world has indeed become a cultural 'melting pot', or whether there are enduring aspects of inter-group relations that limit the extent of such a transformation. We look first at more basic aspects of how members of different groups perceive one another, and then con-sider how these processes act upon those who migrate from one nation to another.

Social Identity Processes

In Chapter 6, we discussed the ways in which individuals in differing social contexts construe themselves, focusing particularly upon the distinction between **independent** and **interdependent self-construals**. While this distinction has particular value to cross-cultural psychologists, it should not be taken as indicating that only those of us who construe ourselves as interdependent are concerned about the reactions of others. Social psychologists have long maintained that processes of social comparison are central to everyone's definition of who one is. A useful formulation was provided by Tajfel's (1981) social identity theory, later reformulated as self-categorization theory (Turner, et al., 1987). According to this formulation, each of us is able to define our-selves in terms of both social identity and personal identity. Social identity is achieved by perceiving oneself as a member of some social groupings that are attractive to us. Each of us has available a range of social identities, based upon age, gender, family, **ethnicity**, nationality, occupation, friendship groups, religious affiliation and so forth. Equally, each of us can define our personal identity on the basis of perceiving differ-ences between ourselves and other individuals. The choices that we make at any one time between a personal or a social identity will be based upon the degree to which they can provide us with a positive self-image. To put it in another way, the need for a positive view of oneself may lead one to a more negative view of others or of groups other than one's own.

Self-categorization theorists understand the choices that we make between personal and social identities as relatively fluid. Through an average day we may perceive ourselves in terms of many different identities, depending upon which is evoked by our individual and social circumstances at the time. From the perspective of self-categorization theory, we should therefore not think of **independent** and **interdependent self-construal** as fixed traits or qualities, but rather as average tendencies to spend more of one's time thinking about oneself in terms of personal identity or in terms of social identities.

If self-categorization theory is to provide us with a useful basis for considering relations between **ethnic groups** and between nations, we need first to consider what evidence there is that the theory is applicable to cultural contexts that differ from the primarily European settings in which it was originally formulated and tested. In Chapter 6, we discussed whether East Asians have the same need for self-enhancement as is typically found among Western respondents. Furthermore, we noted Yuki's (2003) study which indicated that his Japanese respondents were more preoccupied with intra-group relations than with comparing their group with other groups. In another relevant study, De Vries (2003) found that, in ethnically divided Fiji, although Fijians who identified with their in-group did show more in-group bias, they did not derogate their out-group. Reactions to the out-group were predicted by perceptions of prevailing political conditions and social distance.

To determine the strength of these possible limits to the relevance of self-categorization theory, we need direct cross-cultural comparisons of effects. Few such studies have been reported. Chen, Brockner, and Katz (1998) compared the behaviour of randomly composed groups of US and Chinese students. Group members were led to believe that relative to others their group had performed either poorly or well and that they individually had done either poorly or well. In the poor group performance condition, US respondents reacted by rating their in-group lower than was found in other conditions of the experiment. Chinese respondents reacted by rating the out-group lower than was found in other experimental conditions. In other words, US respondents sustained their personal identity by dissociating themselves from their in-group, whereas the Chinese acted to sustain their in-group affiliation by derogating the out-group. These effects were found to be **mediated** by **interdependent self-construal**, such that among those told they had done poorly, respondents high in interdependence favoured their in-group more and their out-group less than those who were more independent. In a second similar study, participants were also given feedback about the performance of the out-group. When the out-group did well and the in-group did not, those with more **interdependent self-construal** were again found to sustain in-group favouritism to a greater extent (Chen, Brockner, & Chen, 2002).

Derlega, Cukur, Kuang, and Forsyth (2002) also obtained cross-cultural support for hypotheses derived from social identity theory. They asked US and a heterogeneous set of non-US students to rate various ways in which they might handle interpersonal, intergroup and international conflicts. **Interdependent self-construal** predicted greater acceptance of the other's viewpoint during interpersonal conflicts, but greater use of threats for conflicts with out-groups. Those with high interdependence also reported greater negative affect in relation to the out-group conflicts. Derlega et al.

suggest that this pattern could arise because those who are high on interdependence identify more strongly with their in-groups. Taken together, these three studies provide us with some confidence that social identity theory and its derivative self-categorization theory do receive support in varying cultural contexts, and furthermore that self-construal measures can help us to understand the effects that are found.

Self-categorization theorists also propose that one is increasingly likely to adopt a given social identity the more similar one is to a prototypical member of a given group. Thus judgements about one's own group identity will draw on images of what is typical of members of different groups. Our concern here is primarily with widely shared images of larger groupings based upon **ethnicity**, '**race**' and nationality. We place **race** in quotation marks because there is no biological evidence for the existence of separate human races (Segall, 1999). Proportions of genetic markers, such as blood groupings and HLA antigens in different human populations, reveal gradual transitions rather than the sharp differences that would be required to identify different races. Continued mingling of populations subsequent to our common origin in Africa has ensured that all persons derive from a common genotypic stock. Each one of us is to a considerable extent African *and* Asian *and* European. Among the many thousands of human genes, social conventions have been created that a few, such as those concerning skin colour and facial characteristics shall be used to define 'racial' groups. However, such groupings have been constructed socially, not biologically. The concept of **ethnicity** provides a better way to describe these different social groupings because it comes closer to reflecting their culturally-constructed basis, even if '**race**' is the more readily apparent one. Both **ethnicity** and nationality are thus social constructs, reflecting the differing social contexts within which persons are socialized. The point at issue in this chapter is to gain an understanding of the factors that lead us to treat these entities as real, identifying with some and rejecting others. We consider nationality first.

Nationality Stereotypes

In earlier chapters, we discussed evidence indicating that national groups differ from one another in terms of prevailing values, beliefs and personality. These findings provide us with what might be considered as relatively accurate, empirically-derived stereotypes. How do these compare with the lay stereotypes prevailing within the general populations of different nations? In discussing the studies reported below, it is important to bear in mind that the lay stereotypes that researchers have detected are not necessarily accurate. More often than not, they are derived from indirect sources such as the mass media, rather than from direct experience. We are not endorsing them, just studying what they are, how they form and how they may affect the behaviour of those who do endorse them.

Hetero-stereotypes

Peabody (1985) asked students in the UK, France, Italy, Germany, Russia and the USA to rate the extent to which various traits were typical of persons from each of the six nations. He found a substantial degree of consensus, particularly between the hetero-stereotype ratings, that is to say the ratings of nations other than one's own. There was agreement for instance that Americans are self-confident, English are self-controlled and Germans are hard-working. Reviewing the published research evidence available at the time, Peabody concluded that the hetero-stereotypes of the students whom he had sampled agreed quite well with the results of empirical studies. In a similar way, Stephan, Stephan, Abalakina, et al. (1996) found consensus across students from six nations that Japanese were hard-working and traditional, Russians were rigid and passive, and Americans were competitive, materialistic and emotional. In a more recent survey McAndrew, Akande, Bridgstock, et al. (2001) surveyed hetero-stereotypes of Australians, British, Canadians, Americans and Nigerians provided by students from these nations and from five further nations in Southern Africa. There was significant agreement between raters from these nations on eight of the nine trait ratings used to measure hetero-stereotypes. The only dimension on which there was disagreement was how selfish or generous were persons from the target nations. As we shall see, this 'morality' dimension is frequently found to be an important basis for making intergroup distinctions, typically favouring the rater's own group.

It is not plausible that those who responded to these surveys had visited all the nations that were rated or had met many persons from them. So, the question arises as to how these representations of nations are created. We can say that they derive from the media, but that does not answer the question of what sources were drawn upon by those who construct the images portrayed by the media. Linssen and Hagendoorn (1994) tested a series of alternative hypotheses as explanations of West European hetero-stereotypes provided by students. By **factor analysing** sets of trait ratings, they identified four dimensions characterizing the ways in which persons from other nations were perceived, naming them as efficiency, dominance, empathy, and emotionality. These dimensions were then correlated with objective national attributes. Understandably, perceived efficiency was predicted by national wealth, and dominance by a nation's political power. Less straightforwardly, empathy was predicted by a nation's smaller size, and emotionality by a nation's more southerly latitude.

The equation of emotionality with southerly latitude, which is often also found within single nations, is most probably related to temperature, and should therefore be reversed in the southern hemisphere. In Chapter 4, we discussed some possible linkages between climate and the types of culture that emerge in warmer climates. These may provide a logical basis for the belief that persons from warmer nations differ on average from those from cooler climates. Sampling students from 26 nations, Pennebaker, Rimé, and Blankenship (1996) tested the belief that persons from the southern part of one's own country are seen as more emotional than those from further north. The predicted effect was found across 21 northern hemisphere nations, but there was no effect in either direction among the five southern hemisphere nations. The effect was stronger in nations further from the equator and stronger in Europe than it was in North America. Pennebaker et al. also asked their respondents to rate themselves on the same scales, and found that there was a significant but weak tendency for those from more southerly locations to see themselves as more emotional than those from further north. Thus, there is a modest grain of truth in these particular stereotypes.

Returning to our topic of national stereotypes, Cuddy, Fiske, Kwan, et al. (2003) sampled students from European nations, asking them to rate persons from their own and all other European Union nations. Their study was designed to test the cross-cultural validity of a model of the structure of stereotypes first developed in relation to gender stereotypes in the USA (Glick & Fiske, 2001). The model is based on the proposition that stereotypes can be classified along two fundamental dimensions, the perceived competence and the perceived warmth of any particular target group. Combination of high and low perceptions of warmth and competence define three possible forms of prejudice, which they named as paternalism, contempt and envy, as well as positive stereotyping which they name as admiration. The results from the European study are portrayed in Box 11.1. The results confirmed Cuddy et al.'s hypotheses that competence ratings would be predicted by a measure of the perceived status of each nation and warmth ratings would be related to a perceived lack of competition with one's own nation. These conclusions concur with those of Linssen and Hagendoorn (1994) in relation to competence, but provide an alternative explanation of the results for warmth.

Box 11.1

Positioning of Shared European Hetero-stereotypes on Two Dimensions

	Low Competence	**High Competence**
High Warmth	('Paternalistic prejudice') • Spain • Italy • Portugal • Greece • Ireland Belgium • • Sweden • France Denmark • • Netherlands Finland • • Luxembourg • Austria	('Admiration') • UK • Germany
Low Warmth	('Contemptuous prejudice')	('Envious prejudice')

Source: Glick & Fiske (2001); Cuddy et al. (2003).

Although there is broad agreement on national hetero-stereotypes, there are also specific factors that will influence the ways in which members of particular nations will characterize each other. Van Oudenhoven, Askervis-Leherpeux, Hannover, et al. (2001) used social identity theory to predict that students' images of one another's nation will reflect the degree to which other nations threaten one's national identity. They proposed that the identity of small nations will be threatened by the existence of larger ones, especially when they speak similar languages, whereas the identity of large nations will not be threatened by the existence of small ones. They took advantage of the fact that Belgium is a smaller nation than neighbouring Germany and France. Furthermore, among Belgians the first language of the Flemish community is Dutch, while the first language of the Walloon community is French. As expected, the Flemish image of Germans comprised more arrogance and less sympathy than did the German image of the Flemish. The contrast between Walloon perceptions of the French and French perceptions of the Walloons was even stronger – a finding that supports the predicted results because both these groups speak French.

While there is thus substantial evidence of consensus as to those national stereotypes that have been most studied, and on some of the factors that influence their formation, Box 11.2 serves to remind us that we should not assume that stereotypes are always fixed and immutable.

Box 11.2

How Changeable are Stereotypes?

Although national hetero-stereotypes may be predictable on the basis of enduring historical, political, and geographical features, they are also open to influence by media coverage of major political events. Haslam, Turner, Oakes, et al. (1992) measured Australian students' stereotypes of Americans at the outbreak of the first Gulf crisis, when Iraq invaded Kuwait. They repeated their measurements six months later, after the military conflict had commenced. The repeat measure showed significant decreases in Australians' ratings of Americans as industrious, straightforward and scientifically-minded, and significant increases in perceptions that they are arrogant, argumentative and tradition-loving.

However, the principal purpose of Haslam et al.'s study was to demonstrate that stereotypes can be changed much more readily, by simple adjustment of the experimental design. Self-categorization theory predicts that our expressed attitudes will vary depending upon the way that we categorize ourselves at a specific point in time. Haslam et al. showed that they could elicit similar and equally large changes in Australian stereotypes of the Americans simply by mentioning the names of other nations, such as Iraq, in the course of their experimental instructions.

This study amplifies earlier work that pointed to stability of stereotypes over time. For example, a series of studies conducted over a period of 50 years with students in the USA pointed to stability of stereotypes regarding ethnic and national groups despite world events that challenged some of them (Gilbert, 1951; Karlins, Coffman & Walters, 1969; Katz & Braly, 1933; Singleton & Kerber, 1980). The work of self-categorization theorists suggests that through life we acquire many differing stereotypic representations of other groups. Which ones are elicited will depend on the social context at a given time. While some persons may hold chronic prejudices, others will focus on positive attributes of another group at some times and negative attributes at other times, depending on the presence or absence of threat, differing audiences and so forth. By using experimental methods, Haslam et al. enlarge our understanding of stereotyping processes. While their study provides some basis for hope that the negative national stereotypes that frequently accompany international conflicts are amenable to change, it is unfortunately equally true that such stereotypes can be fostered and strengthened by biased media coverage based on traditional stereotypes.

Auto-stereotypes

There is value in knowing the prevailing hetero-stereotypes for particular nations. Such information may help, for instance, in understanding individuals' migration decisions or the dynamics of international diplomacy. However, for most individuals the principal relevance of hetero-stereotypes is that they provide a contrast with one's national auto-stereotype. At least at those times when one is thinking of oneself in terms of one's nationality, social identity theory asserts that we will seek to define our nation and co-nationals more positively than other nations and their co-nationals. However, Peabody (1985) observed that the auto-stereotypes in his samples were in fact no more positive than the hetero-stereotypes. This was also the case in the McAndrew et al. (2001) study, except that the Nigerian auto-stereotype was much *more* positive than the Nigerian hetero-stereotype and the US auto-stereotype was much *less* positive than the US hetero-stereotype. These divergences may have occurred because respondents were students and students do not necessarily always identify with those whom they see as typical of their nation. Students from many nations endorse more radical values than those that they would attribute to their nation as a whole. Where this is so, they would be likely to identify less strongly with their own nation.

Consistent with this reasoning, Smith, Giannini, Helkama, et al. (2005) found that identification with one's nation varied substantially between their student samples from nine European nations, with the lowest scores being from German respondents. However, in all samples, individuals' identification with their nation correlated with a more positive auto-stereotype. This was especially true for those with an **interdependent self-construal**. Stephan, Stephan, Abalakina et al. (1996) also tested predictions from social identity theory. On their measure, Japanese, Russian and US respondents all perceived positive traits as more typical of persons from their nation and negative traits as less typical of them than of persons from other nations.

Major political events may also contribute to the divergence of auto-stereotypes from hetero-stereotypes. The data collected by Peabody (1985) and the more recent data of Stephan et al. (1996) indicate that, despite the end of the Cold War, Western respondents continue to hold a negative hetero-stereotype of Russians, seeing them as typically serious, firm, hard-working and persistent. In contrast, Russians see themselves as generous, rash, frank and impractical (Peabody & Shmelyov, 1996). We currently lack systematic data from respondents with the type of everyday contact with Russians that would illuminate their self-perceived emotionality and spontaneity.

There are some negative aspects of most nations' identity that cannot be readily denied. Social identity theory predicts that under such circumstances, one will seek out alternative bases of comparison between one's group and other groups. Poppe and Linssen (1999) reported an instance of this type. Sampling schoolchildren from six nations in Central and Eastern Europe, they found that persons from Italy, Germany and the UK were perceived as higher on a series of positive qualities that the researchers summarized as greater competence. However, the schoolchildrens' auto-stereotypes emphasized a second set of traits that were summarized as representing the superior moral qualities of their nation. These effects were strongest where the rater saw his or her own nation as small and powerless. Poppe (2001) was able to confirm some of the causal relationships between these variables by collecting further data one year later. Where the economic circumstances of the raters' nation had declined, the schoolchildren perceived persons from the more successful nations as even less moral.

A positive sense of one's national identity can also be fostered by focusing on key events within one's nation's history. Liu, Lawrence, Ward, and Abraham (2003) asked students within Malaysia and Singapore to identify the ten key events in their nation's history. The events listed by ethnic Chinese, Indian and Malay respondents within these two nations were rather similar, focusing mainly on the achievements of independence and national statehood. Liu et al. argue that this 'hegemonic' view of shared history enhances identification with one's nation rather than with one's ethnic identity. However, in Taiwan, although there is a shared view of history, that history is evaluated in contrasting ways, depending on the point in history at which the respondent's family moved to Taiwan, leading to alternative identifications with either a Chinese or a Taiwanese identity and representation of Taiwanese history (Huang, Liu & Chang, 2004).

Other types of historical circumstance also foster contested views of history. For instance, Liu, Wilson, McClure, and Higgins (1999) found that *pakeha* (Caucasian) and Maori New Zealand students gave very different listings of key events in their nation's history, and of their significance. Liu et al. suggest that Maori empowerment is generating a contested rather than a hegemonic view of New Zealand history. Many inhabitants of European nations currently see no conflict between identifying with their nation and identifying with being a European, perhaps as a way of overcoming their historical legacy of wars with one another. In contrast, identification with being British is negatively correlated with identification with being European (Cinnirella, 1997; Smith et al., 2005). Some time ago, Gergen (1973) argued that social psychology should be seen as a type of social history, recording how we currently relate to one another, without assuming that what researchers find now will necessarily remain the same in the future. Studies of national and supranational identities reveal a further role for history in psychology: the way that we represent our past national history constrains our contemporary identity choices.

Ethnic Stereotyping

Research into **ethnic** stereotypes differs substantially from that into national stereotypes. The focus has been largely upon hetero-stereotypes and even within that field has strongly emphasized negative attitudes, which are more typically described as prejudices. Furthermore, **ethnic** communities within different nations are rarely the same, so that stereotypes have typically been studied within a single nation, which gives little detailed information as to the extent to which such stereotypes transcend national boundaries.

While the early US research into the authoritarian personality by Adorno et al. (1950) has been subject to much later criticism, it has encouraged subsequent researchers to give attention to the fact that those who endorse prejudiced stereotypes of one **ethnic** community are often also prejudiced against other minority communities. Thus we have current measures of right wing authoritarianism (Altemeyer, 1988), subtle and blatant prejudice (Pettigrew & Meertens, 1995), and ethnic tolerance (Berry & Kalin, 1995).

Generalized measures of prejudice do have their usefulness, but they also risk diverting attention from the way in which we *all* maintain images of ethnic groups other than our own. Going beyond personal factors, there are also *situational* factors that play a role, particularly with regard to prejudiced *behaviours*. For example, an early study of ethnic prejudice showed that the majority of Caucasian-Americans in a southern US town interacted with African-Americans in the work situation where interaction was required and expected, but did not interact with them in the city where segregation was the norm (Minard, 1952). Indeed, the distinction that Pettigrew draws between subtle and blatant prejudice (Pettigrew, 1998) combines a personality and situational perspective on prejudice. In societies such as the Netherlands where it is not 'politically correct' among the more educated middle classes to express blatant prejudice, the situational pressures cause prejudice towards ethnic minorities to be expressed in more subtle and indirect ways.

By using measures of generalized prejudice, we also direct our attention towards particularly prejudiced persons and away from the specific content of the stereotypes attributed to particular groups. In thinking about the ways in which particular **ethnic groups** may actually be perceived, it is useful to draw again on Glick and Fiske's (2001) model of types of prejudice. Box 11.3 shows the different ways in which **ethnic groups** within the US were rated (Fiske, Cuddy, Glick, & Xu, 2002). Berry and Kalin's (1995) analysis of a Canadian national survey also indicated that the population as a whole had a shared evaluation of their relative preference for different **ethnic groups**, with European **ethnicities** being most favoured. In their sample, the difference between more tolerant and more intolerant individuals was that the intolerant made much sharper distinctions between those **ethnic groups** they favoured and those they rejected.

Box 11.3

Positioning of US Ethnic Stereotypes along two Dimensions

	Low Competence	High Competence
High Warmth	('Paternalistic prejudice')	('Admiration')
		Black Professionals •
	Migrant Workers •	Asians •
	Hispanics •	
		• Jews
	• Poor Whites • Poor Blacks	• Arabs
Low Warmth	('Contemptuous prejudice')	('Envious prejudice')

Source: Fiske, Cuddy, Glick, & Xu (2002).

An alternative approach to the study of prejudice is to study the processes whereby prejudicial judgements are created. Media portrayals of **ethnic groups** can certainly contribute to this process, through repetitive portrayals of association between **ethnicity** and social problems. Similar processes occur in face-to-face relations. Verkuyten (2001) conducted focus groups in which Dutch adults were asked to discuss their multi-cultural neighbourhood. Four strategies for arriving at critical judgements of **ethnic minorities** were identified: describing behaviour as abnormal, identifying behaviour as transcending moral standards, presenting extreme examples of behaviours as typi-cal, and asserting that certain behaviours deviated from the cultural norms of a given **ethnic minority**. Other researchers have sought to explain prejudice by examining some of the more specific beliefs that are associated with prejudice. Several lines of investigation have been developed, which we examine in turn.

Integrated Threat Theory Stephan and Stephan (1996) hypothesized that prejudice towards **ethnic groups** may be associated with any or all of four different perceived threats, namely, realistic threats, symbolic threats, intergroup anxiety or negative stereotypes. Realistic threats could include perceived competition for jobs, threats to one's health or environmental pollution. Symbolic threats would be perceived threats to the values and norms of one's cultural group. Intergroup anxiety would be a threat related, for instance, to past conflicts or to minimal prior contact. Negative stereotypes could lead to expectations of difficult or unpleasant contact. Stephan, Ybarra, Martinez, et al. (1998) asked students in Spain to rate their level of negative emotions towards Moroccan immigrants, while students in Israel rated their negative emotions toward Ethiopian and Russian immigrants. They also rated each of the four types of threat that they experienced. For perceptions of Moroccans and Ethiopians, the strongest predictors of the respondents' negative emotions were intergroup anxiety and nega-tive stereotyping. For perceptions of the Russians, the significant predictors were inter-group anxiety and symbolic threat. In a similar study, Stephan, Diaz-Loving, and Duran (2000) found that the attitudes of US students towards Mexicans were best pre-dicted by intergroup anxiety, while Mexican student attitudes towards the USA were predicted by both intergroup anxiety and negative stereotypes. Intergroup anxiety is thus the most consistent predictor of negative emotion, but we need to look more closely at the bases of this anxiety.

Realistic Conflict Theory Esses, Dovidio, Jackson, and Armstrong (2001) have conducted studies in North America that focus upon the first of Stephan and Stephan's four threats. The 'zero-sum' belief that more jobs for immigrants necessarily means that there are fewer jobs for non-immigrants has been repeatedly found to predict levels of rated reluctance to admit immigrants. Furthermore, when messages endorsing or deny-ing the truth of zero-sum beliefs are given to respondents, their rated reluctance to admit immigrants is caused to rise or to fall in accordance with the effect of these mes-sages on zero-sum belief. Thus, like stereotypes, the expression of prejudiced attitudes can be experimentally manipulated.

Jackson, Brown, Brown, and Marks (2001) also compared the predictive power of prejudice and perceived threats. They drew on data from the Eurobarometer, an annual public opinion survey focused upon representative samples from each nation within the European Union. Jackson et al. compared various predictors of whether respondents had asserted that immigrants should be returned to their country of origin. In 14 of the 15 nations sampled, the perceived threat of 'encroachment' was a significant predictor. Encroachment is defined in terms that place it within Stephan and Stephan's category of symbolic threats – a threat to our values and normal ways of life. In contrast, self-rated racism proved to be a significant predictor in only 11 nations. Beliefs that some limits should be placed on acceptance of immigrants, and a belief that immigrants do not make valued contributions were predictive in nine nations. The differing cultural contexts of nations in Europe and varying rates of immigration are reflected in the fact that these predictors accounted for markedly different amounts of variance in each nation, ranging from 11% in Ireland to 45% in France. This study also illustrates the way in which specific beliefs can account for more variance in effects than a simple overall measure of prejudice.

Social Dominance Orientation   Sidanius and Pratto (1999) have formulated a theory as to the way in which different groups within a nation will relate to one another. They propose that groups with higher status will endorse a set of attitudes and beliefs that justify their privileged status, such as the 'just world' hypothesis, which is a belief that those with lower status in society are there because of their own failures, thus making 'internal' attributions for their disadvantaged position and ignoring social injustices. Those who endorse this 'social dominance orientation' (SDO) will identify with their group and see less reason to take a concerned interest in other groups. Members of lower status groups may also endorse SDO beliefs, but if they do so they will identify less with their own group and, where possible, seek to move to higher status groups. SDO theory was initially formulated within the USA and support for its validity was found there in relation to both gender and **ethnicity**. SDO predictions have been subsequently tested in Canada, Israel and Taiwan (Levin & Sidanius, 1999; Pratto, Liu, Levin, and Sidanius et al., 2000). In each nation, the researchers developed locally relevant measures of sexism, ethnic prejudice, conservatism and support for hegemony. The SDO measure was positively correlated with these measures and with identification with high status in-groups in almost all instances. Exceptions were that SDO did not predict **ethnic** prejudice in relation to marriage partners in Taiwan, whereas in Israel it did predict **ethnic** prejudice in relation to marriage partnerships with Jews, but not with Arabs. Thus, there is evidence for the general validity of predictions derived from SDO theory, but local circumstances do place some limits on its scope.

More recently, SDO has been used to clarify responses by groups within Lebanon to the 2001 attack on the World Trade Center in New York. Identification with an Arab identity correlated negatively with SDO and positively with the feeling that the September 11 attack was justified (Levin, Henry, Pratto, & Sidanius, 2003). In the authors' view, support for the attack is more accurately interpreted in terms of a rejection of US dominance, rather than in terms of a clash of cultural values (Sidanius, Henry, Pratto, & Levin, 2004). SDO has sometimes been presented as though it is an alternative measure of personality-based prejudice. However, Esses, Dovidio, Jackson, and Armstrong (2001) found that within the USA, SDO correlated significantly with zero-sum beliefs about job competition, but only weakly with prejudiced attitudes toward black or Asian immigrants. Furthermore, the relationship between SDO and negative attitudes towards immigration was **mediated** by an experimentally manipulated measure of zero-sum job competition. Thus, SDO is better thought of as a set of beliefs about intergroup relations rather than as a personality-based indicator of prejudice. SDO theory has particular relevance to the key issues of immigration and multiculturalism, since migrants are typically assigned a low initial status. SDO also appears to be akin to the conservatism pole of Schwartz's (1992) **individual-level** dimension of conservation versus openness to change and Leung and Bond's (2004) measure of social cynicism.

Individualistic Groups versus Collectivistic Groups

Thus far, our discussion of the ways in which groups within a society relate to one another has made few connections with concepts employed by cross-cultural psychologists. However, there are some clear ways in which such links can and should be made (Smith & Long, in press). If social identity rests upon group memberships, we may expect different approaches to intergroup relations within collectivist cultures than in individualistic cultures. At the **individual level**, we may expect **interdependent self-construal** to predict stronger degrees of in-group bias. For example, among Chinese and Malay students in Singapore, only those scoring high on **interdependent self-construal** showed in-group bias (Lee & Ward, 1998).

In thinking about the nature of intergroup relations in nations with more collectivist cultures, we must come back to the ambiguities in the definition of collectivism. Is it the case that collectivism is primarily relational, and that members of collectivist groups are mostly preoccupied with what goes on within their group and are relatively indifferent to what happens outside that group? Alternatively, is collectivism more a matter of category membership, such that group members are constantly aware of the ebb and flow of their relations with other groups? The answer to these questions may differ in different parts of the world. Even among Western researchers into social identity theory, it is now proposed that comparison of one's group with other groups is more salient in some settings than in others. Hinkle and Brown (1990) proposed that the culture of different groups varies along two orthogonal dimensions. Firstly, groups may be individualistic or collective in orientation, depending upon the degree to which their activities are integrated and interdependent. Secondly, groups may be relational or separate. In other words their reason for existence may involve comparison with other groups, as in the case of a sports team, or may be unrelated to other groups, as in the case of a family. This typology of groups closely parallels Kağıtçıbaşı's (1996b) typology of self-construals that we discussed in Chapter 5.

Hinkle and Brown predicted that bias towards one's in-group would only be found in groups that were collectivist and relational. Using **individual-level** measures of interdependence and relational orientation, evidence in favour of this prediction has been found among groups in one individualist nation, the UK (Brown, Hinkle, Ely, et al., 1992) and in one collectivist nation, Brazil (Torres, 1996). Further tests of this model are required, but there may be difficulty in testing it within different cultures, simply because the extent to which different types of group do compare themselves with one another may vary between cultures. This problem was already apparent in

Torres' study. Affiliation to one's social class was found to be much more relational among Brazilian school children than among UK schoolchildren.

Honour Cultures

In some collectivist cultures, a relational orientation towards other groups is particularly salient. If some offence to the dignity or reputation of a member of one's group is given, it will be the responsibility of appropriate members of one's group to exact a suitable penalty from the person or group that has given offence. Honour cultures are said to exist in parts of Mediterranean Europe and the Middle East, Latin America, and South Asia. In cultures of this type the concept of honour has a distinctive meaning. In order to contrast the understanding of honour in an individualist and a collectivist culture, Mosquera, Manstead, and Fischer (2000, 2002) obtained free descriptions of situations having relevance to honour, its loss or its enhancement from schoolchildren and adults in the Netherlands and Spain. In the Netherlands, honour was understood to be associated with self-achievements and autonomy. In contrast, in Spain, honour was linked with one's family and with interdependence with others. Honour was considered a more important concept in Spain and was more strongly associated with the emotions of pride, shame, and anger. The Spanish concept of *pundonor* and related concepts such as Greek *philotimo* refer to a personal dignity or honour, which is maintained by fulfilling one's obligations to the members of one's in-group. These obligations include loyalty and generous hospitality to those who are favoured, but also firm defence of the group's honour in face of a threat or insult. As we noted in Chapter 8, an interesting reflection of this different understanding is found in comparisons of insults. In the Netherlands, swear words mostly target the individual, but in Turkey they also target the person's family members, stressing the entanglement of the individual's honour with that of the immediate family (Uskul & Semin, 2004).

Traditional honour cultures are said to have developed in pastoral cultures (Peristiany, 1965). The dispersed nature of pastoral herds makes theft of cows, sheep or camels relatively easy and traditional law enforcement difficult. Informal means of sanctioning those who offended against one's group therefore arose. Central values in such cultures were male valour and the protection of female virtue. Breaches of the honour code would elicit vengeance, including honour killings where the offence given was great, for instance in a case of sexual infidelity, or flight from an arranged marriage. These retributions were normative and would be approved by one's in-group members.

While honour killings are less frequent than in former times, contemporary studies indicate continuing, distinctive attributes of honour cultures within the USA (Nisbett & Cohen, 1996). Cohen and Nisbett (1997) mailed job application letters to companies from someone who had supposedly participated in an honour-related killing. Responses from companies in the south and west of the USA were more positive than were those from the north and east. They also sent information relating to an honour killing to newspapers. The stories created by newspapers in the south and west were more sympathetic. Cohen and Nisbett were able to show that these results were not simply attributable to a more favourable response to violence in general – the differences found were distinctive to honour-related episodes. Traditions can even influence law.

Until quite recently, saving one's own or one's family's honour was considered an ameliorating circumstance in honour killings in the Turkish penal code.

Vandello and Cohen (2003) asked students in Brazil and the USA to rate the damage to a man's reputation that would be caused by his female partner's infidelity. They also rated the extent to which that reputation could be restored through the use of violence and the extent to which the woman should accept her partner's violent response. Responses to these questions were significantly more in accord with the norms of an honour culture among respondents from Brazil and the southern USA than were those from respondents in the north of the USA. Similar results were obtained when Vandello and Cohen staged an experiment in which a naïve subject witnessed a man's apparent violence towards a woman. Both the man and the woman were actually experimental accomplices. Respondents from the northern USA expressed less tolerance of the violence than did those from the southern USA and formed a more favourable impression of the victim when she condemned the violence rather than blaming herself for its occurrence.

Not all collectivist cultures are honour cultures. The elements of honour cultures have not been identified in East Asian cultures, for example. If there are in fact distinctive forms of collectivist cultures, we shall need to understand more fully how they have arisen and to take account of those differences in analysing what occurs when individuals migrate from (or to) these varying types of collectivist cultural contexts.

Religion and Intergroup Relations

In the contemporary world a substantial number of violent conflicts are found between groups for whom religious affiliation is a major source of identity. Often, one protagonist in these conflicts is an individualistic group or nation in which Judaeo-Christianity is espoused, while the other is a relatively collectivistic group or nation in which Islam is espoused. Analysis of these conflicts requires more detailed treatment than can be provided here, but protection of honour is often one among many of the issues at stake. In addressing these conflicts, cross-cultural psychologists can provide some types of information that can contribute to a fuller understanding of their dynamics. Huntington (1996) portrays these conflicts as a fundamental clash of civilizations, with religion as a central component in that clash. As we saw in earlier chapters, there is indeed a contrast in the **nation-level** distribution of values around the world. However, this distribution does not map very closely onto the distribution of religious affiliations. Furthermore, an **individual-level** study sampling from 11 nations showed no significant differences in the correlation between self-rated religiosity and the Schwartz values espoused by adherents to the monotheistic religions of the world, Christianity, Islam and Judaism (Huismans, 1994). Those who rated themselves as more religious endorsed tradition, conformity and benevolence most strongly.

Of course, it may be the case that those who become most actively involved in intergroup conflicts differ from the general population. Khan and Smith (2003) compared the **individual-level** Schwartz values espoused by members of two groups in Pakistan. Both groups had a Moslem membership, but one group was actively engaged in politically-motivated terrorism. Members of the terrorist group scored significantly higher on hedonism, stimulation and power values, while the other group scored higher on benevolence, universalism and conformity values. Terrorist group members also scored high on **independent self-construal**. The implication of these studies is that it is an oversimplification to analyse contemporary conflicts in terms of clashes based upon religion. They are better thought of as intergroup conflicts, driven by some of the factors discussed earlier in this chapter such as social dominance, inequality, realistic threat and honour.

Montiel and Shah (2004) investigated the ways in which our perspective on such conflicts is coloured by relevant group loyalties. They chose to sample students from the Philippines, which has a Christian majority and a Moslem minority, and from Malaysia, which has a Moslem majority and a Christian minority. Christian and Moslem respondents from both countries were asked to respond to one or other version of a scenario in which a suicide bomber is described either as a terrorist or as a freedom-fighter, who bombs a building and kills many people. As they predicted, Montiel and Shah found no effect of nationality or of religious affiliation on ratings of the qualities of the bomber. However, members of minority groups in both nations responded significantly more positively to the freedom-fighter label and less positively to the terrorist label than did members of the majority groups.

Thus, it is the experience of being a minority group member rather than religious affiliation that proved to be a key causal variable in this setting. Migrants are very frequently also in a minority group and we next consider their experiences.

Migration

People move from one cultural context to another for a wide variety of reasons. These range from the coercive impetus of flight from war or persecution to the freely taken choice to move to another location to take up a new job or to live closer to one's relatives. We noted in Chapter 1 that the largest element in contemporary migration is movement from rural to urban locations. Ruback, Pandey, Begum, et al. (2004) surveyed migrants who were slum-dwellers in New Delhi, Dhaka and Islamabad. The most frequent reason for moving to the city was to search for work, but many respondents also attributed their move to fate. Attribution to fate was related to perceived lack of personal control and was not associated with religion or with degree of poverty.

Migrants from rural to urban contexts can experience many of the difficulties that are faced by those who migrate from one nation to another. However, most studies of migration have been focused upon international migration. In the contemporary world, persons from a great range of cultural backgrounds are to be found in the larger cities of the twenty-first century. In addition to nations such as Canada, Israel, Australia, New Zealand, and the USA that are openly seeking certain kinds of immigrants, many other population movements are occurring. We find Japanese in Brazil, Bangladeshis in Japan, Vietnamese in Finland, Senegalese in Italy, Turks in Germany, Croatians in Sweden, Surinamese in the Netherlands, Filipinos in Hong Kong, and North African Arabs in France. We find Kazakh Poles who speak no Polish and Russian Germans who speak no German re-migrating to Germany and to Poland, respectively. It is a kaleidoscopic mix!

In gaining the best understanding of the processes that attend these cultural transfusions, we need conceptual models that capture the core processes that are involved. We have touched on two such models in this chapter already, namely Zangwill's concept of the melting pot and the social psychological formulation of social identity theory. The first of these suggests an inexorable process of cultural blending, while the second underlines the way that host populations may not always be welcoming to immigrants. Current research is mostly formulated in terms of the process of **acculturation**.

Assessing Acculturation

Given its practical importance, it is no surprise that the study of **acculturation** has become a major area of investigation in recent years. We focus first on how best to define it.

Conceptual Issues

Although there was some earlier interest in the topic, a widely accepted definition of **acculturation** is the one first formulated by three anthropologists, Redfield, Linton, and Herskovits (1936):

> Acculturation comprehends those phenomena which result when groups of individuals having different cultures come into continuous first hand contact, with subsequent changes in the original culture patterns of either or both groups ... under this definition acculturation is to be distinguished from culture change, of which it is but one aspect, and assimilation, which is at times a phase of acculturation. (pp. 149–52)

A notable aspect of this definition is that it is focused upon cultures, not upon individuals, and that it envisages acculturation as a process in which either one or both parties experiences cultural change. Thus, in order to make use of it, we need to keep in mind our discussions in earlier chapters of the levels of analysis issue. Extensive migration into a particular nation may or may not cause changes in the culture patterns of that nation. For instance, in recent decades, migration has had a major influence on the range of cuisine that is offered by restaurants in many nations. This change can in turn affect also what people choose to eat at home. However, the major focus of **acculturation** researches has been upon immigrants rather than upon members of the host nation. Culture-level processes tell us little about the experiences of these individual migrants, or of host-nation persons with whom they have varying degrees of contact.

In order to focus on these experiences, we need to conceptualize the process of psychological or **individual-level acculturation**. We already discussed Ward et al.'s (2001) distinction between **psychological adaptation** and **socio-cultural adaptation** in Chapter 10, and these concepts give a valuable indication that worthwhile measures of **acculturation** require attention both to the individual's experience and to that individual's contact with other cultural groups.

The simplest conceptualization of **acculturation** used by researchers has been to equate it with assimilation. Scales have been devised that comprise, for instance, items measuring the extent to which members of a specific immigrant group speak English, eat typical American foods, watch English language television stations, and so forth. An example of this type is the widely used Suinn-Lew Asian Self-Identity **Acculturation** Scale (Suinn, Ahuna, & Khoo, 1992). Scales of this type have been increasingly criticized on the grounds that they fail to separate adequately those who are actively engaged in both cultural groups from those who are not much involved in either group. For instance, in answer to the question 'With whom do you now associate in your community?', the answer on a five-point scale 'About equally Anglo groups and Asian groups' scores three, and confounds some respondents who are isolated from both communities with others who are actively engaged in both. In answer to the same question, 'Almost exclusively, Anglos, Blacks, Hispanics and other non-Asian groups' scores five, and would identify those who are actively avoiding their own ethnic group. Because of these anomalies, scores on this scale would be unlikely to predict degree of **socio-cultural adaptation**.

Berry (1997) has popularized an alternative model of **acculturation** that is depicted in Box 11.4, and which is now used frequently by researchers from many nations. He distinguishes four **acculturation** strategies on the basis of the degree to which an immigrant seeks to maintain the characteristics of their culture of origin and the degree to which they seek to engage with the majority culture. Berry identifies a multitude of factors that may lead particular immigrants to adopt one or other of these four orientations towards **acculturation**. It is likely that all immigrants face considerable difficulties when first arriving at their chosen destination. The most obvious difficulties are those associated with language skills, the loss of former support networks, the need for accommodation and for employment. Numerous studies have now been reported which test the proposition that immigrants whose responses fall into the 'integration' category will fare best on a variety of measures of adjustment, while those who favour assimilation will also do better than those who favour separation or marginalization. However, while it is widely believed that these hypotheses are supported (Berry & Sam, 1997), the associations found between favoured **acculturation** style and measures of adaptation have varied from one study to another and are not always in the predicted direction (Rudmin, 2005). Integration may indeed be the optimal **acculturation** style, but if it is, we need a clearer understanding of why the measures that have been used have failed to yield clearer results. We discuss several reasons in the sections that follow.

The use of the verb 'favour' in the preceding paragraph reflects the way in which Berry describes his model. As Box 11.4 shows, the **acculturation** strategies are defined by what the immigrant *values*. However, immigrants are rarely able to make an entirely free choice as to the position that they can take up at their chosen destination. The positions open to them will be constrained by the attitudes of the majority population, the policies of their host nation, and the resources that are consequently made available to them. As the earlier parts of this chapter have underlined, majority populations are by no means always welcoming to those immigrants whom they perceive as out-groups, and may be willing to accept them only if they accept substantial status loss and enter more menial roles than those they held in their country of origin. They are often also more inclined to accept those minorities whom they consider to be not very different from themselves.

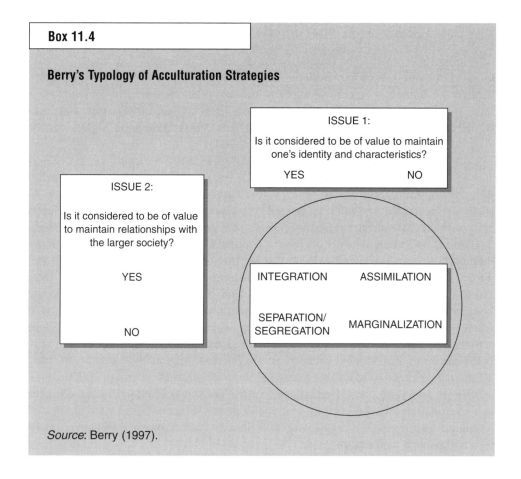

Box 11.4

Berry's Typology of Acculturation Strategies

ISSUE 1:

Is it considered to be of value to maintain one's identity and characteristics?

YES   NO

ISSUE 2:

Is it considered to be of value to maintain relationships with the larger society?

YES

NO

INTEGRATION   ASSIMILATION

SEPARATION/
SEGREGATION   MARGINALIZATION

Source: Berry (1997).

To understand these issues more clearly, some recent researchers have followed Berry's early lead (Berry & Annis, 1974) by surveying the preferences of majority nation respondents as well as those of immigrant groups. Van Oudenhoven, Prins, and Buunk (1998) found that Moroccan and Turkish immigrants in the Netherlands both favoured integration, while majority Dutch respondents favoured assimilation most strongly, but were also favourable to integration. Zagefka and Brown (2002) found that Turks in Germany favoured integration, and that Germans preferred that the Turks integrate. However, the German respondents believed that the Turks preferred separation. In fact, some other studies have found that separation is indeed favoured by Turks in Germany (Piontkowski, Florack, Hoelker, & Obdrzalek, 2000) as well as by lower status Turks in Canada (Ataca & Berry, 2002). German and Israeli majority respondents favoured integration of ethnic Germans and Jews re-migrating from Russia, respectively, whereas Finns favoured assimilation of ethnic Finnish returnees (Jasinskaya-Lahti, Liebkind, Horenczyk, & Schmitz, 2003).

An alternative measure of majority preferences has been developed by Bourhis, Moise, Perreault, and Senecal (1997). This measure parallels Berry's four categories, but adds a fifth, individualism. Those who endorse the individualism option would be those who assert that immigrants should be evaluated on the basis of their personal qualities, not on the basis of their affiliation with **ethnic** categories. Using this measure, it has been found that majority preferences also vary, depending upon whether a particular minority is positively valued by the majority. Montreuil and Bourhis (2001) found that French Canadian students endorsed integration and individualism more strongly for European French immigrants, but assimilation, segregation or exclusion more strongly for Haitians. Similarly, Israeli students favoured integration and individualism for Russian and Ethiopian immigrants, but assimilation, segregation or exclusion for Israeli Arabs (Bourhis & Dayan, 2004).

Majority attitudes toward **ethnic minorities** rest on the degree of perceived difference of the 'other' (Montreuil & Bourhis, 2001), which together with perceived social status of the immigrant group, serves as the basis of an 'ethnic hierarchy' (Schalk-Soekar & van de Vijver, 2004). In general, the more different an immigrant group is perceived to be, the greater is the rejection of that group. For instance, an early study in France showed that a greater degree of prejudice was experienced by North Africans than by Portuguese immigrants, even though the former speak French while the latter do not (Malewska-Peyre, 1980). A paradox inherent in integration rather than assimilation is that maintenance of original cultural features tends to reinforce the immigrant's perceived 'difference' from the majority culture. This is particularly true where religious difference is the case. For example, Islamic schools and other religious activities of Moslem immigrants are supported by multicultural policies in many European states, but Moslem immigrants are rejected more as they assume an overt Moslem identity, often as a consequence of these activities (Kağıtçıbaşı, 1997b).

Majority preferences are often reflected in the policies enacted by the government in a given nation. Box 11.5 provides an adult's personal memoir of a Dutch childhood immigrant experience in New Zealand at a time 50 years ago, when the government policies favoured assimilation.

Box 11.5

Assimilation Pressures

'We...came to New Zealand when 'assimilation' was the official culture. We weren't Dutch, the Government called us 'new New Zealanders'. We bought into it, but our Dutch accents set us apart. We wanted desperately to be the same as everyone else. Our parents had left the Netherlands for good. To help us adjust, English was spoken at home. In our own eyes we were 'kiwis', although we were obviously foreign. Our parents' accents were an embarrassment. It was a shock to find out later from former classmates that we had one too. We hated being labelled as Dutch.

For a long time, I thought it was just the way we were. There was sort of fellow feeling with the few other Dutch children at school, but you didn't feel inclined to get too close to them. Dutch children that came to visit were more like surrogate cousins than friends. It only dawned on me later that it wasn't the way we were, but how others defined us and shaped our attitudes. It was like the adoptions of the time – forget your past and your other identity, you're one of us now. Don't hang out with your former kind.

(Continued)

Box 11.5 Continued

I'm ashamed to admit it, but a Dutch accent still sets off alarm bells in my head. I'm nervous about Dutch clubs, people who call themselves Dutchies. My defences go up. Not so much as they used to, because I've been back to Holland. There, people are normal, relaxed, not trying to impress anyone'.

Source: De Bres (1997).

Measurement Issues

While Berry's typology of strategies does capture important aspects of the immigration experience, a second aspect of current debate on its validity concerns how these orientations may best be validly measured. The four acculturation strategies have typically been assessed by asking respondents to what extent they agree with a series of statements, each of which includes *both* of the elements that define that strategy. For instance, one of the statements used by Montreuil and Bourhis (2001) was, 'Immigrants should maintain their own heritage culture while also adopting the Quebecois culture'. This was one of three statements that the authors used to measure preference for integration. Items like this contain two separate elements, which poses difficulties for respondents, since they may agree with one half more than with the other half. Overlap between the questions defining each strategy also means that the measures are not independent of one another (Rudmin, 2005).

Items representing marginalization are even more problematic because they ask respondents whether or not they agree with two negative statements that take the form, 'Immigrants should not do X and they should not do Y'. In some languages, like Mandarin, one indicates agreement with a negatively worded question by saying 'yes', but in others including English, one would indicate agreement by saying 'no'. For instance, an English speaker would answer 'Should Moslem immigrants not have Islamic schools?' with 'No', if they agreed that they should not. The scope for confusion is evident. Sampling Turkish Dutch schoolchildren as well as adults, Arends-Toth and van de Vijver (2003) compared the predictive ability of measures of this type with simplified measures that ask one question at a time. The simplified items proved more psychometrically satisfactory. Future studies will benefit from improved measurements of this type.

Further Ambiguities in the Study of Acculturation

There are further issues that must be addressed if we are to gain the best possible understanding of the acculturation process. We shall discuss three such issues here. Firstly, as was indicated in Box 1.1, back in Chapter 1, the nations in the world that are currently receiving the largest numbers of immigrants, namely, the USA, Canada, and Australia, are those identified by Hofstede as highly individualistic, although some other nations are actually receiving a higher percentage of immigrants relative to their overall population. Conversely, most immigrants are drawn from nations with more collectivistic cultures. Does this cultural contrast give us an incomplete or distorted overall picture of acculturation processes? What happens when persons migrate from an individualistic culture to another individualistic culture or from a collectivist one to another collectivist one? We have little information that bears on these questions.

Van Oudenhoven, van der Zee, and Bakker (2002) located immigrants from the rural Frisian region of the Netherlands who had migrated to destinations including the USA, Canada, South Africa, Australia and New Zealand 50 years ago. The majority had achieved integration. However, they found a higher proportion than is typical of respondents who neither sought to maintain links with Dutch culture nor to participate in majority activities. According to Berry's model, these respondents would be classified as marginalized, and we should expect that they would have adjusted poorly. However, they were found to be contented with their new life, reporting fewer adaptation problems than the other migrants. Van Oudenhoven et al. suggest that the individualistic values of these migrants meant that they valued their independence, and that they exemplify a fifth 'independent' **acculturation** strategy.

A second issue that requires attention has to do with the distinction between majority and minority groups within a nation. In many nations there are numerous differing minority groups and in locations such as South Africa, Hong Kong, Israel and southwestern USA, 'minorities' are actually a numerical majority. In some of these locations, particular groups are not faced with a simple choice as to whether to sustain links with their culture of origin or to seek links with the majority. In Israel, for instance, religious affiliations and ethnic affiliations are interwoven in a way that poses dilemmas to groups with multiple minority status. Horenczyk (2004) clarified this situation by obtaining measures not only of group members' preferred strategies, but also of their perceptions of what other groups want them to do. He studied Christian Arabs, who prefer separation from Moslem Arabs, but whom they perceived as wanting them to integrate or assimilate. Conversely, Christian Arabs favour integration with the Jewish population, but perceived Jews as preferring separation from them. In a social nexus, one's options are not only a matter of one's preferences, but also constrained by what members of the other groups prefer.

A third and particularly important issue concerns the basis upon which the adjustment of immigrant groups shall be evaluated. Very few studies have included comparison groups of non-migrants. Without data on adjustment from non-migrant groups, it is difficult to evaluate correctly the meaning of data from migrants. Georgas, Berry, Shaw, et al. (1996) administered a measure of endorsement of family values to urban and rural Greeks, Greeks who had migrated to Germany, the Netherlands and Canada and to English Canadians. Family values were most endorsed by Greeks, especially those still in Greece, and least endorsed by European Canadians. Younger respondents in all samples endorsed family values less strongly. Greeks who had migrated to Canada showed stronger retention of family values than those who had migrated to Germany or to the Netherlands. This confirmed the prediction by Georgas et al. that, because Canadian government policy favours integration, indigenous values would be more strongly retained there. Ataca and Berry (2004) surveyed Turkish married couples in Turkey and in Canada, as well as Canadian married couples. The Turkish couples in Canada favoured separation (from Canadian culture, not from each other!). They scored lower on measures of both **psychological** and **socio-cultural adaptation** than the Canadian couples, and unsurprisingly were also lower on **socio-cultural adaptation** than the couples back in Turkey. The integration strategy was shown to be a significant predictor of high **socio-cultural adaptation**, while marginalization predicted poor **psychological adaptation**. This study is of particular value because it focuses upon couples, and family relations are frequently important in providing a secure base during the **acculturation** process, as we shall see in the next section.

Acculturation Processes

Acculturation is a long-lasting process. Researchers have typically attempted to address the challenge that this timeframe poses by surveying samples that include earlier and later generations of immigrants into a country. Unfortunately, this gives only a partial solution to the problem because those who migrate to a given country at different points in history may often do so for different reasons and may also experience different types of response from majority groups when they arrive. They are therefore not directly comparable with one another. In the absence of long-term follow-up studies, we can at best gain snapshots of the various processes that may occur. Consider some of the myriad possibilities: a single adult arrives and after some delay finds employment; a couple arrive and one partner finds work while the other remains at home; a family arrives, one parent finds work and the children begin attending school; a family arrives and locates within a community that already contains relatives and co-nationals; a couple arrives, one of whom is already a national of the nation in which they arrive. Each of these scenarios will elicit a distinctive profile of acculturative processes.

A particularly important element in several of these scenarios is the contrast between relatively private, family-based settings and relatively public, work and school-based settings. Arends-Toth and van de Vijver (2004) predicted that **acculturation** processes will be more rapid in public than in private settings and that **acculturation** strategies may vary between them. They found that their respondents among the Dutch majority population favoured the assimilation of Turkish Dutch immigrants in both public and private settings, but that the Turkish Dutch favoured integration in public settings and separation in private settings.

One of the most critical points in the **acculturation** process is the boundary between immigrant parents and their children. While separation may be preferred at least in the home domain, schooling provides an incentive towards more comprehensive assimilation or integration. Phalet and Schonpflug (2001) showed that immigrant parents were more successful in transmitting their achievement values to their children in Germany than in the Netherlands, and that Turkish parents were more successful in this respect than Moroccan parents. Across these samples, parents who endorsed collectivist values were those who most successfully transmitted their values. However, by using a broader range of measures among four immigrant groups in Germany and one in Israel, Nauck (2001) showed that differing indices of **acculturation**, such as retention of original language, ethnic identification, and reliance on one's own **ethnicity**-based networks, do not correlate positively with one another. The outcome measure that is used makes a crucial difference in the conclusions drawn about the immigrant experience!

The key role of second generation youth in the **acculturation** process has led a group of researchers to initiate the International Comparative Survey of Ethno-Cultural Youth (ICSEY), sampling several immigrant groups within each of nine nations. The full results are not yet published, but Sam (2000) has reported initial data from Norway. Sampling more than 500 adolescents of Vietnamese, Chilean, Pakistani and Turkish ethnicity, Sam also found that criteria of adjustment were each explained by a different set of predictors. Life satisfaction was explained by traditional family structure, preference for a separation strategy and endorsement of both a Norwegian and a strong **ethnic identity**. In contrast, positive mental health status was predicted by preference for an assimilation strategy and low **ethnic identity**. Positive self-esteem was predicted by rejection of a marginalization strategy. The results of the broader ICSEY survey will help to clarify the extent to which these results reflect the distinctive context of Norway or are more pan-cultural in their applicability.

A further stage in the process of cultural retention is illustrated by a study comparing mate preferences of South Asians born in Canada with Euro-Canadians. The South Asians had significantly stronger preference for qualities traditionally favoured in India, namely, good social class, family reputation, dowry, parental approval and association with a similar caste (Lalonde, Hymie, Pannu, & Tatla, 2004). Preference for these attributes was **mediated** by the respondent's level of **interdependent self-construal**, being stronger the more interdependent the respondent. Within the South Asian sample preference for these traditional qualities was also **mediated** by a measure of family connectedness.

In a study that also emphasized the role of the family, Rosenthal and Feldman (1992) contrasted first, second and third generation Chinese migrants to Australia and the USA, including in addition a control group in Hong Kong. Maintenance of Chinese cultural practices within the family declined in the first generation of migrants, but fell no further in later generations, whereas **ethnic** identification did not fall at all. This set of findings is consistent with an integration strategy, with maintenance of Chinese culture in private settings and adoption of local practices in public settings, although this study included no actual measure of **acculturation** strategies.

Detailed analyses of conversations within multigenerational Chinese families in New Zealand give clues as to some of the ways in which such a balance can be struck. Ng, He, and Loong (2004) identified instances of what he called 'brokering', in other words communications that encourage members of the family to speak in a language that the other party can understand. Typically, a child might describe in English an achievement one day at school. The parent would then encourage the child to explain the achievement to a grandparent in Chinese, so that it could be shared with all. In an earlier study, Ng, Loong, He, et al. (2000) showed that, in less acculturated families, there was a greater proportion of remarks addressed to the family as a whole, whereas in more acculturated families the proportion of remarks addressed to individuals was greater. Thus, the overall process of **acculturation** is marked and sometimes fostered by subtle differences in communication patterns.

Other factors may also be associated with progress toward **socio-cultural adaptation**, although it is difficult to know whether they are best thought of as contributing to its cause or its consequences. Kurman and Ronen-Eilon (2004) tested the extent to which knowledge of majority Israeli beliefs, as measured by Leung and Bond's (2004)

Social Axioms Survey predicted the **socio-cultural adaptation** of Ethiopian and Russian immigrants in Israel. Interestingly, positive adaptation was more strongly predicted by the difference between immigrants' beliefs and beliefs that immigrants *attributed* to the majority than by the actual differences between their beliefs. Yamada and Singelis (1999) predicted that among ethnic minority groups in Hawaii, those who scored high on integration (which they termed biculturalism) would be those who scored high on both **independent** and **interdependent self-construal**. The hypothesis was supported.

Who Does the Acculturating?

In evaluating what **acculturation** researchers have achieved, it is useful to think back to Redfield et al.'s (1936) definition of **acculturation**. This specified that **acculturation** involved changes in either or both of the cultural groups in contact. **Acculturation** research to date has focused almost entirely on the changes made by immigrants. In what way have majority populations changed in response to increased ethnic heterogeneity? In Chapter 12, we discuss evidence relating to overall changes in national populations, but we have little evidence for the influence of multiculturalism on these types of change. The closest that we can come to understanding majority responses to multiculturalism is by considering tests of the contact hypothesis.

The Contact Hypothesis

A major determinant of successful **acculturation** is inevitably the degree and quality of contact with the majority group, either interpersonally or through the media. In the light of the studies of prejudice and in-group loyalty, it is evident that having contact with persons from other groups does not guarantee improved relations with them. There is a long history of investigations into the types of interpersonal and intergroup contact that foster positive outcomes for both parties. The contact hypothesis was first advanced by Allport (1954), who proposed that good outcomes would occur where contact between groups was on the basis of equal status, where contact was approved or encouraged by higher authorities, where contact is cooperative rather than competitive, and where it lasts long enough for the parties to get acquainted. Pettigrew and Tropp (2000) reported a **meta-analysis** of 200 tests of the contact hypothesis, some of which concerned intercultural contact. They concluded that the hypothesis is supported, but that it is important to determine how contact is perceived by those involved. For instance, parties may not agree as to whether a series of contacts is based on equal status. Key situations involving contact with immigrants, such as schooling and work, can provide the circumstances for prolonged cooperative contacts that are approved by authority. Achieving perceived equality of status can be more problematic, even where such equality is mandated by government or institutional policies.

   Increasing rates of current immigration to many nations poses the question as to how governments can best ensure that contacts of these kinds can be created, in order that the positive contributions available from immigrants can be best utilized, and levels of intergroup prejudice can consequently be reduced. The choice between multiculturalist and assimilationist policies in nations with high immigration is open to influence by political rhetoric and by particular events that gain salience in the media. The role of psychologists will continue to be one of detailing the consequences of the differing policies that are adopted.

Summary

Our identities are rooted in the groups with which we are affiliated, and in the way that we compare these groups with other relevant groups. We maintain stereotypic conceptions of ethnic groups and of nations, which have some value in guiding relations with their members, but can amount to prejudice where they are resistant to contrary evidence. It is unclear whether members of some cultures are more rejecting of out-groups than others or whether there are certain cultural groups in which the defence of a group's honour is particularly paramount. In practical terms, it is more important to focus on the factors that determine levels of prejudice against minorities. Prejudice derives from perceived threats and from a desire to maintain existing forms of social dominance.

Migration presents the greatest contemporary challenge to cross-cultural psychology. Berry's fourfold classification of psychological **acculturation** strategies has guided the development of the field, but better measures are required, as well as fuller attention to host-nation attitudes and policies. Successful **acculturation** rests upon a match between preferred strategies of immigrants and their host populations. Integration appears most frequently to be effective, though it entails some dilemmas; studies with control groups and wider sampling of destinations are required before we can draw firmer conclusions. Families provide a basis for cultural transmission and for support during the **acculturation** process. Success in overcoming prejudice and other barriers to **acculturation** depends upon the existence of adequate opportunities for facilitative contacts between immigrants and members of the host nation endorsed and sustained by social norms and policies.

Further Reading

1 Berry, J.W., & Sam, D.L. (1997). Acculturation and adaptation. In J.W. Berry, M.H. Segall, & C. Kağıtçıbaşı (Eds.) *Handbook of cross-cultural psychology* (2nd ed., Vol. 3, pp. 291–326). Needham Heights, MA: Allyn & Bacon.
2 Chryssochoou, X. (2004). *Cultural diversity: Its social psychology*. Oxford, UK: Blackwell.
3 Sam, D.L., & Oppedal, B. (2004). Acculturation as a developmental pathway. www.wwu.edu/~culture
4 Schoenpflug, U. (2002). Acculturation, ethnic identity and coping. www.wwu.edu/~culture
5 Ward, C., Bochner, S., & Furnham, A. (2001). *The psychology of culture shock*. Hove, UK: Routledge. Chapters 9 and 10.

Study Questions

1 How do you account for the stereotypes that you hold about persons from your own nation and the ways in which you believe that persons from your nation are seen by those from other nations?

2 Discuss the extent to which ethnic prejudices towards one or more minority groups in your nation are underpinned by Stephan's four types of threat: realistic threats, symbolic threats, intergroup anxiety and negative stereotypes.

3 How does the concept of honour cultures advance our understanding of collectivism? What is the basis of honour in your culture of origin?

4 Assess the utility of Berry's fourfold classification of acculturation strategies. How could this classification be improved or extended?

5 What is the value of non-migrant comparison groups in the study of acculturation?

12

Global Change

> Dislocation is the norm rather than an aberration in our time, but even in the unlikely event that we spend an entire lifetime in one place, the fabulous diverseness with which we live reminds us constantly that we are no longer the norm or the centre, that there is no one geographic centre pulling the world together and glowing with the allure of the real thing (Eva Hoffman, *Lost in translation*, 1989)

Over the past few billion years, life on earth has slowly evolved a myriad of life forms, each of which is propagated through genetic inheritance, for just so long as that particular life form can prosper within current environmental circumstances. Over the past few thousand years, humans have made much greater use than any other species of an additional form of evolution, which supplements rather than replaces genetic transmission. Through the processes of speech and writing, it has become possible for discoveries made by one generation to be passed to later generations, whether this is accomplished through parental training, schooling, attention to media or peer pressure. Some indications are also found that chimpanzees are able to retain and transmit inventions to other members of their troop, and thus to create different chimpanzee cultures at different locations, which may well diverge over time as further inventions are made (Byrne, Barnard, Davidson, et al., 2004; Castro & Toro, 2004).

However, these culture-building processes are far more extensive among humans. Thus human populations are subject to processes of cultural evolution that are far more rapid than those fostered by Darwinian evolution. Life for all of us is very different from that experienced by our forebears 500 years ago, and no one can say in what ways current social structures will differ from those that may exist 500 years ahead. It remains to be seen to what extent there will prove to be genetic limits on the possibilities of human cultural evolution.

Convergence and Modernity

In the preceding chapters we have explored the processes whereby differing environments and restricted contacts led to the creation of many cultures in different parts of the world, characterized by differing emphases on a wide variety of social phenomena. In Chapters 10 and 11, we reviewed evidence as to the ways that increasing contacts may be pushing us towards developing integrated multicultural nations rather than hegemonic monocultural nations. However, there is no current consensus that this process is occurring and some hold the contrary belief that increasing globalization is counteracting the protection of cultural diversity.

In this chapter, we consider current evidence for and against a more global process of cultural homogenization. Researchers in the 1960s devoted considerable attention to the study of what they termed modernity. Their focus was upon the imperatives created by the industrialization and consequent urbanization of society. For instance, Kerr, Dunlop, Harbison, and Myers (1960) asserted that 'the logic of industrialism will eventually lead us all to a common society, where ideology will cease to matter' (p. 12). In a systematic test of such ideas, Inkeles and Smith (1974) surveyed the presence of 'modern' attributes among adults in six nations experiencing economic development, namely, Argentina, Chile, India, Israel, Nigeria and Pakistan. Box 12.1 summarizes the attributes found in this and other studies conducted in developing nations during the 1960s and 1970s that were more often present among 'modern' persons than among less 'modern' persons.

Box 12.1

Twenty Correlates of Modernity

A sense of personal efficacy	Cognitive and behavioural flexibility
Low integration with relatives	Future orientation
Egalitarian attitudes	Field independence
Openness to innovation and change	Empathetic capacity
Belief in gender equality	Need for information
Achievement motivation	Propensity to take risks
Individualistic orientation	Non-local orientation
Independence or self-reliance	Secularized beliefs
Active participation	Preference for urban life
Tolerance of and respect for others	Educational and occupational aspirations

Source: Yang (1988).

In the terms that we have been using in this book, the modern person appears to have a good deal in common with a person with independent rather than **interdependent self-construal**. However, as Yang (1988) points out, few of the studies on modernity that he summarized sampled more than one nation and the results actually varied substantially from one study to another. The historical circumstances of a nation are likely to colour the ways in which modernity will be expressed. For example, Yang (1986) described the personality changes occurring in Chinese individuals as they emerged from their distinctive cultural heritage. He contrasted the traditional, 'social-oriented' character with the modern, 'individual-oriented' character. Among other changes, he noted movements from a submissive disposition to an enjoyment orientation, from an inhibited disposition to an autonomous disposition and from an effeminate disposition to an expressive disposition. None of these changes appear in his 1988 summary of the modern person, as they were not reflected in studies from other nations.

Modernity is not so much a convergence on a single point, more a process of parallel evolution with convergence on some characteristics, continuing distinctiveness on others. The modern person is more of an abstraction than a template for individualism. Furthermore, as we saw in Chapter 11, those who migrate from rural settings to urban settings, whether within their nation or internationally do not simply change all their prior values and behaviours. Yang (1988) concluded that convergent aspects of modernization are best summarized in terms of what he called 'specific-functional' adaptations. In other words, in order to survive in an urban industrial setting rather than a rural agrarian setting, certain adaptations are essential, whereas others are not. To hold down a job in a factory or office requires many of the listed attributes of modernity. In contrast, living with one's family within an industrialized society does not require the same degree of change, so that we may expect family life to show fewer changes than aspects of life that are related to employment.

The early studies of modernity focused upon industrialization, but industrialization is not the only contemporary stimulus for cultural change. Other socio-economic factors, in particular urbanization, entail important modifications in lifestyles that have a bearing on attitudinal and behavioural changes. For example, in an early study on psychological aspects of modernization in Turkey, Kağıtçıbaşı (1973) found that rural to urban mobility and the socio-economic status of the family were the main factors associated with individual modernity in young people. We stressed the importance of global urbanization in Chapter 1.

In the almost twenty years that have passed since Yang (1988) summarized the literature, communications media have become much more heavily internationalized, and may be expected to have as great an impact within the home as at work. Eighty-five per cent of all film audiences throughout the world currently watch films made in the USA (United Nations Development Programme, 2004). The number of television sets in the world is now equal to 24% of the world's population (United Nations Development Programme, 2004). Given the numbers of persons typically having access to a television set, this gives exposure of popular channels to very large numbers of persons. Furthermore, satellite communication technology has enabled the creation of a small number of channels with global reach, such as CNN. Television networks also buy one another's footage and programmes as well as create programmes that copy popular formats developed by other networks. Cumulatively, this centralization of the sources of media output provides a strong impetus toward the adoption of 'modern' values, and the rejection of values that are locally distinctive or 'old-fashioned'. The style and content of this standardized media coverage is Western, and the penetration of this media coverage increases with a nation's wealth. So, much of the value and other psychological change arising from exposure to such mass media will not only reinforce the changes arising directly from economic modernization, but also impinge on areas of behaviour that are less directly related to the acquisition of wealth.

For instance, Boski, van de Vijver, Hurme, and Miluska (1999) showed video clips to students in Poland, the USA, Finland and the Netherlands. The clips showed various Polish persons greeting one another, and included shots of men (both young and old) greeting women by kissing their hand. This has been a customary procedure in Poland for the past several hundred years and the clips were actually recorded in 1994. Respondents were asked to estimate when the video clips were shot and rate how typical they were. Poles estimated that the clips were contemporary and saw them as more typical of scenes that they are familiar with than did respondents from the other nations. Non-Polish respondents also rated the clips as having been filmed between seven and nine years ago. In other words, they saw them as not typical of contemporary behaviour. Ten years later, hand kissing in Poland has become restricted to rather formal occasions, just as men in the UK no longer greet women by raising their hat (if they wear one at all), Christmas has become a holiday in non-Christian Japan, Christmas trees become New Year trees in Turkey, and the Brazilian martial art of *capoeira* is popular with Polish students (and those in many other nations). None of these and many other similar changes can be attributed to industrialization, but they can plausibly be linked to the globalization of the media. These changes can be thought of as instances of the ways that specific behaviours take on new meanings over time, such that what is 'modern' or popular at one time is not so at a later time. Thus, they may not indicate an underlying value change, but a continuing wish to appear to be modern or in fashion. The more standardized media content comes to define how one acts in modern ways. Thus, Kağıtçıbaşı (1996b, p. 97) has noted that the 'convergence' prediction of modernization theory may in fact be occurring, not so much because industrialization requires individualism or because **independent self-construal** is any more psychologically healthy, but rather because of the diffusion of the Western model to the rest of the world as the desirable model to emulate.

The attempts to identify modernity that we have reviewed thus far in this chapter provide some initial guidelines, but if we are to understand the processes of cultural change, we require data that has been collected over a suitable period of time. It is also important to distinguish between **individual-level** change and **nation-level** change. **Nation-level** change can occur over time even when individuals are not showing changes. This will typically occur as generations succeed one another, if younger generations are socialized to different sets of values than those of the generations that preceded them. In practice, **individual-level** change often also occurs and where such changes are widespread they may accelerate the process of **nation-level** change.

A preliminary indication of **nation-level** change was already provided by Hofstede (1980). The first survey providing data that contributed to his classic study were collected between 1967 and 1969, while the second took place between 1971 and 1973. Comparing **nation-level** means for data collected during these two time periods, Hofstede found that significant increases in the items defining individualism occurred in 18 of the 19 nations for which he had data from both surveys. During this four-year period, the national wealth of every one of these 18 nations had increased. The nineteenth nation was Pakistan. During this period Pakistani national wealth had decreased, and Hofstede noted that individualism scores also decreased. There are many possible reasons as to why the changes that Hofstede detected may have occurred, including events within the IBM company itself. However, the study provides us with encouragement to explore further the possible causal effect of wealth upon **nation-level** individualism over longer time periods. Hofstede also found significant changes on some of the other items in his survey, but these were smaller and did not relate consistently with his other **nation-level** dimensions.

The changes that Hofstede detected illustrate another point that is crucial to a contemporary understanding of cultural change. The early researchers into modernity focused upon nations undergoing rapid economic development, implicitly assuming that this was where cultural change was most evident. Developing nations were portrayed as somehow 'catching up' with the relatively static culture of the rich nations of the world. However, within Hofstede's 19 nations, the nation that showed the largest increase in individualism was actually the UK. While this particular result may not prove replicable, it alerts us to the need to sample widely if we are to gain a full picture of the various types of cultural change currently underway. Box 12.2 illustrates one aspect of cultural change over the past half-century in a not-atypical village in the UK. In 1939, the village comprised a community focused upon agriculture, populated by farmers and agricultural workers and those whose work sustained the local population. By 2000, the village had become a dormitory for professionals who either worked from home or commuted to nearby towns. These changes are not simply an effect of migration, but also reflect a change in the range of occupational roles that existed at these two points in history.

Box 12.2

The Changing Complexion of a Small British Village

Occupation	Persons in work, 1939	Persons in work, 2000
Farmers	4	3
Agricultural workers	25	6
Domestic workers	9	1
Public sector workers	5	1
Business employees	3	1
Health workers	2	1
Teachers	2	1
Policeman	1	1
Catering trade	2	5
Artists/Craftspersons	1	4
Entrepreneurs	1	7
Professionals	0	15
Total at work	55	46

Source: Gainsborough (2000).

The Inglehart Project

Collaborative work by social scientists over the past two decades has now made it possible to form a much more comprehensive picture of cultural change. This development has occurred because the opinions on a wide variety of topics of representative samples of adults in an increasing range of nations have been surveyed on a periodic basis. The first development in this direction was the initiation of the 'Eurobarometer' survey in 1970. The nations included in these surveys have increased as the European Union has been expanded to include additional nations, and the surveys continue to the present time. The World Values Survey, a similar project focused upon a broader range of nations, was initiated in 22 nations in 1981 and repeated in 43 nations in 1990–93, with 1,000 respondents from each nation. The nations in the World Values Survey with highest GDP were Sweden, Japan and Switzerland, while those with the lowest GDP were China, India and Nigeria. Much of the raw data from these surveys is available on websites as a free resource to researchers (http://wvs.isr.umich.edu; www.worldvaluessurvey.org; http://www.europa.eu.int/comm/public_opinion), and the country means for the more recent World Values Survey are also available in book form (Inglehart, Basanez, & Moreno, 1998). Several of the multiple-nation studies discussed in previous chapters have derived their data from this source, but have focused solely on the data collected at a single point in time.

The principal analysis of cultural change derived from these data has been that by Inglehart (1997), an American political scientist whose original attraction to the field was focused on attempts to understand changing voting patterns. Over two decades of research, his project has achieved a much broader relevance. Inglehart's hypothesis is that global value change currently comprises not one but two types of change. Firstly, he identifies the types of change delineated by earlier investigations of modernity. Secondly, he identifies the emergence of a set of 'post-modern' values, especially among the richer nations in his sample. Post-modern values are expected to arise in circumstances where economic security and political stability have become sufficiently established that people start to take them for granted. The concept of **post-modernity** has been much debated by social scientists, but has received little attention from psychologists.

There is little current agreement as to the defining characteristics of **post-modernity**. For present purposes it is sufficient to focus on a set of values that Inglehart identifies as 'post-materialist', which comprise a core element within the broader conceptions of **post-modernity** that are under current debate. To test his formulation, Inglehart first selected items within the databank that were relevant to these concepts, and then conducted both a pan-cultural **individual-level factor analysis** and a **nation-level factor analysis** of country means for these items. The analyses conducted at each level yielded two similar factors, thus making it possible for him to justify use of similar concepts at both levels in further exploration of his results. The first factor was named as Rational-Legal Authority versus Traditional Authority. The rational-legal pole of this factor corresponds to modernity and is defined by high loadings on achievement motivation, thrift, determination, interest in politics and acceptance of abortion. The second factor was named as Well-being versus Survival. In later analyses to be described shortly, the well-being pole was renamed as Self-Expression, and the specific items defining it were also changed. In terms of the more recent definition, agreement with the items below defines the Survival pole, whereas disagreement defines the post-materialist, Self-Expression pole (Inglehart & Baker, 2000):

- Respondent gives priority to economic and physical security over self-expression and quality of life.
- Respondent describes self as not very happy.
- Respondent has not signed and would not sign a petition.
- Homosexuality is never justifiable.
- You have to be very careful about trusting people.

The databank that Inglehart has analysed is even larger than those collected by Hofstede and Schwartz, exceeding 165,000 responses. It also includes a much broader range of items and is derived from nationally representative samples. Both of Inglehart's dimensions correlate positively with Hofstede's **individualism-collectivism** dimension and with national wealth (per capita GDP), as his model would lead us to expect. The correlations with GDP are rather higher than those with individualism: +0.60 with rational-legal authority and +0.78 with self-expression values. Indeed, we noted already in Chapter 4 Diener and Oishi's (2004) linkage of subjective well-being and national GDP. Nations with high scores for post-materialism have populations that express greater happiness. Similarly high correlations are obtained between well-being and Schwartz's (2004) **nation-level** scores for Autonomy. Joint **factor analysis** of well-being, individualism and autonomy scores yields a first factor accounting for as much as 78% of the overall variance (Inglehart & Oyserman, 2004).

Value Change over Time

Having identified suitable dimensions to test his model of change, Inglehart then compared the scores obtained in the 1990 survey with those obtained in the 1981 survey. This was only possible for the 21 nations that were common to both surveys. For each nation, the percentage of respondents who endorsed materialist values was subtracted from the percentage who endorsed post-materialist values. Box 12.3 shows that in 19 of the 21 nations there was an increase in the proportion of those endorsing post-materialist values. Although materialists in 11 of the nations still outnumbered post-materialists, the trend was clear. The magnitude of change did vary but was not noticeably greater in the less affluent nations than in the more affluent ones. The large change in the reverse direction in South Africa is likely to be attributable to the violence and instability that prevailed there during the relevant nine-year period.

To gain a fuller understanding of these changes, Inglehart (1997) returned to the World Values Survey databank and determined whether it contained additional opinion items or reports of particular behaviours that were positively correlated with endorsement of post-materialist values. Forty such items were identified, many of them related to forms of political participation, which had been included in the survey because of the original concerns of those who constructed it. In order to obtain the broadest possible summary of change towards post-materialism, Inglehart then determined the proportion of changes that had occurred towards or away from post-materialism, within each of the 21 nations. Box 12.4 shows that a very high proportion of the changes were indeed in the predicted direction within 18 of the 21 nations. However, in Argentina, Hungary and South Africa, there were reversed trends.

Box 12.3

Percentage Endorsement of Post-materialist Values

Nation	1981	1990	Net Shift
Finland	21	23	+2
Netherlands	−2	26	+28
Canada	−6	14	+20
Iceland	−10	−14	−4
Sweden	−10	9	+19
West Germany	−11	14	+25
UK	−13	0	+13
France	−14	4	+18
Belgium	−16	2	+18
South Africa	−16	−33	−17
Mexico	−19	−14	+5
Ireland	−20	−4	+16
Argentina	−20	−6	+14
Norway	−21	−19	+2
USA	−24	6	+30
Japan	−32	−19	+13
South Korea	−34	−34	0
Italy	−39	7	+46
Spain	−41	−6	+35
Northern Ireland	−45	−7	+38
Hungary	−50	−41	+9

Source: Inglehart (1997). Percentages are for those endorsing post-materialist values *minus* those endorsing materialist values.

Inglehart points out that each of these nations experienced political upheaval during the 1980s, whereas the remaining nations that are listed in Box 12.3 did not.

Another way to interpret the results in Box 12.4 is to note that South Africa, Hungary and Argentina were at the time the three least affluent nations in Inglehart's sample of 21. Although the 1990 sample did include additional developing nations, the range of the 1981 survey was more restricted. It could therefore be the case that what Inglehart detected in these three nations would also be found in other less affluent nations, whether or not they experienced the types of turbulence that occurred there in the 1980s. We must consider data from additional sources in order to check whether this is so.

More recently, these conclusions have been tested with a larger sample of nations and over longer periods of time. Inglehart and Baker (2000) drew upon data collected in the third World Values Survey, which was conducted in 65 nations between 1995 and 1998. Within this enlarged sample they identified a further 24 items whose **nation-level** scores correlated with the traditional versus rational-legal dimension,

Box 12.4

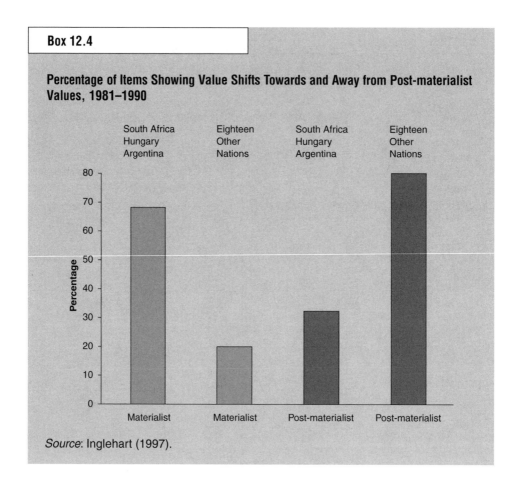

Percentage of Items Showing Value Shifts Towards and Away from Post-materialist Values, 1981–1990

Source: Inglehart (1997).

and 31 items that correlated significantly with the survival versus self-expression dimension. Clearly, these dimensions are not dependent upon the idiosyncrasies of wording of one or two items. The directional trends identified in the earlier data were confirmed. Within the enlarged sample, Inglehart and Baker were able to show that change from traditional authority towards endorsement of rational-legal authority was correlated with a lower percentage of agricultural workers and a higher percentage of industrial workers. On the other hand, endorsement of the cluster of post-materialist self-expression values correlated +0.72 with the percentage of the labour force employed in organizations providing services.

They also again found that responses within a minority of nations had moved in the reverse direction. Movement away from secular-rational authority was found in South Africa, Brazil, Argentina and Bulgaria. Movement away from self-expression was found in Russia, Belarus, Estonia, Lithuania and Latvia. These are all nations that have experienced economic adversity during the relevant period and the effects found within them underlines that the current overall trends are not irrevocable and can be reversed.

Inglehart and Baker (2000) also caution against the view that what is occurring is a simple convergence of values. They note that while values in many nations are changing in a parallel direction, the positioning of nations within the two-dimensional space defined by their dimensions retains the regional groupings that were found in former times. These groupings are defined by historical affiliation with differing religious beliefs. Thus we continue to observe clustering of nations that are historically Protestant, Catholic, Orthodox, Confucian and Islamic. These findings for values probably also hold true for beliefs, with some dimensions associated in part with wealth, but with considerable variance across cultures due to other factors associated with other non-economic features of societies, such as religious heritage (Leung & Bond, 2004). These continuities concur with the conclusions of Georgas et al. (2004), discussed in Chapter 4, that wealth and religion are major **eco-cultural** determinants of culture and of culture change. Inglehart and Baker also find evidence that when other predictors are par-tialled out, having experienced a period of communist rule shows a significant effect on the values that are currently espoused.

Alternative Sources of Data on Cultural Change

The data derived from the World Values Survey provide by far the most comprehen-sive information currently available on value change. However, no single survey can provide comprehensive coverage and the weakness of this database is that the sample underrepresents the less affluent regions of the world. There is change data from only three African nations and none from any Arab nation. A second weakness is that only in 11 of the 65 nations is change surveyed for more than a nine-year period.

Recently, Allen, Ng, Ikeda, Jawan, et al. (2004) reported an attempt to survey cultural change in eight nations over 20 years. They were able to draw on a survey of values reported by Ng, Hossain, Ball, Bond et al. (1982). In this early study, students in nine East Asian and Pacific island nations completed a 40-item version of the Rokeach Value Survey, the instrument that later provided a basis for Schwartz's well-known value survey. Two value dimensions were identified within the 1982 data, which were characterized as representing Submissive versus 'Dionysian' values and Inner Strength versus Materialistic values. The first of these dimensions is the one that is of particular interest. Examples of submissive values were obedience, politeness and emphasis on national security. Examples of Dionysian values were endorsement of an exciting life and of mature love.

In testing for culture change, Allen et al. (2004) sought to sample from students in the same nations and at the same universities that had previously been sampled, who were studying the same subjects and who completed the same survey. This proved pos-sible in some nations, while in others the most similar available option was selected. Data were received from eight of the nine nations originally sampled. Analysis of the new data set indicated that the first of the two-value dimensions could be used to par-tially summarize the data, whereas the second dimension could not because it had a different structure. Change scores were therefore computed on the first dimension. The results showed that students from those nations that had endorsed Dionysian values in 1982, namely, Australia, New Zealand and Japan, did so even more strongly in 2002. Students in Hong Kong and Taiwan were positioned midway between Dionysian and submissive values in 1982, but by 2002 they had moved towards greater endorsement of Dionysian values. In contrast, values among students in the three remaining nations,

Bangladesh, Malaysia and Papua New Guinea, which were already submissive, had become more so by 2002. Thus, in sampling nations that range from very wealthy to much less wealthy, Allen et al. identified a trend towards a polarization of values, rather than a unidirectional change. We can only speculate as to the closeness of the linkage between Dionysian values and Inglehart's concept of self-expression, but there is at least some overlap. In both studies, we find value change moving in opposite directions when we compare the richest and the poorest nations within each sample.

Both Inglehart and Allen et al. are interested in testing alternative explanations of why the changes that they detected occur. Given the strong association between nations' wealth and the cultural values that prevail within them, the key question is whether we can establish any kind of causal relationship between the two. Inglehart (1997) constructed a four-item index of achievement motivation from the measures available to him and used it to show that his index was a significant predictor of economic growth among the 43 nations in his sample. However, as his achievement index was derived from data collected at the same time as the change measures, this tells us only that the two variables are associated with one another, without making it possible to infer any causal linkages. As we noted in Chapter 4, Hofstede (1980) employed a better strategy, **cross-lagged panel analysis**, which draws on measures of both the variables in which one is interested, both from an earlier date and from a later date. By exploring the different correlations between these measures one can infer which causal linkages are more plausible. Hofstede concluded that wealth causes the development of individualism, not the reverse. Allen et al. (2004) used a similar method, finding that their values measure in 1982 did not predict per capita GDP in 2002, whereas per capita GDP in 1982 did predict value change in 2002. Thus, Hofstede's conclusion is supported.

The simple statement that wealth has a significant effect on cultural change leaves open the question of how that change may occur. Allen et al. suggest that a nation's wealth affects at least some of the values that individuals form during childhood. To test this prediction, they computed correlations between national per capita GDP in every alternate year from 1959 to 2000 and each sample's endorsement of Dionysian values. As predicted the correlations for the 1982 sample were strongest for the late 1960s and the early 1970s, in other words in the first ten years of respondents' lives. In a similar way, the correlations for the 2002 sample were strongest from the late 1980s onward, again during the first ten years of these respondents' lives. This type of data analysis leaves open various possible causal mechanisms, but encourages us to examine family dynamics and early schooling practices. For instance, one could hypothesize that wealth affects the type of family dynamics that develop, or that wealth affects the presence or absence of schooling, or that wealth affects exposure to the more globalized media.

Political Change and Cultural Change

A further way in which we can seek understanding of cultural change is to examine the consequences of some of the major political changes that have occurred in recent decades. From the perspective of psychology, these events can be thought of as large scale and poorly controlled field experiments. We shall consider three: the reunification of Germany, the return of Hong Kong to China, and the Chinese government's one-child policy.

Oettingen, Little, Lindenberger, and Baltes (1994) compared the self-efficacy perceptions and school performance of schoolchildren in East and West Berlin, shortly after the reunification of East and West Germany in 1989. The children in the formerly communist eastern sector of the city had much lower perceptions of their own ability to influence their levels of achievement than did the children in West Berlin. However, among East Berlin children, there was a much stronger correlation between perceived efficacy and actual school grades. Oettingen et al. suggest that these differences are caused by different teaching methods. In East Berlin, children would receive public performance feedback in class, with feedback being based on the teacher's evaluation. In West Berlin, the factors affecting efficacy and school grades are more diverse, so that the correlation between the two is weaker. In a further study, Little, Oettingen, Stetsenko, and Baltes (1995) reported similar data collected from schoolchildren in Moscow and in Los Angeles. Consistent with expectation, the correlation between grades and self-efficacy from the Moscow children resembled that from East Berlin, whereas the correlation from Los Angeles was even lower than that from West Berlin.

In the years following the reunification of Germany, this group of researchers has continued to sample schoolchildren within Berlin, where teaching is now conducted throughout the city in the manner previously restricted to the Western sectors. They have found that East Berlin children continue to experience lower personal efficacy, but that the correlations between efficacy and school grades have declined to the levels found in West Berlin (Little, Lopez, Oettingen, & Baltes, 2001). In a similar way, repeated surveys of German factory workers by Frese, Kring, Soose, and Zempel (1996) showed a gradual increase in initiative-taking among East German workers, rising to the level found among West German workers. These studies thus demonstrate the ability of political change to create cultural change.

The change in the status of Hong Kong in 1997 from British colony to a Special Autonomous Region within China also provided researchers with an opportunity to conduct valuable research. Since the change in Hong Kong's political status guaranteed its continuing autonomy, the change was less radical than that which occurred in East Germany. As the time for change of status approached, the issue facing Hong Kong Chinese was whether to sustain their identity as a Hong Kong Chinese, or whether to see themselves more inclusively as Chinese. Choices as to how to identify oneself with changing political contexts are likely to be crucial to an understanding of cultural change because identifications will influence whom one seeks to associate with and consequently what types of influence one will be exposed to. Those who changed towards the more inclusive identification, as Chinese, were those who favoured Confucian values over modern values and who saw human nature as fixed rather than malleable (Chiu & Hong, 1999; Hong et al., 1999; Lam et al., 1999). Thus political change opens up possibilities for value change.

A third instance of politically-driven cultural change is provided by the one-child policy of the Chinese government. On the basis of a review of relevant studies, Chang, Schwartz, Dodge, and McBride-Chang (2003) concluded that parents in one-child families are less authoritarian and more concerned that their children do well in school, while only children are more self-centered, aggressive and extroverted than is found in Chinese multiple-child families. Chang (2004) interviewed parents of 328 Chinese single-child families, asking them what types of social behaviours were desirable in their child. Only 24% endorsed traditional Chinese 'good child' behaviours, such as self-constraint, obedience and listening to others. In contrast, 87% of parents endorsed 'pro-social leadership' behaviours, such as making friends, getting along with others and being a leader. Most strikingly, there were hardly any gender differences in the behaviours that parents preferred to see in their child, or in the behaviours that that they would regard as problematic. When asked whether their parenting was guided by the Confucian values of collectivism or self-restraint, not one parent agreed that they were. Some of these emphases no doubt reflect the trends towards modernity that we have discussed in this chapter. However, the apparent reduction in gender differences is more likely to be a consequence of the single-child policy.

The studies of political change that we have reviewed indicate some significant cultural effects. However, there are other studies that indicate no such effects. Silbereisen and Wiesner (2002) review a broad range of studies of German reunification. Their conclusion mirrors Yang's (1988) concept of specific-functional adaptation; that is to say, political changes do create cultural change where specific institutional changes directly require those changes. An example is the studies of Berlin schoolchildren's response to a centrally imposed change in teaching styles. In other domains of life, political change does not have such immediate effects. For instance, the timing of adolescents' first romantic attachment showed no effect of the political change. Furthermore, Silbereisen and Wiesner provide instances of the ways in which culture patterns once established may persist, even when the original reason for their existence is gone. The *jugendweihe* youth initiation ceremony, initiated under the much-disliked state communist regime, remains a popular event, perhaps because it provided an opportunity for sociability and celebration despite adverse economic circumstances. In evaluating the studies of the effects of German reunification, we must bear in mind that it is possible that changes may have occurred which preceded the start of the research studies. Clandestine watching of West German television in East Germany was widespread before reunification and may have contributed to some types of adolescent value change. Field experiments have their limitations as a source of unambiguous causal connections.

Families and Cultural Change

We have discussed the role of family in maintaining cultural continuity in Chapter 5. In considering current global change, we need to discuss whether the family is less influential than it was in former times. In many of the nations of Europe and in North America, a large and growing proportion of children are born to unmarried mothers and many children grow up living with a single parent. Furthermore, in many of the nations where the **family model of interdependence** has prevailed for generations, schooling has become much more widespread. Both of these social changes open up alternative sources of socialization. In his analysis, Inglehart (1997) predicted that one element in the emergence of post-modern values would be a decline in emphasis on the family. However, this prediction was contradicted by the data. In 16 of 19 nations surveyed, the percentage agreeing that 'a child needs a home with both a father and a mother to grow up happy' increased between 1981 and 1990. Other survey items also detected increased support for the value of the family. Inglehart interprets this result in terms of widespread public awareness that children of single parents are at greater risk for a variety of social pathologies. This knowledge itself is derived from the increased dissemination of psychological knowledge that is associated with widely adopted educational curricula in modern economies.

Rather than seeing family breakdown simply as a cause of cultural change, it is preferable to see families as subject to processes of cultural evolution that parallel those occurring in other segments of society. In Chapter 5, we presented evidence for the emergence of the **family model of psychological interdependence**. This model asserts that decreased level of material interdependency among family members does not necessarily imply emotional distance (Kağıtçıbaşı, 1990, 1996b). A study of family relations in 16 nations confirmed these expectations. Georgas, Mylonas, Bafiti, Poortinga, et al. (2001) found no differences between frequency of communication among family members in more and in less affluent nations. Among more geographically dispersed families in the more affluent nations, communication was more often by telephone or e-mail, whereas in the less affluent nations it was more often face-to-face. These results held true not just for the nuclear family but also for the extended family. A more recent study with samples from 27 nations (Georgas, Berry, van de Vijver, & Poortinga, 2006) also confirmed the distinctness of the material and emotional family interdependencies and showed that material family interdependence is stronger in collectivistic societies whereas emotional roles are important everywhere. The human functions served by families appear to be resilient across recent times.

Migration and Cultural Change

Cultural change has been examined in this chapter so far primarily in terms of economic and political factors. We must also take account of the currently important issue of migration. In Chapter 11, we focused primarily on the experiences of migrants. However, as we noted at that time, the **acculturation** process does not entail changes only within migrants, but also within the majority population. In surveying such cultural change, we must take account of two factors relating to migration. Firstly, when Inglehart analysed the data from representative national samples of different nations, the samples surveyed in 1990 will not have been so ethnically homogeneous as those surveyed in 1981. In Chapter 1, we noted annual migration rates to and from certain nations. Box 12.5 gives a clearer picture of the longer-term effects of migration in each continent. Europe contains the largest number of migrants, but the increase over the past decade has only been five million, compared to 13 million in North America. Migrants from collectivist nations are not especially likely to have been strong contributors to the growth of post-modern values in the more wealthy nations to which they have mostly migrated. More likely, their presence in these samples may have masked a stronger effect among majority groups within those nations.

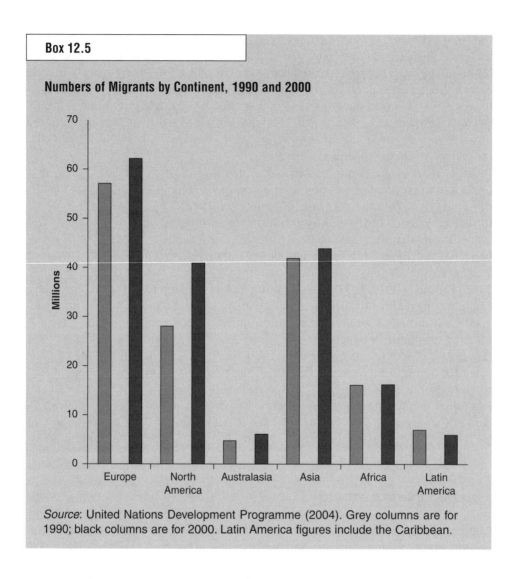

Box 12.5

Numbers of Migrants by Continent, 1990 and 2000

Source: United Nations Development Programme (2004). Grey columns are for 1990; black columns are for 2000. Latin America figures include the Caribbean.

More importantly, the increasing presence and visibility of **ethnic minorities** within previously homogeneous populations poses challenges to the majority population. Just as was the case for the Hong Kong Chinese in 1997, members of majority populations find themselves faced with an increasing choice of identities. Should they adopt a more inclusive multi-ethnic identity or a more exclusive, ethnically-restrictive identity? As we saw in the preceding chapter, adherence to exclusive majority identities creates problems for minorities. It also postpones rather than resolves the contemporary problem of how best to address cultural difference. Governments of some nations with particularly long experience of diversity have found ways to encourage the adoption of inclusive multiple identities. For instance in Belgium, more than 90% of the population now identify themselves as either Flemish or Walloon *and* Belgian, while 75% of those living in Spain see themselves as having both a regional identity *and* a Spanish identity (United Nations Development Programme, 2004).

Majority response to the presence of migrant communities within their nation requires not just the rejection of exclusive identities, but also the reconstrual of what it means to say that one is for instance French, German, American or Australian. Does a majority person's construal of nationalities such as these include implicit assumptions about skin colour, language fluency or knowledge of historically-rooted conceptions of politeness? Arnett (2002) suggests that globalization will encourage us all to think of ourselves in terms of a broader range of identities. Focusing specifically upon the young, he notes an increasing tendency to think of oneself as a citizen of the world, as well as a citizen of a specific nation. In this way, holding a bi-cultural identity could become the norm rather than the exception. However, the studies that he reviews concern relatively affluent student groups, who derive their entertainment from globalized media sources. It would be premature to assume that these types of effects will occur more widely throughout the population in the foreseeable future. It is more likely that poverty, disease and natural disasters will continue to preoccupy large segments of the world's population, rendering those among them who do not migrate relatively immune to the factors currently inducing cultural change.

Finally, we do well to consider that the cultural changes that we have identified appear to be driven mostly by increasing wealth. The world's population currently faces the enormous challenges posed by uncontrolled global warming and by failures in disease control. If adequate responses to these challenges are not forthcoming in future years, a reverse in economic fortunes could well be followed by the collapse of post-modern values and the evolution of values that are more responsive to times of adversity. We have noted already the ways in which values in those parts of the world that experienced particular turbulence or economic failure moved in a contrary direction. History is not reversible, but neither is the future a simple extrapolation of the present.

Summary

Early studies equated modernity with the development of industrialized, individualistic cultures. More recent studies confirm wealth as a significant causal factor of cultural change, but identify different types of change in more affluent and less affluent contexts. The communications revolution and its globalization may be as potent a cause of change as industrialization. Post-materialist values have become more salient, especially within affluent nations over the past decade. The types of value change that have occurred are best thought of as specific-functional adaptations to the requirements of contemporary societies. Consequently, not all values are changing. Impetus for change is provided by globalized media, political change and migration, while the role of the family in maintaining cultural continuity is less clear. Changes within less affluent nations have been less well studied, and appear to be quite different in kind.

Further Reading

1 Arnett, J.J. (2002). The psychology of globalization. *American Psychologist, 57*, 774–83.
2 Inglehart, R. (1997). *Modernization and post-modernization: Cultural, economic and political change in 43 societies.* Princeton, NJ: Princeton University Press.
3 United Nations Development Programme (2004). *Human development report.* New York: Oxford University Press.
4 Yang, K.S. (1988). Will societal modernization eventually eliminate cross-cultural psychological differences? In M.H. Bond (ed.) *The cross-cultural challenge to social psychology* (pp. 67–85). Newbury Park, CA: Sage.

Study Questions

1 Discuss the concept of specific-functional adaptation. What adaptations have you made to your behaviour since becoming a student at university and why?
2 What do you understand to be post-modern values and what evidence do you see for their growth in your country?
3 How can migration become a stimulus to cultural change?

13

The Unfinished Agenda

> There is a tide in the affairs of men, which, taken at the flood, leads on to fortune (Shakespeare, *Julius Caesar*)

Having read the preceding chapters, you will have become acquainted with a broad range of studies that have advanced our understanding of cultural effects on social psychological processes. We should like to conclude this book by discussing with you some of the views that you may have formulated in making sense of the complex material that we have placed before you.

The way in which most of us try to make sense of a new body of information is to relate it to conceptual frameworks with which we are already familiar. Sometimes these frameworks can help but if they do not match well enough with the new material, they can be a hindrance. Since we do not have the opportunity for a two-way interchange with you, we propose instead to share with you some comments on particular ways of reacting to the field that we have encountered frequently in discussions with students and with colleagues. We cannot claim that we have any irrefutable grasp of the right way to grasp these issues, but we do claim relevant experience in thinking them through over long periods of time. We comment in turn on six frequent reactions to the complexity of our field.

Topics for Discussion

Now that We have Valid Individual-level Measures of Beliefs and Values, there is No Further Use for Nation-level Measures

As psychologists we need and are supported in our explorations by having at our disposal social psychological constructs whose applicability in many cultural groups has been amply demonstrated. Many of these helpful individual-level constructs have been discussed throughout this text. They range from the Big Five personality variables, values, beliefs, self-construals, general self-efficacy and self-esteem to emerging relationship-focused constructs, like role complexity (McAuley, Bond, & Kashima, 2002), authority ranking (Caralis & Haslam, 2004), mate preferences (Shackelford et al., 2005) and relationship harmony (Kwan et al., 1997). We can treat these constructs as building blocks in social psychological theories, linking their strength to socialization inputs or to situational variables in predicting behaviour.

Nation-level constructs, like Georgas et al.'s (2004) affluence or Bond et al.'s (2004) societal cynicism, are higher-order variables that define the context in which the socialization of our social understandings and behaviour occurs. In these respects, they are no different than group or organizational characteristics that allow us to distinguish groups or organizations from one another. When these constructs are integrated into a comprehensive theory, such as that of Schwartz (1992) on values, they are appealing in their scientific promise.

Our capacity to map the cultural world in these various ways is aesthetically gratifying. As with any set of variables in science, however, the value of these culture maps lies in their ability to help us understand causal linkages among the phenomena of interest – their antecedents, their associated characteristics and their consequences, ultimately for individual social behaviour. So, for example, we need to know what historical and ecological conditions promote Schwartz's (1994) embeddedness value domain, as opposed to his other six **nation-level** domains of value; what are the political, social, familial and interpersonal ideologies associated with embeddedness; what individual-level value, belief and other domains are socialized to be stronger in these more conservative cultures; do social processes occur in the same ways for cultures that are high or low in embeddedness or does cultural embeddedness amplify or restrain these processes?

'Hard' measures of cultural variation, like the GINI coefficient of economic inequality or the sex ratio of females to males, are more readily available when comparing national cultures and they have been widely used for their convenience value. They provide linkages with the social scientific perspectives of economics, political science or sociology and have an established truth value appealing to those social psychologists who are beginning to grapple with culture.

'Soft' measures of culture are derived by aggregating individual measures, be these reports about one's self or about the society in which one lives (Bond, 1997b). Hofstede's (1980) dimension of **individualism-collectivism** was derived from a **factor analysis** of *self-reported values* averaged within each nation, and compared across 40 nations; asking respondents to rate a different but equally interesting target, Fischer (2004b) has shown that Schwartz's individual-level values can be rated *for my cultural group*. Fischer averaged these ratings within each nation, and compared the results across nine nations. Whatever their target, these types of aggregated measures have an uncertain feel among the social scientists using them because they are derived from individual judgements and because of their recent entrance into social scientific discourse.

However, we must not prejudge the potential of soft measures of culture for cross-cultural work in social psychology. We have already seen the usefulness of the Schwartz **nation-level** value domains in suggesting important ways of understanding culture beyond that provided by the integrative 'hard' measure of affluence used by Georgas et al. (2004). Wong and Bond (2005) have also shown the predictive power of soft measures over and above that of GNP in explaining the strength of emotional intensity and the length of emotions across 30 cultural groups. It seems that some of these soft measures do take us beyond what is provided by the currently available hard measures. We can expect that the range of the soft measures currently available will widen as more social psychological measures are developed. With more nations entering the scientific conversation, much more extensive and representative data sets will become available for exploration of how soft **nation-level** measures can enlarge our understanding of human social behaviour.

A Person can be both Individualist and Collectivist

Well, yes, but also no. The answer depends on how we construe and measure these concepts. A growing number of studies do report apparently conflicting findings of individualistic orientations from so-called collectivistic nations. The interpretation may be that there is a **nation-level** shift towards individualism with modernization (Georgas, 1999), or that some societies, such as Japan, have been wrongly labelled as collectivistic (Matsumoto, 1999; Takano & Osaka, 1999), or that some individuals are both independent and interdependent (Oyserman et al., 2002). There are a number of issues involved. Some of these are methodological, others are conceptual, and sometimes they are mixed together. For example, often the samples comprise university students, who are hardly representative of the societies that they are assumed to represent. Students tend to be younger and more educated, without family responsibilities etc., which make them more individualistic in their outlook. Indeed, when within-country comparisons are conducted, significant variations are found across social classes and geographic/urban-rural differences (Marshall, 1997; Ayçiçegi & Harris, 2005).

What changes with modernization? As we discussed in Chapter 5, Kağıtçıbaşı (1997a) distinguished *normative* from *relational* **individualism-collectivism**. The former refers to societal norms and values, the latter refers to interpersonal relations. Thus normative **individualism-collectivism** has to do with attitudes opposing or endorsing the importance of family/group over the individual, whereas relational **individualism-collectivism** has to do with the interpersonal distance or separateness/connectedness of individuals. What seems to happen with modernization is a shift from conservative and hierarchical normative collectivism to a more democratic normative individualism. This is a *normative* cultural change, but it may or may not translate into shifts from connectedness to separateness at the **individual-level**.

It is possible, therefore, to find apparently conflicting orientations in some groups, such as Turkish students having individualistic values but at the same time displaying high levels of connectedness (Göregenli, 1997). Similarly, **acculturation** studies show that in Western societies immigrants from collectivist backgrounds shift to more individualistic values and behaviour patterns in the public sphere, but remain strongly interconnected in the private sphere of the family (Arends-Toth & van de Vijver, 2004; Kwak, 2003). Thus, what *type* of **individualism-collectivism** we are talking about needs to be clarified in order not to resort to a logically problematic attribution of *both* individualist and collectivist identity to a person at the same time. Nevertheless, given the flexibility of human beings and the powerful situational demands acting upon them, it is also possible for the same person to act in an individualist or a collectivist way with different people at different times and circumstances (Kağıtçıbaşı, 1994). Along these lines, **individualism-collectivism** may be construed in probabilistic terms regarding the greater or lesser likelihood of 'sampling [from individuals' repertoire] the individualist or collectivist themes in constructing their social behaviour' (Triandis, 1995, p. 61).

Another issue of both a conceptual and a methodological nature has to do with the measurement of independence/interdependence at the **individual-level**. Independence scales often include some items that reflect autonomy and some that reflect separateness, the assumption being that these two characteristics are inevitably linked. Inversely, interdependence scales often contain items that measure both connectedness and lack of autonomy, assuming again that these are inherently linked. Yet, if as we have argued in this volume, connectedness and autonomy are distinct and independent concepts, then these scales are in fact bi-dimensional rather than uni-dimensional, thereby decreasing their reliability. Particularly in collectivistic 'cultures of relatedness' some more modern, urban, educated people can be both autonomous and related, yet these characteristics are often operationalized in measurement to reflect independence and interdependence. In this sense, can we call such persons both individualistic and collectivistic? We find it preferable to say that there is a confusion in conceptualization and operationalization. A better understanding of what we mean by individualist or collectivist or what content we attribute to these concepts would clarify matters. Construal and measurement of more specific attributes rather than broad inclusive categories such as **individualism-collectivism** would be more useful.

Researchers have Focused too Narrowly on Individualism-collectivism

There are good reasons why a focus on the cultural dimension that comprises **individualism-collectivism** and its two important correlates of power distance and wealth have been fruitful. As we have seen, changes in wealth appear to be major determinants of contemporary changes in both values and behaviours. However, it is plain that a cross-cultural psychology with such a singular focus cannot hope to explain the world's continuing diversity. The study by Georgas et al. (2004) identified religious affiliation as a correlate of cultural variation that was independent of the cluster of attributes associated with **individualism-collectivism**. Huismans (1994) compared the relation between self-rated religiosity and the Schwartz values endorsed by Catholic, Protestant, Orthodox, Jewish and Moslem respondents, sampling from 11 nations. Very similar value profiles were found for religious persons in each of these categories. Religious persons score high on tradition and conservation and low on hedonism and stimulation. Consequently, we cannot explain Georgas et al.'s results solely in terms of economic differences. The fact that nations in which one or other of these religious affiliations predominates have a shared distinctiveness must derive from something other than value endorsement that is driven by economic forces. A likely candidate is the intricately interwoven patterns of individual religious observance and institutional supports for that observance that exist within a given nation. These supports include the use of particular types of curriculum and distinctive styles of schooling (Hofstede, 1986), provision of public holidays based upon religious observances, the value emphases provided by media coverage and mosques, temples, ashrams, and churches that enable particular kinds of observance.

The neglect of religious affiliation as an explanation of cultural differences is one aspect of the minimal attention so far given to rules and roles as elements of culture. In Chapter 4, we noted the current study by Gelfand et al. (2004), which examines nations that vary in terms of 'situational constraint'. A culture high in situational constraint is one in which persons adhere closely to rule and role prescriptions, whereas in a culture low in situational constraint there is greater latitude for deviance. While results of this study are not yet available, the concepts may prove to have some common elements with existing but neglected value dimensions. High constraint nations may score higher on Hofstede's Uncertainty Avoidance dimension and on the Chinese Culture Connection (1987) Confucian Work Dynamism dimension. This latter dimension featured strong emphasis on fulfilling the role obligations of filial piety, one important element of role requirements in all cultural traditions.

Further attention to dimensions such as these may aid the development of the field. However, in our search for additional dimensions relevant to culture, we must avoid the assumption that all dimensions have equal relevance to what occurs in all parts of the world. Hofstede (2001) suggested that the reason why Uncertainty Avoidance emerged in his analysis, but not in that by the Chinese Culture Connection (1987) is because Uncertainty Avoidance is more relevant to a strong concern with truth in Western nations. Conversely, he suggested Confucian Work Dynamism has more relevance to Pacific Asian nations, where he claims there is greater concern with virtue. His suggestion may or may not prove correct, but it underlines the importance of also seeking out those aspects of culture thought to have more local **emic** relevance, as we have described this focus throughout this book.

Cross-cultural Psychologists have not paid enough Attention to Indigenous, Emic Approaches

The studies that we have emphasized have been predominantly those that analyse comparative data from a set of nations, using concepts derived from the overarching conceptual frameworks that have emerged over the past several decades. During this same time period, other researchers have sought to identify distinctive ways of understanding the psychological processes that occur within their own specific national groups. We have noted examples of such **emic** analyses, particularly from Japan (Yamaguchi, 2004), Korea (Schmidt-Atzert & Park, 1999), the Philippines (Enriquez, 1993), Mexico (Diaz-Guerrero, 1993), the southern USA (Cohen & Nisbett, 1997) and China (Cheung, et al., 1996). More extensive summaries of the achievements of indigenous psychologists are also available (Sinha, 1997; Kim, Yang & Hwang, in press).

From our perspective, indigenous studies pose two questions. Firstly, are the processes that have been identified in specific locations actually unique to those locations, or can similar processes be identified in other cultures, even though they may be less obvious there? If **emic** processes are actually more general than was first thought, then we may hope that they can contribute to the development of the cross-cultural field. Secondly, are there other indigenous concepts or areas of study that would repay broader attention? We address these questions in turn.

There are at least six instances in which concepts first identified indigenously have proved to have some degree of validity when operational measures of these concepts are incorporated into studies undertaken in wider contexts. Yamaguchi's (2004) measure of the *amae* relationship style has shown significant relationships to hypothesized constructs in the USA, as has Cheung et al.'s (2003) Chinese personality dimension of interpersonal relatedness and Kwan et al.'s (1997) measure of relationship harmony.

Diaz-Guerrero's (1993) measure of Mexican 'historic socio-cultural premises' were endorsed in Turkey (Ayçiçegi, 1993). Leung's (1987) measure of animosity reduction as a predictor of conflict resolution style was formulated in Hong Kong, but showed significant effects in Israel (Bond et al., 1992), and in Nigeria and Canada (Gire & Carment, 1993). Cohen and Nisbett's (1997) concept of honour culture was found applicable in Brazil (Vandello & Cohen, 2003). We should note too that if the theories and measures employed in mainstream social psychology are thought of as comprising an indigenous psychology of the USA, many of these concepts and measures have found extensive and valid application elsewhere. This reconceptualization of American studies as **emic** underlines the mutual benefit of linking **emic** to **etic** approaches.

Numerous other studies have been conducted that provide a basis for further exploration. Some researchers have identified values thought to be distinctive to particular nations or regions. Hamid (2004) developed a measure of *budi* values in Malaysia. *Budi* values concern generosity, respect, sincerity and righteousness. Hamid found that, among his Malay student respondents, *budi* values accounted for variance additional to that explained by the Schwartz value survey items. Boski (in press) identified humanism and *sarmatism* as key Polish values. Humanism is defined in terms of a concern for personal relationships combined with endorsement of personal responsibility and a rejection of materialism. This conception has something in common with Kağıtçıbaşı's definition of **autonomous-relational self-construal**. *Sarmatism* entails a mix of impulsive self-assertion and social hedonism, deriving from values espoused in times past by the Polish nobility, and is less clearly linked with other more widely used value measures. Noorderhaven and Tidjani (2001) investigated whether there are distinctive values among students in six nations in sub-Saharan Africa, compared to those in eight other nations. **Nation-level** analysis indicated that among the Africans the strongest emphases were on the importance of religion, respect for rules, the value of sharing with others and a pessimistic view of human nature. Some of these values may not be covered in a more universal measure like the Schwartz value survey, but that question remains to be tested empirically.

While there may prove to be some distinctive values that can account for variance not captured by existing comprehensive value surveys, it is more likely that indigenous psychology will deepen our understanding by identifying distinctive norms and roles than by identifying distinctive values. This is because, particularly in the less studied regions of the world, behaviour is likely to be governed less by individual values and more by traditional role requirements and the necessities for survival. Dols (1993) identified the presence of what he termed 'perverse norms' in Spanish society. These are norms that are widely endorsed but not being enforced. The existence of such norms enables persons in positions of authority to maximize their discretionary power over others, by choosing when norms shall be enforced and when deviance shall be tolerated. Perverse norms are likely to be characteristic of cultures that are high on power distance but low on situational constraint, though no cross-cultural studies assessing their characteristics have yet been reported. Within lower power distance nations, a different type of norm, first identified by Feather (1994) in Australia as the 'tall poppy syndrome' is more likely to prevail. This describes the negative reactions that an individual may receive if they are excessively assertive or successful. In Scandinavian nations this phenomenon is often referred to as the *Jante* law (Fivelsdal & Schramm-Nielsen, 1993) and in Hong Kong as 'red eye disease' (Bond, 1993). More attention to the distinctiveness of roles and norms across cultures is required. It is reflective of our discipline's individualistic and subjectivist bias (Sampson, 1981) that so little attention has been paid to these external, shared determinants of social behaviour.

Cross-cultural Psychologists should do more to Demonstrate the Practical Applications of their Findings

A special 'millennium' issue of the *Journal of Cross-Cultural Psychology* featured a symposium on the present state and future of cross-cultural psychology held at the 1998 congress of the International Association for Cross-Cultural Psychology. This was designed to do some stocktaking of cross-cultural psychology and to foresee progress in the years to come. The relatively unrealized potential for applications was discussed (Kağıtçıbaşı & Poortinga, 2000). We certainly need to do more, but a broad range of applications has already been achieved. We discuss these under four headings.

Providing Information that Enhances Understanding of the Nature of Cultural Differences and their Importance A basic aspect of any scientific investigation is to provide accurate information. Cross-cultural psychology has two tasks in this area. Firstly, studies can and do challenge the validity of derogatory ethnic and national stereotypes, by publicizing empirically-based information on the values, beliefs and life experiences of different groups. Secondly, studies can and do challenge those who adopt a culture-blind perspective, asserting that cultural differences either do not exist or can be ignored with impunity. This book can be seen as a challenge of this type, to those who assert that a valid psychology can be created by making studies within a single cultural group or nation. More specific challenges to psychologists are to move away from **imposed-etic** uses of psychometric instruments and develop locally valid instruments (Lonner, 1990; van de Vijver & Hambleton, 1996).

Information and concepts derived from cross-cultural psychology are available to all, for use in ways that may serve their specific needs. Opinion surveys such as the annual Eurobarometer inform political debate within the European Union. Surveys of cultural variations in definition of human rights in 35 nations (Doise, Spini, & Clemence, 1999; Doise 2001) provide a basis for formulations of ethical codes and for evaluations of UN programmes. Advertisers have taken much note of the concepts of individualism and collectivism, formulating their advertisements with appeals relevant to values prevailing within their target populations (Aaker & Schmitt, 2001; Aaker & Williams, 1998; de Mooij, 1998).

Training Persons in the Skills of Cross-cultural Interaction As we have seen, increasing numbers of persons are engaged in activities where cross-cultural effectiveness is required. Preparatory training programmes have been provided and evaluated for expatriate business persons, student sojourners, aid and development workers, tourist hospitality providers, police officers, military personnel, immigrants and many others (Brislin, 1990; Ward et al., 2001). Providing information on cultural differences is a necessary, but rarely a sufficient practice in achieving effective cross-cultural interactions. As we explored in Chapter 10, while briefings and cultural assimilators can provide infor-mation, different forms of experiential training can enhance their effectiveness (Earley, 1987). Key elements in the success or failure of training programmes appear to be their duration and the degree to which their focus is closely related to the circum-stances in which the trainees will be involved. A token investment of time and resources is unlikely to have more than a short-term effect.

Working Multiculturally   There have been many applications of cross-cultural psychology in the fields of health and education in different parts of the world and also within mul-ticultural nations such as the USA (Harkness & Keefer, 2000). A general lesson from these types of interventions is that unless a culturally sensitive approach is used, not much is accomplished. In this context there is a growing need for culturally informed psycholo-gists to take part in efforts to promote health, education, gender parity, and the like in the majority, non-Western world. Together with health workers, pediatricians, education specialists, and others, psychologists can and should also work in the projects of inter-national agencies such as UNICEF and the World Health Organization to contribute to human well-being globally. It has long been lamented (Jahoda, 1986) that cultural psy-chologists and anthropologists have benefited more from developing country children than those children have benefited from social scientists. It may be time to repay this debt by serving them better with our accumulated knowledge and expertise. This is one direction to follow in applying a culturally sensitive psychology usefully. It would con-tribute to *endogenous* (that is, from within) development at human and societal levels, as proposed by UNESCO (Huynh, 1979; Tripathi, 1988). This type of approach must encompass *both* culturally relevant *and* globally shared knowledge.

Achieving this type of collaborative linkage is never easy. A key element in the situ-ation is that one party to the collaboration is typically of higher social status and paid much more than the other party. This differential can set in motion a downward spi-ral (Carr, 2003). The less well-paid party feels unjustly treated and therefore holds back their contribution. This leads the well-paid party to evaluate the less well-paid party negatively and to attempt to compensate by increasing their own contribution. This in turn leads to further reduced ownership of the project and contribution from the less well-paid party. Unless this cycle is halted, both parties will become disillusioned and the project will fail, because the involvement of the less-well paid party is crucial to its long-term success. Carr's analysis is focused on technical aid workers in Africa, but it is equally applicable to all types of multinational enterprise. Leung, Wang, & Smith (2001) identified similar effects in joint venture hotels in China. The key to arresting such downward spirals lies in adequate prior training about this dynamic and continued alertness to redressing problems that arise in day-to-day relationships.

Equally important issues arise within the fields of psychotherapy and counselling. Effective diagnosis and treatment of distress requires awareness of the cultural context in which it arises. If therapists and counsellors do not share the same cultural back-ground as their clients, they require additional trained expertise in identifying cultur-ally appropriate styles of understanding and response so as to intervene more effectively (Pedersen et al., 1996).

Advising Key Negotiators and Decision-makers   We have discussed in previous chapters the massive recent increase in travel and in migration. Researchers into the processes of

acculturation are able to provide crucial information on the consequences of different government policies concerning immigration and community relations. While many governments have recently been implementing more restrictive policies concerning admission of migrants, the policies in force concerning minority groups already present varies more widely between nations. Those nations such as Canada, Australia and New Zealand that have established official policies of multiculturalism have done so with knowledge of the work of relevant **acculturation** researchers.

Diplomacy and business negotiations provide a second field in which advice from specialists is crucial. Published accounts of negotiations tend to emphasize occasions when spectacular misunderstandings have occurred, due either to mistranslations, misreading of non-verbal cues, or incompatibility of styles of negotiation (Glenn, Wittmeyer & Stevenson, 1997). Factors contributing to successful negotiations are less newsworthy, but there is little doubt that culturally-informed negotiators more often succeed.

In some cases, advice can be more methodological than substantive. A multinational business company running the same training programme for its employees throughout the world enquired why the programme was always less successful in Europe than in North America and Asia. The explanation provided was that European trainees, consistent with their cultural socialization in assertiveness, showed lower **acquiescent response bias** in their ratings of the training programme. The evaluation form was redesigned, so that the training could be more accurately evaluated.

Cultural Differences are Disappearing, so our Field has No Future

It is debatable whether cultural differences are disappearing. Firstly, what is culture? From a social psychological perspective, culture is a set of shared constraints and affordances, both ecological and societal, which influence human social behaviour. Through the socialization process, these channelling factors leave their imprints in the 'software' of the individual, and are studied as the values, beliefs, attitudes, self-construals, personality factors and attributional schemata that underpin behaviour.

Often, we study cultural differences by measuring and comparing these individual psychological reflections of culture in the members of various cultural groups. The World Values Survey is a classic example of this approach. Should the cross-national profile of values or any other psychological measure narrow across nations over time, one might then conclude that cultural differences were diminishing with respect to that measure. Suffice it to say that there is scant data yet available to begin supporting this contention. Representative, longitudinal studies across an adequately wide range of cultural groupings and tapping a comprehensive set of psychological constructs lie in a distant future.

Change in these psychological factors will depend in part on changes in the ecological and societal conditions that combine with the biological bases of behaviour to produce the range of differences that we now observe across and within cultural groups. Are these conditions narrowing? Are cross-national differences in affluence, in democratization, in the gender ratio, in the fertility of land, in the exposure to natural disasters and so forth narrowing? This seems unlikely. If not, then there would seem to be no basis in fact to conclude that cross-culturalists are chasing diminishing ephemera.

Additionally, this line of reasoning overlooks the important role of reflexivity in the formula leading to cultural convergence. One important consequence of globalization has been the apparently paradoxical resurgence of individuals' ethnic consciousness and seeking of distinctiveness. Paralleling the growth in demands for freedom and human rights are insistent voices claiming the right to protect and honour one's cultural heritage and traditions. There is a growing awareness that, 'cultural identities have been suppressed, sometimes brutally, as state policy – through religious persecutions and ethnic cleansings, but also through everyday exclusion and economic, social and political discrimination' (United Nations Development Programme, 2004, p. 1). In reaction to this growing sense of injustice, 'People want the freedom to practice their own religion openly, to speak their language, to celebrate their ethnic or religious heritage without fear of ridicule or punishment or diminished opportunity' (United Nations Development Programme, 2004, p. 1). Cultural consciousness is on the rise!

These struggles bring attendant challenges for modern states to manage these claims while still maintaining national harmony and coherence. Many ensconced beliefs, called a series of 'myths' by the UN's Human Development Report, stand in the way of realizing this unity within diversity. For example, myth 1 holds that: 'People's ethnic identities compete with their attachment to the state, so there is a trade-off between recognizing diversity and unifying the state.' The UN report then proceeds to refute each of these myths in turn, hoping to change peoples' attitudes and nations' policies towards recognizing ethnic groups within their borders.

For present purposes, however, the issue is whether greater, rather than lesser endorsement of cultural diversity will burgeon from this current ideological struggle. If this likely outcome occurs, we expect that interest in cross-cultural studies will escalate. More relevant for present purposes, we also expect that ethnic accentuation will occur in those domains of social life where ethnic group practices do not break the laws of the state or threaten the sovereignty of the nation. These domains are currently being negotiated in those many nations where culture and **ethnicity** are part of contemporary public discourse. We expect that more and more nations will become involved in these issues. Forces of diversification rather than convergence will then be added to the future of cross-cultural studies:

> Where harmony is fecund, sameness is barren. Things accommodating each other on equal terms is called blending in harmony, and in so doing they are able to flourish and grow, and other things are drawn to them. But when same is added to same, once it is used up, there is no more. There is no music in a single note, no decoration in a single item, no relish in a single taste. (*Discourses of the States*, China, 4th century BCE)

Glossary of Key Constructs

Acculturation. Originally used to refer to the process by which contact between two cultures leads to changes in both cultures. Now more frequently used to describe the ways that members of migrant groups adapt to the new cultural environment.

Acquiescent Response Bias. The tendency to agree with rather than disagree with many or all of the statements and questions that are presented by a researcher.

Autonomous-relational Self-construal. A dimension of self-perception that emphasizes both one's capacity for autonomous action and the importance of relatedness with others.

Citizen Mean. A score representing an attribute of the average member of a nation, computed using data that has first been analysed at the individual-level and then aggregated to the nation-level.

Correspondence Bias (also known as the Fundamental Attribution Error). The belief that a person's behaviour in a given situation is due to (corresponds to) their personal qualities, rather than being due to the type of situation in which it occurs.

Cross-lagged Panel Analysis. A technique for testing which of two variables causes the other to change over time. Measures of both variables collected at two points in time are compared. If the correlation of variable A at time 1 predicts variable B at time 2, but variable A at time 2 does not predict variable B at time 1 as strongly, then A can be said to have had a causal impact on B.

Cultural Orientation. A general term used in this book to refer to any one of the various measures that are currently used to characterize relevant individual-level attributes that reflect cultural characteristics, such as self-construal, values or beliefs.

Cultural Psychology. An approach to the study of culture that emphasizes the interrelatedness of persons and their specific contexts. This orientation towards psychological study requires emic research methods and makes no assumption that results will lead to identification of causal relationships or will be comparable with those from other contexts.

Culture. A concept with numerous definitions, applicable to all levels in the analysis of social systems. The culture of a system comprises shared ways of understanding the meanings of events occurring within the system. In this book we have sought to avoid labelling nations as cultures, even though very many of the studies that we discuss do base their sampling on nations. Nations do have many of the characteristics of cultures, but many nations are too culturally diverse to qualify as having a unified culture. Nations are better thought of as multicultural systems.

Culture and Personality. An early research tradition, in which it was assumed that distinctive personality types could be used to characterize whole cultures.

Decentring. A translation procedure that tries to provide phrases that have equivalent meanings in each culture rather than using literal translations for each word.

Eco-cultural Theories. Theories that predict the types of culture that will arise in differing environmental and socio-political circumstances.

Ecological Fallacy. The false belief that the relationship between two variables must be the same at different levels of analysis. Usually used to refer to an illegitimate extrapolation from nation-level relationships to individual-level relationships.

Ecological Mean. A nation-level mean score on some variable.

Emic and Etic Studies. Emic studies are those that draw material from the immediate context being studied and make no assumption about the cross-cultural generality of what is discovered. Etic studies are those that make a provisional assumption that the phenomena being studied are comparable and universal.

Ethnicity/Ethnic Group. Ethnicity is a problematic concept used to identify sub-cultural groups on the basis of criteria such as ancestry, skin colour and other attributes. A person's self-identified ethnic identity does not always coincide with his or her ethnicity as identified by others.

Factor Analysis. A statistical technique used to search for the underlying structure of the responses to a test or survey that indicates the extent to which different items have received similar responses and can therefore be grouped together as 'factors' tapping the same underlying construct.

Family Model of Independence. A system of intergenerational relationships which supports the separateness, independence and autonomy of the offspring.

Family Model of Interdependence. A system of intergenerational relationships which gives distinctive emphasis to continuing relatedness and interdependence between the generations.

Family Model of Psychological Interdependence. A system of intergenerational relationships which gives emphasis both to continuing relatedness and to the autonomy of action by the offspring.

Field Dependence. Relative inability to identify a stimulus hidden within a broader field (background) of more complex stimuli.

Field Independence. The ability to identify a stimulus hidden within a broader, more complex, set of stimuli, thus separating the figure from the field (background). Considered to reflect analytical ability.

Imposed-etic Studies. Studies that take an etic measure developed in one cultural context and apply it to other contexts without first assessing its appropriateness or its equivalence of meaning.

Independent Self-construal. A self-perception that emphasizes one's autonomy and separateness from others.

Individualism-Collectivism. Hofstede's nation-level dimension, defined by many authors in varying ways. The central element concerns the continuity of group affiliations in collectivist cultures, compared with the negotiability of group affiliations in individualist cultures. Some authors also use these constructs at the individual-level, reflecting separateness-relatedness, independence-interdependence, and the upholding of individual or group loyalties.

Individual-level Studies. Studies in which the data from each individual respondent is treated as a separate case.

Indigenous Psychology. An emic approach, whose goal is to achieve understanding of a particular nation or culture, using concepts that are developed locally rather than drawing on those provided from mainstream psychology.

Interdependent Self-construal. A self-perception that emphasizes one's relatedness to others.

Meta-analysis. A statistical technique for summarizing the results of a series of related studies. Even though studies may have used different measurement scales, each can be analysed to yield an 'effect size', which is an estimate of the extent of change reported on whatever measure was used, minus the change found for any control or comparison group.

Moderation and Mediation. A moderator variable is a variable whose presence is shown to increase or decrease the strength of relationship between two other variables. A mediator variable is one that is shown to partially or wholly explain the relationship between two other variables. Within cross-cultural psychology, mediators are typically measures of cultural orientation, which are sometimes shown to be able to explain differences that have been identified between samples drawn from different nations.

Nation-level Studies. Studies in which all the data from each national sample on each available variable is first averaged and then analysed treating each nation as a single case.

Nomological Net. The network of correlations between a new measure and existing measures. This matrix is useful for assessing the validity of the new measure.

Population Mean. The individual-level mean score of a population on some measure. However, if means from two or more nations are compared without first establishing the structure of the measure in each population separately, comparisons are likely to be invalid.

Psychological Adaptation (to culture contact). Adaptation to a new cultural context by someone from a different cultural context, as indicated by the reported subjective experiences of the newcomer, for instance by measures of anxiety, strain, depression and relationship difficulties.

Post-modernity. A set of values and behaviours, first identified among some members of the more affluent nations of the world. Post-modernity represents a progression from life that is dominated by the imperatives of work and the scarcity of money. It includes increased hedonism, political and moral liberalism, concern for the environment, and a search for distinctive modes of self-expression.

Race. A term frequently used in everyday discourse and social perception, but which has no defensible biological basis. In this book, we prefer to refer to ethnicity.

Reliability. In its technical sense, this term is used by psychologists to characterize a measure in two ways. Firstly, do responses to the separate items making up a scale correlate with one another in a consistent manner, i.e., inter-item consistency? Secondly, does the measure yield the same scores from the same individuals when completed at a later time, i.e., test-retest consistency?

Smallest Space Analysis. A statistical technique analogous to factor analysis which does not make the same, more restrictive statistical assumptions that are made in factor analysis. The technique rests on ordinal measurement rather than interval scale measurement.

Socio-cultural Adaptation. Adaptation to a new cultural context by learning how the local system operates and acquiring the necessary skills and procedures to get things done in that less familiar cultural context.

Unpackaging. A metaphor that is useful to cross-cultural researchers. Cultures differ from one another in numerous ways. By using more specific measures of cultural orientation, researchers are sometimes able to show that it is their specific measure that can explain the differences between cultural groups that they have found. This technique can eliminate a variety of possible alternative explanations for the differences. Also used more generally to refer to unravelling of overlapping characteristics or explanations.

Validity. The extent to which a measure has been shown to measure the attributes that it is intended to measure and not those that it is not been developed to measure.

Value of Children. The type of value placed upon the having of children in one's family, in other words the types of satisfactions children provide to their parents and families. The economic or utilitarian value of having children is contrasted with the emotional satisfaction or value that parents experience from having children.

Within-subject Standardization. A procedure used by cross-cultural psychologists to discount acquiescent or reactive response bias. Each respondent's score for response to a particular survey item is calibrated against the mean for that respondent's responses to all other items. This procedure can only be used when the survey has included a broad range of items that are expected to yield responses that are independent from one another. It is important to be clear that this technique differs in an important way from other standardizations that researchers sometimes make for other purposes. For example, within-sample standardization is used when the intention is to equalize scores between two samples before further analyses are undertaken.

References

Aaker, J., & Schmitt, B. (2001). Culture-dependent assimilation and differentiation of the self: Preferences for consumption symbols in the United States and China. *Journal of Cross-Cultural Psychology*, *32*, 561–76.

Aaker, J., & Williams, P. (1998). Empathy versus pride: The influence of emotional appeals across cultures. *Journal of Consumer Research*, *25*, 241–61.

Abe, J.A.A. (2004). Self-esteem, perception of relationships and emotional distress: A cross-cultural study. *Personal Relationships*, *11*, 231–47.

Abel, T.M., & Hsu, F.L.K. (1949). Some aspects of the personality of Chinese as revealed by the Rorschach test. *Rorschach Research Exchange and Journal of Projective Techniques*, *13*, 285–301.

Abrams, D., Ando, K., & Hinkle, S. (1998). Psychological attachment to the group: Cross-cultural differences in organizational identification and subjective norms as predictors of workers' turnover intentions. *Personality and Social Psychology Bulletin*, *24*, 1027–39.

Adair, W.L., Okumura, T., & Brett, J.M. (2001). Negotiation behavior when cultures collide: The United States and Japan. *Journal of Applied Psychology*, *86*, 371–85.

Adorno, T.W., Frenkel-Brunswik, E., Levinson, D.J., & Sanford, R.N. (1950). *The authoritarian personality.* New York: Harper.

Agarwal, R., & Misra, G. (1986). A factor analytic study of achievement goals and means: An Indian view. *International Journal of Psychology*, *21*, 717–31.

Albert, R.D., & Ha, I.A. (2004). Latino/Anglo-American differences in attributions to situations involving touching and silence. *International Journal of Intercultural Relations*, *28*, 253–80.

Albright, L., Malloy, T.E., Qi, D., Kenny, D.A. et al. (1997). Cross-cultural consensus in personality judgments. *Journal of Personality and Social Psychology*, *73*, 270–80.

Al Issa, A. (2003). Sociocultural transfer in L2 speech behaviors: Evidence and motivating factors. *International Journal of Intercultural Relations*, *27*, 581–602.

Allen, M.W., Ng, S.H., Ikeda, K., Jawan, J.A., et al. (2004). 'Two decades of cultural value change and economic development in eight East Asian and Pacific island nations'. Paper given at the congress of the International Association for Cross-Cultural Psychology, Xi'an, China.

Allik, J., & McCrae, R.R. (2004). Toward a geography of personality traits: Patterns of profiles across 36 cultures. *Journal of Cross-Cultural Psychology*, *34*, 13–28.

Allport, G.W. (1954). *The nature of prejudice.* Reading, MA: Addison-Wesley.

Allport, G.W., & Odbert, H. (1936). Trait names: A psycho-lexical study. *Psychological Monographs*, *47* (1), (whole No. 21).

Altemeyer, B. (1988). *Enemies of freedom: Understanding right-wing authoritarianism.* San Francisco, CA: Jossey-Bass.

Ambady, N., Koo, J., Lee, F., & Rosenthal, R. (1996). More than words: linguistic and non-linguistic politeness in two cultures. *Journal of Personality and Social Psychology*, *70*, 996–1011.

Amir, Y., & Sharon, I. (1987). Are social psychological laws cross-culturally valid? *Journal of Cross-Cultural Psychology*, *18*, 383–470.

Andersen, P.A., Hecht, M., Hoobler, G.D., & Smallwood, M. (2002). Nonverbal communication across cultures. In W.B. Gudykunst & B. Mody (Eds.), *Handbook of international and intercultural communication* (pp. 88–106). Thousand Oaks, CA: Sage.

Andolšek, D.M., & Štebe, J. (2004). Multinational perspectives on work values and commitment. *International Journal of Cross-Cultural Management*, *4*, 181–208.

Archer, D., & Gartner, R. (1984). *Violence and crime in cross-cultural perspective.* New Haven, CT: Yale University Press.

Archer, J. (in press). Cross-cultural differences in physical aggression between partners. *Personality and Social Psychology Review.*

Arends-Toth, J., & van de Vijver, F. (2003). Multiculturalism and acculturation: Views of Dutch and Turkish Dutch. *European Journal of Social Psychology, 33*, 249–266.

Arends-Toth, J., & van de Vijver, F. (2004). Domains and dimensions in acculturation: Implicit theories of Turkish Dutch. *International Journal of Intercultural Relations, 28*, 19–35.

Argyle, M. (2001). The development of social psychology at Oxford. In G. C. Bunn, A.D. Lovie, & G.D. Richards (Eds.), *Psychology in Britain: Historical essays and personal reflections* (pp. 333–43). Leicester: BPS Books.

Argyle, M., Henderson, M., Bond, M.H., et al. (1986). Cross-cultural variations in relationship rules. *International Journal of Psychology, 21*, 287–315.

Aries, P. (1962). *Centuries of childhood: A social history of family life* (R. Baldick, Trans.). New York: Knopf.

Arnett, J.J. (1992). Reckless behavior in adolescence: A developmental perspective. *Developmental Review, 12*, 339–73.

Arnett, J.J. (2002). The psychology of globalization. *American Psychologist, 57*, 774–83.

Aron, A., Aron, E.N., & Smollan, D. (1992). Inclusion of Other in the Self scale and the structure of interpersonal closeness. *Journal of Personality and Social Psychology, 63*, 596–612.

Asch, S. (1956). Studies of independence and conformity: A minority of one against a unanimous majority. *Psychological Monographs, 70* (9), (whole No. 416).

Ataca, B., & Berry, J.W. (2002). Psychological, sociocultural, and marital adaptation of Turkish immigrant couples in Canada. *International Journal of Psychology, 37*, 13–26.

Ataca, B., & Berry, J.W. (2004). 'Comparative study of acculturation and adaptation among Turkish immigrants in Canada'. Unpublished manuscript, Bogazici University, Istanbul.

Au, K. (1999). Intra-cultural variation: Evidence and implications for international business. *Journal of International Business Studies, 30,* 799–812.

Au, K. (2000). Intra-cultural variation as another construct of international management: A study based on secondary data of 42 countries. *Journal of International Management, 6,* 217–38.

Au, K., & Cheung, M.W.L. (2002). Consequences of intra-cultural variation: An exploratory study of job autonomy in 42 countries. In P. Boski, F. van de Vijver, & A.M. Chodynicka (Eds.), *New directions in cross-cultural psychology* (pp. 261–77). Warsaw, Poland: Polish Academy of Sciences.

Au, T.K. (2004). Making sense of differences: Language, culture and social reality. In S.H. Ng, C.N. Candlin, & C.Y. Chiu (Eds.), *Language matters: Communication, culture and identity* (pp. 139–53). Hong Kong: City University of Hong Kong Press.

Aycan, Z., Kanungo, R.N., Mendonca, M., You, K., Deller, G., Stahl, G., & Kurshid, A. (2000). Impact of culture on human resource management practices: A ten country comparison. *Applied Psychology: An International* Review, *49*, 192–221.

Ayçiçegi, A. (1993). 'The effects of the mother training program'. Unpublished master's thesis, Bogaziçi University, Istanbul, Turkey.

Ayçiçegi, A., & Harris, C.L. (2005). Variations in individualism-collectivism among Turkish urban and rural residents and immigrants to North America. *Journal of Cross-Cultural Psychology, 36,*

Aydin, B., & Oztutuncu, F. (2001). Examination of adolescents' negative thoughts, depressive mood, and family environment. *Adolescence, 36*, 77–83.

Bandura, A. (2002). Social cognitive theory in cultural context. *Applied Psychology: An International Review, 51*, 269–90.

Barry, H., Child, I., & Bacon, M. (1959). Relation of child training to subsistence economy. *American Anthropologist, 61*, 31–63.

Bartholomew, K., & Horowitz, L.M. (1991). Attachment styles in young adults: A test of a four category model. *Journal of Personality and Social Psychology, 62*, 226–44.

Bass, B.M. (1997). Does the transactional-transformational leadership paradigm transcend organizational and national boundaries? *American Psychologist, 52*, 130–9.

Beauvois, J-L., & Dubois, N. (1988). The norm of internality in the explanation of psychological events. *European Journal of Social Psychology, 18*, 299–316.

Bechts, M.C., & Vingerhoets, A.J.J.M. (2002). Crying and mood change: A cross-cultural study. *Cognition and Emotion, 16*, 87–101.

Benedict, R. (1932). Configuration of culture in North America. *American Anthropologist, 34,* 1–27.

Benedict, R. (1946). *The chrysanthemum and the sword*. Boston, MA: Houghton Mifflin.

Benet-Martínez, V., & John, O.P. (1998). *Los Cinco Grandes* across cultures and ethnic groups: Multitrait-multimethod analyses of the Big Five in Spanish and English. *Journal of Personality and Social Psychology, 75*, 729–50.

Berger, P.L. (1967). *The sacred canopy: Elements of a sociological theory of religion.* New York: Anchor.

Berno, T. (1999). When a guest is a guest: Cook islanders view tourism. *Annals of Tourism Research, 26*, 656–75.

Berry, J.W. (1969). On cross-cultural comparability. *International Journal of Psychology, 4*, 119–28.

Berry, J.W. (1976). *Human ecology and cognitive style: Comparative studies in cultural and psychological adaptation.* New York: Sage.

Berry, J.W. (1979). A cultural ecology of social behaviour. In L. Berkowitz (ed.), *Advances in experimental social psychology*, (Vol. 12, pp. 177–206). New York: Academic Press.

Berry, J.W. (1997). Immigration, acculturation and adaptation. *Applied Psychology: An International Review, 46*, 5–34.

Berry, J.W. (2001). Contextual studies of cognitive adaptation. In M. Collis & S. Messick (Eds.), *Intelligence and personality: Bridging the gap in theory and measurement* (pp. 319–33). Mahwah, NJ: Erlbaum.

Berry, J.W., & Annis, R.C. (1974). Acculturative stress: The role of ecology, culture and differentiation. *Journal of Cross-Cultural Psychology, 5*, 382–406.

Berry, J.W., & Kalin, R. (1995). Multicultural and ethnic attitudes in Canada: An overview of the 1991 national survey. *Canadian Journal of Behavioral Science, 27*, 301–20.

Berry, J.W., & Sam, D.L. (1997). Acculturation and adaptation. In J.W. Berry, M.H. Segall, & Ç. Kağıtçıbaşı (Eds.), *Handbook of cross-cultural psychology* (2nd ed., Vol. 3, pp. 291–326). Needham Heights, MA: Allyn & Bacon.

Binet, A., & Henri, V. (1894). De la suggestibilité naturelle chez les enfants. *L'Année Psychologique, 1*, 404–6.

Black, J.S., & Porter, L.W. (1991). Managerial behaviors and job performance: A successful manager in Los Angeles may not succeed in Hong Kong. *Journal of International Business Studies, 22*, 99–113.

Bloom, B.S. (1977). *Human characteristics and school learning.* New York: McGraw Hill.

Blos, P. (1979). *The adolescent passage.* New York: International Universities Press.

Bochner, S. (1994). Cross-cultural differences in the self-concept: A test of Hofstede's individualism-collectivism distinction. *Journal of Cross-Cultural Psychology, 25*, 275–83.

Bochner, S., & Coulon, L. (1997). A culture assimilator to train Australian hospitality industry workers serving Japanese tourists. *Journal of Tourism Studies, 8*, 8–17.

Bond, M.H. (1979). Dimensions used in perceiving peers: Cross-cultural comparisons of Hong Kong, Japanese, American, and Filipino university students. *International Journal of Psychology, 14*, 47–56.

Bond, M.H. (1986). *The psychology of the Chinese people.* Hong Kong: Oxford University Press.

Bond, M.H. (1988). Finding universal dimensions of individual variation in multi-cultural surveys of values: The Rokeach and Chinese value surveys. *Journal of Personality and Social Psychology, 55*, 1009–15.

Bond, M.H. (1991a). *Beyond the Chinese face.* Hong Kong: Oxford.

Bond, M.H. (1991b). Chinese values and health: A cross-cultural examination. *Psychology and Health: An International Journal, 5*, 137–52.

Bond, M.H. (1993). Emotions and their expression in Chinese culture. *Journal of Nonverbal Behaviour, 17*, 245–62.

Bond, M.H. (1996a). 'The Hofstede dimensions and their successors in empirical retrospect'. Paper presented at the International Congress of Psychology, Montreal, Canada, August.

Bond, M.H. (1996b). Chinese values. In M.H. Bond (ed.), *The handbook of Chinese psychology* (pp. 208–226). Hong Kong: Oxford University Press.

Bond, M.H. (ed.) (1997a). *Working at the interface of cultures: Eighteen lives in social science.* London: Routledge.

Bond, M.H. (1997b). Adding value to the cross-cultural study of organizational behavior: Reculer pour mieux sauter. In P.C. Earley, & M. Erez (Eds.), *New perspectives in industrial/organizational psychology* (pp. 256–75). San Francisco: New Lexington Press.

Bond, M.H. (2002). Reclaiming the individual from Hofstede's ecological analysis: A 20-year Odyssey. *Psychological Bulletin, 128*, 73–77.

Bond, M.H. (2004). Culture and aggression: From context to coercion. *Personality and Social Psychology Review, 8*, 62–78.

Bond, M.H., & Cheung, T.S. (1983). The spontaneous self-concept of college students in Hong Kong, Japan and the United States. *Journal of Cross-Cultural Psychology, 14,* 153–71.

Bond, M.H., & Cheung, M.K. (1984). Experimenter language choice and ethnic affirmation by Chinese trilinguals in Hong Kong. *International Journal of Intercultural Relations, 8,* 347–56.

Bond, M.H., & Forgas, J.P. (1984). Linking person perception to behavioral intention across cultures: The role of cultural collectivism. *Journal of Cross-Cultural Psychology, 15,* 337–52.

Bond, M.H., Kwan, V.S.Y., & Li, C. (2000). Decomposing a sense of superiority: The differential social impact of self-regard and regard-for-others. *Journal of Research in Personality, 34,* 537–53.

Bond, M.H., Leung, K., & 67 co-authors (2004). Culture-level dimensions of social axioms and their correlates across 41 cultures. *Journal of Cross-Cultural Psychology, 35,* 548–70.

Bond, M.H., Leung, K., & Schwartz, S.H. (1992). Explaining choices in procedural and distributive justice across cultures. *International Journal of Psychology, 27,* 211–25.

Bond, M.H., Nakazato, H., & Shiraishi, D. (1975). Universality and distinctiveness in dimensions of Japanese person perception. *Journal of Cross-Cultural Psychology, 6,* 346–57.

Bond, M.H., & Tornatsky, L.C. (1973). Locus of control in students from Japan and the United States: Dimensions and levels of response. *Psychologia, 16,* 209–13.

Bond, M.H., & Yang, K.S. (1982). Ethnic affirmation versus cross-cultural accommodation: The variable impact of questionnaire language on Chinese bilinguals in Hong Kong. *Journal of Cross-Cultural Psychology, 13,* 169–85.

Bond, R., & Smith, P.B. (1996). Culture and conformity: A meta-analysis of studies using Asch's (1952b, 1956) line judgment task. *Psychological Bulletin, 119,* 111–37.

Bordia, P., & Blau, G. (2003). Moderating effect of allocentrism on the pay referent comparison-pay level satisfaction relationship. *Applied Psychology: An International Review, 52,* 499–514.

Boski, P. (in press). Humanism-materialism: Centuries-long Polish cultural origins and 20 years of research in cultural psychology. In U. Kim, K.S. Yang, & K.K. Hwang (Eds.), *Scientific advances in indigenous and cultural psychology: Empirical, philosophical and cultural contributions.* Cambridge: Cambridge University Press.

Boski, P., van de Vijver, F.J.R., Hurme, H., & Miluska, M. (1999). Perception and evaluation of Polish cultural femininity in Poland, the United States, Finland and the Netherlands. *Cross-Cultural Research, 33,* 131–61.

Bosland, N. (1985). 'The cross-cultural equivalence of the power distance-, uncertainty avoidance-, individualism-, and masculinity-measurement scales'. Working paper, Institute for Research on Intercultural Cooperation.

Bourhis, R.Y., & Dayan, J. (2004). Acculturation orientations towards Israeli Arabs and Jewish immigrants. *International Journal of Psychology, 39,* 118–31.

Bourhis, R.Y., Moise, L.C., Perreault, S., & Senecal, S. (1997). Towards an interactive acculturation model: A social psychological approach. *International Journal of Psychology, 32,* 369–86.

Bowen, E.S. (1964). *Return to laughter.* Garden City, NY: Doubleday.

Bresnahan, M.J., Levine, T.R., Shearman, S.M. et al. (2003). A multimethod, multitrait validity assessment of self-construal in Japan, Korea and the United States. *Human Communication Research, 31,* 33–59.

Brett, J.M., & Okumura, T. (1998). Inter- and intracultural negotiation: US and Japanese negotiators. *Academy of Management Journal, 41,* 495–510.

Brew, F.P., & Cairns, D.R. (2004). Styles of managing interpersonal workplace conflict in relation to status and face concern: A study with Anglos and Chinese. *International Journal of Conflict Management, 15,* 19–94.

Brislin, R.W. (1990) (Ed.). *Applied cross-cultural psychology.* Newbury Park, CA: Sage.

Brislin, R., Lonner, W.J., & Thorndike, R.M. (1973). *Cross-cultural research methods.* New York: Wiley.

Brislin, R.W., Cushner, K., Cherrie, K., & Yong, M. (1986). *Intercultural interactions: A practical guide.* Beverly Hills, CA: Sage.

Brockner, J. (2003). Unpacking country effects: On the need to operationalize the psychological determinants of cross-national differences. In R.M. Kramer & B.M. Staw (Eds.), *Research in Organizational Behavior* (Vol. 25, pp. 333–67). Greenwich, CT: JAI Press.

Brockner, J., Ackerman, G., Greenberg, J., Gelfand, M., Francesco, A.M., Chen, Z.X., et al. (2001). Culture and procedural justice: The influence of power distance on reactions to voice. *Journal of Experimental Social Psychology, 37,* 300–15.

Brockner, J., Chen, Y.R., & Chen, X.P. (2002). Individual-collective primacy and in-group favouritism: Enhancement and protection effects. *Journal of Experimental Social Psychology, 38,* 482–91.

Brockner, J., Chen, Y.R., Mannix, E.A., Leung, K., & Skarlicki, D.P. (2000). Culture and procedural fairness: When the effects of what you do depend on how you do it. *Administrative Science Quarterly, 45*, 138–59.

Bronfenbrenner, U. (1979). *The ecology of human development: Experiments by nature and design.* Cambridge, MA: Harvard University Press.

Brown, J.D., & Kobayashi, C. (2002). Self-enhancement in Japan and America. *Asian Journal of Social Psychology, 5*, 145–67.

Brown, R.J., Hinkle, S., Ely, P.C., et al. (1992). Recognizing group diversity: Individualist-collectivist and autonomous-relational social relations and their implications for intergroup processes. *British Journal of Social Psychology, 31*, 327–42.

Burns, T., & Stalker, G.M. (1961). *The management of innovation.* London: Tavistock.

Buss, D.M. (1989). Sex differences in human mate preferences: Evolutionary hypotheses tested in 37 cultures. *Behavioral and Brain Sciences, 12*, 1–49.

Buss, D.M., & 49 co-authors (1990). International preferences in selecting mates: A study of 37 cultures. *Journal of Cross-Cultural Psychology, 21*, 5–47.

Buss, D.M., Shackelford, T.K., Kirkpatrick, L.A., Choe, J.C. et al. (1999). Jealousy and the nature of beliefs about infidelity: Tests of competing hypotheses about sex differences in the United States, Korea and Japan. *Personal Relationships, 6*, 125–50.

Buss, D.M., Shackelford, T.K., & Leblanc, G.J. (2000). Number of children desired and preferred spousal age difference: Context-specific mate preference patterns across 37 cultures. *Evolution and Human Behavior, 21*, 323–31.

Byrne, R.W., Barnard, P.J., Davidson, L., Janik, V.M. et al. (2004). Understanding culture across species. *Trends in Cognitive Sciences, 8*, 341–46.

Campbell, D.T. (1970). Natural selection as an epistemological model. In R. Naroll & R. Cohen (Eds.), *A handbook of method in cultural anthropology* (pp. 51–85). New York: Natural History Press.

Caralis, C., & Haslam, N. (2004). Relational tendencies associated with broad personality dimensions. *Psychology and Psychotherapy: Theory, Research and Practice, 77*, 397–402.

Cargile, A., & Bradac, J. (2001). Attitudes toward language. In W.B. Gudykunst (Ed.), *Communication Yearbook 25* (pp. 347–82). Mahwah, NJ: Erlbaum.

Carr, S.C. (2003). Poverty and justice. In S.C. Carr & T.S. Sloan (Eds.), *Poverty and psychology: Emergent critical practice* (pp. 45–68). New York: Kluwer Academic/Plenum.

Cashmore, J.A., & Goodnow, J.J. (1986). Influences on Australians' parents' values: Ethnicity and socio-economic status. *Journal of Cross-Cultural Psychology, 17*, 441–54.

Castro, L., & Toro, M.A. (2004). The evolution of culture: From primate social learning to human culture. *Proceedings of the National Academy of Sciences of the United States of America, 101* (27), 10235–40.

Cattaneo, C. (1864). Dell'antitesi come metodo di psicologia sociale. *Il Politecnico, 20*, 262–70.

Cavill, S. (2000). Psychology in practice: Welfare of refugees. *The Psychologist, 13*, 552–4.

Chan, H.L. (2004). The relationship between societal factors and universal mate preferences: A cross-cultural study. Unpublished Bachelor's thesis, Chinese University of Hong Kong.

Chan, S.C.N. (1995). Cultural values and country health. Unpublished Bachelor's thesis, Chinese University of Hong Kong.

Chan, S.K.C., Bond, M.H., Spencer-Oatey, H., & Rojo-Laurilla, M.A. (2004). Culture and relationship promotion in service encounters: Protecting the ties that bind. *Journal of Asia-Pacific Communication, 14*, 245–60.

Chang, L. (2004). Socialization and social adjustment of single children in China. *International Journal of Psychology, 39*, 390.

Chang, L., Arkin, R.M., Leong, F.T., Chan, D.K.S., & Leung, K. (2004). Subjective overachievement in American and Chinese college students. *Journal of Cross-cultural Psychology, 35*, 152–73.

Chang, L., Schwartz, D., Dodge, K., & McBride-Chang, C. (2003). Harsh parenting in relation to child emotion regulation and aggression. *Journal of Family Psychology, 17*, 598–606.

Chao, R.K. (1994). Beyond parental control and authoritarian parenting style: Understanding Chinese parenting through the cultural notion of training. *Child Development, 65*, 1111–20.

Chen, C.C. (1995). New trends in reward allocation preferences: A Sino-US comparison. *Academy of Management Journal, 38*, 408–28.

Chen, C.C., Chen, Y.R., & Xin, K.R. (2004). Guanxi practices and trust in management: A procedural justice perspective. *Organization Science, 15*, 200–9.

Chen, Y.R., Brockner, J., & Chen, X. (2002). Individual-collective primacy and in-group favouritism: Enhancement and protection effects. *Journal of Experimental Social Psychology, 38,* 482–91.

Chen, Y.R., Brockner, J., & Katz, T. (1996). Towards an explanation of cultural differences in in-group favouritism: the role of individual versus collective primacy. *Journal of Personality and Social Psychology, 71,* 613–25.

Chen, X.Y., He, Y.F., De Oliviera, A.M., et al. (2004). Loneliness and social adaptation in Brazilian, Canadian, Chinese and Italian children: A multinational comparative study. *Journal of Child Psychology and Psychiatry, 45,* 1373–84.

Chen, X.Y., Zapulla, C., Lo Coco, A., et al. (2004). Self-perceptions of competence in Brazilian, Canadian, Chinese and Italian children: Relations with social and school adjustment. *International Journal of Behavioral Development, 28,* 129–38.

Cheung, F.M., Leung, K., Zhang, J-X., et al. (2001). Indigenous Chinese personality constructs: Is the five factor model complete? *Journal of Cross-Cultural Psychology, 32,* 407–33.

Cheung, F.M., Cheung, S.F., Wada, S., & Zhang, J. (2003). Indigenous measures of personality assessment in Asian countries: A review. *Psychological Assessment, 15,* 280–9.

Cheung, F.M., Cheung, S.F., Leung, K., Ward, C., & Leong, F. (2003). The English version of the Chinese Personality Assessment Inventory. *Journal of Cross-Cultural Psychology, 34,* 433–52.

Cheung, F.M., Leung, K., Fan, R., Song, W.Z., Zhang, J.X., & Zhang, J.P. (1996). Development of the Chinese Personality Assessment Inventory (CPAI). *Journal of Cross-Cultural Psychology, 27,* 181–99.

Chinese Culture Connection (1987). Chinese values and the search for culture-free dimensions of culture. *Journal of Cross-Cultural Psychology, 18,* 143–64.

Chirkov, V., Kim, Y., Ryan, R., & Kaplan, U. (2003). Differentiating autonomy from individualism and independence: A self-determination theory perspective on internalization of cultural orientations and well being, *Journal of Personality and Social Psychology, 84,* 97–110.

Chirkov, V.I., & Ryan, R.M. (2001). Parent and teacher autonomy-support in Russian and US adolescents: Common effects on well-being and academic motivation. *Journal of Cross-Cultural Psychology, 32,* 618–35.

Chiu, C.Y., & Hong, Y.Y. (1999). Social identification in a political transition: The role of implicit beliefs. *International Journal of Intercultural Relations, 23,* 297–318.

Choi, I., Nisbett, R.E., & Norenzayan, A. (1999). Causal attribution across cultures: Variation and universality. *Psychological Bulletin, 125,* 47–63.

Choi, I., Nisbett, R.E., & Smith, E.E. (1997). Culture, category salience and inductive reasoning. *Cognition, 65,* 15–32.

Choi, I., & Nisbett, R.E. (2000). Cultural psychology of surprise: Holistic theories and recognition of contradiction. *Journal of Personality and Social Psychology, 79,* 890–905.

Choi, S.C., & Lee, S.J. (2002). Two-component model of chemyon-oriented behaviors in Korea: Constructive and defensive chemyon. *Journal of Cross-Cultural Psychology, 33,* 332–45.

Chou, K-L. (2000). Emotional autonomy and depression among Chinese adolescents. *Journal of Genetic Psychology, 161,* 161–9.

Church, A.T., & Katigbak, M.S. (1992). The cultural context of academic motives: A comparison of Filipino and American college students. *Journal of Cross-Cultural Psychology, 23,* 40–58.

Church, A.T., & Katigbak, M. (2002). Indigenisation of psychology in the Philippines. *International Journal of Psychology, 37,* 129–48.

Church, A.T., Katigbak, M.S., & Reyes, J-A.S. (1996). Toward a taxonomy of trait adjectives in Filipino: Comparing personality lexicons across cultures. *European Journal of Personality, 10,* 3–24.

Cinnirella, M. (1997). Towards a European identity? Interactions between the national and European social identities manifested by university students in Britain and Italy. *British Journal of Social Psychology, 36,* 19–31.

Claes, M. (1998). Adolescents' closeness with parents, siblings and friends in three countries: Canada, Belgium and Italy. *Journal of Youth and Adolescence, 27,* 165–84.

Cogan, J.C., Bhalla, S.K., Sefadedeh, A., & Rothblum, E. (1996). A comparison study of United States and African students on perceptions of obesity and thinness. *Journal of Cross-Cultural Psychology, 27,* 98–113.

Cohen, D. (1997). Ifs and thens in cross-cultural psychology. In R.S. Wyer Jr. (Ed.), *The automaticity of everyday life* (pp. 121–131). Mahwah, NJ: Erlbaum.

Cohen, D., & Nisbett, R.E. (1997). Field experiments examining the culture of honor: The role of institutions in perpetuating norms about violence. *Personality and Social Psychology Bulletin, 23,* 1188–99.

Cohen, S., Doyle, W.J., Turner, R., Alper, C.M., & Skoner, D.P. (2003). Sociability and susceptibility to the common cold. *Psychological Science, 14,* 389–95.

Cohen, S., & Williamson, G.M. (1991). Stress and infectious disease in humans. *Psychological Bulletin, 109,* 5–24.

Cole, M. (1996). *Cultural psychology: A once and future discipline.* Cambridge, MA: Harvard University Press.

Collins, B.E. (1974). Four components of the Rotter Internal-External scale: Belief in a difficult world, a just world, a predictable world, and a politically responsive world. *Journal of Personality and Social Psychology, 29,* 381–91.

Colquitt, J.A., Conlon, D.E., Wesson, M.J., Porter, C.O.L.H., & Ng, K.Y. (2001). Justice at the millennium: A meta-analytic review of 25 years of organizational justice research. *Journal of Applied Psychology, 86,* 425–45.

Conroy, M., Hess, R.D., Azuma, H., & Kashiwagi, K. (1980). Maternal strategies for regulating children's behavior: Japanese and American families. *Journal of Cross-Cultural Psychology, 11,* 153–72.

Costa, P.T., Jr., & McCrae, R.R. (1992). *Revised NEO Personality Inventory (NEO-PI – R) and NEO Five Factor Inventory (NEO – FFI).* Odessa, FL: Psychological Assessment Resources.

Costa, P.T., Jr., Terracciano, A., & McCrae, R.R. (2001). Gender differences in personality traits across cultures: Robust and surprising findings. *Journal of Personality and Social Psychology, 81,* 322–31.

Cousins, S. (1989). Culture and selfhood in Japan and the US. *Journal of Personality and Social Psychology, 56,* 124–31.

Crockett, L.J., & Silbereisen, R. (Eds.), (2000). *Negotiating adolescence in times of social change.* Cambridge, UK: Cambridge University Press.

Cuddy, A.J.C., Fiske, S.T., Kwan, V., et al. (2003). 'Is stereotyping culture-bound? A cross-cultural comparison of stereotyping principles reveals systematic similarities and differences'. Unpublished paper, Princeton University.

Cukur, C.S., Guzman, M.R.T., & Carlo, G. (2004). Religiosity, values and horizontal and vertical individualism-collectivism: A study of Turkey, the United States and the Philippines. *Journal of Social Psychology, 144,* 613–34.

Cullen, J.B., Parboteeah, K.P., & Hoegl, M. (2004). Cross-national differences in managers' willingness to justify ethically suspect behaviors: A test of institutional anomie theory. *Academy of Management Journal, 47,* 411–21.

Darroch, R., Meyer, P.A., & Singarimbun, M. (1981). *Two are not enough: the value of children to Javanese and Sundanese parents.* Honolulu, HI: East-West Population Institute.

Dasen, P.R. (1988). Développement psychologique et activités quotidiennes chez les enfants Africains (Psychological development and daily activities of African children). *Enfance, 41,* 3–24.

Dawson, R. S. (1978). *The Chinese experience.* London: Weidenfeld & Nicolson.

Day, R.D., Peterson, G.W., & McCracken, C. (1998). Predicting spanking of younger and older by mothers and fathers. *Journal of Marriage and the Family, 60,* 79–94.

Deater-Deckard, K., & Dodge, K.A. (1997). Externalizing behaviour problems and discipline revisited: Nonlinear effects and variation by culture, context, and gender. *Psychological Inquiry, 8,* 161–75.

De Bres, J. (1997). 'The boat people'. Unpublished manuscript.

Dekovic, M., Pels, T., & Model, S. (Eds.), (2004). *Unity and diversity in child rearing: Family life in a multicultural society.* Lewiston, NY: Edwin Mellen.

De Mooij, M. (1998). *Global marketing and advertising: Understanding cultural paradoxes.* Thousand Oaks, CA: Sage.

Den Hartog, D.N., House, R.J., Hanges, P.J., Dorfman, P.W., & Ruiz-Qintanilla, S.A. (1999). Emics and etics of culturally-endorsed implicit leadership theories: Are attributes of charismatic-transformational leadership universally endorsed? *Leadership Quarterly, 10,* 219–56.

Dennis, T.A., Cole, P.M., Zahn-Waxler, C., & Mizuta, I. (2002). Self in context: Autonomy and relatedness in Japanese and US mother-preschooler dyads. *Child Development, 73,* 1803–17.

De-Raad, B., Perugini, M., Hrebickova, M. Szarota, P. (1998). Lingua franca of personality: Taxonomies and structures based on the psycholexical approach. *Journal of Cross-Cultural Psychology, 29,* 212–32.

Derlega, V.J., Cukur, C.S., Kuang, J.C.Y., & Forsyth, D.R. (2002). Interdependent construal of self and the endorsement of conflict resolution strategies in interpersonal, intergroup and international disputes. *Journal of Cross-Cultural Psychology, 33,* 610–25.

Deshpande, S.P., & Viswesvaran, C. (1992). Is cross-cultural training of expatriate managers effective? A meta-analysis. *International Journal of Intercultural Relations, 16,* 295–310.

Deutsch, M. (1975). Equity, equality, and need: What determines which value will be used as the basis of distributive justice? *Journal of Social Issues, 31,* 137–50.

De Vries, R.E. (2003). Self, in-group and out-group evaluation: bond or breach? *European Journal of Social Psychology, 33,* 609–21.

Diaz-Guerrero, R. (1993). Mexican ethnopsychology. In U. Kim, & J.W. Berry (Eds.), *Indigenous psychologies: Research and experience in cultural context* (pp. 44–55). Thousand Oaks, CA: Sage.

Dibiase, R., & Gunnoe, J. (2004). Gender and culture differences in touching behavior. *Journal of Social Psychology, 144,* 49–62.

Dickson, M.W., Resnick, C., & Hanges, P.J. (in press). Systematic variation in culturally-endorsed prototypes of effective leadership based on organizational form. *Leadership Quarterly.*

Diener, E., & Diener M. (1995). Cross-cultural correlates of life satisfaction and self-esteem. *Journal of Personality and Social Psychology, 68,* 653–63.

Diener, E., & Oishi, S. (2004). Are Scandinavians happier than Asians? Issues in comparing nations on subjective well-being. In F. H. Columbus (Ed.), *Politics and economics of Asia* (Vol. 10, pp. 1–25). Hauppauge, NY: Nova Science.

Dion, K.K., & Dion, K.L. (1995). Cultural perspectives on romantic love. *Personal Relationships, 3,* 5–17.

Doi, T. (1973). *The anatomy of dependence.* Tokyo: Kodansha.

Doise, W. (2001). *Droits de l'homme et force des idées.* Paris: Presses Universitaires de France.

Doise, W., Spini, D., & Clemence, A. (1999). Human rights studies as social representations in a cross-national context. *European Journal of Social Psychology, 29,* 1–29.

Dols, J.M.F. (1993). Perverse norm: Theoretical hypotheses. *Psicothema, 5,* 91–101, supplement S.

Durkheim, E. (1898). Réprésentations individuelles et réprésentations collectives. *Révue de Métaphysique, 6,* 274–302.

Dwairy, M. (1998). *Cross-cultural counseling: The Arab-Palestinian case.* New York: Haworth.

Dyal, J.A. (1984). Cross-cultural research with the locus of control construct. In H.M. Lefcourt (Ed.), *Research with the locus of control construct* (Vol. 3, pp. 209–306). New York: Academic Press.

Earley, P.C. (1987). Intercultural training for managers: A comparison of documentary and interpersonal methods. *Academy of Management Journal, 30,* 685–98.

Earley, P.C. (1993). East meets West meets Mideast: Further explorations of collectivistic versus individualistic work groups. *Academy of Management Journal, 36,* 319–48.

Earley, P.C. (1999). Playing follow the leader: Status-determining traits in relation to collective efficacy across cultures. *Organizational Behavior and Human Decision Processes, 80,* 192–212.

Earley, P.C. (2002). Redefining interactions across cultures and organizations: Moving forward with cultural intelligence. In B.M. Staw & R.M. Kramer (Eds.), *Research in Organizational Behaviour* (Vol. 24, pp. 271–99). Amsterdam, NL: Jai-Elsevier.

Earley, P.C., & Gibson, C.B. (2002). *Multinational work teams: A new perspective.* Mahwah, NJ: Erlbaum.

Earley, P.C., Gibson, C.B., & Chen, C.C. (1999). 'How did I do, versus how did we do?': Cultural contrasts in performance feedback use and self-efficacy. *Journal of Cross-Cultural Psychology, 30,* 594–619.

Earley, P.C., & Mosakowski, E. (2000). Creating hybrid team cultures: An empirical test of international team functioning. *Academy of Management Journal, 43,* 26–49.

Ekman, P. (1972). Universals and cultural differences in facial expressions of emotion. In J. Cole (Ed.), *Nebraska Symposium on Motivation* (Vol. 19, pp. 207–82). Lincoln, NE: University of Nebraska Press.

Ekman, P., Sorenson, E.R., & Friesen, W.V. (1969). Pan-cultural elements in facial displays of emotion. *Science, 164,* 86–88.

Ekman, P., Friesen, W.V., O'Sullivan, M., et al. (1987). Universals and cultural differences in the judgment of facial expressions of emotion. *Journal of Personality and Social Psychology, 53,* 712–717.

Elder, G.H. (1974). *Children of the great depression: Social change and life experience.* Chicago: University of Chicago Press.

Elfenbein, H.A., & Ambady, N. (2002). On the universality and cultural specificity of emotion recognition: A meta-analysis. *Psychological Bulletin, 128,* 203–25.

Elfenbein, H.A., & Ambady, N. (2003). Cultural similarity's consequences: A distance perspective on cross-cultural differences in emotion recognition. *Journal of Cross-Cultural Psychology, 34,* 92–110.

Elron, E. (1997). Top management teams within multinational corporations: Effects of cultural heterogeneity. *Leadership Quarterly, 8,* 393–412.

Ember, C.R., & Ember, M. (1994). War, socialization, and interpersonal violence: A cross-cultural study. *Journal of Conflict Resolution, 38,* 620–46.

Enriquez, V. (1993). Developing a Filipino psychology. In U. Kim & J. W. Berry (Eds.), *Indigenous psychologies: Research and experience in cultural context* (pp. 152–69). Thousand Oaks, CA: Sage.

Ervin, S.M. (1964). Language and TAT content in bilinguals. *Journal of Abnormal and Social Psychology, 68,* 500–7.

Esses, V.M., Dovidio, J.F., Jackson, L.M., & Armstrong, T.L. (2001). The immigration dilemma: The role of perceived group competition, ethnic prejudice and national identity. *Journal of Social Issues, 57,* 389–412.

Farh, J.L., Earley, P.C., & Lin, S.C. (1997). Impetus for action: A cultural analysis of justice and organizational behaviour in Chinese society. *Administrative Science Quarterly, 42,* 421–44.

Farh, J.L., Tsui, A.S., Xin, K., & Cheng, B.S. (1998).The influence of relational demography and *guanxi:* The Chinese case. *Organization Science, 9,* 471–98.

Farh, J.L., Zhong, C.B., & Organ, D.W. (2004). Organizational citizenship behaviour in the People's Republic of China. *Organization Science, 15,* 241–53.

Farr, R.M. (1996). *The roots of modern social psychology.* Oxford, UK: Blackwell.

Fawcett, J.T. (1983). Perceptions of the value of the children: Satisfactions and costs. In R. Bulatao, R.D. Lee, P.E. Hollerbach, & J. Bongaarts (Eds.), *Determinants of fertility in developing countries* (Vol. 1, pp. 347–69). Washington DC: National Academy Press.

Feather, N.T. (1994). Attitudes toward high achievers and reactions to their fall: Theory and research concerning tall poppies. In M.P. Zanna (Ed.), *Advances in Experimental Social Psychology* (Vol. 26, 1–73). Orlando, FL: Academic Press.

Feldman, R.E. (1978). Response to compatriot and foreigner who seek assistance. *Journal of Personality and Social Psychology, 10,* 202–14.

Felson, R.B. (1978). Aggression as impression management. *Social Psychology Quarterly, 41,* 205–13.

Fey, C. (2005). Opening the black box of motivation: A cross-cultural comparison of Sweden and Russia. *International Business Review,* 14 (3).

Fijneman, Y.A., Willemsen, M.E., Poortinga, Y.H., et al. (1996). Individualism-collectivism: An empirical study of a conceptual issue, *Journal of Cross-Cultural Psychology, 27,* 381–402.

Fischer, R. (2004a). Organizational reward allocation: A comparison of British and German organizations. *International Journal of Intercultural Relations, 28,* 151–64.

Fischer, R. (2004b). *My values or my culture's values: The importance of referent choice for cross-cultural comparisons.* Manuscript submitted for publication.

Fischer, R., & Mansell, A. (2004). 'Commitment across cultures: A meta-analysis of affective commitment levels and the relationship with turnover intentions'. Unpublished manuscript, Victoria University of Wellington, New Zealand.

Fischer, R., & Smith, P.B. (2003). Reward allocation and culture: A meta-analysis. *Journal of Cross-Cultural Psychology, 34,* 251–68.

Fischer, R., & Smith, P.B. (2004). Values and organizational justice: Performance and seniority-based allocation criteria in the United Kingdom and Germany. *Journal of Cross-Cultural Psychology, 35,* 669–88.

Fisek, G.O. (1991). A cross-cultural examination of proximity and hierarchy as dimensions of family structure. *Family Process, 30,* 121–33.

Fiske, A.P. (1991). *Structures of social life: The four elementary forms of human relations.* New York: Free Press.

Fiske, D.W. (1949). Consistency of the factorial structures of personality ratings from different sources. *Journal of Abnormal and Social Psychology, 44,* 329–44.

Fiske, S.T., Cuddy, A.J.C., Glick, P., & Xu, J. (2002). A model of (often mixed) stereotype content: Competence and warmth respectively follow from perceived status and competition. *Journal of Personality and Social Psychology, 82,* 878–902.

Fivelsdal, E., & Schramm-Nielsen, J. (1993). Egalitarianism at work: Management in Denmark. In D.J. Hickson (ed.), *Management in Western Europe: Society, culture and organisation in 12 nations* (pp. 27–45). Berlin: de Gruyter.

Flanagan, C.A. (2000). Social change and the 'social contract' in adolescent development. In L.J. Crockett & R.K. Silbereisen (Eds.), *Negotiating adolescence in times of social change* (pp. 191–8). New York: Cambridge University Press.

Fleeson, W. (2004). Moving personality beyond the person-situation debate: The challenge and the opportunity of within-person variability. *Current Directions in Psychological Science, 13*, 83–7.

Forgas, J.P., & Bond, M.H. (1985). Cultural influences on the perception of interaction episodes. *Personality and Social Psychology Bulletin, 11*, 75–88.

Frese, M., Kring, W., Soose, A., & Zempel, J. (1996). Personal initiative at work: Differences between East and West Germany. *Academy of Management Journal, 39*, 37–63.

Freud, S. (1923/1961). *The ego and the id.* London: Hogarth.

Fridlund, A.J., & Duchaine, B. (1996). 'Facial expressions of emotion' and the delusion of the hermetic self. In R. Harré & W.G. Parrott (Eds.), *The emotions: Social, cultural and biological dimensions* (pp. 259–84). London: Sage.

Friedlmeier, W., Hofer, J., Chasiotis, A., Campos, D., & Nsamenang, B. (2004). 'Comparisons between loglinear models and irt models to test the validity of projective tests'. Paper presented at the 17th International Congress of the International Association for Cross-Cultural Psychology, Xi'an, China, August.

Friedman, M., & Rosenman, R.H. (1975). *Type A behavior and your heart.* Greenwich, CT: Fawcett.

Friesen, W.V. (1972). 'Cultural differences in facial expressions in a social situation: An experimental test of the concept of display rules'. Unpublished doctoral dissertation, University of California, San Francisco.

Fu, G., Lee, K., Cameron, C.A., & Xu, F. (2001). Chinese and Canadian adults' categorization and evaluation of lie- and truth-telling about pro-social and anti-social behaviours. *Journal of Cross-Cultural Psychology, 32*, 720–7.

Fu, P.P., Kennedy, J.C., Tata, J., Yukl, G.A., & 11 co-authors (2004). The impact of societal cultural values and individual social beliefs on the perceived effectiveness of managerial influence strategies: A meso approach. *Journal of International Business Studies, 35*, 284–305.

Furnham, A., Moutafi, J., & Baguma, P. (2002). A cross-cultural study on the role of weight and waist to hip ratio on female attractiveness. *Personality and Individual Differences, 32*, 729–45.

Gabrenya, Jr., W.K. (1999). Psychological anthropology and the 'levels of analysis' problem: We married the wrong cousin. In J.C. Lasry, J.G. Adair, & K.L. Dion (Eds.), *Latest contributions to cross-cultural psychology* (pp. 333–51). Lisse, NL: Swets & Zeitlinger.

Gabrielidis, C., Stephan, W.G., Ybarra, O., Pearson, V.M.S., & Villareal, L. (1997). Cultural variables and preferred styles of conflict resolution: Mexico and the United States. *Journal of Cross-Cultural Psychology, 28*, 661–77.

Gainsborough, J. (2000). *Alciston at the close of the millennium: Sixty years in the life of a Sussex downland village.* Alciston, UK: Alciston Parish Meeting.

Gallois, C., Giles, H., Jones, E., Cargile, A.C., & Ota, H. (1995). Accommodating intercultural encounters: Elaborations and extensions. In R.L. Wiseman (Ed.), *Intercultural communication theory* (pp. 115–47). Thousand Oaks, CA: Sage.

Gannon, M.J., & Poon, J.M.L. (1997). The effect of alternative instructional approaches on cross-cultural training outcomes. *International Journal of Intercultural Relations, 21*, 429–46.

Gass, S.M., & Varonis, E.M. (1985). Variation in native speaker speech modification to non-native speakers. *Studies in Second Language Acquisition, 7*, 37–58.

Gausden, J. (2003). 'The giving and receiving of feedback in central Eastern European cultures'. MSc dissertation, University of Salford, UK.

Geertz, C. (1973). *The interpretation of cultures.* New York: Basic Books.

Geertz, C. (1975). *The social history of an Indonesian town.* Westport, CT: Greenwood.

Gelfand, M.J., Nishii, L.H., Holcombe, K.M., Dyer, N., Ohbuchi, K.I., & Fukuno, M. (2001). Cultural influences on cognitive representations of conflict: Interpretations of conflict episodes in the United States and Japan. *Journal of Applied Psychology, 86*, 1059–74.

Gelfand, M., Nishi, L., Raver, J., & Lim, B.C. (2004). *Cultural tightness-looseness: A multilevel theory.* Unpublished manuscript, University of Maryland.

Georgas, J. (1999). Family as a context variable in cross-cultural psychology. In J. Adamopoulos & Y. Kashima (Eds.), *Social psychology and cultural context* (pp. 163–175). Beverly Hills, CA: Sage.

Georgas, J., & Berry, J.W. (1995). An ecocultural taxonomy for cross-cultural psychology. *Cross-Cultural Research, 29*, 121–57.

Georgas, J., Berry, J.W., Shaw, A., Christakopoulou, S., & Mylonas, K. (1996). Acculturation of Greek family values. *Journal of Cross-Cultural Psychology, 27*, 329–38.

Georgas, J., Berry, J.W., van de Vijver, F., Kağıtçıbaşı, Ç., & Poortinga, Y.H. (2005). *Families across cultures: A 30-nation psychological study.* Cambridge, UK: Cambridge University Press.

Georgas, J., Mylonas, K., Bafiti, T., Poortinga, Y.H. et al. (2001). Functional relationships in the nuclear and extended family: A 16-culture study. *International Journal of Psychology, 36*, 289–300.

Georgas, J., van de Vijver, F., & Berry, J.W. (2004). The ecocultural framework, ecosocial indices and psychological variables in cross-cultural research. *Journal of Cross-Cultural Psychology, 35*, 74–96.

Gergen, K.J. (1973). Social psychology as history. *Journal of Personality and Social Psychology, 26*, 309–20.

Giacobbe-Miller, J.K., Miller, D.J., & Victorov, V.I. (1998). A comparison of Russian and US pay allocation decisions, distributive justice judgments and productivity under different payment conditions. *Personnel Psychology, 51*, 137–63.

Gilbert, G.M. (1951). Stereotype persistence and change among college students. *Journal of Abnormal and Social Psychology, 46*, 245–54.

Giles, H., Coupland, N., & Coupland, J. (1991). Accommodation theory: Communication, context and consequence. In H. Giles, N. Coupland, & J. Coupland (Eds.), *Contexts of accommodation: Developments in applied sociolinguistics* (pp. 1–68). Cambridge: Cambridge University Press.

Giles, H., Coupland, N., & Wiemann, J.M. (1992). 'Talk is cheap, but my word is my bond': Beliefs about talk. In K. Bolton & H. Kwok (Eds.), *Sociolinguistics today: Eastern and western perspectives.* London: Routledge.

Gire, J.T., & Carment, D.W. (1993). Dealing with disputes: The influence of individualism-collectivism. *Journal of Social Psychology, 133*, 81–95.

Glenn, E.S., Wittmeyer, D., & Stevenson, K.A. (1997). Cultural styles of persuasion. *International Journal of Intercultural Relations, 1*, 52–66.

Glick, P., & Fiske, S.T. (2001). Ambivalent sexism. In M.P. Zanna (Ed.), *Advances in experimental social psychology* (Vol. 33, pp. 115–88). San Diego, CA: Academic Press.

Goffman, E. (1959). *The presentation of self in everyday life.* New York: Doubleday.

Goldberg, L.R. (1981). Language and individual differences: The search for universals in personality lexicons. In L. Wheeler (Ed.), *Review of Personality and Social Psychology* (Vol. 2, pp. 141–65). Beverly Hills, CA: Sage.

Goldberg, L.R. (1990). An alternative 'Description of personality': The Big-Five factor structure. *Journal of Personality and Social Psychology, 59*, 1216–29.

Goleman, D. (1996). *Emotional intelligence.* London: Bloomsbury.

Goodwin, R., & Tang, C.S.K. (1996). Chinese personal relationships. In M.H. Bond (Ed.), *Handbook of Chinese psychology* (pp. 294–308). Hong Kong: Oxford University Press.

Goody, E.N. (1978). Introduction. In E.N. Goody (Ed.), *Questions and politeness.* Cambridge: Cambridge University Press.

Göregenli, M. (1997). Individualist-collectivist tendencies in a Turkish sample. *Journal of Cross-Cultural Psychology, 28*, 787–94.

Goswami, U., Porpodas, C., & Wheelwright, S. (1997). Children's orthographic representations in English and Greek. *European Journal of Psychology of Education, 3*, 273–92.

Graham, J.A., & Argyle, M. (1975). A cross-cultural study of the communication of extra-verbal meaning by gesture. *International Journal of Psychology, 10*, 56–67.

Graham, J.L., Mintu, A.T., & Rodgers, W. (1994). Explorations of negotiation behaviours in ten foreign cultures, using a model developed in the United States. *Management Science, 40*, 72–95.

Graham, J.L., & Mintu Wimsat, A.T. (1997). Culture's influence on business negotiations in four countries. *Group Decision and Negotiation, 6*, 483–502.

Greenfield, P.M., & Childs, C.P. (1977). Weaving, color terms, and pattern representation: Cultural influences and cognitive development among the Zinacantecos of Southern Mexico. *International Journal of Psychology, 11*, 23–48.

Greenfield, P.M., Keller, H., Fuligni, A., & Maynard, A. (2003). Cultural pathways through universal development. *Annual Review of Psychology, 54*, 461–90.

Greenfield, P.M., Maynard, A.E., & Childs, C.P. (2003). Historical change, cultural learning, and cognitive representation in Zinacantec Maya Children. *Cognitive Development, 18*, 455–87.

Greenfield, P., Trumbull, E., & Rothstein-Fisch, C. (2003). Bridging cultures. *Cross-Cultural Psychology Bulletin, 37*, 1–2, 6–16.

Greenwald, A.G., & Farnham, S.D. (2000). Using the implicit association test to measure self-esteem and self-concept. *Journal of Personality and Social Psychology, 79*, 1022–38.

Gregersen, H.B, Hite, J.M., & Black, J.S. (1996). Expatriate performance appraisal in US multi-national firms. *Journal of International Business Studies, 27*, 711–38.

Grossman K.E., Grossman K., & Zimmerman P. (1999). A wider view of attachment and exploration. In J. Cassidy & P.R. Shaver (Eds.), *Handbook of attachment: Theory, research, and clinical applications* (pp. 760–86). New York: Guilford Press.

Grotevant, H.D., & Cooper, C.R. (1986). Individuation in family relationships. *Human Development, 29*, 82–100.

Gudykunst, W.B., & Lee, C.M. (2003). Assessing the validity of self-construal scales: A response to Levine et al. *Human Communication Research, 29*, 253–74.

Gudykunst, W.B., Gao, G., Schmidt, K.L., Nishida, T., et al. (1992). The influence of individualism-collectivism, self-monitoring and predicted-outcome value on communication in in-group and out-group relationships. *Journal of Cross-Cultural Psychology, 23*, 196–213.

Gudykunst, W.B., Matsumoto, Y., Ting-Toomey, S., Nishida, T., Kim, K., & Heyman, S. (1996). The influence of cultural individualism-collectivism, self-construals and individual values on communication styles across cultures. *Human Communication Research, 22*, 510–43.

Guisinger, S., & Blatt, S.J. (1994). Individuality and relatedness: Evolution of a fundamental dialectic. *American Psychologist, 49*, 104–11.

Guthrie, G.M., & Bennett, A.B. (1971). Cultural differences in implicit personality theory. *International Journal of Psychology, 6*, 305–12.

Haberstroh, S., Oyserman, D., Schwarz, N., Kuhnen, U., & Ji, L.J. (2002). Is the interdependent self more sensitive to question context than the independent self? Self construal and the observation of conversational norms. *Journal of Experimental Social Psychology, 38*, 323–9.

Hall, E.T. (1966). *The hidden dimension.* New York: Doubleday.

Hamid, A.H. (2004). 'Cultural values as a predictor of personality, work values and causal attributions in Malaysia'. Unpublished doctoral dissertation, University of Sussex, UK.

Hara, K., & Kim, M.S. (2004). The effect of self-construals on conversational indirectness. *International Journal of Intercultural Relations, 28*, 1–18.

Hardin, E.E., Leong, F.T.L., & Bhagwat, A.A. (2004). Factor structure of the self-construal scale revisited: Implications for the multidimensionality of self-construal. *Journal of Cross-Cultural Psychology, 35*, 327–45.

Harkness, S. (1992). Parental ethnotheories in action. In I.E. Sigel, A.V. MacGillicuddy-DeLisi, & J.J. Goodnow (Eds.), *Parental belief systems* (pp. 373–91). Hillsdale, NJ: Erlbaum.

Harkness, S., & Keefer, C.H. (2000). Contributions of cross-cultural psychology in research and interventions in education and health. *Journal of Cross-Cultural Psychology, 31*, 92–109.

Harper, J.E.T., & Cormeraie, S. (1992). 'C'est trop Anglais, Monsieur'. CRICCOM Papers, 2. Horsham, UK: Roffey Park Management Institute.

Harris, M. (1979). *Cultural materialism: The struggle for a science of culture.* New York: Vintage.

Harwood, J., Giles, H., & Bourhis, R. (1994). The genesis of vitality theory: Historical patterns and discoursal dimensions. *International Journal of the Sociology of Language, 108*, 167–206.

Harwood, R.L., Handwerker, W.P, Schoelmerich, A., & Leyendecker, B. (2001). Ethnic category labels, parental beliefs, and the contextualized individual: An exploration of the individualism-sociocentrism debate. *Parenting: Science and Practice, 1*, 217–36.

Harwood, R.L., Miller, J.G., & Izarry, N.L. (1995). *Culture and attachment: Perceptions of the child in context.* New York: Guilford.

Harzing, A.W. (1995). The persistent myth of high expatriate failure rates. *International Journal of Human Resource Management, 6*, 457–74.

Harzing, A-W., & Maznevski, M. (2002). The interaction between language and culture: A test of the cultural accommodation hypothesis in seven countries. *Language and Intercultural Communication, 2*, 120–39.

Hasegawa, T., & Gudykunst, W.B. (1998). Silence in Japan and the United States. *Journal of Cross-Cultural Psychology, 29*, 668–84.

Håseth, K.J. (1996). The Norwegian adaptation of the State-Trait Anger Expression Inventory. In C.D. Spielberger, I.G. Sarason, et al. (Eds.), *Stress and emotion: Anxiety, anger and curiosity* (Vol. 16). Washington, DC: Taylor & Francis.

Haslam, N., & Fiske, A.P. (1999). Relational Models Theory: A confirmatory factor analysis. *Personal Relationships, 6*, 241–50.

Haslam, N., Reichert, T., & Fiske, A.P. (2002). Aberrant social relations in the personality disorders. *Psychology & Psychotherapy: Theory Research and Practice, 75*, 19–31.

Haslam, S.A., Turner, J.C., Oakes, P.J., et al. (1992). Context-dependent variation in social stereotyping: 1. The effects of intergroup relations as mediated by social change and frame of reference. *European Journal of Social Psychology, 22*, 3–20.

Hatfield, E., & Rapson, R.L. (1996). *Love and sex: Cross-cultural perspectives*. Needham Heights, MA: Allyn & Bacon.

He, W., Chen, C.C., & Zhang, L.H. (2004). Reward allocation preferences of Chinese employees in the new millennium: The effects of ownership reform, collectivism and goal priority. *Organization Science, 15*, 221–31.

Heine, S. J. (2003). Making sense of East Asian self-enhancement. *Journal of Cross-Cultural Psychology, 34*, 596–602.

Heine, S.J. (in press). Where is the evidence for pancultural self-enhancement? A reply to Sedikides, Gaertner and Toguchi. *Journal of Personality and Social Psychology*.

Heine, S.J., & Lehman, D.R. (1999). Culture, self-discrepancies and self-satisfaction. *Personality and Social Psychology Bulletin, 25*, 915–25.

Heine, S.J., Lehman, D.R., Markus, H.R., & Kitayama, S. (1999). Is there a universal need for self-regard? *Psychological Review, 106*, 766–94.

Heine, S.J., Lehman, D.R., Peng, K.P., & Greenholz, J. (2002). What's wrong with cross-cultural comparisons of subjective Likert scales? The reference group effect. *Journal of Personality and Social Psychology, 82*, 903–18.

Heine, S.J., & Renshaw, K. (2002). Interjudge agreement, self-enhancement and liking: Cross-cultural divergences. *Personality and Social Psychology Bulletin, 28*, 578–87.

Heine, S.J., Takata, T., & Lehman, D.R. (2000). Beyond self-presentation: Evidence for self-criticism among Japanese. *Personality and Social Psychology Bulletin, 26*, 71–8.

Heise, D.R., & Calhan, C. (1995). Emotion norms in interpersonal events. *Social Psychology Quarterly, 58*, 223–40.

Herskovits, M. (1948). *Man and his works: The science of cultural anthropology*. New York: Knopf.

Hillier, S., Huq, A., Loshak, R., Marks, F., & Rahman, S. (1994). An evaluation of child psychiatric services for Bangladeshi parents. *Journal of Mental Health, 3*, 332–7.

Hinkle, S., & Brown, R.J. (1990). Intergroup comparisons and social identity: Some links and lacunae. In D. Abrams & M. Hogg (Eds.), *Social identity theory: Constructive and critical advances*, pp. 48–70. Hemel Hempstead, UK: Harvester-Wheatsheaf.

Ho, D.Y.F. (1976). On the concept of face. *American Journal of Sociology, 81*, 867–84.

Hodes, M., Jones, C., & Davies, H. (1996). Cross-cultural differences in maternal evaluation of children's body shapes. *International Journal of Eating Disorders, 19*, 257–63.

Hofer, J., & Chasiotis, A. (2003). Congruence of life goals and implicit motives as predictors of life satisfaction: Cross-cultural implications of a study of Zambian male adolescents. *Motivation and Emotion, 27*, 251–72.

Hofer, J., & Chasiotis, A. (2004). Methodological considerations of applying a TAT-type picture-story test in cross-cultural research: A Comparison of German and Zambian adolescents. *Journal of Cross-Cultural Psychology, 35*, 224–42.

Hoffman, L. (1989). *Lost in translation: A life in a new language*. London: Heineman.

Hoffman, L.W. (1987). The value of children to parents and childrearing patterns. In Ç. Kağıtçıbaşı (Ed.), *Growth and progress in cross-cultural psychology* (pp. 159–70). Lisse, NL: Swets & Zeitlinger.

Hoffman, L.W., & Youngblade, L.M. (1998). Maternal employment, morale, and parenting style: Social class comparisons. *Journal of Applied Developmental Psychology, 19*, 389–413.

Hofstede, G. (1980). *Culture's consequences: International differences in work-related values*. Beverly Hills, CA: Sage.

Hofstede, G. (1983). Dimensions of national cultures in fifty countries and three regions. In J. Deregowski, S. Dzuirawiec, & R. Annis (Eds.), *Expiscations in cross-cultural psychology* (pp. 335–55). Lisse, NL: Swets & Zeitlinger.

Hofstede, G. (1986). Cultural differences in teaching and learning. *International Journal of Intercultural Relations, 10*, 301–20.

Hofstede, G. (2001). *Culture's consequences: Comparing values, behaviours, institutions and organizations across nations* (2nd ed.). Thousand Oaks, CA: Sage.

Hofstede, G. (2004). The universal and the specific in cross-cultural management. In D. Tjosvold & K. Leung (Eds.), *Cross-cultural management: Foundations and future* (pp. 29–42). Aldershot, UK: Ashgate.

Hofstede, G., Bond, M.H., & Luk, C.L. (1993). Individual perceptions of organizational cultures: A methodological treatise on levels of analysis. *Organizational Studies, 14,* 483–503.

Hofstede, G., & McCrae, R.R. (2004). Personality and culture revisited: Linking traits and dimensions of culture. *Cross-Cultural Research, 38,* 52–88.

Hofstede, G., Neuyen, B., Ohayv, D.D., & Sanders, G. (1990). Measuring organizational cultures: A qualitative and quantitative study across 20 cases. *Administrative Science Quarterly, 35,* 286–315.

Hogan, R. (1982). A socioanalytic theory of personality. In M. Page (ed.), *Nebraska Symposium on Motivation* (Vol. 30, pp. 56–89). Lincoln, NB: University of Nebraska Press.

Hogan, R. (1996). A socioanalytic perspective on the five-factor model. In J.S. Wiggins (Ed.), *The five-factor model of personality: Theoretical perspectives* (pp. 163–79). New York: Guilford.

Holland, R.W., Roeder, U.R., van Baaren, R.B., Brandt, A.C., & Hannover, B. (2004). Don't stand so close to me: The effects of self-construal on interpersonal closeness. *Psychological Science, 15,* 237–42.

Holtgraves, T. (1997). Styles of language use: Individual and cultural variability in conversational indirectness. *Journal of Personality and Social Psychology, 73,* 624–37.

Holtgraves, T., & Yang, J. (1990). Politeness as universal: Cross-cultural perceptions of request strategies and inferences based on their use. *Journal of Personality and Social Psychology, 59,* 719–29

Holtgraves, T., & Yang, J. (1992). Interpersonal underpinnings of request strategies: General principles and differences due to culture and gender. *Journal of Personality and Social Psychology, 62,* 246–56.

Hong, Y.Y., Chiu, C.Y., Yeung, G., & Tong, Y.Y. (1999). Social comparison during political transition: Interaction of entity versus incremental beliefs and social identities. *International Journal of Intercultural Relations, 23,* 257–79.

Hong, Y.Y., & Chiu, C.Y. (2001). Toward a paradigm shift: From cross-cultural differences in social cognition to social-cognitive mediation of cultural differences. *Social Cognition, 19,* 181–96.

Hong, Y.Y., Morris, M.W., Chiu, C.Y., & Benet-Martinez, V. (2000). Multicultural minds: A dynamic constructivist approach to culture and cognition. *American Psychologist, 55,* 709–20.

Horenczyk, G. (2004). 'The complexity of acculturation orientations and their assessment'. Paper presented at the congress of the International Association for Cross-Cultural Psychology, Xian, China.

Hornsey, M., & Gallois, C. (1998). The impact of interpersonal and intergroup communication accommodation on perceptions of Chinese students in Australia. *Journal of Language and Social Psychology, 17,* 323–47.

House, R.J., Hanges, P.J., Ruiz-Quintanilla, S.A., Dorfman, P.W., Javidan, M., & GLOBE associates (1999). Cultural influences on leadership and organizations: Project GLOBE. In W.H. Mobley, M.J. Gessner, & V. Arnold (Eds.), *Advances in Global Leadership* (Vol. 1, pp. 71–114). Stamford, CT: JAI Press.

House, R.J., Hanges, P.J., Javidan, M., Dorfman, P.W., Gupta, V., & GLOBE associates (2004). *Leadership, culture and organizations: The GLOBE study of 62 nations.* Thousand Oaks, CA: Sage.

Huang, L.L., Liu, J.H., & Chang, M. (2004). The 'double identity' of Taiwanese Chinese: A dilemma of politics and culture rooted in history. *Asian Journal of Social Psychology, 7,* 149–68.

Huang, X., & van de Vliert, E. (2004). Job level and national culture as joint roots of job satisfaction. *Applied Psychology: An International Review, 53,* 329–48.

Huang, X., & van de Vliert, E. (2003). Where intrinsic job satisfaction fails to work: National moderators of intrinsic motivation. *Journal of Organizational Behaviour, 24,* 159–79.

Hui, C., Lee, C., & Rousseau, D.M. (2004). Employment relationships in China: Do workers relate to the organization or to people? *Organization Science, 15,* 232–40.

Hui, C.H. (1988). Measurement of individualism-collectivism. *Journal of Research in Personality, 22,* 17–36.

Hui, C.H., & Cheng, I.W.M. (1987). Effects of second language proficiency of speakers and listeners on person perception and behavioural intention: A study of Chinese bilinguals. *International Journal of Psychology, 22,* 421–30.

Hui, C.H., Triandis, H.C., & Yee, C. (1991). Cultural differences in reward allocation: Is collectivism the explanation? *British Journal of Social Psychology, 30,* 145–57.

Hui, M., Au, K., & Fock, H. (2004). Empowerment effects across cultures. *Journal of International Business Studies, 35,* 46–60.

Huismans, S. (1994). The impact of differences in religion on the relation between religiosity and values. In A.M. Bouvy, F. van de Vijver, P. Boski, & P. Schmitz (Eds.), *Journeys into cross-cultural psychology* (pp. 255–67). Lisse, NL: Swets & Zeitlinger.

Huntington, S.P. (1996). *The clash of civilizations and the remaking of world order.* New York: Simon & Schuster.

Huynh, C.T. (1979). *The concept of endogenous development centred on man.* Paris: UNESCO.

Imamoglu, E.O., Kuller, R., Imamoglu, V., & Kuller, M. (1993).The social psychological worlds of Swedes and Turks in and around retirement. *Journal of Cross-Cultural Psychology, 24,* 26–41.

Inglehart, R. (1997). *Modernization and post-modernization: Cultural, economic and political change in 43 nations.* Princeton, NJ: Princeton University Press.

Inglehart, R., & Baker, W.E. (2000). Modernization, cultural change and the persistence of tradi- tional values. *American Sociological Review, 65,* 19–51.

Inglehart, R., Basanez, M., & Moreno, A. (1998). *Human values and beliefs: Political religious, sexual and economic norms in 43 nations: Findings from the 1990–1993 World Values Survey.* Ann Arbor, MI: University of Michigan Press.

Inglehart, R., & Klingemann, H.D. (2000). Genes, culture, democracy, and happiness. In E. Diener & E.M. Suh (Eds.), *Culture and subjective well-being* (pp. 165–183). Cambridge, MA: MIT Press.

Inglehart, R., & Oyserman, D. (2004). Individualism, autonomy and self-expression: The human development syndrome. In H. Vinken, J. Soeters, & P. Ester (Eds.), *Comparing cultures: Dimensions of culture in a comparative perspective* (pp. 74–96). Leiden, NL: Brill.

Inkeles, A., & Smith, D.H. (1974). *Becoming modern: Individual change in six developing countries.* Cambridge, MA: Harvard University Press.

Ishii, K., Reyes, J.A., & Kitayama, S. (2003). Spontaneous attention to word content versus emo- tional tone: Differences among three cultures. *Psychological Science, 14,* 39–46.

Israel, J., & Tajfel, H. (1972). *Context of social psychology: A critical assessment.* London: Academic Press.

Iyengar, S.S., & Lepper, R. (1999). Rethinking the value of choice: a cultural perspective on intrin- sic motivation. *Journal of Personality and Social Psychology, 76,* 349–66.

Jackson, J.S., Brown, K.T., Brown, T.N., & Marks, B. (2001). Contemporary immigration policy orien- tations among dominant group members in Western Europe. *Journal of Social Issues, 57,* 431–56.

Jahoda, G. (1986). A cross-cultural perspective on developmental psychology. *International Journal of Behavioural Development, 9,* 417–37.

Jasinskaya-Lahti, I., Liebkind, K., Horenczyk, G., & Schmitz, P. (2003). The interactive nature of acculturation: Perceived discrimination, acculturation attitudes and stress among young ethnic repatriates in Finland, Israel and Germany. *International Journal of Intercultural Relations, 27,* 79–97.

Ji, L. J., Schwarz, N., & Nisbett, R.E. (2000). Culture, autobiographical memory and behavioural frequency reports: Measurement issues in cross-cultural studies. *Personality and Social Psychology Bulletin, 26,* 586–94.

Ji, L.J., Nisbett, R.E., & Su, Y.J. (2001). Culture, change and prediction. *Psychological Science, 12,* 450–6.

Ji, L.J., Peng, K.P., & Nisbett, R.E. (2000). Culture, control and perception of relationships in the environment. *Journal of Personality and Social Psychology, 78,* 943–55.

Jones, D., & Hill, K. (1993). Criteria of facial attractiveness in five populations. *Human Nature, 4,* 271–96.

Jones, E., Gallois, C., Barker, M., & Callan, V. (1994). Evaluations of interactions between students and academic staff: Influence of communication, accommodation, ethnic group and status. *Journal of Language and Social Psychology, 13,* 158–91.

Jose, P.E., Huntsinger, C.S., Huntsinger, P.R., & Liaw, F-R. (2000). Parental values and practices rel- evant to young children's social development in Taiwan and the United States. *Journal of Cross- Cultural Psychology, 31,* 677–702.

Jurowski, C., & Gursoy, D. (2004). Distance effects on residents' attitudes towards tourism. *Annals of Tourism Research, 31,* 296–312.

Kağıtçıbaşı, Ç. (1970). Social norms and authoritarianism: A Turkish–American comparison. *Journal of Personality and Social Psychology, 16,* 444–51.

Kağıtçıbaşı, Ç. (1973). Psychological aspects of modernization in Turkey. *Journal of Cross-Cultural Psychology*, 4, 157–74.

Kağıtçıbaşı, Ç. (1978). Cross-national encounters: Turkish students in the United States. *International Journal of Intercultural Relations*, 2, 141–60.

Kağıtçıbaşı, Ç. (1982a). *The changing value of the children in Turkey* (Publ. No. 60–E). Honolulu: East-West Center.

Kağıtçıbaşı, Ç. (1982b). Sex roles, value of children and fertility in Turkey. In Ç. Kağıtçıbaşı (Ed.), *Sex roles, family and community in Turkey* (pp. 151–180). Bloomington, IN: Indiana University Press.

Kağıtçıbaşı, Ç. (1982c). Old-age security value of children: Cross-national socio-economic evidence. *Journal of Cross-Cultural Psychology*, 13, 29–42.

Kağıtçıbaşı, Ç. (1990). Family and socialization in cross-cultural perspective: A model of change. In J. Berman (Ed.), *Cross-cultural perspectives: Nebraska symposium on motivation*, 1989 (pp. 135–200). Lincoln, NE: Nebraska University Press.

Kağıtçıbaşı, Ç. (1994). A critical appraisal of individualism and collectivism: Toward a new formulation. In U. Kim, H.C. Triandis, Ç. Kağıtçıbaşı, S.-C.Choi, & G. Yoon (Eds.), *Individualism and collectivism: Theory, method and applications* (pp. 52–65). Thousand Oaks, CA: Sage.

Kağıtçıbaşı, Ç. (1996a). The autonomous-relational self: A new synthesis. *European Psychologist*, 1(3), 180–6.

Kağıtçıbaşı, Ç. (1996b). *Family and human development across cultures: A view from the other side.* Hillsdale, NJ: Erlbaum.

Kağıtçıbaşı, Ç. (1997a). Individualism and collectivism. In J.W. Berry, M.H. Segall, & Ç. Kağıtçıbaşı (Eds.), *Handbook of cross-cultural psychology* (2nd ed., Vol. 3, pp. 1–49). Needham Heights, MA: Allyn & Bacon.

Kağıtçıbaşı, Ç. (1997b). Whither multiculturalism? *Applied Psychology: An International Review*, 46, 44–9.

Kağıtçıbaşı, Ç. (1998). The value of children: A key to gender issues. *International Child Health*, 9, 15–24.

Kağıtçıbaşı, Ç. (1999). The model of family change: A rejoinder. *International Journal of Psychology*, 34, 15–17.

Kağıtçıbaşı, Ç. (2002). Rites of passage to adulthood: Adolescence in the western world: Essay review of *Negotiating Adolescence in times of social change. Human Development*, 45, 136–40.

Kağıtçıbaşı, Ç. (2005). Autonomy and relatedness in cultural context: Implications for self and family. *Journal of Cross-Cultural Psychology*, 36, 403–22.

Kağıtçıbaşı, Ç., & Ataça, B. (2005). Value of children, family and self: A three-decade portrait from Turkey. *Applied Psychology: An International Review*, 317–37.

Kağıtçıbaşı, Ç., & Poortinga, Y.H. (2000). Cross-cultural psychology: Issues and overarching themes. Millennium Special Issue of the *Journal of Cross-Cultural Psychology*, 31, 129–47.

Kanagawa, C., Cross, S.E., & Markus, H.R. (2001). 'Who am I': The cultural psychology of the conceptual self. *Personality and Social Psychology Bulletin*, 27, 90–103.

Karau, S.J., & Williams, K.D. (1993). Social loafing: A meta-analytic view of social integration. *Journal of Personality and Social Psychology*, 65, 681–706.

Kardiner, A., & Linton, R. (1945). *The individual and his society.* New York: Columbia University Press.

Karlins, M., Coffman, T.L., & Walters, G. (1969). On the finding of social stereotypes: Studies in three generations of college students. *Journal of Personality and Social Psychology*, 13, 1–16.

Kashima, E.S., & Hardie, E.A. (2000). The development and validation of the relational, individual and collective self-aspects (RIC) scale. *Asian Journal of Social Psychology*, 3, 19–48.

Kashima, Y. (1998). Culture, time and social psychology of cultural dynamics. *Cross-Cultural Psychology Bulletin*, 32 (2), 8–15.

Kashima, Y., & Kashima, E. (1998). Culture and language: The case of cultural dimensions and personal pronoun use. *Journal of Cross-Cultural Psychology*, 29, 461–86.

Kashima, Y., Kashima, E., Chiu, C.Y., et al. (2005). Culture, essentialism and agency: Are individuals universally believed to be more real entities than groups? *European Journal of Social Psychology*, 35, 147–70.

Katigbak, M.S., Church, A.T., Guanzon-Lapena, M.A., Carlota, A.J., & del Pilar, G.H. (2002). Are indigenous personality dimensions culture specific? Philippine inventories and the five-factor model. *Journal of Personality and Social Psychology*, 82, 89–101.

Katz, D., & Braly, K.W. (1933). Racial prejudice and social stereotypes. *Journal of Abnormal and Social Psychology*, 30, 175–93.

Keller, H. (1997). Evolutionary approaches. In J.W. Berry, Y. Poortinga, & J. Pandey (Eds.), *Handbook of cross-cultural psychology* (2nd ed., Vol. 1, pp. 215–56). Needham Heights, MA: Allyn & Bacon.

Keller, H., & Greenfield, P.M. (2000). History and future of development in cross-cultural psychology. *Journal of Cross-Cultural Psychology, 31*, 52–62.

Keller, H., & Lamm, B. (2005). Parenting as the expression of socio-historical time: The case of German individualization. *International Journal of Behavioral Development, 29*, 238–46.

Keller, H., Lohaus, A., Völker, S., Cappenberg, M., & Chasiotis, A. (1999). Temporal contingency as an independent component of parenting behaviour. *Child Development, 70*, 474–85.

Keller, H., Papaligoura, Z., Kunsemueller, P., Voelker, S., Papaeliou, C., Lohaus, A., Lamm, B., Kokkinaki, N., Chrysikou, E.G., & Mousouli, V. (2003). Concepts of mother–infant interaction in Greece and Germany. *Journal of Cross Cultural Psychology, 34*, 677–89.

Kelley, H.H. (1952). Two functions of reference groups. In G.E. Swanson, T.M. Newcomb, & E.L. Hartley (Eds.), *Readings in social psychology* (pp. 410–14). New York: Holt Rinehart.

Kennedy, J.C., Fu, P.P., & Yukl, G.A. (2003). Influence tactics across twelve cultures. In W.H. Mobley & P.W. Dorfman (Eds.), *Advances in Global Leadership* (Vol. 3, pp. 127–47). Oxford, UK: Elsevier.

Kerr, C., Dunlop, J.T., Harbison, F.H., & Myers, C.A. (1960). *Industrialism and industrial man.* Cambridge, MA: Harvard University Press.

Khan, N., & Smith, P.B. (2003). Profiling the politically violent in Pakistan: Self-construals and values. *Peace and Conflict: Journal of Peace Psychology, 9*, 277–95.

Kickul, J., Lester, S.W., & Belgio, E. (2004). Attitudinal and behavioral outcomes of psychological contract breach: A cross-cultural comparison of the United States and Hong Kong Chinese. *International Journal of Cross-Cultural Management, 4*, 229–52.

Kim, M.S. (1994). Cross-cultural comparisons of the perceived importance of interactive constraints. *Human Communication Research, 21*, 128–51.

Kim, M.S., Hunter, J.E., Miyahara, A., Horvath, A.M., Bresnahan, M., & Yoon, H.J. (1996). Individual versus culture-level dimensions of individualism-collectivism: Effects on preferred conversational styles. *Communication Monographs, 63* (1), 29–49.

Kim, U., & Berry, J.W. (Eds.), (1993). *Indigenous psychologies: Research and experience in cultural context.* Thousand Oaks, CA: Sage.

Kim, U., Yang, K.S., & Hwang, K.K. (Eds.), (in press). *Scientific advances in indigenous and cultural psychology: Empirical, philosophical and cultural contributions.* New York: Springer.

Kim, Y., Butzel, J.S., & Ryan, R.M. (1998). 'Interdependence and well-being: A function of culture and relatedness needs'. Paper presented at The International Society for the Study of Personal Relationships, Saratoga Spring, NY.

Kirkman, B.L., & Shapiro, D.L. (2001). The impact of team members' cultural values on cooperation, productivity and empowerment in self-managing work teams. *Journal of Cross-Cultural Psychology, 32*, 597–617.

Kitayama, S., Duffy, S., Kawamura, T., & Larsen, J.T. (2003). Perceiving an object and its context in three cultures: A cultural look at New Look. *Psychological Science, 14*, 201–6.

Kitayama, S., & Ishii, K. (2002). Word and voice: Spontaneous attention to emotional utterances in two languages. *Cognition and Emotion, 16*, 29–59.

Kitayama, S., Markus, H.R., & Kurokawa, M. (2000). Culture, emotion and well-being: Good feelings in Japan and the United States. *Cognition and Emotion, 14*, 93–124.

Kitayama, S., Markus, H.R., Matsumoto, H., & Norasakkunkit, V. (1997). Individual and collective processes in the construction of the self: Self-enhancement in the United States and self-criticism in Japan. *Journal of Personality and Social Psychology, 72*, 1245–67.

Ko, J.W., Price, J.L., & Mueller, C.W. (1997). Assessment of Meyer and Allen's three component model of organizational commitment in South Korea. *Journal of Applied Psychology, 82*, 961–73.

Kohn, M.L., Naoi, A., Schoenbach, C., Schooler, C., & Slomczynski, K.M. (1990). Position in the class structure and psychological functioning in the United States, Japan and Poland. *American Journal of Sociology, 95*, 964–1008.

Kravitz, D.A., & Martin, B. (1986). Ringelmann rediscovered: The original article. *Journal of Personality and Social Psychology, 50*, 936–41.

Kroeber, A.L., & Kluckhohn, C. (1963). *Culture: A critical review of concepts and definitions.* New York: Random House.

Kuhn, M.H., & McPartland, R. (1954). An empirical investigation of self attitudes. *American Sociological Review, 19*, 68–76.

Kuhnen, U., Hannover, B., Roeder, U., et al. (2001). Cross-cultural variations in identifying embedded figures: Comparisons from the United States, Germany, Russia and Malaysia. *Journal of Cross-Cultural Psychology, 32*, 365–71.

Kuppens, P. Kim-Pricto, C., & Diener, E. (in press). Culture and the structure of emotional experience. *Cross-Cultural Research.*

Kurman, J. (2003). Why is self-enhancement low in certain collectivist cultures? An investigation of two competing explanations. *Journal of Cross-Cultural Psychology, 34*, 496–510.

Kurman, J., & Ronen-Eilon, C. (2004). Lack of knowledge of a culture's social axioms and adaptation difficulties among immigrants. *Journal of Cross-Cultural Psychology, 35*, 192–208.

Kwak, K. (2003). Adolescents and their parents: A review of intergenerational family relations for immigrant and non-immigrant families. *Human Development, 46*, 15–36.

Kwan, V.S.Y., Bond, M.H., & Singelis, T.M. (1997). Pancultural explanations for life satisfaction: Adding relationship harmony to self-esteem. *Journal of Personality and Social Psychology, 73*, 1038–51.

Lalonde, R.N., Hynie, M., Pannu, M., & Tatla, S. (2004). The role of culture in interpersonal relationships: Do second generation South Asian Canadians want a traditional partner? *Journal of Cross-Cultural Psychology, 35*, 503–24.

Lam, S.F., Lau, I.Y., Chiu, C.Y., Hong, Y.Y., & Peng, S.Q. (1999). Differential emphases on modernity and Confucian values in social categorization: The case of Hong Kong adolescents in political transition. *International Journal of Intercultural Relations, 23*, 237–56.

Lam, S.S.K, Hui. C., & Law, K.S. (1999). Organizational citizenship behavior: Comparing perspectives of supervisors and subordinates across four international samples. *Journal of Applied Psychology, 84*, 594–601.

Lam, S.S.K., Schaubroeck, J., & Aryee, S. (2002). Relationship between organizational justice and employee work outcomes: A cross-national study. *Journal of Organizational Behavior, 23*, 1–18.

Lansford, J.E., Deater-Deckard, K., Dodge, K.A., Bates, J.E., & Pettit, G.S. (2003). Ethnic differences in the link between physical discipline and later adolescent externalizing behaviors. *Journal of Child Psychology and Psychiatry, 44*, 1–13.

Lau, S., & Cheung, P.C. (1987). Relations between Chinese adolescents' perception of parental control and organization and their perception of parental warmth. *Developmental Psychology, 23*, 726–9.

Lau, S., Lew, W.J.F., Hau, K.T., Cheung, P.C., & Berndt, T.J. (1990). Relations among perceived parental control, warmth, indulgence, and family harmony of Chinese in Mainland China, *Developmental Psychology, 26*, 674–7.

Lawson, S., & Sachdev, I. (2000). Codeswitching in Tunisia: Attitudinal and behavioral dimensions. *Journal of Pragmatics, 32*, 1343–61.

Le Bon, G. (1895). *Psychologie des foules*. Paris: F. Olean.

Lee, K., Allen, N.J., Meyer, J.P., & Rhee, K.Y. (2001). The three component model of organization commitment: An application to South Korea. *Applied Psychology: An International Review, 50*, 596–614.

Lee, L., & Ward, C. (1998). Ethnicity, idiocentrism-allocentrism and intergroup perceptions. *Journal of Applied Social Psychology, 28*, 109–23.

Lee, Y.T., & Duenas, G. (1995). Stereotype accuracy in multicultural business. In Y.T. Lee, L.J. Jussim, & C.R. McCauley (Eds.), *Stereotype accuracy: Towards appreciating group differences* (pp. 157–86). Washington, DC: American Psychological Association.

Lehman, D.R., Chiu, C.Y, & Schaller, M. (2004). Psychology and culture. *Annual Review of Psychology, 55*, 689–714.

Lenneberg, E.H., & Roberts, J.M. (1956). The language of experience: A study in methodology. *International Journal of American Linguistics*, (Memoir 13, Supplement 22), 1–33.

Leung, K. (1987). Some determinants of reactions to procedural models for conflict resolution: A cross-national study. *Journal of Personality and Social Psychology, 53*, 898–908.

Leung, K. (1997). Negotiation and reward allocation across cultures. In P.C. Earley & M. Erez (Eds.), *New perspectives on international industrial/organizational psychology* (pp. 640–75). San Francisco, CA: New Lexington.

Leung, K., & Bond, M.H. (1984). The impact of cultural collectivism on reward allocation. *Journal of Personality and Social Psychology, 47*, 793–804.

Leung, K., & Bond, M.H. (1989). On the empirical identification of dimensions for cross-cultural comparisons. *Journal of Cross-Cultural Psychology, 20*, 133–52.

Leung, K., & Bond, M.H. (2004). Social axioms: A model of social beliefs in multi-cultural perspective. In M.P. Zanna (Ed.), *Advances in Experimental Social Psychology* (Vol. 36, pp. 119–97). San Diego, CA: Elsevier Academic Press).

Leung, K., Bond, M.H., & 7 co-authors. (2002). Social axioms: The search for universal dimensions of beliefs about how the world functions. *Journal of Cross-Cultural Psychology, 33*, 286–302.

Leung, K., & Park, H.J. (1986). Effects of interactional goal on choice of allocation rules: A cross-national study. *Organizational Behavior and Human Decision Processes, 37*, 111–20.

Leung, K., Smith, P.B., Wang, Z.M., & Sun, H. (1996). Job satisfaction in joint venture hotels in China: An organizational justice analysis. *Journal of International Business Studies, 27*, 947–63.

Leung, K., Wang, Z.M., & Smith, P.B. (2001). Job attitudes and organizational justice in joint venture hotels in China: The role of expatriate managers. *International Journal of Human Resource Management, 12*, 926–45.

Leung, S.K., & Bond, M.H. (2001). Interpersonal communication and personality: Self and other perspectives. *Asian Journal of Social Psychology, 4*, 69–86.

Levin, S., Henry, P.J., Pratto, F., & Sidanius, J. (2003). Social dominance and social identity in Lebanon: Implications for support of violence against the West. *Group Processes and Intergroup Relations, 6*, 353–68.

Levin, S., & Sidanius, J. (1999). Social dominance and social identity in the United States and Israel: In-group favoritism or out-group derogation? *Political Psychology, 20*, 99–126.

LeVine, R.A. (1989). Cultural environments in child development. In N. Damon (Ed.), *Child development today and tomorrow*. San Francisco, CA: Jossey-Bass.

Levine, R.V., & Bartlett, C. (1984). Pace of life, punctuality and coronary heart disease in six countries. *Journal of Cross-Cultural Psychology, 15*, 233–55.

Levine, R.V., & Norenzayan, A. (1999). The pace of life in 31 countries. *Journal of Cross-Cultural Psychology, 30*, 178–205.

Levine, R.V., Norenzayan, A., & Philbrick, K. (2001). Cross-cultural differences in helping strangers. *Journal of Cross-Cultural Psychology, 32*, 543–60.

Levine, R.V., Sato, S., Hashimoto, T., & Verma, J. (1995). Love and marriage in eleven cultures. *Journal of Cross-Cultural Psychology, 26*, 554–71.

Levine, T.R., Bresnahan, M.J., Park, H.S., Lapinski, M.K., et al. (2003). Self-construal scales lack validity. *Human Communication Research, 29*, 210–52.

Levinson, J.D., Peng, K.P., & Wang, L. (2004). 'Let's make a deal: Understanding the cultural basis of contract formation'. Paper presented at International Congress of Psychology, Beijing, August.

Lewin, K. (1936). Some socio-psychological differences between the United States and Germany. *Character and Personality, 4*, 265–93.

Li, H.Z. (2002). Culture, gender and self-close-others connectedness in Canadian and Chinese samples. *European Journal of Social Psychology, 32*, 93–104.

Li, H.Z. (2004). Culture and gaze direction in conversation. *RASK, 20*, 3–26.

Lim, F., Bond, M.H., & Bond, M.K. (in press). Social and psychological predictors of homicide rates across nations: Linking societal and citizen factors to the killing of others. *Journal of Cross-Cultural Psychology*.

Lin, C.-Y.C., & Fu, V.R. (1990). A comparison of child-rearing practices among Chinese, immigrant Chinese, and Caucasian-American parents. *Child Development, 61*, 429–33.

Lind, E.A., Tyler, T.R., & Huo, Y.J. (1997). Procedural context and culture: Variation in the antecedents of procedural justice judgments. *Journal of Personality and Social Psychology, 73*, 767–80.

Lindsey, D.T., & Brown, A.M. (2002). Color naming and the phototoxic effects of sunlight on the eye. *Psychological Science, 13*, 506–12.

Linsky, A.S., Bachman, R., & Straus, M.A. (1995). *Stress, culture, and aggression*. New Haven, CN: Yale University Press.

Linville, P., Fischer, G.W., & Yoon, C. (1996). Perceived covariation among the features of in-group and out-group members: The out-group covariation effect. *Journal of Personality and Social Psychology, 70*, 421–36.

Linssen, H., & Hagendoorn, L. (1994). Social and geographic factors in the explanation of the content of European nationality stereotypes. *British Journal of Social Psychology, 33*, 165–82.

Li-Ripac, D. (1980). Cultural influences on clinical perception: A comparison between Caucasian and Chinese-American therapists. *Journal of Cross-Cultural Psychology, 11*, 327–42.

Little, T.D., Lopez, D.F., Oettingen, G., & Baltes, P.B. (2001). A comparative-longitudinal study of action-control beliefs and school performance: On the role of context. *International Journal of Behavioral Development, 25*, 237–45.

Little, T.D., Oettingen, G., Stetsenko, A., & Baltes, P.B. (1995). Children's action-control beliefs about school performance: How do American children compare with German and Russian children? *Journal of Personality and Social Psychology, 69,* 686–700.

Liu, J.H., Lawrence, B., Ward, C., & Abraham, S. (2003). Social representations of history in Malaysia and Singapore: On the relationship between national and ethnic identity. *Asian Journal of Social Psychology, 5,* 3–20.

Liu, J.H., Wilson, M., McClure, J., & Higgins, T. (1999). Social identity and the perception of history: cultural representations of Aotearoa/New Zealand. *European Journal of Social Psychology, 29,* 1021–47.

Lo, S., & Aryee, S. (2003). Psychological contract breach in a Chinese context: An integrative approach. *Journal of Management Studies, 40,* 1005–20.

Lonner, W.J. (1990). An overview of cross-cultural testing and assessment. In R.W. Brislin (Ed.), *Applied cross-cultural psychology* (pp. 56–76). Newbury Park, CA: Sage.

Lück, H. (1987). A historical perspective on social psychological theories. In G.R. Semin & B. Krahé (Eds.), *Issues in contemporary German social psychology* (pp. 16–35). London: Sage.

Lunt, P. (2003). The histories of social psychology. *Social Psychological Review, 5* (2), 3–19.

Lutz, C. (1988). *Unnatural emotions: Everyday sentiments on a Micronesian atoll and their challenge to Western theory.* Chicago, IL: University of Chicago Press.

Lynn, R., & Hampson, S.L. (1975). National differences in extraversion and neuroticism. *British Journal of Clinical and Social Psychology, 14,* 223–40.

Maccoby, E.E., & Martin, J.A. (1983). Socialization in the context of the family: Parent-child interaction. In E.M. Hetherington (Ed.), *Handbook of child psychology: Socialization, personality, and social development* (Vol. 4, pp. 1–102). New York: Wiley.

Mahler, M. (1972). On the first three phases of the separation-individuation process. *International Journal of Psychoanalysis, 53,* 333–8.

Malewska-Peyre, H. (1980). 'Conflictual cultural identity of second generation immigrants'. Paper presented at the Workshop on Cultural Identity and Structural Marginalization of Migrant Workers, European Science Foundation.

Malinowski, B. (1927). *Sex and repression in savage society.* London: Humanities Press.

Man, D.C., & Lam, S.S.K. (2003). The effects of job complexity and autonomy on cohesiveness in collectivistic and individualistic work groups: A cross-cultural analysis. *Journal of Organizational Behavior, 24,* 979–1001.

Mandal, M.K., Bryden, M.P., & Bulman-Fleming, M.B. (1996). Similarities and variations in facial expressions of emotion: Cross-cultural evidence. *International Journal of Psychology, 31,* 49–58.

Marsh, A.A., Ambady, N., & Elfenbein, H.A. (2003). Non-verbal 'accents': Cultural differences in facial expressions of emotion. *Psychological Science, 14,* 373–6.

Markus, H.R., & Kitayama, S. (1991). Culture and the self: Implications for cognition, emotion, and motivation. *Psychological Review, 98,* 224–53.

Markus, H.R., & Kitayama, S. (2003). Culture, self, and the reality of the social. *Psychological Inquiry, 14,* 277–83.

Marriott, H. (1993). Spatial arrangements in Japanese–Australian business communication. *Journal of Asia Pacific Communication, 4,* 107–26.

Marshall, R. (1997). An investigation of variances of individualism across two cultures and three social classes. *Journal of Cross-Cultural Psychology, 28,* 490–5.

Mascolo, M.F., Misra, G., & Rapisardi, C. (2004). Individual and relational conceptions of self in India and the United States. In M.F. Mascolo & J. Li (Eds.), *Culture and developing selves: Beyond dichotomization* (pp. 9–26). San Francisco, CA: Jossey Bass.

Masuda, T., & Nisbett, R.E. (2001). Attending holistically versus analytically: Comparing the context sensitivity of Japanese and Americans. *Journal of Personality and Social Psychology, 81,* 922–34.

Matsumoto, D. (1999). Culture and self: An empirical assessment of Markus and Kitayama's theory of independent and interdependent self-construal. *Asian Journal of Social Psychology, 2,* 289–310.

Matsumoto, D., Consolacion, T., Yamada, H., et al. (2002). American–Japanese cultural differences in judgments of emotional expressions of different intensities. *Cognition and Emotion, 16,* 721–47.

Matsumoto, D., & Kudoh, T. (1993). American-Japanese cultural differences in attributions of personality based on smiles. *Journal of Non-verbal Behavior, 17,* 231–43.

Matsumoto, D., & Kupperbusch, C. (2001). Idiocentric and allocentric differences in emotional expression, experience and the coherence between expression and experience. *Asian Journal of Social Psychology, 4,* 113–31.

Matsumoto, D., Leroux, J.A., Bernhard, R., & Gray, H. (2004). Unraveling the psychological correlates of intercultural adjustment potential. *International Journal of Intercultural Relations, 28*, 281–309.

McAndrew, F.T., Akande, A., Bridgstock, R., et al. (2001). A multicultural study of stereotyping in English speaking countries. *Journal of Social Psychology, 140*, 487–502.

McArthur, L.Z., & Berry, D.S. (1987). Cross-cultural agreement in perceptions of baby-faced adults. *Journal of Cross-Cultural Psychology, 18*, 165–92.

McAuley, P., Bond, M.H., & Kashima, E. (2002). Towards defining situations objectively: A culture-level analysis of role dyads in Hong Kong and Australia. *Journal of Cross-Cultural Psychology, 33*, 363–80.

McAuley, P.C., Bond, M.H., & Ng, I.W.C. (2004). Antecedents of subjective well-being in working Hong Kong adults. *Journal of Psychology in Chinese Societies, 5*, 25–49.

McClelland, D.C. (1961). *The achieving society*. Princeton, NJ: Van Nostrand.

McCrae, R.R. (2000). Trait psychology and the revival of personality-and-culture studies. *American Behavioral Scientist, 44*, 10–31.

McCrae, R.R., Costa, P.T. Jr., Pilar, G.H., Rolland, J.P., & Parker, W.D. (1998). Cross-cultural assessment of the five-factor model: The Revised NEO Personality Inventory. *Journal of Cross-Cultural Psychology, 29*, 171–88.

McCrae, R.R., Costa, P.T. Jr., & Yik, M.S.M. (1996). Universal aspects of Chinese personality structure. In M.H. Bond (ed.), *The handbook of Chinese psychology* (pp. 189–207). Hong Kong: Oxford.

McCrae, R.R., Terracciano, A., et al. (2005). Universal features of personality traits from the observer's perspective: Data from 50 cultures. *Journal of Personality and Social Psychology, 88*, 547–61.

McCrae, R.R., Yik, M.S.M., Trapnell, P.D., Bond, M.H., & Paulhus, D.L. (1998). Interpreting personality profiles across culture: Bilingual, acculturation, and peer rating studies of Chinese undergraduates. *Journal of Personality and Social Psychology, 74*, 1041–55.

McDougall, W. (1908). *Introduction to social psychology*. London: Methuen.

McLoyd, V.C. (1990). The impact of economic hardship on black families and children: psychological distress, parenting, and socioemotional development. *Child Development, 61*, 311–46.

Mead, M. (1928). *Coming of age in Samoa*. New York: Morrow.

Meaning of Working International Research Team. (1987). *The meaning of work: An international view*. New York: Academic Press.

Mesquita, B., & Frijda, N.H. (1992). Cultural variations in emotions: A review. *Psychological Bulletin, 112*, 179–204.

Meyer, J.P., & Allen, N.J. (1997). Commitment in the workplace: Theory, research and applications. Thousand Oaks, CA: Sage.

Milgram, S. (1961). *Obedience to authority: An experimental view*. New York: Harper, Row.

Miller, J.G. (1997). Cultural conception of duty: Implications for motivation and morality. In D. Munro, J.F. Schumaker, & A.C. Carr (Eds.), *Motivation and Culture* (pp. 178–92). New York: Routledge.

Miller, J.G. (1984). Culture and the development of everyday social explanation. *Journal of Personality and Social Psychology, 46*, 961–78.

Miller, J.G., Bersoff, D.M., & Harwood, R.L. (1990). Perceptions of social responsibilities in India and the United States: Moral imperatives or personal decisions? *Journal of Personality and Social Psychology, 58*, 33–47.

Minard, R.D. (1952). Race relationships in the Pocahontas coal field. *Journal of Social Issues, 8* (1), 29–44.

Mischel, W. (1968). *Personality and assessment*. New York: Wiley.

Mischel, W. (1977). The interaction of person and situation. In E. Magnusson & N.S. Endler (Eds.), *Personality at the crossroads: Current issues in interactional psychology* (pp. 333–52). Hillsdale, NJ: Erlbaum.

Miyamoto, Y., & Kitayama, S. (2002). Cultural variations in correspondence bias: The critical role of attitude diagnosticity of socially constrained behavior. *Journal of Personality and Social Psychology, 83*, 1239–48.

Montiel, C.J., & Shah, A.A. (2004). Effects of political labeling and perceiver's dominant group position on trait attributions of terrorist/freedom-fighter. *International Journal of Psychology, 39*, 11.

Montreuil, A., & Bourhis, R.Y. (2001). Majority acculturation orientations toward 'valued' and 'devalued' immigrants. *Journal of Cross-Cultural Psychology, 32*, 698–719.

Moos, R.H., & Moos, B.S. (1981). *Family environment scale manual*. Palo Alto, CA: Consulting Psychologists' Press.

Morelli, G.A., Rogoff, B., & Angelillo, C. (2003). Cultural variation in young children's access to work or involvement in specialized child-focused activities. *International Journal of Behavioral Development*, 27, 264–74.

Morling, B., Kitayama, S., & Miyamoto, Y. (2002). Cultural practices emphasize influence in the United States and adjustment in Japan. *Personality and Social Psychology Bulletin*, 28, 311–23.

Morris, D., Collett, P., Marsh, P., & O'Shaughnessy, M. (1979). *Gestures, their origins and distribution*. Briarcliff Manor, NY: Stein & Day.

Morris, M.W., Menon, T., & Ames, D.R. (2001). Culturally conferred conceptions of agency: a key to social perception of persons, groups and other actors. *Personality and Social Psychology Review*, 5, 169–82.

Morris, M.W., Williams, K.Y., Leung, K., Larrick, R., Mendoza, M.T., Bhatnagar, D., et al. (1998). Conflict management style: Accounting for cross-national differences. *Journal of International Business Studies*, 29, 729–47.

Morrison, E.W., Chen, Y.R., & Salgado, S.R. (2004). Cultural differences in newcomer feedback-seeking: A comparison of the United States and Hong Kong. *Applied Psychology: An International Review*, 53, 1–22.

Moscardo, G., & Pearce, P.L. (1999). Understanding ethnic tourists. *Annals of Tourism Research*, 26, 416–34.

Moscovici, S. (1972). Society and theory in social psychology. In J. Israel & H. Tajfel (Eds.), *The context of social psychology: A critical assessment* (pp. 17–68). London: Academic Press.

Mosquera, P.M.R., Manstead, A.S.R., & Fischer, A.H. (2000). The role of honor-related values in the elicitation, communication and experience of pride, shame and anger: Spain and the Netherlands compared. *Personality and Social Psychology Bulletin*, 26, 833–44.

Mosquera, P.M.R., Manstead, A.S.R., & Fischer, A.H. (2002). Honor in the Mediterranean and Northern Europe. *Journal of Cross-Cultural Psychology*, 33, 16–36.

Muensterberger, W. (1969). Orality and dependence: Characteristics of Southern Chinese. In W. Muensterberger (ed.), *Man and his culture: Psychoanalytic anthropology after 'Totem and taboo'* (pp. 295–329). New York: Taplinger.

Mundy-Castle, A.C. (1974). Social and technological intelligence in Western and non-Western cultures. *Universitas: University of Ghana, Legos*, 4, 42–56.

Munene, J.C. (1995). 'Not on seat': An investigation of some correlates of organizational citizenship behavior in Nigeria. *Applied Psychology: An International Review*, 44, 111–22.

Munroe, R.L., Munroe, R.H., & Shimmin, H. (1984). Children's work in four cultures: determinants and consequences. *American Anthropologist*, 86, 342–8.

Munroe, R.L., Munroe, R.H., & Winters, S. (1996). Cross-cultural correlates of the consonant-vowel (cv) syllable. *Cross-Cultural Research*, 30, 60–83.

Muramoto, Y. (2003). An indirect enhancement in relationship among Japanese. *Journal of Cross-Cultural Psychology*, 34, 552–66.

Murdock, G.P. (ed.), (1967). *Ethnographic atlas*. Pittsburgh, PA: University of Pittsburgh.

Murray, H.A. (1938). *Explorations in personality*. New York: Oxford University Press.

Nagashima, S., Fujiwara, K., Harano, K., Saito, K., & Hori, H. (1967). A study on the relationships of self-concepts to adjustment: Development and construction of self-differential for adults, high school students, and middle school students. *Bulletin of the Faculty of Education, Tokyo University of Education, 13*, 59–83. (In Japanese).

Nakane, C. (1973). *Japanese society*. London: Penguin.

Nauck, B. (2001). Intercultural contact and intergenerational transmission in immigrant families. *Journal of Cross-Cultural Psychology*, 32, 159–73.

Nelson, G.L., el Bakary, W., & al Batal, M. (1993). Egyptian and American compliments: A cross-cultural study. *International Journal of Intercultural Relations*, 17, 293–314.

Nelson, G.L., al Batal, M., & el Bakary, W. (2002). Directness versus indirectness: Egyptian Arabic and US English communication style. *International Journal of Intercultural Relations*, 26, 39–57.

Nelson, M.R., & Shavitt, S. (2002). Horizontal and vertical individualism and achievement values: A multimethod examination of Denmark and the United States. *Journal of Cross-Cultural Psychology*, 33, 439–58.

Neto, F., Mullet, E., Deschamps, J.C., Barros, J., et al. (2000). Cross-cultural variations in attitudes toward love. *Journal of Cross-Cultural Psychology*, 31, 626–35.

Newman, L.S. (1993). How individualists interpret behavior: Idiocentrism and spontaneous trait inference. *Social Cognition, 11,* 243–69.

Ng, S.H., & He, A.P. (2004). Code-switching in tri-generational family conversations among Chinese immigrants in New Zealand. *Journal of Language and Social Psychology, 23,* 28–48.

Ng, S.H., He, A.P., & Loong, C.S.F. (2004). Tri-generational family conversations: Communication accommodation and brokering. *British Journal of Social Psychology, 43,* 449–64.

Ng, S.H., Hossain, A., Ball, P., Bond, M.H., et al. (1982). Human values in nine countries. In R. Rath, H.S. Asthana, D. Sinha, & J.B.P. Sinha (Eds.), *Diversity and unity in cross-cultural psychology* (pp. 196–205). Lisse, NL: Swets and Zeitlinger.

Ng, S.H., Loong, C.S.F., He, A.P., Liu, J.H., & Wetherall, A. (2000). Communication correlates of individualism and collectivism: Talk directed at one or more addressees in family conversations. *Journal of Language and Social Psychology, 19,* 26–45.

Nisbett, R.E., & Cohen, D. (1996). *Culture of honor: The psychology of violence in the south.* Boulder, CO: Westview.

Nisbett, R.E., Peng, K.P., Choi, I., & Norenzayan, A. (2000). Culture and systems of thought: Holistic versus analytic cognition. *Psychological Review, 108,* 291–310.

Noels, K., Clément, R., & Gaudet, S. (2004). Language and the situated nature of ethnic identity. In S.H. Ng, C.N. Candlin, & C.Y. Chiu (Eds.), *Language matters: Communication, culture and identity* (pp. 245–66). Hong Kong: City University of Hong Kong Press.

Noorderhaven, N.G., & Tidjani, B. (2001). Culture, governance and economic performance: An explorative study with a special focus on Africa. *International Journal of Cross-Cultural Management, 1,* 31–52.

Norenzayan, A., Choi, I., & Nisbett, R.E. (2002). Cultural similarities and differences in social inference: Evidence from behavioral predictions and lay theories of behavior. *Personality and Social Psychology Bulletin, 28,* 109–20.

Norenzayan, A., Smith, E.E., Kim, B.J., & Nisbett, R.E. (2002). Cultural preferences for formal versus intuitive reasoning. *Cognitive Science, 26,* 653–84.

Norman, W.T. (1963). Toward an adequate taxonomy of personality attributes: Replicated factor structure in peer nomination personality ratings. *Journal of Abnormal and Social Psychology, 66,* 574–83.

Nsamenang, A.B. (1992). *Human development in cultural context: A third world perspective.* Newbury Park, CA: Sage.

Oerter, R., Oerter, R., Agostiani, H., Kim, H.O., & Wibowo, S. (1996). The concept of human nature in East Asia: Etic and emic characteristics. *Culture and Psychology, 2,* 9–51.

Oettingen, G., Little, T.D., Lindenberger, U., & Baltes, P.B. (1994). Causality, agency and control beliefs in East versus West Berlin children: A natural experiment in the control of context. *Journal of Personality and Social Psychology, 66,* 579–95.

Oetzel, J.G., Ting-Toomey, S., Masumoto, T., Yochi, Y., Pan, X.H., Takai, J., & Wilcox, R. (2001). Face and facework in conflict: A cross-cultural comparison of China, Germany, Japan and the United States. *Communication Monographs, 68,* 235–58.

Oetzel, J.G., & Ting-Toomey, S. (2003). Face concerns in interpersonal conflict: A cross-cultural empirical test of the face negotiation theory. *Communication Research, 30,* 599–624.

Oguri, M., & Gudykunst, W.B. (2002). The influence of self-construals and communication styles on sojourners' psychological and sociocultural adjustment. *International Journal of Intercultural Relations, 26,* 577–93.

Ohbuchi, K., Fukushima, O., & Tedeschi, J.T. (1999). Cultural values in conflict management: Goal orientation, goal attainment and tactical decision. *Journal of Cross-Cultural Psychology, 30,* 51–71.

Ohbuchi, K., Tamura, T., Quigley, B.M., Tedeschi, J.T., Madi, N., Bond, M.H., & Mummendey, A. (2004). Anger, blame, and dimensions of perceived norm violation: Culture, gender, and relationships. *Journal of Applied Social Psychology, 34,* 1587–603.

Oishi, S. (2000). Goals as cornerstones of subjective well-being: Linking individuals and cultures. In E. Diener & E.M. Suh (Eds.), *Culture and subjective well-being* (pp. 87–112). Cambridge, MA: Bradford.

Oishi, S., Diener, E., Napa Scollon, C., & Biswas-Diener, R. (2004). Cross-situational consistency of affective experiences across cultures. *Journal of Personality and Social Psychology, 86,* 460–72.

Orano, P. (1902). *Psicologia sociale.* Bari: Laterza.

Osgood, C.E., May, W.H., & Miron, M.S. (1975). *Cross-cultural universals of affective meaning.* Urbana, IL: University of Illinois Press.

Oyserman, D., Coon, H.M., & Kemmelmeier, M. (2002). Rethinking individualism and collectivism: Evaluation of theoretical assumptions and meta-analyses. *Psychological Bulletin, 128,* 3–72.

Oyserman, D., Sakamoto, I., & Lauffer, A. (1998). Cultural accommodation: Hybridity and the framing of social obligation. *Journal of Personality and Social Psychology, 74,* 1606–18.

Özgen, E. (2004). Language, learning and color perception. *Current Directions in Psychological Science, 13,* 95–8.

Peabody, D. (1985). *National characteristics.* Cambridge: Cambridge University Press.

Peabody, D., & Shmelyov, A.G. (1996). Psychological characteristics of Russians. *European Journal of Social Psychology, 26,* 507–12.

Pearce, P.L. (1981). 'Environment shock': A study of tourists' reaction to two tropical islands. *Journal of Applied Social Psychology, 11,* 268–80.

Pearson, V.M.S., & Stephan, W.G. (1998). Preferences for styles of negotiation: A comparison of Brazil and the US. *International Journal of Intercultural Relations, 22,* 67–83.

Pedersen, P., Draguns, J., Lonner, W.J., & Trimble, J. (1996). *Counseling across cultures.* Thousand Oaks, CA: Sage.

Pelto, P. (1968). The difference between 'tight' and 'loose' societies. *Transaction, 5,* 37–40.

Pennebaker, J.W., Rimé, B., & Blankenship, V.E. (1996). Stereotypes of emotional expressiveness of northerners and southerners: A cross-cultural test of Montesquieu's hypotheses. *Journal of Personality and Social Psychology, 70,* 372–80.

Peristiany, J.G. (Ed.), (1965). *Honor and shame: The values of Mediterranean society.* London: Weidenfeld & Nicholson.

Pettigrew, T.F. (1998). Reactions toward the new minorities of Western Europe. *Annual Review of Sociology, 24,* 77–103.

Pettigrew, T.F., & Meertens, R.W. (1995). Subtle and blatant prejudice in Western Europe. *European Journal of Social Psychology, 25,* 57–75.

Pettigrew, T., & Tropp, L.R. (2000). Does intergroup contact reduce prejudice? Recent metanalytic findings. In S. Oskamp (Ed.), *Reducing prejudice and discrimination* (pp. 93–114). Mahwah, NJ: Erlbaum.

Phalet, K., & Claeys, W. (1993). A comparative study of Turkish and Belgian youth. *Journal of Cross-Cultural Psychology, 24,* 319–43.

Phalet, K., & Schönpflug, U. (2001). Intergenerational transmission of collectivism and achievement values in two acculturation contexts: The case of Turkish families in Germany and Turkish and Moroccan families in the Netherlands. *Journal of Cross-Cultural Psychology, 32,* 186–201.

Piaget, J. (1948). *The moral judgment of the child.* Glencoe, IL: Free Press.

Pierson, H.D., & Bond, M.H. (1982). How do Chinese bilinguals respond to variations of interviewer language and ethnicity? *Journal of Language and Social Psychology, 1,* 123–39.

Pike, K. (1967). *Language in relation to a unified theory of the structure of human behavior.* The Hague, NL: Mouton.

Piker, S. (1998). Contributions of psychological anthropology. *Journal of Cross-Cultural Psychology, 29,* 9–31.

Piontkowski, U., Florack, A., Hoelker, P., & Obdrzalek, P. (2000). Predicting acculturation attitudes of dominant and non-dominant groups. *International Journal of Intercultural Relations, 24,* 1–26.

Pittam, J., Gallois, C., Iwawaki, S., & Kroonenberg, P. (1995). Australian and Japanese concepts of expressive behavior. *Journal of Cross-Cultural Psychology, 25,* 451–73.

Poortinga, Y.H., & van Hemert, D.A. (2001). Personality and culture: Demarcating between the common and the unique. *Journal of Personality, 69,* 1033–60.

Poppe, E. (2001). Effects of changes in GNP and perceived group characteristics on national and ethnic stereotypes in central and Eastern Europe. *Journal of Applied Social Psychology, 31,* 1689–708.

Poppe, E., & Linssen, H. (1999). In-group favoritism and the reflection of realistic dimensions of difference between nation states in Central and East European nationality stereotypes. *British Journal of Social Psychology, 38,* 85–103.

Pratto, F., Liu, J.H., Levin, S., Sidanius, J., et al. (2000). Social dominance orientation and the legitimation of inequality across cultures. *Journal of Cross-Cultural Psychology, 31,* 369–409.

Pruitt, D.G., & Carnevale, P.J. (1993). *Negotiation in social conflict.* Pacific Grove, CA: Brooks-Cole.

Ralston, D.A., Vollmer, G.R., Srinvasan, N., Nicholson, J.D., Tang, M, & Wan, P. (2003). Strategies of upward influence: A study of six cultures from Europe, Asia and America. *Journal of Cross-Cultural Psychology, 32,* 728–35.

Ramirez-Esparza, N., Gosling, S., Pennebaker, J., & Benet-Martínez, V. (in press). Do bilinguals have two personalities? A special case of cultural frame-switching. *Journal of Research in Personality*.

Rao, A., & Hashimoto, K. (1996). Intercultural influence: A study of Japanese expatriate managers in Canada. *Journal of International Business Studies, 27*, 443–66.

Rea, A. (2004). Now you're talking my language. *The Psychologist, 17*, 580–2.

Redding, S.G. (1990). *The spirit of Chinese capitalism*. Berlin, Germany: De Gruyter.

Redfield, R., Linton, R., & Herskovits, M.J. (1936). Memorandum on the study of acculturation. *American Anthropologist, 38*, 149–152.

Redford, P.C., & Smith, P.B. (2004). 'Culture, context and anger expression: A three-nation study'. Unpublished paper, University College, Winchester, UK.

Reisinger, Y., & Turner, L.W. (2002). *Cross-cultural behaviour in tourism: Concepts and analysis*. Oxford: Elsevier.

Remland, M.S., Jones, T.S., & Brinkman, H. (1995). Interpersonal distance, body orientation and touch: Effects of culture, gender and age. *Journal of Social Psychology, 135*, 281–97.

Rice, T.W., & Steele, B. (2004). Subjective well-being across time and space. *Journal of Cross-Cultural Psychology, 35*, 633–47.

Ricks, D.A. (1993). *Blunders in international business*. Cambridge, MA: Blackwell.

Rivers, W.H.R. (1901). Introduction and vision. In A.C. Haddon (ed.), *Reports of the Cambridge anthropological expedition to the Torres Straits* (Vol. 2, part 1). Cambridge: Cambridge University Press.

Roe, R., Zinovieva, I., Dienes, E., & ten Horn, L.A. (2003). A comparison of work motivation in Bulgaria, Hungary and the Netherlands: Test of a model. *Applied Psychology: An International Review, 49*, 658–87.

Rogoff, B. (1990). *Apprenticeship in thinking: Cognitive development in social context*. New York: Oxford University Press.

Rohner, R.P. (1975). *They love me, they love me not: A worldwide study of the effects of parental acceptance and rejection*. New Haven, CT: Human Relations Area Files, Yale University.

Rohner, R. (1984). Toward a conception of culture for cross-cultural psychology. *Journal of Cross-Cultural Psychology, 15*, 111–38.

Rohner, R.P., & Pettengill, S.M. (1985). Perceived parental acceptance-rejection and parental control among Korean adolescents, *Child Development, 56*, 524–8.

Rokeach, M. (1973). *The nature of human values*. New York: Free Press.

Rosenthal, D.A., & Feldman, S.S. (1992). The nature and stability of ethnic identity in Chinese youth: Effects of length of residence in two cultural contexts. *Journal of Cross-Cultural Psychology, 23*, 214–27.

Ross, E.A. (1908). *Social psychology*. New York: MacMillan.

Ross, L. (1977). The Intuitive psychologist and his shortcomings: Distortions in the attribution process. In L. Berkowitz (Ed.), *Advances in Experimental Social Psychology, 10*, 174–221. New York: Academic Press.

Ross, M., Xun, W.Q.E., & Wilson, A.E. (2002). Language and the bicultural self. *Personality and Social Psychology Bulletin, 28*, 1040–50.

Rothbaum, F., Pott, M., Azuma, H., Miyake, K., & Weise, J. (2000). The development of close relationships in Japan and the United States: path of symbiotic harmony and generative tension. *Child Development, 71*, 1121–42.

Rothbaum, F., & Tsang, B.Y.P. (1998). Lovesongs in the US and China: On the nature of romantic love. *Journal of Cross-Cultural Psychology, 29*, 306–19.

Rothbaum, F., Weisz, J., Pott, M., Miyake, K., & Morelli, G. (2000). Attachment and culture: Security in the United States and Japan. *American Psychologist, 55*, 1093–104.

Rotter, J.B. (1966). Generalized expectancies for internal versus external control of reinforcement. *Psychological Monographs, 80*, Whole No. 609, 1–28.

Rousseau, D.M., & Schalk, R. (2000). *Psychological contracts in employment: Cross-national perspectives*. Thousand Oaks, CA: Sage.

Ruback, R.B., Pandey, J., Begum, H.A., Tariq, N., & Kamal, A. (2004). Motivations for and satisfaction with migration: An analysis of migrants to New Delhi, Dhaka and Islamabad. *Environment and Behavior, 36*, 814–38.

Rudmin, F. (2005). 'Debate in science: The case of acculturation'. Unpublished manuscript, University of Tromso, Norway.

Rusbult, C.E., Farrell, D., Rogers, G., & Mainous, A.G. (1988). Impact of exchange variables on exit, voice, loyalty and neglect: An integrative model of responses to declining job satisfaction. *Academy of Management Journal, 31,* 599–627.

Russell, J.A. (1994). Is there universal recognition of emotion from facial expression? *Psychological Bulletin, 115,* 102–41.

Ryan, R.M. (1993). Agency and organization: Intrinsic motivation, autonomy and the self in psychological development. In J. Jacobs (Ed.), *Nebraska symposia on motivation* (Vol. 40, pp. 1–55). Lincoln, NE: University of Nebraska Press.

Ryan, R.M., & Deci, E.L. (2000). Self-determination theory and the facilitation of intrinsic motivation, social development and well-being. *American Psychologist, 55,* 68–78.

Ryan, R.M., & Lynch, J.H. (1989). Emotional autonomy versus detachment: Revisiting the vicissitudes of adolescence and young adulthood. *Child Development, 60,* 340–56.

Salamon, S. (1977). Family bonds and friendship bonds: Japan and West Germany. *Journal of Marriage and the Family, 39,* 807–20.

Sam, D.L. (2000). Psychological adaptation of adolescents with immigrant backgrounds. *Journal of Social Psychology, 140,* 5–25.

Sampson, E.E. (1981). Cognitive psychology as ideology. *American Psychologist, 36,* 730–3.

Sanchez-Burks, J., Lee, F., Choi, I., Nisbett, R., et al. (2003). Conversing across cultures: East–west communication styles in work and non-work contexts. *Journal of Personality and Social Psychology, 85,* 363–72.

Saucier, G., & L. R. Goldberg (2001). Lexical studies of indigenous personality factors: Premises, products, and prospects. *Journal of Personality, 69,* 847–79.

Sawyer, J. (1967). Dimensions of nations: Size, wealth, and politics. *American Journal of Sociology, 73,* 145–72.

Schalk-Soekar, R.G.S., & van de Vijver, F.J.R. (2004). Attitudes toward multiculturalism of immigrants and majority members in the Netherlands. *International Journal of Intercultural Relations, 28,* 533–50.

Scherer, K.R. (1997). The role of culture in emotion-antecedent appraisal. *Journal of Personality and Social Psychology, 73,* 902–22.

Scherer, K.R., Banse, R., & Wallbott, H.G. (2001). Emotion inferences from vocal expression correlate across languages and cultures. *Journal of Cross-Cultural Psychology, 32,* 76–92.

Scheu, U.D. (2002). Cultural constraints in bilinguals' code-switching. *International Journal of Intercultural Relations, 24,* 131–50.

Schimmack, U., Oishi, S., & Diener, E. (2005). Individualism: A valid and important dimension of cultural differences between nations. *Personality and Social Psychology Bulletin, 9,* 17–31.

Schmidt-Atzert, L., & Park, H.S. (1999). The Korean concepts dapdaphada and uulhada: A cross-cultural study of the meaning of emotions. *Journal of Cross-Cultural Psychology, 30,* 646–54.

Schmitt, D.P. (2003). Universal sex differences in the desire for sexual variety: Tests from 52 nations, six continents and 13 islands. *Journal of Personality and Social Psychology, 85,* 85–104.

Schmitt, D.P. (2004). Patterns and universals of mate poaching across 53 nations: The effects of sex, culture and personality on romantically attracting another person's partner. *Journal of Personality and Social Psychology, 86,* 560–84.

Schmitt, D.P., and 120 co-authors (2003). Are men universally more dismissing than women? Gender differences in romantic attachment across 62 cultural regions. *Personal Relationships, 10,* 307–31.

Schmitt, D.P., and 110 co-authors (2004). Patterns and universals of adult romantic attachment across 62 cultural regions: Are models of self and of other pancultural constructs? *Journal of Cross-Cultural Psychology, 35,* 367–402.

Scholz, U., Gutiérrez-Doña, B., Sud, S., & Schwarzer, R. (2002). Is general self-efficacy a universal construct? Psychometric findings from 25 countries. *European Journal of Psychological Assessment, 18,* 242–51.

Schwartz, S.H. (1992). Universals in the content and structure of values: Theoretical advances and empirical tests in 20 countries. In M.P. Zanna (Ed.), *Advances in experimental social psychology* (Vol. 25, pp. 1–65). Orlando, FL: Academic.

Schwartz, S.H. (1994). Beyond individualism and collectivism: New cultural dimensions of values. In U. Kim, H.C. Triandis, Ç. Kağıtçıbaşı, S.C. Choi, & G. Yoon (Eds.), *Individualism and collectivism: Theory, method and applications* (pp. 85–119). Thousand Oaks, CA: Sage.

Schwartz, S.H. (1999). A theory of cultural values and some implications for work. *Applied Psychology: An International Review, 48,* 23–47.

Schwartz, S.H. (2004). Mapping and interpreting cultural differences around the world. In H. Vinken, J. Soeters, & P. Ester (Eds.), *Comparing cultures: Dimensions of culture in a comparative perspective* (pp. 43–73). Leiden, NL: Brill.

Schwartz, S.H., & Bardi, A. (2001). Values hierarchies across cultures: Taking a similarities perspective. *Journal of Cross-Cultural Psychology, 32,* 268–90.

Schwartz, S.H., Bardi, A., & Bianchi, G. (2000). Value adaptation to the imposition and collapse of communist regimes in Eastern Europe. In S.A. Renshon & J. Duckitt (Eds.), *Political psychology: Cultural and cross-cultural perspectives* (pp. 217–37). London: Macmillan.

Schwartz, S.H., Melech, G., Lehmann, A., Burgess, S., Harris, M., & Owens, V. (2001). Extending the cross-cultural validity of the theory of basic human values with a different method of measurement. *Journal of Cross-Cultural Psychology, 32,* 519–42.

Schwartz, S.H., & Sagiv, L. (1995). Identifying culture-specifics in the content and structure of values. *Journal of Cross-Cultural Psychology, 26,* 92–116.

Sedikides, C., & Brewer, M.B. (Eds.), (2001). *Individual self, relational self, collective self.* Philadelphia, PA: Psychology Press.

Sedikides, C., Gaertner, J., & Toguchi, Y. (2003). Pan-cultural self-enhancement. *Journal of Personality and Social Psychology, 84,* 60–79.

Segall, M.H. (1999). Why is there still racism if there is no such thing as 'race'? In W.J. Lonner, D.L. Dinnel, D.K. Forgays & S.A. Hayes (Eds.), *Merging past, present and future in cross-cultural psychology* (pp. 14–26). Lisse, NL: Swets & Zeitlinger.

Segall, M.H., Dasen, P.R., Berry, J.W., & Poortinga, Y.H. (1999). *Human behaviour in global perspective.* Boston, MA: Allyn & Bacon.

Seki, K., Matsumoto, D., & Imahori, T.T. (2002). The conceptualization and expression of intimacy in Japan and the United States. *Journal of Cross-Cultural Psychology, 33,* 303–19.

Semin, G.R., Gorts, C.A., Nandram, S., & Semin-Goossens, A. (2002). Cultural perspectives on the linguistic representation of emotion and emotion events. *Cognition and Emotion, 16,* 11–28.

Seymour, P.H.K., Aro, M., & Erskine, J.M. (2003). Foundation literacy acquisition in European orthographies. *British Journal of Psychology, 94,* 143–74.

Shackelford, T.K., Schmitt, D.P., & Buss, D.M. (2005). Universal dimensions of human mate preferences. *Personality and Individual Differences, 39,* 477–58.

Sherif, M. (1966). *Group conflict and cooperation: Their social psychology.* London: Routledge.

Shirts, G. (1995). Beyond ethnocentrism: Promoting cross-cultural understanding with BAFA BAFA. In S.M. Fowler & M.G. Mumford (Eds.), *Intercultural sourcebook: Cross-cultural training methods* (Vol. 1, pp. 93–100). Yarmouth, MN: Intercultural Press.

Shoda, Y., & Mischel, W. (1996). Towards a unified, intra-individual dynamic conception of personality. *Journal of Research in Personality, 30,* 414–28.

Shuter, R. (1976). Proxemics and tactility in Latin America. *Journal of Communication, 26,* 46–52.

Shweder, R.A. (1991). *Thinking through culture: Expeditions in cultural psychology.* Cambridge MA: Harvard University Press.

Shweder, R.A., & Bourne, E.J. (1982). Does the concept of the person vary cross-culturally? In A.J. Marsella & G.M. White (Eds.), *Cultural conceptions of mental health and therapy* pp. 97–137. Dordrecht, NL: Riedel.

Sidanius, J., Henry, P.J., Pratto, F., & Levin, S. (2004). Arab attributions for the attack on America: The case of Lebanese subelites. *Journal of Cross-Cultural Psychology, 35,* 403–16.

Sidanius, J., & Pratto, F. (1999). *Social dominance: An intergroup theory of social hierarchy and oppression.* Cambridge: Cambridge University Press.

Siegman, A.W. (1994). Cardiovascular consequences of expressing and repressing anger. In A.W. Siegman & T.W. Smith (Eds.), *Anger, hostility, and the heart* (pp. 173–97). Hillsdale, NJ: Erlbaum.

Silbereisen, R.K., & Wiesner, M. (2002). Lessons from research on the consequences of German unification: Continuity and discontinuity of self-efficacy and the timing of psychosocial transitions. *Applied Psychology: An International Review, 51,* 291–317.

Singelis, T.M. (1994). The measurement of independent and interdependent self-construals. *Personality and Social Psychology Bulletin, 20,* 580–91.

Singelis, T.M., Bond, M.H., Sharkey, W.F., & Lai, S.Y. (1999). Unpackaging culture's influence on self-esteem and embarrassability: The role of self-construals. *Journal of Cross-Cultural Psychology, 30,* 315–41.

Singelis, T.M, Her, P., Aaker, J., Bhawuk, D.P.S., Gabrenya, W., Gelfand, M., Harwood, J., Tanaka-Matsumi, J., & Vandello, J. (2003). *Ethnic and regional differences in social axioms.* Unpublished manuscript California State University, Chico.

Singelis, T.M., Hubbard, C., Her, P., & An, S. (2003). Convergent validation of the social axioms survey. *Personality and Individual Differences, 34,* 269–82.

Singelis, T.M., Triandis, H.C., Bhawuk, D., & Gelfand, M. (1995). Horizontal and vertical dimensions of individualism and collectivism: A theoretical and measurement refinement. *Cross-Cultural Research, 29,* 240–75.

Singleton, R., Jr., & Kerber, K.W. (1980). Topics in social psychology: Further classroom demonstrations. *Teaching Sociology, 7,* 439–52.

Sinha, D. (1997). Indigenous psychology. In J.W. Berry, Y. H. Poortinga, & J. Pandey (Eds.), *Handbook of cross-cultural psychology* (2nd ed., Vol. 1, pp. 129–69). Needham Heights, MA: Allyn & Bacon.

Smith, P.B. (2004a). Nations, cultures and individuals: New perspectives and old dilemmas. *Journal of Cross-Cultural Psychology, 35,* 6–12.

Smith, P.B. (2004b). Acquiescent response bias as an aspect of cultural communication style. *Journal of Cross-Cultural Psychology, 35,* 50–61.

Smith, P.B. (2005). Is there an indigenous European social psychology? *International Journal of Psychology, 40* (3).

Smith, P.B., & Bond, M.H. (1998). *Social psychology across cultures* (2nd ed.). Hemel Hempstead, UK: Prentice Hall.

Smith, P.B., Dugan, S., & Trompenaars, F. (1996). National culture and managerial values: A dimensional analysis across 43 nations. *Journal of Cross-Cultural Psychology, 27,* 231–64.

Smith, P.B., Giannini, M., Helkama, K., Maczynski, J., & Stumpf, S. (2005). Identification and relational orientation predictors of positive national auto-stereotyping. *International Review of Social Psychology, 18,* 65–90.

Smith, P.B., & Long K.M. (in press). Social identity theory in cross-cultural perspective. In R.J. Brown & D. Capozza (Eds.), *Social identities: Motivational, emotional, cultural influences.* Hove, UK: Psychology Press.

Smith, P.B., Peterson, M.F., Leung, K., & Dugan, S. (1998). Individualism-collectivism and the handling of disagreement: A 23-nation study. *International Journal of Intercultural Relations, 22,* 351–67.

Smith, P.B., Peterson, M.F., et al. (2005). 'National culture, managerial reliance on guidance sources and effectiveness of change procedures'. Unpublished manuscript, University of Sussex.

Smith, P.B., Peterson, M.F., & Schwartz, S.H. et al. (2002). Cultural values, sources of guidance and their relevance to managerial behavior: A 47-nation study. *Journal of Cross-Cultural Psychology, 33,* 188–208.

Smith, P.B., & Schwartz, S.H. (1997). Values. In J.W. Berry, M.H. Segall, & Ç. Kağıtçıbaşı (Eds.), *Handbook of cross-cultural psychology* (2nd ed., Vol. 3, pp. 77–108). Needham Heights, MA: Allyn & Bacon.

Smith, P.B., Trompenaars, F., & Dugan, S. (1995). The Rotter locus of control scale in 43 countries: A test of cultural relativity. *International Journal of Psychology, 30,* 377–400.

Snyder, M. (1987). *Public appearances/private realities: The psychology of self-monitoring.* New York: Freeman.

Solomon, M. (1993). Transmission of cultural goals: Social network influences on infant socialization. In J. Demick, K. Bursik, & R. DiBiase (Eds.), *Parental development* (pp. 135–56). Hillsdale, NJ: Erlbaum.

Sommer, S.M., Bae, S.H., & Luthans, F. (1996). Organizational commitment across cultures: The impact of antecedents on Korean employees. *Human Relations, 49,* 977–93.

Spreitzer, G.M., Perttula, K.H., & Xin, K.R. (2005). Traditionality matters: An examination of the effectiveness of transformational leadership in the United States and Taiwan. *Journal of Organizational Behavior, 26,* 205–27.

Steele, M.S., & McGarvey, S.T. (1996). Expression of anger by Samoan adults. *Psychological Reports, 79,* 1339–48.

Steinberg, L., & Silverberg, S.B. (1986). The vicissitudes of autonomy in early adolescence. *Child Development, 57,* 841–51.

Stephan, W.G., Diaz-Loving, R., & Duran, A. (2000). Integrated threat theory and intercultural attitudes: Mexico and the United States. *Journal of Cross-Cultural Psychology, 31,* 240–9.

Stephan, W.G., & Stephan, C.W. (1996). Predicting prejudice. *International Journal of Intercultural Relations, 20,* 1–12.

Stephan, W.G., Stephan, C.W., Abalakina, M., et al. (1996). Distinctiveness effects in intergroup perceptions: An international study. In H. Grad, A. Blanco, & J. Georgas (Eds.), *Key issues in cross-cultural psychology* (pp. 298–308). Lisse, NL: Swets & Zeitlinger.

Stephan, W.G., Ybarra, O., Martinez, C.M., et al. (1998). Prejudice toward immigrants to Spain and Israel: An integrated threat analysis. *Journal of Cross-Cultural Psychology, 29,* 559–76.

Sternberg, R.J., & Grigorenko, E.L. (Eds.) (2003). *Culture and competence: Contexts of life success.* Washington, DC: American Psychological Association.

Stewart, S.M., Bond, M.H., Deeds, O., & Chung, S.F. (1999). Intergenerational patterns of values and autonomy expectations in cultures of relatedness and separateness. *Journal of Cross-Cultural Psychology, 30,* 575–93.

Stewart, S.M., Bond, M.H., Kennard, B.D., Ho, L.M., & Zaman, R.M. (2002). Does the Chinese construct of *guan* export to the West? *International Journal of Psychology, 37,* 74–82.

Suinn, R.M., Ahuna, C., & Khoo, G. (1992). The Suinn-Lew Asian self-identity acculturation scale: concurrent and factorial validation. *Educational and Psychological Measurement, 52,* 1041–6.

Super, C.M., & Harkness, S. (1986). The developmental niche: A conceptualization at the interface of child and culture. *International Journal of Behavioral Development, 9,* 545–70.

Sussman, N. (2002). Testing the cultural identity model of the cultural transition cycle: Sojourners return home. *International Journal of Intercultural Relations, 26,* 391–408.

Sussman, N., & Rosenfeld, H. (1982). Influence of culture, language and sex on conversational distance. *Journal of Personality and Social Psychology, 42,* 66–74.

Sweeney, P.D., & McFarlin, D.B. (2004). Social comparisons and income satisfaction. *Journal of Occupational and Organizational Psychology, 77,* 149–54.

Szarota, P. (1996). Taxonomy of the Polish personality-descriptive adjectives of the highest frequency of use. *Polish Psychological Bulletin, 27*(4), 343–51.

Tafarodi, R.W., Lo, C., Yamaguchi, S., et al. (2004). The inner self in three countries. *Journal of Cross-Cultural Psychology, 35,* 97–117.

Tajfel, H. (Ed.) (1981). *Human groups and social categories: Studies in social psychology.* Cambridge: Cambridge University Press.

Tajfel, H., & Turner, J.C. (1979). An integrative theory of intergroup conflict. In W.G. Austin & S. Worchel (Eds.), *The social psychology of intergroup relations* (pp. 33–47). Monterey, CA: Brooks Cole.

Takanishi, R. (2000). Preparing adolescents for social change: Designing generic social interventions. In L.J. Crockett & K. Rainer (Eds.), *Negotiating adolescence in times of social change* (pp. 284–94) Cambridge: Cambridge University Press.

Takano, Y., & Osaka, E. (1999). An unsupported common view: comparing Japan and the US on individualism/collectivism. *Asian Journal of Social Psychology, 2*(3), 311–41.

Takeuchi, R., Yun, S., & Tesluk, P.E. (2002). An examination of crossover and spillover effects of spousal and expatriate cross-cultural adjustment on expatriate outcomes. *Journal of Applied Psychology, 87,* 655–66.

Tanzer, N., Sim, C.Q.E., & Spielberger, C.D. (1996). Experience and expression of anger in a Chinese society: The case of Singapore. In C.D. Spielberger, I.G. Sarason, et al. (Eds.), *Stress and emotion: Anxiety, anger and curiosity* (Vol. 16, pp. 51–65). Washington, DC: Taylor & Francis.

Tarde, G. (1898). *Etudes de psychologie sociale.* Paris: Giard & Brière.

Thomas, D.C. (1999). Cultural diversity and work group effectiveness: An experimental study. *Journal of Cross-Cultural Psychology, 30,* 242–63.

Thomas, D.C. (2002). *Essentials of international management: A cross-cultural perspective.* Thousand Oaks, CA: Sage.

Thomas, D.C., & Au, K.Y. (2002). The effect of cultural variation on the behavioral response to low job satisfaction. *Journal of International Business Studies, 33,* 309–26.

Thomas, D.C., & Inkson, K. (2004). *Cultural intelligence: People skills for international business.* San Francisco, CA: Bennett-Koehler.

Thomas, D.C., & Pekerti, A. (2003). The effect of culture on situational determinants of exchange behavior in organizations: A comparison of New Zealand and Indonesia. *Journal of Cross-Cultural Psychology, 34,* 269–81.

Thomas, D.C., & Ravlin, E.C. (1995). Responses of employees to cultural adaptation by a foreign manager. *Journal of Applied Psychology, 80,* 133–46.

Ting-Toomey, S. (1988). A face negotiation theory. In Y.Y. Kim & W.B. Gudykunst (Eds.), *Theory in intercultural communication* pp. 213–35. Newbury Park, CA: Sage.

Tinsley, C.H. (2001). How negotiators get to yes: Predicting the constellation of strategies used across cultures to negotiate conflict. *Journal of Applied Psychology, 86*, 583–93.

Tinsley, C.H., & Brett, J.M. (2001). Managing workplace conflict in the United States and Hong Kong. *Organizational Behavior and Human Decision Processes, 85*, 360–81.

Tinsley, C.H., & Weldon, E. (2003). Responses to a normative conflict among American and Chinese managers. *International Journal of Cross-Cultural Management, 3*, 183–94.

Torres, A.R.R. (1996). 'Exploring group diversity: Relationships between in-group identification and in-group bias'. Unpublished doctoral dissertation, University of Kent, UK.

Trafimow, D., Triandis, H.C., & Goto, S.G. (1991). Some tests of the distinction between the private self and the collective self. *Journal of Personality and Social Psychology, 60*, 649–55.

Transparency International (2004). *Corruption perceptions index.* http://www.icgg.org

Triandis, H.C. (1995). *Individualism and collectivism.* Boulder, CO: Westview.

Triandis, H.C., Bontempo, R., Villareal, M.J., Asai, M., & Lucca, N. (1988). Individualism and collectivism: Cross-cultural perspectives on self-ingroup relationships. *Journal of Personality and Social Psychology, 54*, 323–38.

Triandis, H.C., Carnevale, P.J., Gelfand, M.J., & 13 co-authors (2001). Culture and deception in business negotiations. *International Journal of Cross-Cultural Management, 1*, 73–90.

Triandis, H.C., Chen, X.P., & Chan, D.K.S. (1998). Scenarios for the measurement of individualism and collectivism. *Journal of Cross-Cultural Psychology, 29*, 275–89.

Triandis, H.C., Leung, K., Villareal, M., & Clack, F.L. (1985). Allocentric versus idiocentric tendencies: Convergent and discriminant validation. *Journal of Research in Personality, 19*, 395–415.

Triandis, H.C., Lisansky, J., Marin, G., & Betancourt, H. (1984). *Simpatía* as a cultural script for Hispanics. *Journal of Personality and Social Psychology, 47*, 1363–75.

Triandis, H.C., McCusker, C., Betancourt, H., Iwao, S., Leung, K., Salazar, J.M., Setiadi, B., Sinha, J.B.P., Touzard, H, & Zaleski, Z. (1993). An etic–emic analysis of individualism and collectivism. *Journal of Cross-Cultural Psychology, 24*, 366–83.

Triandis, H.C., McCusker, C., & Hui, C.H. (1990). Multimethod probes of individualism and collectivism. *Journal of Personality and Social Psychology, 59*, 1006–20.

Tripathi, R.C. (1988). Aligning development to values in India. In D. Sinha & H.S.R. Kao (Eds.), *Social values and development: Asian perspectives* (pp. 315–33). New Delhi: Sage.

Triplett, N. (1898). The dynamogenic factors in pacemaking and competition. *American Journal of Psychology, 9*, 507–33.

Trommsdorf, G. (1985). Some comparative aspects of socialization in Japan and Germany. In I.R. Lagunes & Y.H. Poortinga (Eds.), *From a different perspective: Studies of behavior across cultures* (pp. 231–40). Lisse, NL: Swets & Zeitlinger.

Turner, J.C., Hogg, M.A., Oakes, P.J., Reicher, S., & Wetherell, M.S. (1987). *Rediscovering the social group: A self-categorization theory.* Oxford: Blackwell.

Tylor, E.B. (1871). *Primitive cultures.* London: Murray.

Uleman, J.S., Rhee, E., Bardoliwalla, N., Semin, G.R., & Toyama, M. (2000). The relational self: Closeness to in-groups depends on who they are, culture and the type of closeness. *Asian Journal of Social Psychology, 3*, 1–18.

United Nations. (2002). *International migration report.* New York: Department of Economic and Social Affairs, United Nations.

United Nations Development Programme. (2004). *Human development report.* New York: Oxford University Press. http://hdr.undp.org/reports/global/2004 .

Urry, J. (1990). *The tourist gaze: Leisure and travel in contemporary society.* London: Sage.

Uskul, A., Hymie, M., & Lalonde, R.N. (2004). Interdependence as a mediator between culture and interpersonal closeness for Euro-Canadians and Turks. *Journal of Cross-Cultural Psychology, 35*, 174–91.

Uskul, A., & Semin, G.R. (2004). 'What do insults tell us about cultural identity?' Unpublished manuscript, University of Michigan.

Valsiner, J. (1989). *Human development and culture.* Cambridge, MA: Harvard University Press.

Vandello, J.A., & Cohen, D. (2003). Male honor and female infidelity: Implicit scripts that perpetuate domestic violence. *Journal of Personality and Social Psychology, 84*, 997–1010.

Van der Vegt, G.S., van de Vliert, E., & Huang, X. (in press). Location-level links between diversity and innovative climate depend on national power distance. *Academy of Management Journal.*

Van der Zee, K., Atsam, N., & Brodbeck, F. (2004). The influence of social identity and personality on outcomes of cultural diversity in teams. *Journal of Cross-Cultural Psychology, 35*, 283–303.

Van der Zee, K.I., & van Oudenhoven, J.P.L. (2001). The multicultural personality questionnaire: reliability and validity of self and other ratings of multicultural effectiveness. *Journal of Research in Personality, 35*, 278–88.

Van de Vijver, F.J.R. (1997). Meta-analysis of cross-cultural comparisons of test performance. *Journal of Cross-Cultural Psychology, 28*, 678–709.

Van de Vijver, F., & Hambleton, R.K. (1996). Translating tests: Some practical guidelines. *European Psychologist, 1*, 89–99.

Van de Vijver, F.J.R., & Leung, K. (1997). *Methods and data analysis for cross-cultural research.* Thousand Oaks, CA: Sage.

Van de Vliert, E. (2003). Thermoclimate, culture, and poverty as country-level roots of workers' wages. *Journal of International Business Studies, 34*, 1–15.

Van de Vliert, E., Huang, X., & Levine, R.V. (2004). National wealth and thermal climate as predictors of motives for volunteer work. *Journal of Cross-Cultural Psychology, 34*, 62–71.

Van de Vliert, E., Huang, X., & Parker, P.M. (2004). Do colder and hotter climates make the rich more but the poor less happy and altruistic? *Journal of Environmental Psychology.*

Van de Vliert, E., Ohbuchi, K., van Rossum, B., Hayashi, Y., & van der Vegt, G.S. (in press). Conglomerated contending by Japanese subordinates. *International Journal of Conflict Management.*

Van de Vliert, E., Shi, K., Sanders, K., Wang, Y., & Huang, X. (2004). Chinese and Dutch interpretations of supervisory feedback. *Journal of Cross-Cultural Psychology, 35*, 417–35.

Van de Vliert, E., & Smith, P.B. (2004). Leader reliance on subordinates across nations that differ in development and climate. *Leadership Quarterly, 15*, 381–403.

Van de Vliert, E. (in press). Autocratic leadership around the globe: Do climate and wealth drive leadership culture? *Journal of Cross-Cultural Psychology,*

Van Hemert, D., van de Vijver, F., & Poortinga, Y.H. (2002). The Beck depression inventory as a measure of subjective well-being: a cross-national study. *Journal of Happiness Studies, 3*, 257–86.

Van Nimwegen, T., Soeters, J., & van Luijk, H. (2004). Managerial values and ethics in an international bank. *International Journal of Cross-Cultural Management, 4*, 101–22.

Van Oudenhoven, J.P.L., Askervis-Leherpeux, F., Hannover, B., Jaaersma, R., & Dardenne, B. (2001). Asymmetrical international attitudes. *European Journal of Social Psychology, 32*, 275–89.

Van Oudenhoven, J.P., Mechelse, L., & de Dreu, C.K.W. (1998). Managerial conflict management in five European countries: The importance of power distance, uncertainty avoidance and masculinity. *Applied Psychology: An International Review, 47*, 439–56.

Van Oudenhoven, J.P.L., Mol, S., & van der Zee, K.I. (2003). Study of the adjustment of western expatriates in Taiwan ROC with the multicultural personality questionnaire. *Asian Journal of Social Psychology, 6*, 159–70.

Van Oudenhoven, J.P.L., Prins, K.S., & Buunk, B.P. (1998). Attitudes of majority and minority members towards adaptation of immigrants. *European Journal of Social Psychology, 28*, 995–1013.

Van Oudenhoven, J.P.L., & van der Zee, K.I. (2002). Predicting multicultural effectiveness of international students: The multicultural personality questionnaire. *International Journal of Intercultural Relations, 26*, 679–74.

Van Oudenhoven, J.P.L., van der Zee, K., & Bakker, W. (2002). Culture, identity, adaptation strategy and well being. In D. Gorter & K. van der Zee (Eds.), *Frisians abroad* (pp. 46–56). Ljouwert, NL: Fryske Akademy.

Van Strien, P.J. (1997). The American 'colonization' of northwest European social psychology after World War 2. *Journal of the History of the Behavioral Sciences, 33*, 349–63.

Vassiliou, V., & Vassiliou, G. (1973). The implicative meaning of the Greek concept of *philotimo. Journal of Cross-Cultural Psychology, 4*, 326–41.

Veenhoven, R. (2004). Subjective measures of well-being. Discussion paper 7, World Institute for Development Economics Research, Helsinki, Finland (www.wider.unu.edu).

Veenhoven, R. (1999). Quality of life in individualistic society: A comparison of 43 nations in the early 1990's. *Social Indicators Research, 48*, 157–86.

Verkuyten, M., & Masson, K. (1996). Culture and gender differences in the perception of friendship by adolescents. *International Journal of Psychology, 31*, 207–17.

Verkuyten, M. (2001). 'Abnormalization' of ethnic minorities in conversation. *British Journal of Social Psychology, 40*, 257–78.

Vygotsky, L.S. (1934/1962). *Thought and language.* Cambridge, MA: MIT Press.

Wallbot, H.G., & Scherer, K.R. (1986). How universal and specific is emotional experience: Evidence from 27 nations in five continents. *Social Science Information, 25*, 763–95.

Ward, C. (1987). Mid-life crisis in women – A cross cultural phenomenon? In Ç. Kağıtçıbaşı (Ed.), *Growth and progress in cross-cultural psychology*. Lisse, NL: Swets & Zeitlinger.

Ward, C., Berno, T., & Main (2002). Can the Cross-cultural adaptability inventory predict sojourner adjustment? In P. Boski, F.J.R. van de Vijver & A.M. Chodnicka (Eds.), *New directions in cross-cultural psychology* (pp. 409–23). Warsaw: Polish Psychological Association.

Ward, C., Bochner, S., & Furnham, A. (2001). *The psychology of culture shock*. Hove, UK: Routledge.

Ward, C., Leong, C.H., & Low, M.L. (2004). Personality and sojourner adjustment: An exploration of the big five and the cultural fit proposition. *Journal of Cross-Cultural Psychology, 35*, 137–51.

Ward, C., & Rana-Deuba, A. (1999). Acculturation and adaptation revisited. *Journal of Cross-Cultural Psychology, 30*, 422–42.

Ward, C., & Rana-Deuba, A. (2000). Home and culture influences on sojourner adjustment. *International Journal of Intercultural Relations, 24*, 291–306.

Wasti, S.A. (2003a). The influence of cultural values on antecedents of organizational commitment: An individual-level analysis. *Applied Psychology: An International Review, 52*, 533–54.

Wasti, S.A. (2003b). Organizational commitment, turnover intentions and the influence of cultural values. *Journal of Occupational and Organizational Psychology, 76*, 303–22.

Watson, O. (1970). *Proxemic behavior: A cross-cultural study*. The Hague, NL: Mouton.

Watson, W.E., Johnson, L., & Zgourides, G.D. (2002). The influence of ethnic diversity on leadership, group process and performance: An examination of learning teams. *International Journal of Intercultural Relations, 26*, 11–16.

Watson, W.E., Kumar, K., & Michaelsen, L.K. (1993). Cultural diversity's impact on interaction process and performance: Comparing homogeneous and diverse task groups. *Academy of Management Journal, 36*, 590–602.

Wei, L., & Yue, L. (1996). 'My stupid wife and ugly daughter': The use of pejorative references as a politeness strategy by Chinese speakers. *Journal of Asia Pacific Communication, 7*, 129–42.

Wheeler, L., & Kim, Y. (1997). What is beautiful is culturally good: The physical attractiveness stereotype has different content in collectivist cultures. *Personality and Social Psychology Bulletin, 23*, 795–800.

Wheeler, L., Reis, H.T., & Bond, M.H. (1989). Collectivism-individualism in everyday social life: The Middle Kingdom and the Melting Pot. *Journal of Personality and Social Psychology, 57*, 79–86.

Whiting, B.B. (1976). The problem of the packaged variable. In K.A. Riegel & J.F. Meacham (Eds.), *The developing individual in a changing world* (Vol. 1, pp. 303–9). The Hague, NL: Mouton.

Whiting, J.W.M., & Child, I.L. (1953). *Child training and personality*. New Haven, CT: Yale University Press.

Whiting, B.B., & Whiting, J.W.M. (1975). *Children of six cultures: A psychocultural analysis*. Cambridge, MA: Harvard University Press.

Whorf, B. (1956). *Language, thought, and reality*. Cambridge, MA: Massachusetts Institute of Technology Press.

Wiggins, J.S., & Trapnell, P. D. (1996). A dyadic interactional perspective on the five factor model. In J.S. Wiggins (Ed.), *The five factor model of personality: Theoretical perspectives* (pp. 88–162). New York: Guilford.

Wilkinson, R.G., Kawachi, I., & Kennedy, B.P. (1998). Mortality, the social environment, crime and violence. *Sociology of Health and Illness, 20*, 578–97.

Williams, A., Garrett, P., & Tennant, R. (2004). Seeing the difference, feeling the difference: Emergent adults perceptions of 'good' communication with peers and adolescents. In S.H. Ng, C.N. Candlin, & C.Y. Chiu (Eds.), *Language matters: Communication, culture and identity* (pp. 111–53). Hong Kong: City University of Hong Kong Press.

Williams, J., & Best, D. (1990). *Sex and psyche: Gender and self viewed cross-culturally*. Newbury Park, CA: Sage.

Williams, J.E., Satterwhite, R.C., & Saiz, J.L. (1998). *The importance of psychological traits: A cross-cultural study*. New York: Plenum.

Witkin, H.A. (1950). Individual differences in the case of perception of embedded figures. *Journal of Personality, 19*, 1–15.

Witkin, H.A., & Berry, J.W. (1975). Psychological differentiation in cross-cultural perspective. *Journal of Cross-Cultural Psychology, 6*, 4–87.

Witkin, H.A., Moore, C.A., Goodenough, D.R., & Cox, P.W. (1977). Field-dependent and field-independent cognitive styles and their educational implications. *Review of Educational Research, 47*, 1–64.

Wong, S., & Bond, M.H. (2002). Measuring emotionality across cultures: Self-reported emotional experiences as conceptualizations of self. In R.G. Craven, H.W. Marsh & K.B. Simpson (Eds.), *Proceedings of the second international biennial conference. Self-concept research: Driving international research agendas*. Self Research Center, University of Western Sydney. http://edweb.ews.edu.au/self/Conference_2002.CD_Wong_&_Bond.pdf

Wong, S.S.W., & Bond, M.H. (2005). 'Intensity of feelings and exercise of control as factors influencing the display of joy and anger in 30 cultural groups'. Manuscript submitted, Chinese University of Hong Kong.

World Energy Council. (1999). *The challenge of rural energy poverty in developing countries*. London: World Energy Council. www.worldenergy.org/wec-geis/publications/reports/rural/rural_development_and_energy/

World Health Organization. (2002). *World report on violence and health*. www.who.int/violence_injury_prevention/violence/world_report/wrvh1/en/

World Tourism Organization. (1999). *Compendium of tourism statistics*. Madrid, Spain: World Tourism Organization.

World Tourism Organization. (2004). *Statistics and economic measures of tourism*. http://www.world-tourism.org

Yafee, R. (2003). *A primer for panel data analysis*. Article available online at: http://www.nyu.edu/its/pubs/connect/fall03/yaffee_primer.html

Yamada, A.M., & Singelis, T.M. (1999). Biculturalism and self-construal. *International Journal of Intercultural Relations, 23*, 697–709.

Yamaguchi, S. (2004). Further clarification of the concept of *Amae* in relation to attachment and dependence. *Human Development, 47*, 28–33.

Yang, K.S. (1986). Chinese personality and its change. In M.H. Bond (Ed.), *The psychology of the Chinese people* (pp. 106–70). Hong Kong: Oxford University Press.

Yang, K.S. (1988). Will societal modernization eventually eliminate cross-cultural psychological differences? In M.H. Bond (Ed.), *The cross-cultural challenge to social psychology* (pp. 67–85). Newbury Park, CA: Sage.

Yang, K.S. (2000). Monocultural and cross-cultural indigenous approaches: The royal road to the development of a balanced global psychology. *Asian Journal of Social Psychology, 3*, 241–63.

Yang, K.S., & Bond, M.H. (1980). Ethnic affirmation by Chinese bilinguals. *Journal of Cross-Cultural Psychology, 11*, 411–25.

Yang, K.S., & Bond, M.H. (1990). Exploring implicit personality theories with indigenous or imported constructs: The Chinese case. *Journal of Personality and Social Psychology, 58*, 1087–95.

Yang, K.S., & Lee, P.H. (1971). Likeability, meaningfulness, and familiarity of 557 Chinese adjectives for personality trait description. *Acta Psychologica Taiwanica, 13*, 36–57. (In Chinese.)

Yao, X., & Wang, L. (2004). 'Is normative organizational commitment valuable? Its predictability for turnover'. Unpublished paper, Department of Psychology, Peking University.

Ying, Y.W., & Liese, L.H. (1991). Emotional wellbeing of Taiwan students in the US: An examination of pre to post differential. *International Journal of Intercultural Relations, 15*, 345–66.

Yu, A.B. (1996). Ultimate life concerns, self and Chinese achievement motivation. In M.H. Bond (ed.), *The handbook of Chinese psychology* (pp. 227–46). New York: Oxford University Press.

Yuki, M. (2003). Intergroup comparison versus intra-group relationships: A cross-examination of social identity theory in North American and East Asian cultural contexts. *Social Psychology Quarterly, 66*, 166–83.

Yukl, G.A., Fu, P.P., & McDonald, R. (2003). Cross-cultural differences in perceived effectiveness of influence tactics for initiating or resisting change. *Applied Psychology: An International Review, 52*, 68–82.

Zagefka, H., & Brown, R.J. (2002). The relationship between acculturation strategies, cultural fit and intergroup relations: Immigrant–majority relations in Germany. *European Journal of Social Psychology, 32*, 171–88.

Zangwill, I. (1909). *The melting pot*. New York: Mcmillan.

Zhang, Y.C., Kohnstamm, G., Slotboom, A.M., Elphick, E., & Cheung, P.C. (2002). Chinese and Dutch parents' perceptions of their children's personality. *Journal of Genetic Psychology, 163*, 165–78.

Name Index

Subject Index

acculturation, 216, 237–46, 261, 267, 273
achievement,
  motivation, 122–3, 128–9, 258
  socially-oriented, 122–3, 172–3
acquiescent response bias, 27–8, 34, 37,
    107–9, 134, 147, 192, 196, 273
adaptation, 213
  psychological, 216, 218–9, 237, 242–3
  socio-cultural, 216, 218–9, 237–8, 242–5
advertisements, 208, 271
affluence, see wealth
African Americans, 95–6, 99, 112, 230
Africans, studies including, 44, 84, 120, 138,
    170, 177, 185, 225, 228, 249, 270
aggression, 65, 170
Albania, 190, 209
amae, 162–3, 195
anger, 19, 67, 116–8, 120, 158
animosity reduction, 183, 185, 270
applications, practical, 10, 213–6, 271–3
Arabs, studies including, 155–6, 170, 207,
    209, 232, 240, 242
Argentina, 44, 116, 249, 254–6
Asian Americans, 93, 94, 95, 119, 125, 160,
    164, 208
assimilation, see acculturation
attachment styles, 163, 169–70
Australia, 3, 36, 40, 44, 69, 110, 132, 136,
    154–6, 177, 205–6, 210, 218–9, 225, 227,
    236, 242, 244, 257, 270
Austria, 4, 35, 36, 44, 73, 135
authoritarian personality, 94, 129, 229
autonomous-relational self-construal, 91–3,
    96–7, 99, 109–10, 123, 270
autonomy, 88–92, 97–100, 268; see
    also values

back-translation, 18, 141
Bahrein, 3
Bangladesh, 236, 258
Belarus, 256
Belgium, 44, 123, 135, 184, 189, 227,
    255, 262
beliefs, 48, 61, 104, 111, 146, 245, 265
  dynamic externality, 48, 62
  fate control, 48, 76–7, 99, 130, 192

beliefs, cont.
  reward for application, 48, 192
  religiosity, 48, 192
  social complexity, 48
  social cynicism, 48, 130, 192, 233
  societal cynicism, 47, 62, 145, 266
big five personality factors, 133–45, 219, 265
  agreeableness, 131, 134–8, 144
  conscientiousness, 130–1, 134–8, 144
  extraversion, 68, 130–1, 134–8, 144, 146
  neuroticism, 68, 131, 134–8, 144
  openness to experience, 131, 134–5,
    138, 144
Bolivia, 44
Bosnia, 44
Botswana, 120
Brazil, 32, 44, 116, 147, 161–2, 168, 169, 184,
    233–5, 256, 270
Bulgaria, 44, 176, 256

Canada, 3, 4, 36, 44, 106, 122, 124, 135, 147,
    155, 164, 185, 207, 211–12, 225, 230,
    232, 236, 239–40, 242–4, 255
children, studies of, 17, 81–4, 90–1, 123, 147,
    161, 163, 228, 233–4, 241, 259
Chile, 44, 116, 244, 249
China, 4, 32, 44, 69, 72, 94, 95, 103, 104,
    106, 114, 123–4, 131, 133, 135, 137,
    140–1, 147, 153, 155, 157–8, 160, 162,
    170, 176–8, 180–2, 190, 195–6, 205–6,
    223, 249–50, 253, 259–60, 269
citizen means, 50–3, 58, 59, 61, 62, 63, 66,
    71–2, 110, 120, 142, 147
climate, see temperature
closeness, interpersonal, 162–6
cognition, 112–16, 151–2
collectivism, see individualism-collectivism,
Colombia, 36, 70
communication, 150–60
  direct vs indirect, 153, 155, 186, 190, 218
  electronic, 191
  language issues, 205–9
  non-verbal, 155–8, 210, 250–1
communism, 59–60, 64
conflict, 188
conformity, 20–1, 65, 87, 143

Peter B. Smith is Professor of Social Psychology at the University of Sussex, UK.

Michael Harris Bond is Professor of Psychology at the Chinese
University of Hong Kong, China.

Çiğdem Kağıtçıbaşı is Professor of Psychology at the Koç University
in Istanbul, Turkey.